NARROW GAUGE
IN THE TROPICS

Railroads Past & Present

H. ROGER GRANT AND THOMAS HOBACK, EDITORS

Recent titles in the *Railroads Past and Present* series

NARROW GAUGE
IN THE TROPICS

THE RAILWAYS OF THE DUTCH EAST INDIES, 1864–1942

AUGUSTUS J. VEENENDAAL, JR.

INDIANA UNIVERSITY PRESS

This book is a publication of

Indiana University Press
Office of Scholarly Publishing
Herman B Wells Library 350
1320 East 10th Street
Bloomington, Indiana 47405 USA

iupress.org

Manufactured in the United States of America

Frist printing 2022

Cataloging information is available
from the Library of Congress.

ISBN 978-0-253-06029-7 (hdbk.)
ISBN 978-0-253-06030-3 (web PDF)

CONTENTS

PREFACE

Although there was limited trackage in European—and American—standard gauge in the Dutch East Indies, I have chosen for this book the title *Narrow Gauge in the Tropics*, as the vast majority of railways and tramways in these tropical islands was running on the narrow gauge. After all, of the total of 7,583 km of railways and tramways on Java and Sumatra—figures of 1939—only 266 km were laid to a gauge of 1,435 mm (4 ft 8.5 in), the Stephensonian standard gauge as used worldwide, but known as broad gauge on Java and Sumatra. The rest of the tracks, 6,644 km, were, with very few exceptions, built in 1,067 mm gauge (3 ft 6 in); this was generally known as Indisch Normaalspoor, the East Indies standard gauge.

Remarkably, the railways of the Dutch East Indies have to a great extent escaped the attention of travelers and students of steam locomotives worldwide. Only after World War II, when steam was on its way out almost everywhere in the world and ancient steam traction still survived on a few lines on Java and Sumatra, a universal interest was awakened, resulting in a number of publications that can be found in the bibliography at the end of this book. But world travelers like Charles S. Small and P. Ransome Wallis, who roamed all over the globe in search of steam, make no mention at all of the Java State Railways or its later successor in the Republic of Indonesia. P. B. Whitehouse, another of these international travelers in search of steam, does mention the railways of Indonesia briefly and even includes a single photograph of an engine labeled as a "sturdy survivor of Dutch colonialism," but that is all. On the other hand, an authority on light railways worldwide like W. J. K. Davies does not include the Indonesian light railways in his book. It is clearly high time for a book—in English—about the rail networks of the two Indonesian islands that were covered with railways and tramways during colonial times and of which the core network still survives in use.[1]

I should stress that I have no Indonesian roots and that I have never set foot in the country, although the country's history and economy have always been of great interest to me as a professional historian. My

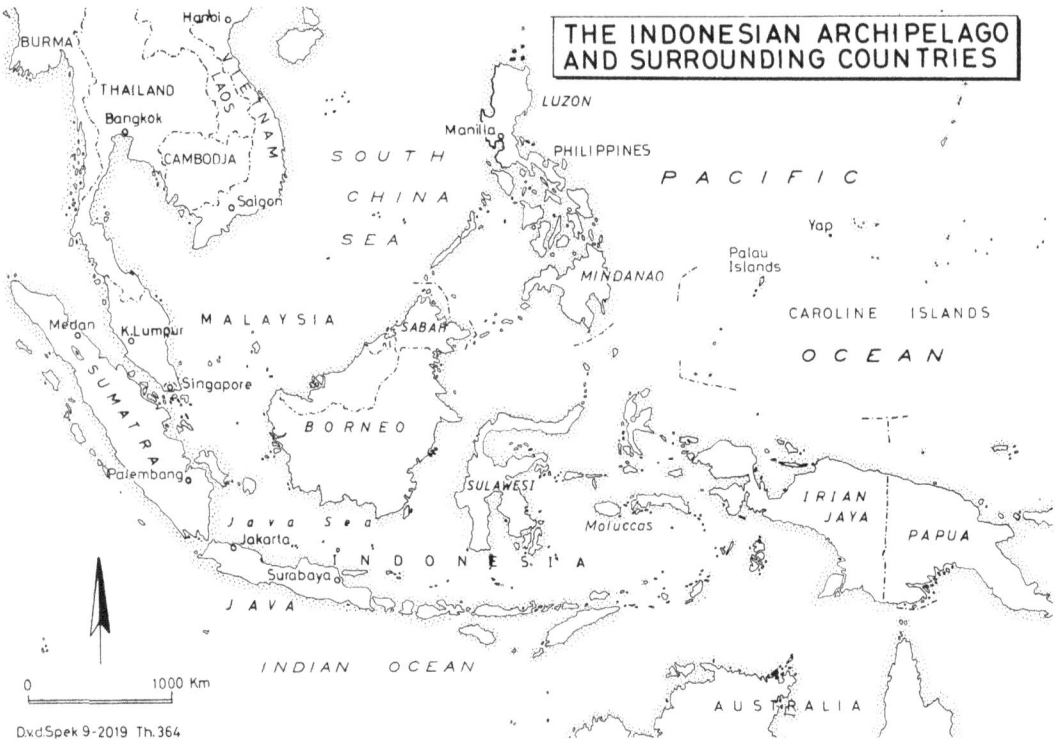

THE INDONESIAN ARCHIPELAGO
AND SURROUNDING COUNTRIES

D.v.d.Spek 9-2019 Th.364

publications in the field of railway history have until now been chiefly limited to my home country, the Netherlands, and the United States of America, more especially the Dutch financial involvement in American railroads in the nineteenth and early twentieth centuries. My publications on Indonesia's railways and their early predecessors are confined to one chapter in a book about Dutch general engineering in Indonesia, published in Dutch and English. The title will be found in the bibliography. However, with that short chapter my appetite was whetted. Although my knowledge of the railways in the Dutch East Indies is only derived from books, journals, and archival materials, I have realized that more than that single chapter would be needed to give an overview of the history of these interesting railways. I also have done some work on Dutch railway engineers and developers, who often had long or short careers in the Indies, in the home country and elsewhere in the world, and this helped me to overcome my hesitation. The resemblance between Dutch and Indonesian railway situations has always struck me, and I have tried to pay attention to that aspect in this book. Over the centuries there has been a distinct influence vice versa on railway matters, positive and negative, but not to be denied. Finally, I noticed during my research that there is nothing about the interesting history of the railways in Indonesia available in English, hence my idea of writing this book.

Contrary to British India, where a vast literature of scholarly works exist on the construction and working of railways in the subcontinent, including many aspects of the influence of railways on the economy, the unification of the many different parts of the country and a host of other aspects where railways have played a sometimes most important role, there is no such literature available for the former Dutch East Indies. Whereas for British India after independence in 1947, Indian scholars have continued to publish important books and articles in this field; Indonesian writers have contributed little since independence after 1945. And from the period before 1942 there is a very limited body of works in Dutch on certain aspects of railway operating in the East Indies, but no general survey of the innumerable effects of railway building in a colonial society. My book is certainly not meant to be the final word in this respect, but it is an attempt to give the railways of Java and Sumatra their rightful place in the history of those islands.[2]

I have tried to keep away from the ongoing and often-acrimonious discussion about the negative or positive effects of Dutch colonialism in Indonesia. I don't feel qualified for this and I do not want to be the judge of the pros and cons of colonialism. My aim is to just show what happened when, where, and why, without a value judgment. I only want to focus on the growth of the railway network and to enumerate the effects of an expanding railway system on a developing country. The rails have been instrumental in the growth of a modern export-oriented economy and as such their role should not be underestimated. After all, the railways are part of the heritage of modern-day Indonesia, and they have played a role in the unification of the country. The railways have also contributed to the setting up of an integrated national market in foodstuffs, rice foremost, and also helped to establish a more nationwide labor market. And the companies themselves were large employers, paying good wages in cash and providing all kinds of perks for their staff, such as schools, medical care, and even old-age pensions or allowances. Moreover, the railway companies were buying goods and demanding services from others beyond their own staff and in this way helped the regional and even national economies.

As this book only covers the colonial period of the railways in the present Indonesian Republic, I have chosen to use the geographical names that were generally in use in that period. In the Gazetteer at the end of the book, the reader will find the present-day equivalents.

Measures used in this book are metric—millimeters (mm), centimeters (cm = 100 mm), meters (m = 100 cm) and kilometers (km = 1,000 meters)—but sometimes the equivalent in British measures are given when appropriate or useful for the reader, as in railway gauges. One inch is

25.4 mm or 2.54 cm, one mile is 1.61 km, and 1 km is 0.62 mile. One metric ton (= 1,000 kg) of weight is 0.9842 imperial ton in the British system; where the word *ton* or *tons* is used in this book, metric tons are meant. A *pikol*, a much-used local measure of weight, is about 61 kg; a *paal*, a regional measure of length, is about 1.507 km or 0.944 mile.

The currency officially used in the Indies was the Dutch silver guilder, indicated as *f* for florin. For most of the period of this book, one US dollar was about *f*2.50, at least until the gold standard was left by both countries in the 1930s. Silver coins were the guilder and rijksdaalder, a coin of *f*2.50 and of about the same value as one US dollar. The 10 guilder gold piece was rare in the Indies.

NOTES

1. About the travels of C. S. Small, see his *Far Wheels*. About Dr. Patrick Ransome Wallis, see his *On Railways at Home and Abroad*. Also Davies, *Light Railways*, and Whitehouse and Allen, *Round the World on the Narrow Gauge*.

2. For British India and its railways, see Kerr, *Building the Railways of the Raj*.

ACKNOWLEDGMENTS

I am fortunate to have been able to collect a fairly large number of publications and images about the railway system of the former Dutch East Indies myself, but without the help of many friends I would have been in trouble. First of all, I have to thank my good friend Remmo Statius Muller, with whom I have published several books on steam locomotives and early railway photography. Without him I could not have written this book. He was most helpful in scanning the many photographs needed from books, journals, and originals, and he managed to bring even old and faded images to new life. His help was also invaluable in explaining several rare intricacies of construction of some of the East Indian locomotives. Another friend, Gerard de Graaf, with his many Indonesian connections, made available a number of photos from his own collection, chiefly images of the many plantation rails. Sjoerd Bekhof also helped me with scanning many images from old books, and Ton Pruissen supplied interesting material. Fellow historian Pim Waldeck presented me with some photographs from his family album. Without their help the book would have been much less interesting and devoid of many pictures. I thank the board of the Stichting NVBS Railverzamelingen for allowing me to use a great number of photos from its collections. As a former keeper of some of these collections, I was only too well aware of the valuable contribution made to the history of rail- and tramways in the Dutch East Indies by these holdings. The Nederlands Spoorwegmuseum (Netherlands Railway Museum) at Utrecht also holds large collections of photographs from the former Dutch East Indies, and the curator, Mrs. Evelien Pieterse, helped me in the selection of suitable images. At the same time the museum's librarian, Miss Kimberley Boucquet, assisted me when I wanted to consult the collection of printed annual reports of the several rail- and tramway companies operating in the Indies. The Koninklijk Instituut voor Taal- Land- en Volkenkunde has placed many early photographs of Java and other islands on its website to be used free of charge, and I have used several of them here.

A fellow historian and friend from my student days, Dick Engelen, read the manuscript and asked many questions and also indicated places where some more explanation could be helpful. I owe him a lot. Another friend, Dick van der Spek, a professional cartographer now living in retirement in Thailand, was again willing to draw the necessary maps to my specifications. Without his maps the book would be useless to most readers without the essential knowledge of the geography of the Indonesian islands, especially Java and Sumatra, where the railways and tramways were located. Dick and I have collaborated before, and as always his maps are clear and indispensable. My good friend and fellow American railroad historian H. Roger Grant was greatly interested in the idea of a book about the railways of the Dutch East Indies. He gave valuable advice and encouraged me to persevere when I was wondering if I would really succeed. Most of all I have to thank my wife, Jannie, who even after more than fifty-seven years of marriage, always listened to my stories about steam locomotives and railways, and every time she had some good suggestions and ideas that I could use. As usual, she also read the manuscript with close attention to the language and punctuation. Whenever she said, "I don't understand this," I knew that that particular paragraph needed more explanation. I owe her a lot.

Ashley Runyon, former acquisitions editor of the Indiana University Press's Railroads Past and Present series, was positive about my proposal right from the start and she was helpful explaining the process of working with IUP, where I had published once many years ago. Her successor Anna Francis, severely hampered by the Covid-19 outbreak with its many restrictions, successfully managed to guide my manuscript through the first stages. I am thankful for their work.

‘t Harde, Netherlands, June 2021

NARROW GAUGE
IN THE TROPICS

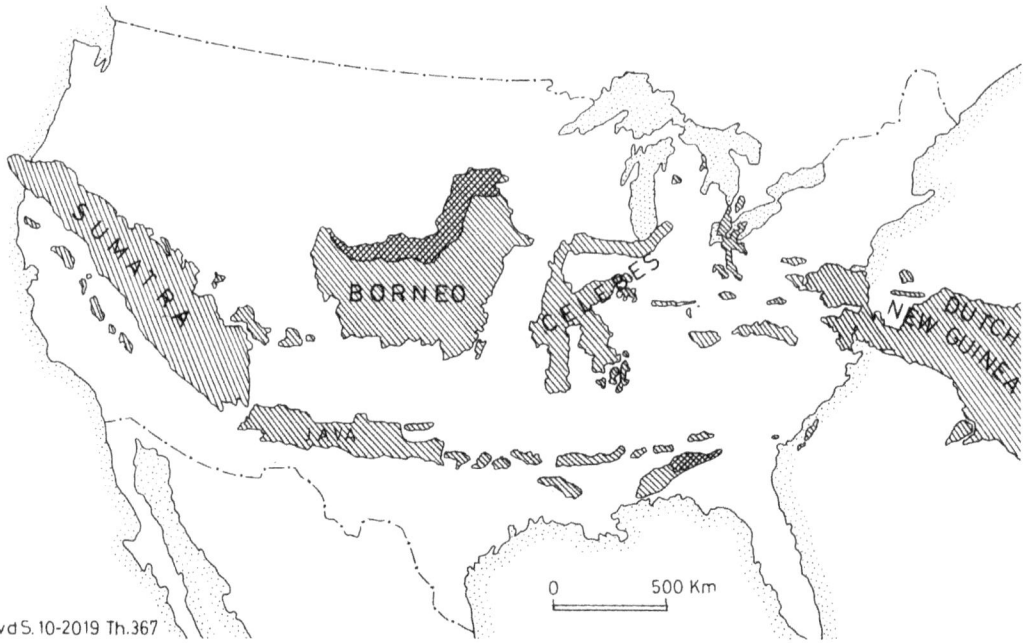

SUMATRA

BORNEO

CELEBES

NEW GUINEA

DUTCH

JAVA

0   500 Km

DvdS. 10-2019 Th.367

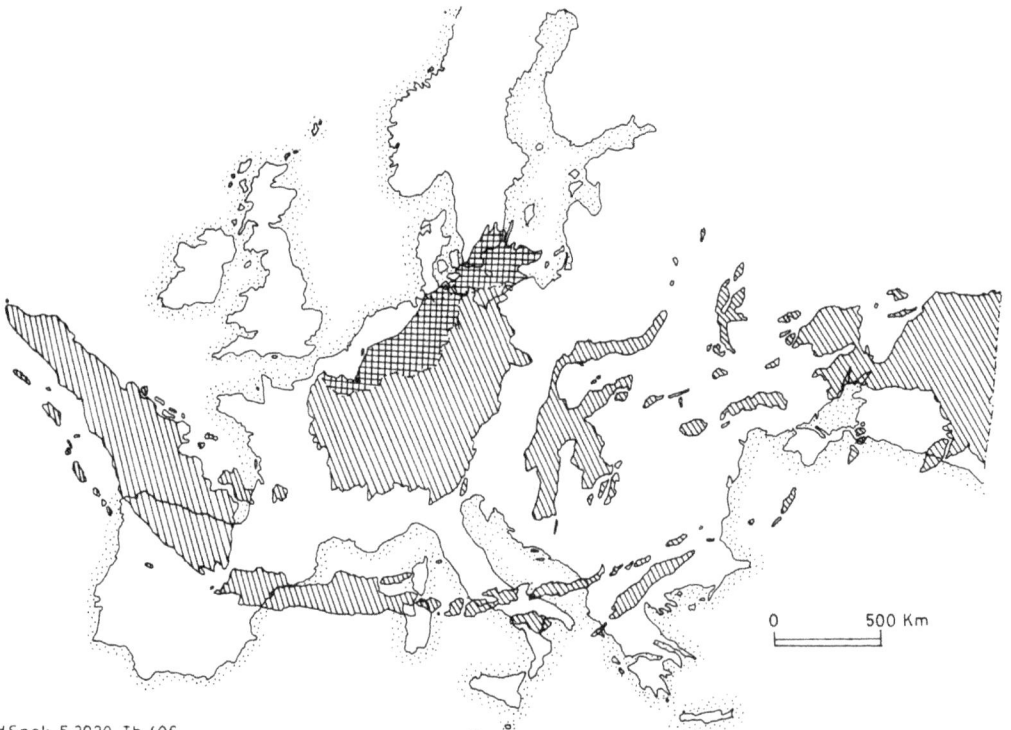

0   500 Km

D.v.d.Spek 5-2020 Th.406

THE DUTCH OR NETHERLANDS EAST INDIES 1

GEOGRAPHY OF THE INDONESIAN ARCHIPELAGO

The Indonesian archipelago in Southeast Asia, straddling the equator, is easily the largest of its kind in the world, with at least 17,508 islands, large and small, populated or uninhabited. Of this approximate total, 13,466 islands are officially localized, registered, and named, but quite a lot are unknown and unregistered, although nowadays the government of the Republic of Indonesia has instituted a program whereby every island will be visited, located exactly with a global positioning system, and given a name and official status. One problem is that because of severe volcanic activity, islands have a tendency to disappear quite suddenly, while new ones grow slowly or quickly out of the sea, resulting in a constant change in the number of islands. Total land surface is about 2 million km^{2}.[1]

This vast archipelago extends from latitude 6° to 11° south and from longitude 95° to 141° east, separating the Indian Ocean from the Pacific Ocean. Superimposed on a map of the contiguous United States of America with the top of the island of Sumatra overlaid on Oregon's coast, the most eastern part of the former Dutch East Indies, the western half of New Guinea, is situated far into the Atlantic Ocean, more than 5,000 km from west to east and 2,000 km from north to south. The two major islands, Java and Sumatra, the only ones where public railways were to be constructed, consist of an almost-impenetrable mountainous core running from west to east on Java and north to south on Sumatra. Some three hundred volcanoes are located in these mountain ranges, chiefly on Java. About sixty are active and all are between 3,000 m and 4,000 m high. These mountain ranges hindered communications well into the twentieth century. The northern part of Java and the eastern part of Sumatra are chiefly made up of a fertile alluvial plain. The population was and is concentrated in these low-lying plains, which are eminently suitable for agriculture.

The prevailing climate is tropical. From April to October the dry monsoon from the east is prevalent; the rest of the year the wet monsoon

Facing top, The Dutch East Indies superimposed on the USA in the same scale.

Facing bottom, The Dutch East Indies superimposed on Europe in the same scale.

from the west brings enormous moisture, annually between 1,500 and 4,000 mm of water, with the mountains receiving as much as 6,000 mm. Rainfall in western Java is more abundant than in the east, which impacts agriculture and the variety of plants that can be grown. El Niño conditions influence the climate unpredictably, with alternating wet and dry periods that affect plant growth and occasionally cause famine in some areas.[2]

This vast island empire was a gigantic colonial possession for the Kingdom of the Netherlands, itself a small but prosperous European country. With the largest colonial empire of all European powers except Great Britain, this kingdom somehow managed to hold on and survived well into the twentieth century. In 1816 the total population of the East Indies was roughly estimated at around 6 million, of which 4.5 million people were living on Java and neighboring Madoera. In 1880 the total population reached about 18 million, with 12.5 million people living on Java. Twenty years later the figures were 42 million and 28.4 million, respectively. This explosive increase was largely due to the so-called Pax Neerlandica that had removed the usual impediments to population growth such as war, famine, and plague. According to the 1930 census, the last under Dutch rule, the total population of the Netherlands East Indies was just under 60 million, of which 242,000 were Europeans and 1,233,000 Chinese. From these figures it is clear that apart from the European segment, the total population has grown enormously under Dutch rule since 1815. The Chinese arrived in the seventeenth century and were admitted and tolerated by the ruling Dutch East India Company, the Verenigde Oostindische Compagnie (VOC). They came as merchants and seafarers but soon settled in coastal towns as shopkeepers and also made themselves useful to the VOC and regional princes and sultans as tax farmers and operators of the opium dens and gambling joints, making them rather unpopular with the local population.

Although not the largest island and with an almost-inaccessible mountainous core full of volcanic activity, Java was and is the most important of all islands, with a population of over 100 million and still growing. Jakarta, known as Batavia in colonial times, is the capital of the Republic of Indonesia; with its 12 million inhabitants—in 2000—it is easily the largest town in the whole country. Soerabaja comes second with about 4 million, and Bandoeng is third with about 3 million. The five biggest towns of the whole archipelago—these three plus Semarang and Cheribon—are all situated on Java. For comparison, in 1815 the home country had a population of 2.5 million, in 1900 it had grown to 5.1 million, and by 1930 its inhabitants numbered 7.9 million. At the time of writing the population of the Kingdom of the Netherlands had grown to over 17 million, making it the most densely populated country of Europe and possibly of the world.

Slavery was normal during the early colonial era; local rulers and white officials had slaves, mostly house servants, but after the end of the English interim rule, the Dutch government prohibited the slave trade in 1818, following Britain (1807) and France (1815) in this respect. Slavery itself was abolished in the British colonies in 1833 and in France five years later. Batavia followed officially in 1860, but at that time slavery, mostly only in the shape of house servants, no longer amounted to much. This abolition could be immediately enforced in Java and in other areas and towns where Dutch rule was established, but certainly not everywhere, as Dutch authority in the Outer Possessions, as they were called, was weak or even nonexistent. The Spice Islands such as Ambon, Ternate, and Banda were also minor centers of population and under Dutch rule since the seventeenth century.[3]

The indigenous population belongs mostly to the Malay race, but a large number of subdivisions prevail, differing from each other in many respects, including language. On East Java Javanese was commonly spoken, including by Europeans who had settled there. In the western, Sundanese part of the island, Sundanese was the common language. To obviate the problem of many different tongues hindering communication, the Malay language, originating in the Malay Peninsula and also spoken in Sumatra, came to be considered as the lingua franca of the whole archipelago and also the language that the Dutch used to communicate with the native population. Their version of Malay was jokingly called "Barracks Malay" and was widely used, although the upper classes of Javanese had to learn Dutch in order to obtain better-paying jobs in administration, railways, and the mercantile world. The Bahasa Indonesia, nowadays the official language of the country, is chiefly High-Malay with a lot of Javanese, Dutch, and other foreign words.

HISTORY: DUTCH SEAFARERS AND MERCHANTS ENTER THE ASIAN TRADE

In the wake of the Portuguese seafarers, Dutch merchants decided to try their luck with Asia's promising trade. A first expedition of four ships was sent out in 1595, and although only three ships came home the following year with a small cargo of spices, the results were seen as positive, and other merchants joined the fray. In 1598 no less than twenty-two ships were outfitted by five different groups of merchants; enormous profits were made on the invested capital, as large as 400 percent. The competition in Holland and Zeeland became so strong that the fight for a place

The first meeting of Dutchmen and Indonesians. Cornelis de Houtman, with his brother Frederick, commander of the first Dutch expedition to the Indies, sets foot on the shores of Java in the Sultanate of Bantam and is greeted by the Shabandar (harbormaster) of the sultan, July 1595. A somewhat romanticized image from an educational print meant for elementary schools, late nineteenth century. (Author's collection)

in this developing and highly profitable trade became intense. This made responsible merchants and government officials of the Dutch Republic think of collaboration instead of competition. Under strong pressure from the States-General, now the undisputed rulers of the northern provinces forming the Republic of the Seven United Netherlands, a single national trading company, the Vereenigde Oostindische Compagnie, or the United East India Company, was founded in 1602. It was the first joint stock company in the world, with a capital of 6.5 million guilders, an unheard-of sum in those days. The VOC had a charter whereby it obtained a monopoly of trade and navigation east of the Cape of Good Hope and west of the Straits of Magellan. In essence it made the VOC a state within the state, with almost-unlimited powers and a near-absolute monopoly in the vital spice trade.[4]

At first the VOC operated from Bantam, the westernmost sultanate of Java, where a cooperative sultan allowed the Dutch—and other foreigners—to maintain a trading factory. In 1619 the city of Jacatra (Jakarta) on Java was besieged successfully; a new town, Batavia, was founded on its remnants. It became the center of operations of the VOC, the nucleus of the Dutch occupation of the Indies for the coming centuries. From there the company extended its activities as far as Japan and Ceylon and chased away all competitors, Portuguese, English, and others. Between

1602 and 1795, the VOC outfitted 4,721 ships for the journey to Asia, of which 3,356 ships returned to the patria. For these ships and for manning the forts, factories, and outposts in Asia, nearly one million men—and a few women—went to the East over these years; only 379,000 of them returned. Many Europeans succumbed to tropical diseases; others remained in the East after their contracts with the VOC had run out, often seeking refuge in the arms of local belles. Mixed-blood children became common, as European wives were hard to get. Of course, a small country such as the Dutch Republic, with a population of 1.6 million at most, was unable to supply the VOC with enough manpower. Large numbers of men from Scandinavia, Denmark, the Baltic countries, England, and the German states filled this void. Unemployment, personal problems in the relational sphere, bad harvests, or simply lust for adventure induced many to sign contracts with the VOC, sometimes with excellent results, but more commonly with early deaths as the outcome. Colonization of Java with white settlers was halfheartedly tried a few times but without lasting results. At the Cape of Good Hope, however, a permanent body of white settlers developed, mostly farmers, small merchants, and shopkeepers catering to the crews of the passing ships, resulting eventually in the Afrikaans/Dutch-speaking Boer segment of the population of the present-day South African Republic.[5]

By the end of the eighteenth century, however, the VOC suffered from ossification of the top-heavy administration, with the cost of maintaining its position in Asia increasing every year. In 1795 the situation became desperate and the new Batavian Republic, successor of the Dutch Republic, took over all assets and liabilities of the VOC, which became a nationalized trading company with a large number of settlements in the East, now wholly owned by the government.[6]

The Batavian Republic, established along the teachings of the French Revolution and soon occupied by French armies and drawn into its wars, was a small power, unable to defend its vast colonial possessions against the English foe, who occupied most of its colonial territories after 1795. In 1802, with the short-lived Peace of Amiens, all possessions, with the exception of Ceylon, were returned to the Batavian government, and a new discussion erupted about what to do with the colonies. However, war between France and Britain resumed in 1803 and the English again occupied the Cape, cutting off the familiar route to the Indies. The Batavian Republic was replaced by the Kingdom of Holland in 1806, with Louis Napoleon, the brother of Emperor Napoleon, taking the throne. Although still independent in name, the country was now just a small part of Napoleon's vast empire and supposed to follow orders from Paris. In 1810 Napoleon, unhappy with his brother who tried to hold on to some measure of independence, simply annexed the Kingdom of Holland; the former

Dutch Republic then became officially part of the French Empire, without any vestige of independence left. A consequence of the lost independence was that British forces occupied Java in 1811 and the Dutch flag was struck. The only place in the world where that flag was still proudly flown through all those turbulent years was Deshima, the little Japanese outpost of the VOC Empire in the Bay of Nagasaki. Nothing changed there until the arrival of Commodore Perry with the American navy in 1852.

A NEW APPROACH

The government of the newly formed Batavian Republic, after 1795 the overlord of the former VOC possessions in East Asia, wished to institute a new form of administration in the East Indies, one more in line with the precepts of the French Revolution and the ideals of liberty, equality, and fraternity of all mankind. To this end Herman Willem Daendels was appointed as governor-general in 1807 and was given wide powers to reorganize the ossified structure of government. After his arrival in Batavia, Daendels began vigorously reorganizing governmental structures, making the central administration in Batavia all important. He also enforced the growth of coffee by the indigenous people but at the same time tried hard to ensure that the money the government paid for this coffee ended up in the hands of the growers, not in those of Chinese intermediaries or the regional aristocracy. In 1811 the Dutch forts and factories in the Indies were occupied by British forces, an interregnum that lasted until 1815.[7]

With the London Agreement of August 13, 1814, Great Britain returned all former Dutch colonies except the Cape of Good Hope and Ceylon to the new government of the Netherlands, now under King Willem I of Orange-Nassau, the son of the last stadtholder of the Dutch Republic. Java and the Moluccas, Malacca, and some factories on the coast of British India became Dutch again. In 1824 with the Treaty of London, Britain also ceded all its possessions and factories on Sumatra. In return the Dutch government gave up its objections to the construction of a trading settlement at Singapore, originally part of the territory claimed by the VOC as part of the Dutch possessions.

After the English had departed, the new government structure consisted of the governor-general as the highest official representing the king of the Netherlands and residing in Batavia. He was assisted by a five-member council of the Indies and a general secretariat that took care of the day-to-day business. Altogether it was a highly centralized form of government, where everything had to be decided by Batavia. Of course, the Dutch minister for the colonies back in The Hague had the final decision and was responsible to the king and, especially after the introduction of the new constitution of the Netherlands in 1848, to Parliament. And

Parliament, often with "Indian specialists" as members, could be severely critical. Although without direct influence on the day-to-day business in the Indies, it could and often did send the minister home.

In the new government structure, following the direction taken by the British interim government, Java was split up into twenty residencies, with a "resident" at the head (in some cases supported by an assistant resident), a few European secretaries, and some indigenous staff. They reported to Batavia, and the governor-general had to sanction all important decisions. Gradually, these civil servants became known as the Binnenlands Bestuur (Internal Civil Administration), and during the nineteenth century, this corps of often-dedicated civil officers developed into an all-embracing civil service, with a strong belief in the importance of its mission to serve not only the interests of the colonial government but also the well-being of the indigenous population. Outside of Java there were only a few Dutch officials stationed in other places—in the Moluccas, at Makassar on Celebes, and at Padang on the west coast of Sumatra.

COMMUNICATIONS BETWEEN COLONY AND MOTHER COUNTRY

Before the opening of the Suez Canal, communication between home country and colony was only possible by sailing vessels around the Cape of Good Hope, and such a journey could take months. Letters and dispatches between Batavia and The Hague were lost with some regularity, and this made the government in Batavia very independent; it even had to be its own master when orders from The Hague were late or lacking. The opening of the English Overland Mail between Alexandria and Suez in Egypt in 1845, with connecting packet boats between England and Alexandria and from Suez to British India and Singapore, accelerated communications considerably, but it remained a troublesome and expensive journey. After the Suez Canal opened in 1869, the first Dutch regular shipping line was established in 1870, with regular sailings from Amsterdam to Batavia with modern steamships, but even then a journey still took weeks. At Port Said a Dutch coaling station was opened, an initiative of Prince Hendrik, younger brother of then-reigning King Willem III and an astute businessman and shipping specialist. It turned out to be a godsend for Dutch steamships to have their own coaling facilities there, and the Dutch soon reached third place—after Britain and France—in the number of ships passing through the new canal.

However, even with steamships, communication was still time-consuming; only the introduction of the telegraph improved matters substantially. This was not trouble free, as most of the telegraph lines were British-owned and -operated, and transmitting secret messages by this medium could be problematic. Only much later did German and French lines become available, making it possible for the Dutch to choose the carrier that promised the best service and the most secrecy.[8]

Both Daendels and his English predecessor had alienated the regional native princes of Java, and unrest caused by their policies continued after the Dutch returned to power. Especially in Jogjakarta—also written as Djokjakarta, or Djokja for short—one of the two large principalities in mid-Java known as the Vorstenlanden, the *soesoehoenan*—sultan—was unhappy with his strictly limited "independence" as the outcome of the measures taken by both governors. And when Batavia got itself mixed up in the disputed succession of the deceased sultan, the majority of the regional aristocracy rebelled. The common people, already angered by the farming out of the road tolls to Chinese entrepreneurs, joined the revolt. A Javanese prince, Diponegoro, a man with an almost-religious aura, became the leader of the rebels, and the Batavian government had the greatest trouble in subduing the revolt in 1830. It took almost five years and great loss of life on both sides, with eight thousand European and seven thousand indigenous military killed or struck down by disease, and an estimated two hundred thousand Javanese dead by famine and sickness. The *soesoehoenan* of Soerakarta, the other of the great princes, had wisely remained neutral in the conflict, but he also had to accept a still more restricted and wholly ceremonial role, with the Dutch representative in his capital the real authority. The role of the Javanese aristocracy as actual rulers was terminated from then on, and the government in Batavia had to be recognized as the only power in the land.[9]

ESTABLISHMENT OF DUTCH RULE

On Java, always the nucleus of Dutch presence, there were no serious disturbances of the peace after the end of the Java War; Dutch rule was acknowledged, albeit grudgingly, by the local sultans and rajahs. In the Buitengewesten, the Outer Possessions, this was different. Well into the nineteenth century the government in Batavia, although formally claiming the overlordship, had left a large number of regional rulers in power. After the 1850s this attitude slowly changed and the Batavian government established actual rule, enforced by military presence if need be. Fear of interference by other European powers also played a role. Britain was always seen as a frequent interloper, meddling in Borneo, for instance; later, Japan and the United States of America were viewed as possible aggressors. Around 1900 the last of the more or less independent sultans and rajahs were brought under the Kompenie, the old East India Company, which was still used in some places as the name for Dutch rule. This process of integration was generally peaceful and executed by the signing of the Korte Verklaring, the Brief Declaration, whereby the local ruler acknowledged the overlordship of the king or queen of the Netherlands as represented by the governor-general in Batavia, while retaining some measure of independence in local affairs. If need be, Dutch rule was enforced with military presence resulting in sometimes-bloody fights such as with the Bali rajahs, who were subjected only after large-scale expeditions from Batavia in 1906 and 1908.[10]

Indonesia as a centrally governed state dates only from the end of World War II. Its present borders did not exist before 1900 and were only slowly determined with the extension of Dutch rule as far as the very limits of the archipelago. Possible outside enemies had been eliminated with agreements and treaties with other powers. Sumatra had been secured with treaties with Great Britain in 1824 and 1871, and agreement over Borneo was reached in 1895. On New Guinea the Dutch government had simply drawn a frontier on the map in a straight north-south line down the middle of the enormous but still largely uncharted island. This border was not challenged and was accepted by Germany for the northeastern half and by Britain for the southeastern part. Both major powers simply acknowledged the fact that the Dutch claimed the western half of this vast island and apparently did not take the trouble to check for themselves if this border was indeed accurate. New Guinea's interior was then unknown, and no whites had ever disturbed the silence in the vast primeval jungle and mountains.[11]

THE CULTIVATION SYSTEM

By 1830, with a deficit of more than 31 million guilders, the financial situation in the East Indies had become desperate and had to be made good by the home government. As the ongoing "war" with Belgium kept the Dutch army on a war footing, government in The Hague anxiously sought a solution for the Indian deficits. King Willem I, who at that time still held executive power in colonial matters, appointed Johannes van den Bosch as governor-general, with the strict order to find a solution for the continuing losses. Van den Bosch was no newcomer in this respect, as he had already done a similar job to clear up the finances of the Dutch West Indies—with no real success, however—but the king trusted him.[12]

Van den Bosch arrived in Batavia in early January 1830 with explicit instructions to improve the financial situation of the colony by whatever means necessary. The existing system of recognizing the individuality of the Javanese farmers in combination with the introduction of free

European entrepreneurs employing local workers had not been a success, so Van den Bosch fell back on the traditional system as operated by the old East India Company, where the governor-general decided which products had to be grown on government-owned lands. To execute the system, the village heads, the *bupatis*, were charged with the actual enforcement of the newly prescribed cultures in their villages. Not more than one-fifth of the village lands were to be used this way, and the mandatory labor of the villagers to care for the government cultures was to be strictly limited so as to leave them time to grow rice and other foodstuffs for the local population on the remaining lands. To facilitate the new organization, a *plantloon*, planting wage, was paid to the local villagers as a reward, a not-to-be-disregarded addition to the income of the small farmers in cash. The Vorstenlanden, the Principalities of Soerakarta and Jogjakarta, were exempt from the system, as these lands were not government owned but rather part of the old feudal lands of both sultans. The system was not too bad and did not put too great a strain on the native population. However, although this was the official policy, local or regional circumstances could make a great difference and the colonial authorities could and did make wrong decisions now and then, while native authorities sometimes misused their position and newly acquired powers. The local population suffered while a number of the aristocratic Javanese regents made a lot of money, helped in some cases by an untrustworthy European resident.

Of course, opponents of the system were many, and they had reason to complain. In some regions there were serious abuses when the population was forced to work more than the stipulated hours, and a number of fairly serious famines in some regions of Java resulted because of a lack of manpower to see to the rice crops. On the other hand the development of the Javanese economy was stimulated by this Cultuurstelsel, or Cultivation System, as it became known, and the enormous population growth during these years may be seen as a sign that not everything in this system was wrong. This is not the place to weigh the pros and cons of the Cultuurstelsel, as scores of books and studies have been published over the years stressing the advantages or negative sides of the system.[13]

Financially, Van den Bosch was indeed successful in regard to the home country's economy, even if the actual results minus the sums expended in Java are open to different explanations and computations. However, modern experts agree that the system worked positively for the home country. In 1832 the first Batig Slot (Colonial Benefits) flowed into the Dutch treasury, then still only a small amount of ƒ761.500. Not much perhaps, but more sizable sums were coming soon. Five years later the total was ƒ20 million, and in 1857 it amounted to no less than ƒ41.7 million, a sum that constituted more than 40 percent of the Netherlands government's total revenue. Throughout the 1850s the Batig Slot made up

32 percent of the Dutch national income, with peaks of over 50 percent in some years. After 1865 this percentage declined slowly to almost nil in 1875, when the Cultivation System was abolished. Altogether, between 1832 and 1875 at least ƒ800 million—possibly more—were transferred from the Indies to the mother country, but hard figures are difficult to come by. The Netherlands government sensibly used these for-the-time gigantic sums. The great canals linking the ports of Amsterdam and Rotterdam with the North Sea were paid, at least partly, with this money, and the railway network constructed by the state after 1860 was financed largely from the Batig Slot. On the other hand, it should not be forgotten that Java (and other districts, to a lesser extent) also profited from the increase in production, the availability of cash for the indigenous population, and the stricter regulation and supervision of the local regents when their rapacious treatment of the population was discovered by the authorities. A possibly unexpected result of the sudden growth of the production of tropical products, sugar and coffee foremost, was the need for a better transportation system than the existing slow and cumbersome oxcarts.[14]

Apart from the Cultivation System, the government had other regular sources of income. One of these was the mining of tin on the island of Banka on the southeastern coast of Sumatra. These mines were developed during the eighteenth century by the old East India Company, and in the nineteenth century they were taken over by the government. In 1853, when the finances of the Batavian government were slowly recovering, the Banka mines yielded some 92,000 pikols (~5.6 million kg), and in 1914 this had grown to more than 255,000 pikols (~15.5 million kg), with a net result of more than 16 million guilders for the treasury. The Billiton Company, a private company established with the support of Prince Hendrik, the brother of King Willem III, operated the tin mines on the neighboring island of Billiton beginning in 1852. The company's production was always less than that of the Banka mines but was generally at a healthy level. As one of the principal shareholders of the Billiton Maatschappij, Prince Hendrik managed to generate a fortune of many millions.[15]

An organization that benefited enormously from the Cultivation System was the Nederlandsche Handel-Maatschappij (NHM, Netherlands Trading Company), another of King Willem I's creations, which monopolized the traffic to and from the Indies for a long time. Established in 1824 with strong support of the king, it was intended to boost the country's exports and imports after the disastrous years of the Continental System imposed by Napoleon, whereby trade and industry in the Netherlands had come to a near standstill. The old East India Company was the great example to follow and the NHM became the banker, broker, and shipping agent of the government in the Netherlands Indies. The NHM sold Java's products; cotton fabrics from the Netherlands were exported to the Indies, and competing British fabrics were charged with high import duties to force them off the market. The shipbuilding industry in the north was also stimulated enormously, as the NHM guaranteed a number of voyages for every ship built by domestic shipyards. Sugar refiners on Java could obtain substantial loans under favorable conditions from the NHM. From the 1850s the company gradually also took over existing cane fields and established new ones. In short, in the first half of the nineteenth century the NHM played a role as a monopolist resembling the old East India Company. Later in the century it would also act as banker to several new railway and tramway companies.

During the times of the East India Company, the VOC bronze duit, or penny, had become the common coin used by the indigenous population. Millions of these small coins had been brought in by the East Indiamen, and they became the established means of paying when cash was needed. With the Muntwet (Coinage Law) of 1854, it had been laid down that in the Indian archipelago the Dutch gulden (guilder) was the only monetary unit to be used, but this did not mean that silver guilders and copper cents were going to be used exclusively everywhere. Ancient and modern Spanish and Portuguese coins were used regionally, and Dutch cents were rare. In the 1890s the decision was made to introduce the cent on a large scale in Java and declare the use of the old duit unlawful. In the last four years of the nineteenth century, newly minted coins of 0.5, 1, and 2.5 cents to a value of more than seven million guilders were introduced and exchanged for the old duiten.

In the Outer Possessions Dutch coins were hardly used at all; on Sumatra's east coast the Straits dollar was the usual currency. Tobacco and other products of the Deli region were generally paid in Straits dollars until around 1905, when the Batavian government declared the Straits dollar illegal in Sumatra; from then on the Dutch silver guilder and rijksdaalder (2.5 guilders) were the only legal tender. Silver coins were minted at the Royal Mint at Utrecht, and from 1885 until the outbreak of World War I in 1914, silver coins valuing more than 25 million guilders were sent.

ROAD CONSTRUCTION ON JAVA, 1800–1850

Governor-General Daendels, sent out by the Batavian Republic, arrived in Batavia in 1808. As noted, he was full of ideas for improvement of both the internal structure of government and at the same time catered for the welfare of the indigenous population. He also clearly saw that to ward off the numerous British competitors, who were looking at the Dutch possessions with a jealous eye, better inland communication was sorely needed to be able to transport troops and equipment quickly to threatened places. Shortly after his arrival, Daendels traveled across Java and saw with his

own eyes how terrible the few existing roads were. These desa—village—roads needed a lot of improvement to make them suitable for vehicular traffic, and they had to be interconnected. He set his mind to the creation of a surfaced road extending from the west of the island at Anjer all the way to Soerabaja and farther east to Banjoewangi, some 1,000 km in all. The first part would be the road from Batavia to Buitenzorg, where the governor-general resided, and from there eastward to Bandoeng. This road was intended to lower transportation costs in general, facilitate the movement of troops, and stimulate new "cultures," new areas for profitable large-scale agriculture.

This first section was to form an integral part of the Grote Postweg, the Great Post Road, 7.5 m wide and surfaced with gravel or rubble to make it fit for use in the wet season. Military engineers selected the best routes and the best locations to cross rivers. Every 5 to 6 paal (a paal is about 1 mile), a government post was established where travelers could change horses. More widely spaced were so-called pasanggrahans, primitive

A *pendopo* along the Great Post Road near Tjiandjoer, before 1880. Here horses could be changed, and light refreshments could be bought from a local merchant. (KITLV collection)

hostelries set up by the government and operated by local managers, more often than not Chinese. In these very simple places travelers could obtain food and (hopefully) clean and bug-free beds. Workers on the road were paid in money or in rice and salt, and the supervisors generally were Europeans, invalids from the army mostly. By mid-1809 the Great Post Road was almost finished and its advantages had become clear to everyone. In earlier days it had taken two weeks in the dry season and three in the wet to reach Soerabaja from Batavia; now travelers needed only nine or ten days to cover the same distance. Letters could be transferred in even less time, six or seven days and express mail in four to five. Twice a week a stagecoach left Batavia for Soerabaja and vice versa, a luxury unknown until then.

After the restoration of Dutch rule, roadbuilding continued, now with the use of forced labor, the hated Heerendiensten. A more southerly road was started in 1854 to pass through Djokja and Solo (Soerakarta), something that had been sorely needed during the Java War in those regions. On all other islands road construction took off much later, with the exception of an early road already built through the Anei Gorge on Sumatra's west coast, connecting Padang on the coast with the interior. It was stupendous work, given the character of the mountainous area, but military considerations played a paramount role in this case.[16]

THE INTERINSULAR TRAFFIC

It will come as no surprise that in a vast archipelago such as this one, shipping had always been the most important way in connecting the several islands and ports. The East India Company had set up an intricate network of interinsular shipping, and some of the indigenous people were skillful navigators and plied the Indonesian waters with their multitude of small but sophisticated vessels. In the nineteenth century Chinese and Arabs also operated shipping lines, sometimes under the Dutch flag though more often under British colors, and the Batavian government had little or no influence over these. After the English interregnum, Singapore became a great competitor to Batavia and attracted most of these vessels. Consequently, yields of the custom duties at Batavia diminished and the importance of the town as a shipping center was marginalized.

After some earlier attempts, a Gouvernements Marine (GM, government navy) was set up in 1861 for both civilian and military duties. All new ships were armed with small caliber cannon, although the personnel remained in civilian service. Apart from these duties the GM vessels were also used for hydrographical purposes, setting up lights and placing buoys in dangerous waters, and for charting the then-still-largely-unknown seas. The laying and maintenance of underwater telegraph cables came also

The *Koningin Sophia*, an 822-ton steamer of the NISM, at the landing stage of Ternate Island around 1880. Queen Sophia was the first wife of King Willem III. (KITLV collection)

into their realm. Steamships were in service with the GM since 1839, but sailing craft remained in use until well into the nineteenth century.[17]

A purely commercial enterprise was the shipping company of a former Dutch naval officer named W. Cores de Vries. Starting in 1850 the company operated regular steamship lines between the more important ports and carried government goods and personnel in return for a subsidy per nautical mile for its regular lines. This agreement did not work well: rates were considered too high, the number of ships—six—too small, and their capacity too limited. In 1865 the government decided not to renew the contract and a call for tenders was issued. The lowest bid was offered by a certain H. O. Robinson, an Englishman, while the Dutch applicant, an Amsterdam firm of good reputation, asked one cent more of subsidy per nautical mile, making a total annual difference for the government of 421 guilders and 56 cents. Although the Amsterdam firm offered to lower its bid to that of Robinson's, the contract went to the Englishman, who transferred his rights to a newly incorporated firm, the Nederlandsch-Indische Stoomvaartmaatschappij (Netherlands Indies Steam Navigation Company), a subsidiary of the British India Steam Navigation Company of London. Despite its Dutch name, this was a British company and apart

from the contracted lines to and from Batavia. It concentrated its services on Singapore, not Batavia, and it also tended to neglect the Buitengewesten, the Outlying Districts that were developing fast in the second half of the nineteenth century.

Most harbors in the archipelago were just river estuaries, without any attempt to facilitate the loading and unloading of ships. Only small vessels could enter the rivers; larger ships had to anchor in the roadstead and unload or load by means of proas or lighters. Only Batavia had been provided with two piers of 800 m as early as 1634 to protect the roadstead from storms. However, the river, the Tjiliwong, continued to silt up, which meant that Batavia as a port was still insufficient; mechanical dredging had to be employed in the 1860s to provide enough draft for the growing number of ever-larger steamships. All other harbors suffered from the same faults.[18]

THE TRANSPORTATION PROBLEM

With the growth of the economy and the enormous increase in the production of sugar, coffee, and other staple products grown under the

Cultivation System, it became clear that the lack of transportation was becoming the greatest hindrance for progress. This problem was felt most in the Vorstenlanden, where sugar production was expanding. Two-wheeled bullock carts were the only means to get the sugar from the mills over primitive roads to the port of Semarang. Serious attempts were made to improve road transport with the importation of camels, but these animals were unable to adapt to the humid tropical climate. A similar experiment with donkeys from the home country failed for the same reason.

Some forward thinkers came early with plans for railways to ease this transportation problem. The first, in 1840, was the director of the East Indies Army Corps of Engineers, Colonel C. van der Wijck, who presented a memorandum to the Batavian government advising the construction of an east–west railway across the length of Java, chiefly as a means to facilitate the defense of the island against internal and external enemies. It was an eminent idea, but he was too early; moreover, there was no detailed knowledge of the terrain such a railway would have to traverse, so nothing more was heard of his plan. And it is good to bear in mind that Van der Wijck's memorandum came only one year after the first railway had been opened in the home country between Amsterdam and Haarlem. The railway was still a novelty, even more so in the Indies.

More serious was the request of the Amsterdam firm Job Dixon & Company late in 1841 for a concession for a railway from Semarang to the Vorstenlanden, the Principalities, the center of sugar and coffee growing. Dixon knew what he was talking about. At the time, his Amsterdam firm, trading under the name of IJzergieterij de Atlas (Iron Foundry the Atlas), was constructing steam locomotives and other equipment for the Holland Railway in the Netherlands. Yet, despite this experience with steam traction, he did not advocate steam for his proposed lines on Java. Instead, he preferred, at least for the first years, traction by animals—bullocks, buffalo, or even horses. He estimated that his proposed company would need a capital of at least 5 million guilders, to be raised privately. To facilitate this, he asked the government for an interest guarantee of 5 percent per annum for this sum. In June 1843 the minister for the colonies, J. C. Baron Baud, dismissed his proposal chiefly for financial reasons. The government was not yet ready to support private enterprise.

Earlier, on May 28, 1842, a royal decree had been published wherein it was explicitly stated that an iron railway was deemed necessary between Semarang and the Principalities "for the advancement of the transportation of goods by means of wagons hauled by buffaloes." Baud had advised against government involvement; in his opinion it was already doing too much while private persons and commercial enterprises were doing too little. He believed whenever a venture seemed qualified to attract private entrepreneurs, one should stimulate these as much as possible. Apparently, the proposed railway was seen as such a venture, but the purse strings were not yet loosened. A call for parties interested in such a railway was issued, but nobody came forward. Baud had to tell the king that without some form of financial support, it would be impossible to get anything done. The lack of dependable maps and complete absence of estimates of expected revenues from the traffic made it simply impossible to even roughly define the cost and probable profitability of such a line; without these essential data, capitalists—Dutch or foreign—were not interested.

With this in mind Baud ordered the Batavian government to have a survey made for a line from Semarang to the Principalities. An officer of the Corps of Engineers, G. H. Uhlenbeck, finished this survey in 1844, but his conclusion was negative: the line was technically possible, but only at great expense. In his final words, it would be "a hazardous, dangerous and not very effective enterprise." Meanwhile, Job Dixon, naturally in the hope of substantial orders for ironwork, had renewed his request for a concession for such a line, this time without interest guarantee; again his request was refused. This refusal was based on the possibility that a new group of businessmen and bankers had demanded a concession for a more extensive network of lines on Java, on the condition that the company would be allowed to cut wood in the government forests free of charge and could dispose of a workforce of five thousand forced laborers per day at the government's expense. When the minister showed much reluctance to grant the second article of this request, the applicants withdrew their demand.

THE GOVERNMENT TAKES THE INITIATIVE

An unexpected outcome of all these frustrated attempts was that Governor-General J. J. Rochussen, although a moderate liberal in his political outlooks, declared officially that he now opined that only the government would ever be able to construct railways and work them and, moreover, that it was now financially possible, without endangering the Batig Slot, the precious cash flow from the Indies to the home country. Minister Baud disagreed with the financial picture as sketched by Rochussen and made it known that he wanted to have a detailed report of the need and practicability of every proposed line. Upon reception of this decision, the governor-general at once ordered David Maarschalk, of the Indian Corps of Engineers, to prepare such a report for a Batavia–Buitenzorg railway line.

More delays followed, and when A. J. Duymaer van Twist succeeded Rochussen in 1851, the new minister for the colonies C. F. Pahud in the Liberal cabinet of J. R. Thorbecke turned out to favor railway construction by private parties, not by government. In 1852 a royal decree was issued in which it was stated that Dutch citizens could obtain a concession for railway construction but without a promise of any financial government support. The stipulation that such a concession would only be granted after an exhaustive report about the practicability and usefulness of the project proved to be the greatest obstacle, as detailed and reliable maps of the interior of Java were nonexistent and economic data unavailable. Many applicants hesitated to invest in a thorough survey of a proposed line without the certainty of its possible rentability. Nothing much came of the decree, and Java remained without the much-needed railway for many more years.[19]

By now the greatest possible disagreement reigned among the Indian specialists and advisors. Pahud, now governor-general, wrote to the Minister for the Colonies Rochussen—they had changed places—that railways were sorely needed for the maintenance of Dutch authority as well as for Java's prosperity, but as a confirmed liberal he saw no role for government. However, he admitted that help from the state would be indispensable, preferably in the shape of an interest guarantee on the capital necessary for construction. Rochussen, still in favor of construction by the state, handed Pahud's message to a newly appointed fact-finding committee of two engineers with deep knowledge of railway matters, L. J. A. van der Kun and D. J. Storm Buysing. Van der Kun was known as one of the few real experts in railway construction, and he was also a great proponent of construction by the state, which was soon to bear fruit in the law of 1860 that ordered the building of a network of some 800 km in the Netherlands as planned by Van der Kun himself. Storm Buysing was author of an authoritative handbook of engineering, water management, and public works, including railways.[20]

In 1860 the two presented their report, and they were outspoken in their conclusion. First, railway construction on Java by private parties was impossible without strong support from the state. And though an interest guarantee might seem the easiest way of support, that would be most unprofitable for the state, as hereby all risks would be shifted onto the state, which would have no power over the way the railway was built and run. Second, in view of this, railway construction should be undertaken by the state itself and, if necessary, the actual running of the line could be farmed out to private parties. They also advised to start immediately with the necessary surveys and drawing up of estimates for the lines that were considered most needed.

This was a pretty clear and well-founded report, and Rochussen then asked the king to send out two new experts—Storm Buysing and Van der Kun did not want to go again—to make a study of the transportation problems between Semarang and the Principalities. He proposed T. J.

Stieltjes and Job Dixon as candidates for the job, and both agreed to travel to Java and see for themselves what could be done. Stieltjes was appointed "advisor in technical matters" with the Department for the Colonies, and Dixon got the title of "engineer in chief for railways and industry" in the Netherlands Indies. The two left immediately for the Indies, accompanied by several others including the engineer N. H. Henket, whom we will meet again later. The group was known as the Commissie voor de Vervoermiddelen (Transportation Committee) and it was assisted by several local officials. Late in 1862 the committee came forward with a comprehensive plan for railways and waterways on Java, but two lines stood out: Semarang–Principalities and Batavia–Buitenzorg.

NOTES

1. Short article in daily newspaper *NRC-Handelsblad*, June 9, 2017.

2. Figures from Reitsma, *Van Stockum's Travellers' Handbook*, 33–38. On agriculture also Boomgaard, "Het Javaanse Boerenbedrijf."

3. Figures from Ravesteijn and Kop, "The Infrastructure of Dutch Colonialism in Indonesia," in Ravesteijn and Kop, eds., *For Profit and Prosperity*, 15–43.

4. These paragraphs are based on Boxer, *Dutch Seaborne Empire, 1600–1800*. Also used is Jong (de), *De Waaier van het Fortuin*. Older but still useful is the short survey by Stapel, *Geschiedenis van Nederlandsch-Indië*. See the history of the Dutch East India Company in Gaastra, *De geschiedenis van de VOC*; also Meilink-Roelofs, *Asian Trade and European Influence*.

5. Guleij and Knaap, eds., *Dutch East India Company Book*. Also Israel, *Dutch Primacy in World Trade*, and Vries (de) and Woude (van der), *First Modern Economy*, 429–56. A useful short survey of the history of the VOC in English is Jacobs, *In Pursuit of Pepper and Tea*.

6. Goor (van), *De Nederlandse Koloniën*. Also Goor (van), *Prelude to Colonialism*, and Wintle, *Economic and Social History*, 214–25.

7. About Daendels's work as governor-general of the Indies, see Jong (de), *De Waaier van het Fortuin*, 164–89.

8. Goor (van), *Prelude to Colonialism*, 115–24.

9. About Prince Diponegoro (or Dipanagara), see Carey, *Power of Prophecy*.

10. Goor (van), *De Nederlandse Koloniën*, 256–58.

11. Ibid., 209–11.

12. Johannes van den Bosch (1780–1844) was an officer in the Army Corps of Engineers and was active in the plans to reform beggars and other unruly persons in the Netherlands. Between 1830 and 1834 he was governor-general of the Dutch East Indies; after his return he was elevated to the nobility as baron and in 1839 was promoted to Count Van den Bosch. Molhuysen and Blok, eds., *Nieuw Nederlandsch Biografisch Woordenboek*, II, 221–27.

13. About the Cultivation System, see Goor (van), *De Nederlandse Koloniën*, 220–30; Jong (de), *De Waaier van het Fortuin*, 203–27; Wintle, *Economic and Social History*, 214–25; Elson, *Village Java under the Cultivation System*. See the figures for the "Batig Slot" in Zanden (van) and Riel (van), *Nederland*, 220–31; the NHM in

Graaf (de), *Voor Handel en Maatschappij*; currency and monetary matters in Potting, "De muntvoorziening in Nederlands-Indië."

14. A Dutch guilder, indicated by *f* for florin, was the currency used in the Dutch East Indies and worth about $0.45 as long as the countries were more or less adhering to the gold standard.

15. Figures from Gonggrijp, *Schets ener economische geschiedenis van Indonesië*, 150–51. About Billiton, see Mollema, *De ontwikkeling van het eiland Billiton.* About Prince Hendrik and the Billiton Maatschappij, see Fasseur, *Indischgasten*, 244.

16. Helsdingen (van), *Daar werd wat groots verricht*, 250–55. Horn-van Nispen, "Road to a New Empire," 68–91.

17. Wijn, *Tot in de verste uithoeken*, 13–24.

18. Veering, "Nodes in the Maritime Network."

19. Reitsma, *Korte geschiedenis*, 5–20. Gerard Hendrik Uhlenbeck (1815–1888), a career officer of the Corps of Engineers (1853–1858), chief of the Waterboard and Public Works in Batavia, minister for the colonies (1862–1863) in the Liberal Cabinet of J. R. Thorbecke. He earned much praise for his reorganization of the Public Works in the Indies. Molhuysen and Blok, eds., *Nieuw Nederlandsch Biografisch Woordenboek*, IV, 1349–53. Jan Jacob Rochussen (1797–1871) was minister of finance from 1840–1843. As such he did much to restore the shaky finances of the kingdom. As governor-general of the Netherlands East Indies (1845–1851), he managed to establish the rule of the Batavian government in some of the Outlying Districts; in 1858 he was asked to form a ministry, moderately liberal as he said, and was himself minister for the colonies until 1861. Ibid., II, 1217–24. Jean-Chrétien Baron Baud (1789–1891) was governor-general of the East Indies 1833–1836 and minister for the colonies 1840–1848; for a time this department was combined with that of the navy.

20. Leopold Johannes Antonius van der Kun (1801–1864) was engineer with the National Waterboard and charged with the construction of the Rhine Railway Amsterdam-Utrecht-Arnhem; later he was first advisor of the government in railway matters. Veenendaal, *Spoorwegen in Nederland*, 56–62; Molhuysen and Blok, eds., *Nieuw Nederlandsch Biografisch Woordenboek*, II, 738–44. Duco Johannes Storm Buysing (1802–1870) was teacher and later professor of water management and public works at the Delft Academy, the predecessor of the present-day Technical University. Ibid., I, 525–27.

Meanwhile, with the Transportation Committee still at work, three businessmen had applied in August 1861 for a concession for a Semarang–Soerakarta–Djokjakarta line, the old plan but somewhat modified. The Indies government asked Stieltjes to advise about this, and his report in January 1862 was negative. He opined that the most productive regions of mid-Java would not be reached by the proposed line and therefore the profitability would be dubious. Other self-styled experts on Java gave their opinions as well, some favorably, others in the negative; the discussions continued, in Batavia and in The Hague.

Finally, a new application for a concession came from the three solid businessmen with strong connections to Java: W. Poolman, A. Fraser and E. H. Kol. It embraced the construction and exploitation of a railway between the three towns mentioned. The initiator of this venture was Willem Poolman, who had a career in the Indies as factor of the Nederlandsche Handel Maatschappij on Java, but he had returned to Amsterdam in 1859 and set up on his own. He was one of the leading businessmen behind the company that was incorporated to work the state-built railway lines in the Netherlands after 1863 and was one of its first directors until 1865, when he concentrated all of his attention—and his private means—on the Indian railway as promoted by him and his fellow applicants. Kol was a member of a prosperous banking family from Utrecht. Fraser was a Scottish banker living in Batavia and factor of the Nederlandsch-Indische Handels Bank there.[1]

The three applicants estimated the necessary capital for construction at 18 million guilders and asked for an interest guarantee of 5 percent from the government. Moreover, they requested permission to attract foreign engineers and craftsmen, as these were hardly available locally. Batavia was always reluctant to permit foreigners to migrate to and settle on Java, hence their request. All three men were well known and respected, were seen as sound entrepreneurs—not fantasts or swindlers—and were fully capable of undertaking and finishing the project. Despite Stieltjes's negative advice, the new governor-general, L. A. J. W. Baron Sloet van de Beele, decided on August 28, 1862, with the reservation of royal permission and formal agreement by law, that Poolman and his friends could make a start. Stieltjes was furious and sent a formal protest straight to Parliament in The Hague in which he asked for a new examination of his reports and postponement of the granting of the concession to Poolman. This was not only inexpedient, as government servants were not allowed to contact Parliament without consent of their superiors, but it also smelled of a personal antagonism between him and Sloet. Stieltjes, when chief of the Waterboard of Overijssel province in the home country, had advised very negatively about a plan for railways in that province as proposed by Sloet, then still only a lawyer with business interests in neighboring Gelderland province. Sloet, now in a powerful position as governor-general, hit back by ignoring Stieltjes's report about the concession and allowing Poolman to begin with his plan. Minister for the Colonies J. D. Fransen van de Putte was not amused by this unheard-of move by Stieltjes and discharged him with dishonor straightaway.[2]

Meanwhile, discussions in The Hague continued. Uhlenbeck, who had earlier made the first survey of the Semarang–Principalities line, was now minister for the colonies, and he was more in favor of all-embracing concessions, not for just one line as Poolman had applied for. He handed the application to a commission of which J. P. de Bordes was a member. De Bordes was already secretary of the Dutch Commission for the Construction of Railways by the state, a result of an 1860 law to make good the arrears in the development of a railway network in the country. Delays resulted from the setting up of this new commission, and while the issue was undecided, Uhlenbeck stepped down as minister early in January 1863; his successor, the liberal J. D. Fransen van de Putte, himself once a planter and owner of sugar mills on Java, acted at once. At his request the applicants agreed to have the interest guarantee lowered from 5 to 4.5 percent, and at the minister's request, a branch to Fort Willem I was added to the project. In this somewhat modified shape, Parliament passed the law after long deliberations in June 1863. The concession in the name of Poolman, Fraser, and Kol was published in the Staatsblad (the official Dutch government publication) on July 6, 1863. The three could set to work.[3]

The most important articles of the concession were the following: duration of the concession would be for ninety-nine years, and at the end of that period the railway with everything included would become the property of the state, free and without charge. After twenty years, and after each consecutive period of ten years thereafter, the state would have the right to take over the railway for a price agreed on by both parties. During the first thirty-three years of exploitation, the state would guarantee 4.5 percent interest on the capital used for construction to a maximum of ƒ630,000 annually. And until ultimo December 1868, the date that the first trains should be running, the state would pay 4.5 percent interest over the capital really paid in. The gauge of the track and the size and weight of the rail to be used would be decided by the governor-general after consultation with the concessionaires. So far this was nothing unusual, as concessions for large public works to be executed by private parties in the Netherlands generally carried the same provisions. One thing was particular to the situation in the Indies: the concessionaires would be free to attract foreign workers, but the governor-general reserved the right to extradite these workers after the railway was finished. The slowness in decision-making about the need for railways as outlined in the above story was nothing special to the Indies, as the same was seen in the home country in those years. Only in 1860, with the law of August 18 of that year, came an end to the interminable discussions and palavers about the construction of railways in the Netherlands.[4]

For the Indies there were two additional grave problems. Although in the Netherlands cartography had advanced strongly since the Napoleonic era and the whole country had been clearly mapped out in great detail by triangulation, in the Indies large parts of the interior even of the island of Java were still terra incognita, making surveys and estimates of expenses a kind of gamble. It is no wonder potential investors were reluctant to risk their money in these ventures with an unknown and possibly negative end. A second problem was the time it took to get messages from Batavia to The Hague and vice versa. Months went by before the home government's decisions, including royal decrees and laws, would reach Batavia. The opening of the Suez Canal in 1869 speeded up this process enormously, and the laying of telegraph cables had an even more beneficial effect. The first land cable was laid between Batavia and Buitenzorg in 1856, followed by the connection between Batavia and Soerabaja in 1858. The first undersea cable between Batavia and Singapore was opened in 1859, but technical problems with this first one went unsolved until 1870.

THE NETHERLANDS INDIES RAILWAY COMPANY

On August 27, 1863, Poolman, Fraser, and Kol, the fresh concessionaires of the railway between Semarang and the Principalities in central Java, incorporated the Nederlandsch-Indische Spoorweg Maatschappij (NIS, Netherlands Indies Railway Company) and transferred their concession to the new company. The official seat of the NIS was to be The Hague in the Netherlands and share capital was set at 14 million guilders, of which 10 million was to be issued at once, which was considered enough for the acquisition of land, the actual construction of the line plus all other necessities such as rolling stock and staff wages. The Amsterdam banking firm Algemeene Maatschappij voor Handel en Nijverheid (General Company for Trade and Industry) was to take care of the sale of the shares on the international money market. The Algemeene Maatschappij had been founded only a short while before and had already embarked upon a series of fantastic ventures, some of them of undoubtedly insufficient earning power. The shady French financier André Langrand Dumonceau was one of the incorporators, and the whole venture closely followed the French Crédit Mobilier banking precepts. One of the first activities of the Algemeene Maatschappij was the floating of a newly incorporated company to undertake the working of the state-built railways in the Netherlands, with a share capital of "only" 6 million guilders, which succeeded despite some serious difficulties. Another newly founded Amsterdam company, the Nederlandsch-Indische Handelsbank (NIHB, Netherlands Indies Commercial Bank), also a child of the Algemeene Maatschappij, supplied 500,000 guilders to the NIS, but despite these participations, sale of the NIS stock did not go according to plan; seven thousand shares remained unsold when the Algemeene Maatschappij went broke and folded in the fall of 1864 amid a great rumpus and incriminations of fraud. One of its leading Dutch financiers absconded to escape creditors and justice.

The remaining unsold shares of the NIS were taken over by the French Crédit Mobilier bank of the Pereire Brothers. This as-yet-unplaced capital amounted to some 6 million guilders and remained in the hands of the bankers for a long time, severely slowing the construction of the line, as almost all materials and equipment had to be bought in Europe and of course paid for. An English syndicate agreed to provide a loan of 4 million guilders at a very high interest rate, a burden for the future, but at least making some money available for construction. As noted before, one provision of the concession was the guarantee of interest to be paid by the government to a maximum of 4.5 percent over a share capital of 14 million guilders at the most. Even that was not enough and the governor-general had to extend a helping hand with an interest-free loan of 3 million guilders in 1868. It would last until 1894 before this last loan had been redeemed. Parliament in The Hague in 1869 extended the period of the interest guarantee to 1906 and raised the annual maximum of this guarantee from 630,000 to 765,000 guilders. And when even this was still not enough, some of the coffee and sugar growers in the Principalities advanced estimated transportation charges to the NIS even before the products in question had been harvested, just to make sure that the company would be able to reach the mills when the harvest was due.

Despite all these financial complications, the first spade of earth could be turned by Governor-General L. A. W. J. Baron Sloet van de Beele on June 17, 1864. Sloet had been a great proponent of the construction of railways on Java, not quite unexpected in view of his earlier career in the

Netherlands, and he had pushed through the decision to grant the concession to Poolman cum suiss. He had even inspected the terrain of the proposed line in person, something exceptional in those days, to ensure that construction of a railway was indeed technically possible. Engineer in chief J. P. de Bordes could begin.[5]

THE ENGINEER IN CHIEF

Jan Philip de Bordes was born in Amsterdam in 1817 and followed a career in the Army Corps of Engineers, practically the only technical education available in the country at the time. His hero in the international engineering fraternity was Ferdinand de Lesseps, whose plans for a canal between the Mediterranean and the Red Sea he supported wholeheartedly. Already in 1857 he had held a public lecture wherein he described with enthusiasm and admiration the technical aspects of a Suez Canal. According to him this was "one of the proudest plans made in this century." In the 1850s, when the discussion about railway construction in the Netherlands was reaching a high pitch, he became involved with several applicants for concessions from the government, one of them a nobleman from Gelderland province named Baron Sloet van de Beele, who would be governor-general of the Indies after 1861. Most of these concessions came to naught, and in 1860 Parliament passed a law authorizing the construction by the state of 800 km of railway in ten years. The money was found in the revenues from the Indies that were flowing in by now. As usual a commission was appointed to supervise this construction with Sloet van de Beele as one of the members and de Bordes as secretary, now discharged from military service. Sloet would serve only one year in this commission, as he was elevated in 1861 to the position of governor-general of the Netherlands East Indies. The commission worked hard and de Bordes was certainly one of the most active, if not the most active, members. However, he was considered too domineering, and his forceful drive and his attention to the smallest details made him distinctly unpopular with the engineers in charge of the construction of the lines. In 1863, just after the first state line in the Netherlands had been opened, de Bordes was asked to become engineer in chief of the Nederlandsch-Indische Spoorweg-Maatschappij, a great honor for a man without experience building a railway line in a foreign, unfamiliar country. In this capacity he was to meet Sloet van de Beele again with the turning of the first sod of earth in June 1864.[6]

THE CONSTRUCTION OF THE FIRST LINE

De Bordes took his work seriously, as he knew that constructing a railway in a tropical and partially mountainous environment was a great challenge of unknown severity. In those years mountains were generally considered well-nigh impassable for railways, even by the foremost members of the international engineering world. He traveled to the Indies by the fastest way possible, by rail through Germany to Vienna, and from there by train over the spectacular Semmering mountain pass to Triëst on the Adriatic (an Austrian port at that time), where he boarded a steamer to take him over the Mediterranean to Alexandria, Egypt. Once there he took the English Overland Mail to Suez and where he boarded a British steamship to India. He had good reasons to choose this route, as he wanted to inspect the Semmering railway in Austria. That spectacular line, opened in 1854, was the first real mountain railway in Europe with steam locomotive traction only, and it had drawn the attention of engineers from all over Europe. It had shown the international engineering fraternity what was possible with the steam railway, that new means of transportation for which no barrier now seemed insurmountable. De Bordes must have taken a good look around and possibly talked with the responsible Austrian engineers, knowledge he could have used later when confronted with similar problems in the Indies. Once in Bombay—now Mumbai—the most important port on the western coast of British India, he inspected another mountain railway, the line from Bombay inland, where it crossed the mountain range known as the Ghats. That formidable barrier had only very recently been conquered by means of a railway with many switchbacks, something that was—fortunately—proven unnecessary in Java. Exceptionally powerful British-built steam locomotives were in use there, but operation of such a line was always a nightmare, expensive, and slow.[7]

Once in Semarang, Java, in 1864, de Bordes could start on his assignment in earnest. One problem that confronted him immediately was the lack of dependable maps of the area to be traversed. He sent out personnel with the necessary expertise and equipment to map out a suitable line, but available European surveyors were few. He himself went out with only two Dutch engineers and two supervisors, later followed by one more engineer and a couple of supervisors. At the start of the work those few were the only technicians available. De Bordes chose the European standard gauge of 4 ft 8.5 in (1,435 mm), a gauge with which he was familiar from his earlier work in the home country. From Semarang the chosen line went east to Goendih by way of Kedoeng Djati over still fairly easy terrain, but from there the mountains would have to be crossed, a serious challenge for a Dutch engineer not experienced in mountain rails. Instead he opted to avoid them as much as possible by means of a rather roundabout line to reach Solo and from there Djokja. The distance from Semarang to Djokja is 115 km as the crow flies, but by rail 166 km were needed to keep away from the active volcanoes Merapi and Merbaboe. The first 25 km to Tangoeng took three years to finish despite the relatively flat terrain.

Tropical rains caused severe flooding, soft soil that could not support the roadbed had to be reinforced, and bridges were needed to cross the many streams and rivers, all hindering progress. Moreover, de Bordes had to work with local Javanese workers, who were unaccustomed to this kind of work and were unwilling to contract for fixed periods. They wanted to be paid by the day and to come to work by the day, making strict planning of work hardly possible. The use of forced labor, known as the Heerendiensten, was out of the question, as this could only be ordered by the government for public works when Javanese farmers could or would not pay the required 20 percent of their harvests as taxes to the government.

Originally it had been the intention to entrust the building of the whole line to a single big European contractor, who would be responsible for the actual construction plus the supply of all rolling stock, as British contractors had executed similar contracts in British India. The NIS opened negotiations with two Dutch firms of contractors in the Indies, Drossaers & Co. and K. H. Verloop, who both had acquired good names. A credit of 150,000 guilders had been advanced to them, but they could not show much result when they had spent already more than 180,000 guilders, and the contract was annulled. Apparently no other contractor, Dutch or foreign, was willing to undertake such work, and when negotiations with others failed, there was no other way than having all construction work done by the staff of the NIS itself. This meant searching for more European personnel, who were difficult to find, expensive, and hard to retain.[8]

Despite these numerous and seemingly insurmountable difficulties, de Bordes managed to overcome all problems, technical and human. He came to be known as a strict but just master, and he always reckoned with the need for his workers to be allowed to go home during harvest time or to attend religious festivals. His labor force was enormous, at several periods some nine thousand men in all, with only a few European engineers and supervisors to control this mass. After 1865 de Bordes switched over to the importation of Chinese coolies, who were paid less than their Javanese colleagues and were consequently eager to stop working when circumstances did not agree with them. But at least they were contracted for a fixed time, making planning of the work possible, and when willing and regularly paid they could work hard. The government allowed this import of foreign workers but only on the condition that they were sent home after the works were finished. The Batavian government was always afraid of large influxes of other Asians and even non-Dutch Europeans. It is not known if these Chinese really went home to China after the opening of the line. Probably most of them just disappeared after their contracts had expired and merged into the existing Chinese communities in most Javanese towns.

Halte Tangoeng, the
temporary terminus
of the NIS line from
Semarang. The official
first train is entering the
simple station on August
10, 1867. This must be a
posed photograph, as
the chief engineer de
Bordes is seen standing
on the platform with
some other dignitaries
from Batavia, but they
can only have reached
that outpost in the flat
Javanese coastal plain
on that same train. Of
the three Europeans in
white tropical uniforms,
de Bordes is the one on
the left with a high sun
helmet, with two officials
of the government next
to him. (NSM collection)

More skilled personnel had to be brought in from Europe, not only
from the Netherlands, as there were never enough Dutchmen willing to
come; Germans also became well-respected members of the workforce.
The more adventurous males of all nations were always attracted to the
opportunities offered by the tropics, and there were always young men
eager to make the choice for a job in the Indies. However, Europeans
could never be attracted in large enough numbers for the lower ranks.
Fortunately, it turned out that Javanese were willing and able to learn
and could be depended on when placed in more responsible positions.
The first fully qualified Javanese locomotive engineer was ready for work
in 1868, and others soon followed. It did not take long before most drivers
and firemen of the NIS were Javanese, and indigenous conductors soon
joined the ranks. But on every train at least one European conductor was
mandatory, as the native colleagues could exert no authority over the
first-class—European—passengers.[9]

Earthworks were heavy in places and every cubic meter of soil had
to be dug out by hand and moved in the traditional Javanese baskets or
in diminutive wheelbarrows, specially fabricated for the relatively small
posture of the laborers. No large machines were available and only human

A bridge for the NIS over the Toentang River near Kedoeng Djati under construction in 1868. The iron girders are ready to be hauled over the wooden falsework with a lot of manpower. (NSM collection)

and animal power could be used. One cutting was 600 m long and in places 19 m deep, while some embankments were 17 to 18 m high. No less than one hundred bridges were necessary, small and large, of which the longest had a span of 50 m, while elsewhere 2 of 20 m each were necessary. All ironwork had to be imported from Belgium and the Netherlands, and because of the lack of experienced riveters, de Bordes had designed two "bridge wagons" to bring long bridge sections from Semarang to the place where they were to be erected, minimizing the need for riveting on the spot. The two four-wheeled wagons had a long, articulated carrying base to support the bridge sections and were built by the relatively unknown firm Evrard of Brussels, Belgium.[10]

Rails came chiefly from England and Belgium, as the Netherlands had no blast furnaces or rolling mills at the time. Stone for bridge abutments and piers and viaducts could be found locally and wood was plentiful in the mountains, although not all wood was suitable for use as ties in the damp climate. Termites were also a perennial nuisance. When in Bombay, de Bordes had seen the use of inland teak for ties, and on Java the local djati, also a kind of teak and known as *ijzerhout* (ironwood), was plentiful and turned out to be excellent for ties and other uses. Djati ties had an

average life of between sixteen and twenty years, very long for wood in a damp tropical climate. Iron rails weighed 26 kilograms per meter, light but strong enough for the expected traffic. Later the NIS went over to heavier rails of 33 kilograms per meter. Signaling was of a very simple pattern, with revolving red/white discs to protect stations and yards only.

At the express wish of the Minister for the Colonies Fransen van de Putte, a branch from Kedoeng Djati to Willem I had been added to the concession, without an enlargement of the capital, adding to the financial woes of the NIS. Willem I, near Ambarawa, was a fortification and arsenal constructed when the Java War was still vividly remembered. At that time of war, it had been found that the transport of men and equipment constituted a great problem, and with the fort and barracks still in operation in the 1860s, it was deemed necessary to have a railway as a dependable supply line. It was a difficult line, with heavy earthworks and gradients as steep as 28‰ and a viaduct of 162 m long across a swampy area. That section of the line was opened in 1873, when the military need for the connection had already diminished. Solo had been reached in 1870 and Djokja, the end of the line, two years later.[11]

Altogether de Bordes earned a lot of respect with the construction of the first railway on Java, thousands of kilometers removed from the

established industrial world. He had introduced a new technology in a remote and strongly isolated area and opened up a future for agriculture and industry, and for the Javanese general population as well, it was truly a pioneering achievement.

LOCOMOTIVES AND ROLLING STOCK

For steam locomotives the engineer in chief had to look to Germany and England, as no domestic suppliers had remained active after the first railways in the Netherlands had been constructed. The first engines de Bordes ordered in 1863 came from the works of August Borsig of Berlin, by that time the leading European locomotive builder. Borsig had set up an iron foundry and machine works in the city of Berlin in 1837 and constructed his first steam locomotive for a German railway in 1841. For the NIS Borsig constructed two 0-4-2 tank engines (or "tanks") of a type then common in Germany, but little is known about these NIS Nos. 1 and 2, as no drawings and only very few photographs have survived. They were fairly small engines with pannier tanks and two outside cylinders and a weight in working order of about 30 tons, as their maximum axle loading could not be more than 10 tons per axle. The light tracks had to settle down during the early years. The two arrived in Semarang in June 1865 and were first used on construction trains and later on the branch to Willem I. A small outsider in the NIS stable was an 0-4-0 tank engine from the Hunslet Engine Works of Leeds, a typical contractor's engine and the Hunslet's first export order. The engine arrived in 1867 as NIS No. 7 and it was sold ten years later to the Batavian government. For a short time it carried the

NIS engine Nr. 1, an 0-4-2 pannier tank supplied by Borsig of Berlin in 1865, photographed together with an 0-4-2 engine with separate tender constructed by Beyer Peacock of Manchester, probably at the Semarang engine shed, around 1867. The number of the BP engine is not visible, as the usual brass number plate on the side of the cab is missing. The proud staff members, both European and Indonesian, are posing with the tools of their trade. (Author's collection) name *JAVA*, but naming of locomotives was soon discarded by the NIS. Another contractor's engine was No. 9, bought secondhand in 1868 from the Dutch contractor Jan van Haaften who was busy with large works in the Netherlands and had a stable of many steam locomotives. No. 9 was constructed by Neilson & Co. of Glasgow in 1863 with a reputed weight of 10 tons and probably also of 0-4-0 wheel arrangement. NIS No. 9 lasted in its new role in tropical surroundings until 1874, but its boiler was used for many more years for pumping purposes. Why anyone took the trouble and the expense of bringing this old and small engine to the other end of the world remains a mystery, as it is unknown that Van Haaften participated in the building of the NIS or in any other great work in the Indies. Neilson had been established in 1837 in Glasgow, Scotland, and from 1855 was known as Neilson & Co., since 1861 operating in large new premises in Springburn, Glasgow, known as Hyde Park Works.[12]

More important were five locomotives for train service ordered from Beyer Peacock & Company of Gorton near Manchester, England. Beyer Peacock was one of the leading locomotive manufacturers in Britain, established in 1854 and renowned for its sturdy yet elegant products. Since 1863 the firm had become the chief supplier of locomotives to the Dutch State Railways and over the years it delivered hundreds of engines to that company, well into the twentieth century. Of course, in view of his earlier work in the Netherlands in the early 1860s, de Bordes must have known that and he possibly even witnessed the opening of the first state-built line in the Netherlands in September 1863 with a locomotive supplied by Beyer Peacock. For passenger and freight trains, the NIS ordered four engines of the 0-4-2 wheel arrangement with separate tender on six wheels, delivered in 1866. They were a standard factory design and could also be seen in other countries. The NIS named them *J. P. de BORDES*, *MERAPI*, *MERBABOE*, and *LAWOE*, after the engineer in charge and three active volcanoes of mid-Java. Nameplates were fixed to the side sheets of the footplate in Javanese script on the left and in Latin script on the right side. Only No. 3, *J. P. de BORDES*, ran with its name until its scrapping in 1910; the other names were soon discarded, reputedly because no one could read the names in Javanese script. After this experiment the NIS abolished name giving, only to take it up again much later. The 0-4-2s had a weight of 31 tons—engine only—in full working order with another 25 tons for the tender when fully loaded.

Three more of the mixed-traffic 0-4-2s followed, again from Beyer Peacock, but this was not yet enough for working the growing traffic, so they were joined by two more in the next year. Three units of the same design followed in 1872, with another two in 1875. But even then this classic—even outmoded—model had not been quite superseded, for in 1880 two units of the same designs arrived and the last two were delivered in

NIS Nr. 29, a compound 0-4-2 engine delivered by Beyer Peacock in 1893 at Solo station. She was one of the series 28–33, the most modern of the long line of 0-4-2s as supplied by Beyer Peacock. A modern touch is the steam-sanding apparatus with a sandbox between chimney—with spark arrester—and dome. The tender is built up with a large crate to store an adequate supply of firewood. Photo from the 1920s. (SNR collection)

1884 by the Gorton Foundry with only minor improvements. By then they were completely outmoded but apparently the NIS was still happy with the design, and the quality of Beyer Peacock products guaranteed long lives. After the forced conversion of the NIS broad gauge lines to Indian standard gauge by the Japanese aggressor during World War II, some of these 0-4-2s were just dumped and were found rusting away in the Javanese jungle many years later.[13]

For the Kedoeng Djati–Willem I mountain line, the NIS turned again to Borsig for two small-wheeled outside-cylindered 0-6-0 tank engines, very German looking and similar to the Nos. 1 and 2, but with three coupled axles instead of two. Nos. 13 and 14 were delivered in 1870, and twelve years later another very similar engine, No. 7, arrived. This was a new No. 7, as the old No. 7, the Hunslet Tank, had been sold by then. The three 0-6-0 tanks spent their whole lives on the mountain line.

All steam locomotives burned coal, but coal had to be imported from Britain and was expensive, although British ships were often loaded with coal as ballast, returning with sugar and other colonial products. Later, coal from Japan and Australia was used, as it was cheaper than fuel brought in the long way from Europe. Only as late as around 1903 the change to wood burning was made as wood was plentiful and cheap. But wood needed more room than coal, so the tenders were then fitted with high racks to store the hardwood blocks safely. Simple workshops for the maintenance of locomotives and rolling stock were established at Semarang, and over the years were slowly extended and better equipped with machinery when the financial situation allowed. In the Indies coal was mined but not yet in sufficient quantities to provide an alternative to imported coal. Coal mines had been opened and developed by the government at Kalangan near Bandjermasin on Borneo since 1849–1850. The mine named *Julia Hermina* was in full operation by 1859, and the coal was chiefly used for fueling the growing number of government steamers.[14]

Rolling stock of the NIS was also inspired by European examples. Passenger coaches were four-wheeled of the conventional type, with side doors for every compartment. The renowned Haarlem firm of J. J. Beijnes was soon involved in constructing carriages for the NIS. In 1866 the company ordered from Beijnes one model carriage and fifty iron frames with wheels, European style buffers, couplings, and other ironwork. The NIS works in Semarang built the superstructures from local hardwoods. Apparently these first orders were fulfilled to satisfaction, as new orders followed in the next years. Three classes were originally carried on trains, but soon a sort of fourth class for natives only was added, although it was never officially called fourth class. It turned out that the indigenous population recognized the opportunities offered by being able to travel, despite predictions that the natives were not interested in leaving their villages. The cheap fare of 1 cent per kilometer and the free 30 kg of luggage meant that they could sell their wares, produce, and animals in the neighboring bigger village or city. On market days these trains were overloaded. Freight vehicles were also four wheeled, with the common side buffers and simple couplers of the hook and chain type, as usual in Europe at the time. These first closed wagons, with an empty weight of between 7 and 8 tons, were allowed to carry about a hundred sacks of raw sugar of 101 kg each. Every year the sugar season was always the high point of freight traffic, but as this lasted on average only about a hundred days, the wagons used for this traffic stood idle for a large part of the year. Only handbrakes were provided, with brakemen riding the roofs of the wagons to apply the brakes on the signal from the locomotive engineer. With long trains, riding the roofs was absolutely necessary, as brakemen at the end of the train often did not hear the whistle signals of the engineer and had to rely on hand signals from their colleagues farther ahead. The locomotives had hand brakes on the tenders only, operated by the fireman. Traffic was limited in the first years, with two or three daily passenger trains and freight trains as needed.[15]

THE BATAVIA–BUITENZORG LINE OF THE NIS

With the negotiations of 1868–1869 between the government in The Hague and the NIS about the raising of the annual interest guarantee from ƒ630,000 to ƒ765,000, the then-minister for the colonies, E. de Waal,

had included a new element in the deal, the concession for the Batavia–Buitenzorg line. The NIS had already requested a concession for that line back in 1864, without interest guarantee. In 1865 the governor-general had granted this concession, but it had taken years to reach agreement over the details and only in 1868 the royal decree for this line was issued. Late in 1868, with the financial arrangements between NIS and the government settled, the final agreement about Batavia–Buitenzorg could be signed. One of the new stipulations, much against the will of de Bordes, was that the line was to be built on the narrow gauge of 1,067 mm (3 ft 6 in), the gauge that later became known in Europe as Cape gauge but as Indian standard gauge in the East Indies. It was generally assumed that the narrow gauge would be cheaper to build, while at the same time guaranteeing enough potential for the expected traffic then and in the future. A wise move, amply proved by later developments.

The governors-general's palace was located in Buitenzorg (Bogor), south of Batavia, and because Batavia was the center of government of the Dutch East Indies, a lot of traffic moved between these two places. The existing roadway some 35 km long was in a very poor condition, especially during the west monsoon. Horses of the post chaises sometimes sank to

There is hardly a soul in sight when the photographer put up his heavy camera to capture the station of Weltevreden, on the NIS line Batavia–Buitenzorg. The station, a single-story brick building with an iron and glass awning over the front doors, was the second one here, opened in 1884. In this shape it served until 1917, when it was enlarged by the State Railways. In 1937 it was renamed Batavia-Koningsplein and is now known as Gambir. Photograph from around 1890. (NSM collection)

their knees in the mud. It was obvious that a better all-weather connection was sorely needed. David Maarschalk, one of the engineers assisting de Bordes, had mapped out a possible line by way of Weltevreden and Meester Cornelis, suburbs of Batavia where most of the hotels, mercantile houses, and government offices were situated. More or less along this plan, construction of the NIS line was started in 1870, and as there were few severe gradients or deep cuttings, progress was good. On the last day of January 1873, Governor-General J. Loudon opened the line for traffic.

Because of the new narrow gauge a completely new set of locomotives and rolling stock had to be acquired. Existing stock could not be used and new specifications had to be drawn up. England was again seen as the best place to find this new equipment, and Beyer Peacock was known as the most experienced with the narrow gauge. Since 1866 this firm had already constructed a number of small 2-4-0 tank engines for the Norwegian government for use on the narrow-gauge lines in that country. Generally, they gave satisfaction, so it was no wonder that the NIS approached Beyer Peacock for similar engines when the first stretch to Weltevreden was nearing completion; Nos. 1–3 arrived from Manchester in 1871. They were 2-4-0 saddle tanks too, but unlike their Norwegian predecessors they had horizontal outside cylinders, with a fixed carrying axle in front instead of a swiveling Bissel truck. To get around curves they had a much shorter wheelbase than the Norsemen. Total weight in working order was about 23 tons, of which 15 tons were available for adhesion. In the same year, three more tank engines arrived, with the same wheel arrangement but smaller and lighter and with side tanks instead of the saddle tanks of the first three. They were intended for local trains with many stops on the first part of the line from Batavia–Benedenstad (Old Town) to Weltevreden and Meester Cornelis. Three more of the larger version of 2-4-0 tanks arrived in 1873 and 1879, joined by two of the smaller side tanks also in 1879. All of these engines came without sanding gear in any form, and it is not known if they were ever equipped with this device.

A slightly modernized version of the same 2-4-0 saddle tanks was ordered from Beyer Peacock in 1884, this time with sanding gear and a better cab for protection of the crew against sun and rain. Two more of the same pattern followed as late as 1898 and 1899. A well-proven design apparently, but by the end of the nineteenth century it was, of course, completely outmoded. The reason for the company to postpone real investment in modern mainline equipment may well lay in the fact that negotiations with the Batavian government about a takeover of the line were already going on since 1881, but as yet without results as the parties involved could not agree about a reasonable price.

With these eleven (twelve after 1884) small engines, the whole traffic could be handled until 1893, when Beyer Peacock supplied two 2-4-2 side

Facing top, There are few photographs of trains on the Batavia–Buitenzorg line in the early NIS days. One of the small Beyer Peacock 2-4-0 tanks is standing in the Batavian terminus circa 1874. The engine in the photograph is Nr. 3, a saddle tank of the series BB-1-3 of 1872. A steam locomotive is still a novelty, and everyone wants to be in the picture: railway staff, military and police personnel, and civilians. (Gerard de Graaf collection)

Facing bottom, NIS Nr. BB-6, also a 2-4-0 tank for the Batavia–Buitenzorg line and supplied by Beyer Peacock in 1872, intended for tram services to the suburbs of Batavia such as Weltevreden and Meester Cornelis. The diminutive engine has side tanks only and sports an enormous smokestack. Locomotive personnel had to be content with only a spectacle plate and a short roof as protection against sun and rain. (Author's collection)

This is how an ancient 2-4-0 tank of the NIS looked in later life. Nr. 336, formerly Nr. BB-12, constructed by Beyer Peacock in 1883, is seen switching at Tjepoe station in East Java. The rerailing jack on the footplate might come in handy in the wilds of Java. Photo by L. J. Biezeveld, June 20, 1938. (SNR collection

tanks intended for the newly introduced expresses between Batavia and Buitenzorg, weighing just over 29 tons and equipped with sanding gear for running in both directions. Apart from these two, apparently not very successful 2-4-2s, all earlier 2-4-0s had long lives after they were transferred to other lines of the NIS when the Batavia–Buitenzorg line was finally taken over by the State Railways in 1913.

The personnel on the footplate of all early engines was protected by a spectacle plate and a short roof but stood in the open on both sides. A

Opening of lines of the NIS

Indian Broad Gauge (1,435 mm)		
Semarang–Tangoeng	25 km	08-10-1867
Tangoeng–Kedoeng Djati	9 km	07-19-1868
Kedoeng Djati–Solo	74 km	02-10-1870
Solo–Djokja	58 km	06-10-1872
Kedoeng Djati–Willem I	37 km	05-21-1873
Indian Standard Gauge (1,067 mm)		
Batavia–Weltevreden	6 km	09-15-1871
Weltevreden–Meester Cornelis	6 km	06-16-1872
Meester Cornelis–Buitenzorg	44 km	01-31-1873

modern touch was that the engines, besides the customary crosshead pump, were also equipped with one of the newfangled injectors for feeding the boiler. Braking was by hand brake only. Another Norwegian influence was the use of the central coupler as designed by Carl Pihl, the Norwegian engineer. This coupler would become standard for all Indian standard gauge (1,067 mm) stock in ever-heavier construction. The numbering of the BB line engines started again with one, but with the addition of the letters BB (Batavia–Buitenzorg) to distinguish them from the broad-gauge stock with the same numbers. The new line was chiefly a passenger line with in the beginning a most insignificant freight traffic.[16]

NOTES

1. About Willem Poolman (1809–1873), see Molhuysen and Blok, eds., *Nieuw Nederlandsch Biografisch Woordenboek*, X, 748–49. While in the Indies he was active in abolitionist groups and strongly favored ending remnants of the former widespread slavery. Alexander Fraser (1816–1904) was a Scottish banker in Dutch service. Apart from his role in the NIS, he was later also one of the incorporators of the Java Spoorweg Maatschappij of 1884. Information about Fraser supplied by Mr. Adriaan Intveld.

2. About Thomas Johannes Stieltjes (1819–1878), ibid., II, 1370–76. He was known as a good officer and an able engineer but was overly critical and did not mince words, irrespective to whom he addressed. Later he would be a member of the Second Chamber of the Dutch Parliament and as such was a severe critic of the Indian government.

3. About Isaac Dignus Fransen van de Putte (1822–1902), ibid., IV, 1099–1101. Twice minister for the colonies (1863–1866 and 1872–1874) and longtime member of Parliament, he did much to improve the government of the colonies. He was influential in the abolition of the Cultivation System and forced labor, and he advocated the construction of railways on Java. He was a true colonial reformer.

4. The terms of the concession in Reitsma, *Korte geschiedenis*, 29–30.

5. Jonker, *Merchants, Bankers, Middlemen*, 259. Veenendaal, *Spoorwegen in Nederland*, 26, 36–37. *Holland's Colonial Call*, "Means of Transport in the Dutch East Indies," 5–6. About Sloet van de Beele (1806–1890), see Molhuysen and Blok, eds., *Nieuw Nederlandsch Biografisch Woordenboek*, V, 751–53. He was governor-general of the Dutch East Indies 1861–1866. Reitsma, *Korte geschiedenis*, 21–24. About the NIHB, see Korthals Altes, *Tussen cultures en kredieten*, 31.

6. About de Bordes, see Molhuysen and Blok, eds., *Nieuw Nederlandsch Biografisch Woordenboek*, I, 413–17. Pieterse, *Sporen van Smaragd*, 13–15.

7. *Encyklopädie des gesamten Eisenbahnwesens*, 6, 3006–08. Veenendaal and Grant, *Rails to the Front*, 96–97.

8. Gratama, "De Nederlandsch-Indische Spoorwegmaatschappij," 287. About the contemporary situation in British India, see Derbyshire, "Building of India's Railways." About the early Dutch contractors of the NIS, see Korthals Altes, *Tussen cultures en kredieten*, 58–61.

9. Pieterse, *Sporen van Smaragd*, 12–17. Veenendaal, "Locomotive of Modernity," 99. Ballegoijen (van) de Jong, *Spoorwegstations op Java*, 15.

10. About Evrard's factory, known since 1881 as the S. A. Franco-Belge pour la Construction de Machines et de Matériel de Chemins de Fer, one of the larger Belgian-French constructors, see Dambly, *Vapeur en Belgique*, vol.1, 54–55. Apart from the bridge wagons, the Evrard firm and its successors constructed only a single steam engine for railways in the Netherlands Indies.

11. Bordes (de), *De spoorweg Samarang-Vorstenlanden*. Also Doorn (van), "De eerste spoorweg op Java," 80–88.

12. The American Whyte system for indicating the wheel arrangements of steam locomotives has been followed in this book. An 0-4-2 engine means a unit with two driven axles, no front pilot axle, and one carrying axle at the rear end. A 4-6-2, in American parlance generally known as a Pacific, is an engine with a front bogie, three driven axles, and a carrying axle under the firebox and cab. The much later giant 2-12-2s of the Java State Railways had a single pilot axle, six driven axles, and a carrying axle at the rear. In American parlance the type became known as Javanics.

13. Mixed traffic engines were intended for both passenger and freight trains.

14. About the coal mine near Bandjermasin, see Kuipers, *In de Indische wateren*, 383–86.

15. Details of all steam locomotives of the NIS in Oegema, *De stoomtractie op Java en Sumatra*, 39–43; Townsley, *Hunslet Engine Works*, 31; Hills, *Beyer Peacock Locomotive Order List*, 10–11; Lowe, *British Steam Locomotive Builders*, 59–64, 502–05; Pierson, *Borsig*; Herder (de), *Nederlandse industrielocomotieven*, 23. About Beijnes and the NIS, see Asselberghs, *Beijnes*, 99.

16. Reitsma, *Korte geschiedenis*, 22–24. For discussions about the most suitable railway gauge for the Indies, see the next chapter. James Loudon (1824–1900) was minister for the colonies 1861–1862 and governor-general of the Netherlands East Indies 1871–1875. Molhuysen and Blok, eds., *Nieuw Nederlandsch Biografisch Woordenboek*, III, 790–95. Oegema, *De stoomtractie op Java en Sumatra*, 50–51.

THE CHOICE OF THE MOST 3
SUITABLE RAILWAY GAUGE
FOR THE EAST INDIES

A NATURAL GAUGE?

As noted, the first railway in the Netherlands East Indies was constructed in the European standard gauge. For de Bordes, the engineer in charge, the use of standard gauge of 4 ft 8.5 in (1,435 mm) must have been an easy choice, almost natural, as he had begun his career in the building of the state railways in his home country. And there had been no discussion about the choice of that gauge for those new lines in the Netherlands, as they were meant to connect with railways in neighboring Hanover, Prussia, and Belgium, all using the Stephensonian standard gauge.

RAILWAY GAUGES IN EUROPE

But was this standard gauge indeed really standard all over the world in the 1860s? In England the struggle between supporters of the Stephensonian standard gauge and the followers of Isambard Kingdom Brunel, who had chosen a gauge of 7 ft for his Great Western Railway (GWR) London–Bristol and beyond, was sharp and acrimonious. A Royal Commission finally decided that the Stephensonian gauge would be the gauge for all new construction in Britain, but for the time being, the GWR was allowed to continue with its own system; it would be 1892 before the last broad-gauge line was converted to standard. For Ireland, then completely under British administration, the choice fell on 5 ft 3 in (1,600 mm) for no clear-cut reasons.

Broad gauge was not confined to England or Ireland, as railways in Tsarist Russia, in the Grand Duchy of Baden, and in Spain and Portugal were constructed in several gauges broader than standard. In Russia, 5 ft (1,524 mm) became the norm; the later often-quoted military strategic reasons for this 5-ft gauge did not decide the issue there. Belgium, France, Austria, and most of the German states apart from the Grand Duchy of Baden adopted the standard gauge.[1]

The gauge problem is clear from this photograph. A double-headed broad-gauge express of the NIS is standing in Semarang-Tawang station, with four-rail track in the foreground to accommodate both broad and Indies standard gauge trains. The two 4-6-0 engines heading the train will have no problems in getting the train away. The large electric headlight, needed for night running, is conspicuous. Photo by L. J. Biezeveld, April 30, 1939. (SNR collection)

COLONIAL RAILWAYS

Early railways in colonial territories meant lines in the British Empire, as other European powers came much later with railroad construction in their dependencies in the tropics. For India, Britain's "Jewel in the Crown," a broad gauge of 5 ft 6 in (1,676 mm) was chosen in 1850 after a first experimental contractor's line in European standard gauge. The wider gauge was deemed safer in the sometimes-cyclonic winds on the Indian subcontinent. It was a questionable assumption, to say the least, but Governor-General Lord Dalhousie decided the issue. He was supposed to know what he was talking about, as he had been president of the Board of Trade in Great Britain; in that capacity he had been in almost-daily contact with the railway companies there. The Great Indian Peninsula Railway opened its first portion of the later mainline out of Bombay in 1852; from then on the wide gauge was considered to be the national one, at least for a time. Later a host of narrow-gauge feeder lines were to be constructed.[2]

In South Africa, in the Natal Colony, the first line was opened in 1860 in standard gauge; another opened in the Cape Colony the following year, also in European standard gauge. Like de Bordes, British engineers in charge of the construction of both lines saw no reason not to use the gauge they were familiar with at home. Tasmania started with a broad-gauge line, as did the Australian territories of Victoria and South

Australia, while New South Wales opted for the Stephensonian standard gauge. No real technical or economic reasons are discernible behind these choices, but interstate competition seems to have decided the issues in Australia. Standard or even wider gauges seemed to have the upper hand worldwide around 1860.

THE NARROW GAUGE

Despite the early choice of the standard Stephensonian gauge in many colonial territories, engineers all over the world were wondering if that width was really the most suitable for mountainous countries or colonial territories with difficult terrain that expected light traffic and a chronic lack of capital. In Great Britain several mine or industrial railways were already operating on a gauge smaller than standard. Most influential of these was the Festiniog Railway in Wales, running from slate quarries in the mountains down to the harbor of Portmadoc, from where the slate was shipped. The line, opened in 1836, was laid with a gauge of 1 ft 11.5 in (597 mm). Loaded trains ran down from the quarries by gravity, and the empty wagons were hauled back by horses. Steam traction was introduced in 1863, and passengers were carried from 1865.[3]

Yet it was not in Britain or in its colonies that the first successful public railway on a narrow gauge was opened but in mountainous Norway. Carl Pihl, state engineer of Norway, was charged with the construction of two lines with low expected traffic. He chose the then-novel and fairly untried gauge of 1,067 mm (3 ft 6 in), clearly not a metric but a British measure. Before making this choice he had approached Sir Charles Fox (1810–1874), one of the foremost British engineers of the time, with the question if steam locomotives of sufficient power would be possible for this gauge. Fox had already long been thinking about the use of gauges narrower than the standard and he set Pihl's mind at rest. The first line, the first narrow-gauge common carrier railway, opened in Norway in 1862; two years later a longer line to the same specifications was added. The success was great and the locomotives, delivered by the British firm of Beyer Peacock, operated without major problems.[4]

With the success of Pihl's lines in Norway, Fox now actively started to promote narrow-gauge railways in British possessions at the other end of the globe. Queensland, Australia, was the first state to adopt the narrow gauge in 1865, again with 3 ft 6 in and again with complete success. Lower costs of construction and lower costs of running the lines were a boon to cash-starved governments, and high speeds were not contemplated. One other and most vociferous promoter of the narrow gauge was Robert F. Fairlie (1831–1885), a Scottish engineer involved in the introduction of steam power on the Festiniog Railway and inventor of a locomotive especially suitable for heavy haulage on narrow-gauge lines, the articulated Fairlie locomotive, which had a limited vogue during the nineteenth century. In 1870 Fairlie arranged a kind of demonstration of the capabilities of the narrow gauge on the Festiniog Railway, where Russian, French, German, Hungarian, and Swedish observers could see what was possible on that gauge with his patented articulated engines. Pihl himself was also present, but it is unknown whether Dutch observers attended the party too.[5]

Meanwhile, the narrow-gauge "craze," as it was called by some opponents, continued. In India a first line with the unusual gauge of 4 ft (1,219 mm) opened in 1863, and another in the 3-ft 6-in gauge in 1865. Much debate was going on which would be the best for India, but the decision was left to the viceroy, Lord Mayo, who had little knowledge of railway matters. He calculated that with four persons sitting abreast, at least a 6-ft internal—6-ft 6-in external—width of the carriage would be necessary. And as his advisors had told him that the track gauge should be at least half the external measure for reasons of stability, 3 ft 3 in was his choice. At that time a bill for introducing the metrical system of weights and measures in British India was in consideration, so the 3-ft 3-in system was changed into meter gauge (1,000 mm or 3 ft 3.4 in). However, the introduction of metric measures nationwide was never implemented and so the Indian narrow-gauge railways, supplementing the broad-gauge lines, were built with a metric gauge in an otherwise wholly British system of measures.[6]

Elsewhere in the world, the narrow-gauge movement gained momentum. In South Africa, in Natal and Cape Colony provinces, the few existing early lines were narrowed to 3 ft 6 in, and all new construction was henceforth in that gauge, which gave the name Cape Gauge for 1,067-mm track, although the Cape was certainly not the first to use it. In Germany Kapspur became the familiar name, and in the Dutch language Kaapspoor was used. Bear in mind, however, that the term *Cape Gauge* is really a misnomer, as the Cape was only a follower, not a pioneer in this respect. Japan chose the 1,067 mm for all its lines in 1872, and in the British Empire, apart from India, 3 ft 6 in was the new gauge for many networks such as in New Zealand and Western Australia, in the African possessions and in Malaya.

In the United States the narrow-gauge fever also caught on, and in the early 1870s the first lines were opened, chiefly with 3 ft (914 mm) gauge. Here not only short feeders were constructed but also long trunk lines intended to cross the continent. The best-known and longest-lived company working with the 3 ft gauge was to become the Denver & Rio Grande Railway in Colorado, of which the first section was opened in 1870. Dutch financiers and engineers must have been familiar with this line, as all construction capital for this early narrow-gauge line came from Amsterdam. General William J. Palmer, the driving force behind the company, had

For its—few—tramway lines with the 600-millimeter gauge, Java State Railways in 1911 ordered three 0-8-0 tanks from Hartmann, supplemented by three more in 1912. One of these is seen blowing off in the transfer station of Rambipoedji for the line to Poeger in East Java. The difference between the 600- and 1,067-millimeter gauges is striking. (Author's collection)

been a regular visitor there and had managed to interest leading Dutch financial houses.[7]

THE GAUGE QUESTION IN THE NETHERLANDS INDIES

Even at the time that the NIS was still under construction, Dutch engineers were wondering if the choice of the European standard gauge for Java had been right. Critics in the Indies and at home ventilated their concerns, and the minister for the colonies in The Hague apparently took these objections seriously. In March 1869 he installed a commission of two members to study the subject. One of the experts was N. H. Henket, at the time already staying in the Indies, and the other was J. A. Kool, new to the Indies but a seasoned railway engineer.[8]

As soon as Kool arrived in Batavia in 1869, where he joined Henket, the two started work. They had been charged explicitly to examine the suitability of a gauge of between 1,000 and 1,100 mm for future railways in the colony. Their report, finished in record time in September 1869, was clearly in favor of a narrower gauge. They recommended using a gauge of

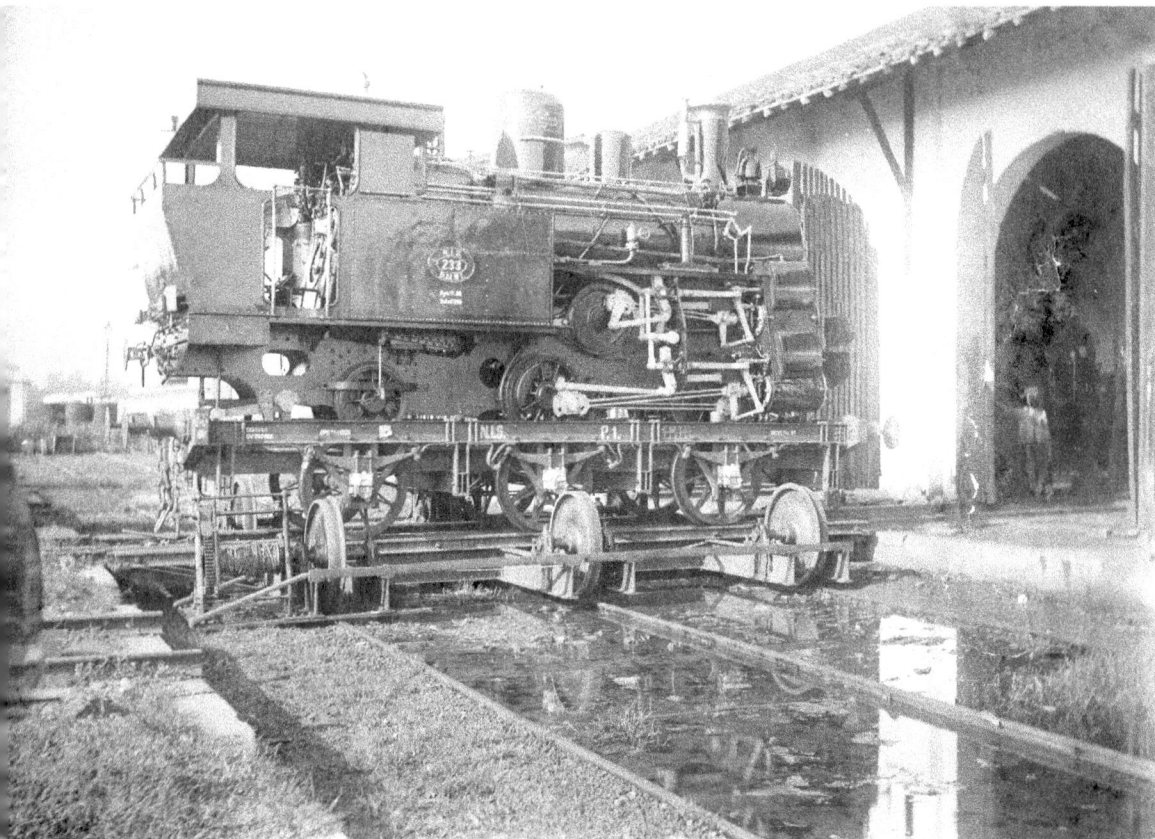

The problem of the two different gauges used by the NIS is clearly illustrated here. On the traverser outside the Djokja works NIS Nr. 233, one of the rack engines for the section Ambarawa (Willem I) to Setjang built on the Indian standard gauge, is standing on a broad-gauge transporter wagon for transfer to the Djokja Works. (NSM collection)

1,000 or 1,067 mm as future standard because it was cheaper to construct in the often-mountainous terrain while at the same time suitable for all transportation needs then and in the future. They recommended also leaving the Semarang–Principalities line in standard gauge, but for the Batavia–Buitenzorg line the narrow gauge should be used. Kool and Henket opted for the 1,067-mm gauge, as for this width rolling stock and locomotives were already in use in countries such as Norway or Queensland and could be readily ordered from well-known British firms.

Although this report was clear enough, other Indian specialists such as T. J. Stieltjes, the perennial critic of the Batavia and Hague governments, opted for a still-smaller gauge of 760 mm (2 ft 6 in). He had seen the Festiniog Railway in Wales in operation and opined that this small gauge would be sufficient for all future needs of Java. Fortunately, the Batavian government decided to ignore him and instead follow the advice of Kool and Henket. The 1,067-mm gauge was officially established as the future standard for all new construction in the Dutch East Indies. Henceforth, this 1,067-mm gauge was called the Indian standard gauge, and the European gauge of the NIS was called the Indian broad gauge. In this book the same terms have been followed.[9]

After this discussion leading to the establishment of the narrow gauge as future standard, nothing much happened for a time. Kool and Henket, still in Batavia, were ordered by royal decree of February 22, 1871, to design a railway network for Java. They opted for two east–west lines on Java, but the expanded committee thought this to be excessive and advised that for the time being only the southernmost line of the Kool-Henket plan would be necessary. The results of these discussions will be found in the next chapter.

NOTES

1. On the development of the railway gauge in different regions of the world, see Puffert, *Tracks across Continents*. For Britain, see Simmons, *Railway in England and Wales*, 45–47. Also Ellis, *British Railway History*, 100–107. For Russia, see Westwood, *History of Russian Railways*. Also Veenendaal, "Baltic States," 25–39. For the situation in the Netherlands, see Veenendaal, *Spoorwegen in Nederland*, 31–34, 67–68.

2. James Andrew Broun Ramsay, tenth earl and first marquess of Dalhousie, a Scottish nobleman, governor-general of India 1847–1856, and president of the Board of Trade in Great Britain before that. Satow and Desmond, *Railways of the Raj*, 11–13. See also Hughes, *Indian Locomotives: Part 1*, 7.

3. For the Festiniog Railway, see Boyd, *Festiniog Railway*. More popular is Winton, *Little Wonder*.

4. Puffert, *Tracks across Continents*, 83–84, 183.

5. Winton, *Little Wonder*, 62.

6. Hughes, *Indian Locomotives: Part 2*, 7.

7. Hilton, *American Narrow Gauge Railroads*, 78–79; Veenendaal, *Slow Train to Paradise*, 63–66.

8. Johan Arthur Kool was born in 1816 in Danzig (then Germany, now Gdansk, Poland), son of a Dutch army officer and a German mother. He followed in the footsteps of his father and became an officer in the Dutch Army Corps of Engineers. His railway career took off in 1845 when he became engineer in chief of the Aachen-Maastricht Railway in the south of Limburg province of the Netherlands and the neighboring Prussian territory. That line was finished in 1853. In 1860, with the start of the construction of railways in the Netherlands by the state, he was appointed engineer in charge of the Maastricht–Venlo line and later for the whole network of state railways south of the great rivers and in 1870 for the whole of the then-largely-finished state system. He died in The Hague in 1873. Molhuysen and Blok, eds., *Nieuw Nederlandsch Biografisch Woordenboek*, II, 707–10.

9. Veenendaal, "Locomotive of Modernity," 92–135. Bruin (de), *Het Indische spoor in oorlogstijd*, 16.

Ever since the start of construction of the NIS in 1864, with its continuous financial problems that could only be solved with the help of the Dutch and East Indies government, the discussion about the pros and cons of railway construction by the state continued unabated. Kool and Henket had not taken position in this respect but only recommended the use of narrow gauge for further construction of railways. Government had followed this recommendation and ordered the NIS to build its second line, Batavia–Buitenzorg, which opened in 1873, to the 1,067-mm gauge. Apart from their report on the most suitable gauge for the Indies, Kool and Henket also came forward with a plan for a relatively comprehensive and interconnected network of lines to be built on Java, altogether some 955 km, plus a number of "desirable" lines to be constructed in the future. Most important of these proposed lines was a railroad south from Buitenzorg, the end of the projected NIS line from Batavia, then east to Bandoeng and from there farther east to Tjilatjap, the only usable harbor on the south coast of the island. From Tjilatjap a line was to be constructed by way of Djokja and Solo through the Principalities to Semarang on the north coast, partly through the region where the broad-gauge NIS was being built at the time. From a halt on the Tjilatjap–Semarang line, a branch was planned by way of Madioen to Soerabaja. One of the desirable extras would be another west–east line along the northern coast, forming a second connection between the major cities. An ambitious plan, overambitious perhaps in view of the strained financial circumstances of the Batavian government and the hesitation of The Hague government to invest more in the colony. The southern line included many kilometers of difficult mountain line and provided at least one link between Batavia, Semarang, and Soerabaja, albeit in a rather roundabout way. A problem of unknown magnitude was that some of the regions to be traversed were hardly known, as no reliable maps existed, which made the difficulties that would be met there impossible to foresee.

By royal decree of February 22, 1871, a new commission was established, with Kool and Henket again as members, now reinforced by J. P. de Bordes, who had just stepped down as engineer in chief of the NIS, plus an officer of the Army Corps of Engineers and two civil servants of the Binnenlands Bestuur (Internal Civil Government) as other members. With uncommon speed this commission was ready with its report and in August 1871 it was published. Two west–east lines were considered necessary, one along the northern coast and the other more to the south through more mountainous terrain. However, because the cost of two lines would be astronomical, only one was to be chosen to start. As the southern line would open up regions that were until now wholly devoid of transportation whatsoever, the commission advocated the construction of the difficult southern line first. Traffic along the north coast could use the existing rivers and the many small ports on the Java Sea where shallow draught vessels would suffice for the existing transportation needs. Undoubtedly, the southern route was considered to be the more expensive, but apart from the need to open up the regions to large-scale agriculture, it would also serve as a means of defense against a possible foreign enemy coming in from the south.

Only de Bordes and one of the civil servants disagreed and recommended the construction of the northern line first, and in Indian broad gauge, no doubt with a connection to the NIS line in mind. Unanimously, the committee recommended construction and working of the line by private parties. Support from the government was to be provided in the shape of an interest guarantee for the necessary capital that was to be found on the international money market. The cost of the lines as suggested was estimated at 73 million guilders.

Surprisingly, Minister of the Colonies Van Bosse acted rapidly and on November 6, 1871, introduced a bill in Parliament in The Hague for the construction of a network of lines to the account of the state. The following lines were proposed:

1. Batavia–Bandoeng;
2. Djokja–Tjilatjap;
3. Pasoeroean–Poerwodadi to a link with the existing NIS line from Semarang; and
4. Soerabaja–Malang, crossing No. 3 somewhere south of Soerabaja.

Clearly, a connection between the western lines and those in the middle of the island was still lacking, but in a later bill this omission was to be rectified. Nothing was mentioned of the most controversial issue—the way these lines were to be worked—but a bill coming in due time would take care of that.

The proposal generated an enormous number of adverse comments and it was soon clear to Van Bosse that his ideas would never be accepted by Parliament in the shape proposed. No one understood why he, himself a proponent of private enterprise, now suddenly advocated construction by the state. In his answer Van Bosse quoted the advice of the East Indies army commander lieutenant-general W. A. Kroesen, the director of Public Works W. F. K. H. van Raders, and of the Council of the Indies. These officials all agreed with the proposed lines, but only Kroesen and Van Raders strongly favored construction by the state. In their opinion private enterprise would never be able to get a real railroad network on Java going, let alone rails in the Outlying Possessions. Only the state was in a position to do this. The Council of the Indies, though, still opined that construction by private parties was to be preferred and also possible. In his answer to Parliament Van Bosse changed his mind and wrote that construction by private parties was recommended but that the state, in case solid and dependable private parties were not forthcoming, could step in and construct the railways. And as no such private parties had come forward, the case was clear and the surveys and necessary expropriation measures could be started. However, this halfhearted system was not well received, and strong opposition continued until July 6, 1872, when the ministry, the third Liberal ministry of J. R. Thorbecke, stepped down on an unrelated issue. I. D. Fransen van de Putte, a strong advocate of private enterprise, succeeded Van Bosse, and he quickly withdrew the proposals of his predecessor.[1]

Fransen van de Putte had made his fortune as a sugar planter on Java and so he knew the problems with transportation of the product from the inland mills to the ports for export to Europe, but he hesitated to involve the government in the controversial issue of railroad construction. However, it was clear that enthusiasm from the side of private business parties for concessions for railways was lukewarm at best. The shaky financial position of the NIS did little to make businessmen and capitalists willing to risk their guilders in new railroads on Java. Yet, some plans matured and concessions for some lines were applied for. One of them came from the NIS itself, and it contained an extension of its Batavia–Buitenzorg line to Bandoeng. A joint British-Dutch combination and several other Dutch parties were also interested in some lines, mostly in the eastern part of the island south of Soerabaja, leading into the center of the sugarcane growing area. All parties requested some measure of support from the government, generally in the shape of a guaranteed interest on the necessary capital. Only David Maarschalk, in a new role, in 1873 requested no interest guarantee for construction of Soerabaja–Pasoeroean–Malang, stipulating only a contract for working the line.[2]

As usual, nothing happened, and the minister wanted first to establish the financial relationship between a possible concessionary and the government. In true Dutch fashion a new commission was formed, consisting of bankers from Amsterdam, Rotterdam, and, surprisingly, Darmstadt in Hessen, Germany. This town was the seat of the Bank für Handel und Industrie, which was heavily involved in the private company working the State Railways in the Netherlands, hence its presence here. Lodewijk Pincoffs, a well-known businessman from Rotterdam, was chairman, and T. J. Stieltjes, known from his earlier adventures in the Indies, was appointed secretary. The commission was charged with finding the best way for government to support private parties willing to undertake construction of railways in the regions known from earlier plans. Its report was presented in September 1873 with a proposed model of a contract between government and private parties. This contract, however, was considered so burdensome for the government that Parliament was strongly opposed; all financial risks seemed to be shifted to the government and all possible rewards to the private company. And risks there were many, as parts of the areas to be traversed were still largely terra incognita. Even the minister, although a dedicated champion of private enterprise, had to concede that this was an impossible approach; the state now simply had to act. "Better state railways than no railways" Fransen van de Putte declared in Parliament in 1874 during his defense of the annual colonial budget. He was ready to introduce a bill for construction of a Soerabaja–Pasoeroean–Malang line by the state, but before that could be done the ministry had stepped down on another issue and Fransen van de Putte was out. On November 2, 1874, W. Baron van Goltstein, his successor, simply introduced a bill for raising the East Indies annual budget by 1 million guilders for construction of the 115-km Soerabaja–Malang line.[3]

It was now up to the new incumbent to defend the bill against a most hostile Second Chamber. The debate was opened February 18, 1875, and Van Goltstein began with stating that financial considerations were the chief reason for changing over to construction by the state, as all available alternatives were obviously worse. He deemed it wise to start with the relatively short Soerabaja–Malang line through well-known territory that could later form part of the much-larger network. His estimate of the cost of construction was 10 million guilders spread over four years, and this sum included the cost of surveying the other planned lines as well. Now all earlier arguments against railroad building with public money by the state were heard repeatedly, while some members were most negative about the government's ability to undertake and successfully finish such a grand project. Since Daendels's Great Post Road, nothing comparable had been undertaken by the government. An inefficient and ignorant administration had been the cause of harbors silting up, road bridges slowly collapsing, and roads not being maintained adequately. With such a bad record, how would it be possible for the Batavian government to construct a railroad in this tropical country, a project of unknown magnitude and most uncertain future? Van Goltstein countered with the remark that one just had to travel in the Netherlands to see how well the state had been able to build a railway network there, even better and cheaper than private enterprise had done so far. On the other hand, in the Indies a lot of major and minor projects had indeed gotten bogged down over the years in endless discussions, fruitless negotiations with interested parties, structural indecision, and too much caution among leading government officials. The opposition certainly had a point.[4]

Others, the ex-resident Van Herwerden foremost among them, attacked the minister on the grounds that this large-scale expenditure on railways would in the end only benefit private businessmen and planters, who were chiefly foreigners and only intent on exploiting the riches of the colony. He declared: "Let us once again be warned! The opening up of Java to people from everywhere by providing a railway network will soon mean that we will be flooded with foreigners. Very soon, and earlier than one might imagine, it will lead to a loss of sovereignty in the East Indies." A far-fetched argument for sure. Another opponent jokingly called the proposed railway the "Rijks Pleizierbaan," the state pleasure route, to indicate that in his opinion it had no economic or military usefulness whatsoever.[5]

In his defense of the bill the minister referred to British India, where the private railway companies had been supported by an almost unlimited 5 percent government guarantee on their invested capital. Because of this guarantee, the companies, mostly working with capital from Britain, had no incentive to practice any economy, and expensive and much-too-lavish building was the result. British capitalists were only too eager to supply the money with such a guarantee of a regular income, and large amounts of money from the Indian tax revenues were paid out in this way to British investors, something that no one could really defend. Therefore, in 1869 a decision of historic proportions was made in London: from now on the state was to build new lines and operate them as well, but war in Afghanistan and severe famines in India frustrated these plans. However, some lines had indeed already been built and operated by the government in a very efficient manner, showing that the state could construct railways as well as private parties, or possibly even better. From 1879 a mixed system was followed with most private investors being bought out, which put ownership of the railways largely in government hands. Operation would be by private companies, with a possible guarantee of 4 percent for the

Soekaboemi, south of Buitenzorg on the line of the Java State Railways to Bandoeng, got its first station in 1882. It is a simple wooden building but with an overall roof for protection against sun and rain. The layout of the tracks was, for the time, fairly elaborate, with a real freight shed. This photograph dates from around 1884, not long after opening. (NSM collection)

few remaining shareholders. According to Van Goltstein this early and now abolished guarantee system of British India was not an example to be followed by the Dutch government. The British Indian state had shown that construction by the state was quite possible and even to be preferred.[6]

To appease some of his opponents, the minister declared that the working of the proposed line was to be left to a later debate. That helped him to obtain a majority of 44 to 21 votes in the Second Chamber of Parliament. In the Senate the same warmed-over objections were heard again, but the bill passed into law on April 5, 1875, and was published in the Official State Bulletin the next day. All applicants for railway concessions on Java were notified that no concessions would be granted when financial support from the government was requested.

THE STATE AS RAILWAY BUILDER

David Maarschalk was appointed chief of construction of the Soerabaja–Malang line, as he seemed to be the only engineer available to tackle the difficult assignment. Maarschalk was born in The Hague in 1829 as son of a public prosecutor and followed a military career. A cadet at the Royal Military Academy of Breda since 1843, he was appointed lieutenant in the Corps of Engineers of the Dutch East Indies in 1847 and sailed for Batavia.

He slowly climbed the ranks until being promoted to lieutenant-colonel in 1867. In 1868, at his own request, he was discharged; as a civilian engineer he succeeded de Bordes, becoming chairman of the NIS and chief engineer of that company. In that capacity he finished the line into the Principalities and designed and built the Batavia–Buitenzorg line. In 1874 Minister Van Goltstein recalled him to the Netherlands to be his advisor for the planned state railway construction in the Indies. After the passing of the law in Parliament, he was sent back to Batavia and on June 27, 1875, the governor-general appointed him chief engineer and head of the State Railway Organization. Officially, he and his staff were subordinated to the director of the Burgerlijke Openbare Werken (BOW, Public Works) in Batavia, but with a considerable freedom of action. This time the endless bickering between civil servants and the limitless discussions about the best way to handle a subject, resulting in delay or abandonment, was avoided. Maarschalk was the boss and he decided without meddling by others. His later successors were not so fortunate.[7]

Once in Batavia, Maarschalk had to recruit his staff; he was lucky to be able to count on the support of several experienced Dutch civil engineers and officers of the Corps of Engineers. He seemed to have a preference for the latter, as the engineers from the Delft Polytechnic were in his eyes only good for nothings, a rather sweeping statement, of course, in view of the many eminent Delft engineers involved in the building of the state railways in the home country. His second in command was D. N. Meyners, also an ex-army officer, who had already built up some railway experience with the NIS. H. G. Derx, from that company's construction staff, and P. Maas Geesteranus were chosen as section engineers. Twelve others in different capacities were appointed in the same royal decree and sent out to the East immediately. Once in Batavia more European personnel, chiefly Dutch with the odd German or Englishman, were recruited, and Maarschalk was fortunate to get some really experienced surveyors as well. A governmental survey for a coal railway on Sumatra's west coast under J. L. Cluysenaer had just been finished, and some specialists of Cluysenaer's staff were happy to join Maarschalk's new team in the same capacities. One of them was J. W. IJzerman, civil engineer, who would have a great career in the Indies. Locally a large number of Indo-European and indigenous personnel for clerical and more menial duties were recruited. Despite all these appointments, it should be borne in mind that there was practically no existing organization for Maarschalk to fall back upon. He had to start with nothing, and everything had to be built up from scratch.

Maarschalk has been compared to Daendels, a man with unbridled energy and capacity for work, who expected the same from his team members, which did not always ensure smooth relations with his coworkers and subordinates on the shop floor or out in the Javanese jungle. Despite

Nr. 21, an early 0-6-0 tank of the Java State Railways, delivered by Sharp Stewart in 1880. Originally numbered 16, she was intended for the mountain lines, but she was found too light for those duties. By the time this photograph was taken, she had been rebuilt with a new boiler and in this shape would last well into the post–WW II years. Photo from the 1920s or 1930s. (SNR collection)

these adverse opinions, he turned out to be a masterful engineer and one eminently adapted to working in a tropical climate and the mountainous regions to be traversed. He also had the knack of being able to work with largely unskilled indigenous personnel. He was recalled in 1878 to The Hague to give advice about possible extensions of the railroad network on Java. While there he founded the Technisch Bureau of the Ministry for the Colonies, a purchasing office for public works in the East Indies. It was fully operational by 1880 and coordinated all orders to be placed in Europe for railway equipment, rails, bridges, rolling stock, and locomotives, down to the smallest things such as nuts and bolts. This way a clear standard was established for all these things, ensuring that equipment and materials could be exchanged between lines, and once tested and admitted by the government inspectors, all these things could be reordered again and again without time-consuming new inspections and trials. The later private steam tramway companies also gladly made use of the bureau for their equipment. In 1920 the bureau changed its name to Oost-Indische Centraal Aankoop Dienst (East Indian Central Purchasing Service) and continued in the same functions but at a lower intensity. In Britain the office of the Crown Agents played much the same role.[8]

Maarschalk was back in Java late in 1878, now as inspector-general of all railways on the island and was honorably discharged as such in 1880. He

A more modern and much heavier six-coupled tank engine was the series 85–104, delivered by Hartmann in 1897–1898. Their weight was over 26 tons, but maximum speed was still set at only 30 kilometers per hour. L. J. Biezeveld saw this veteran in April 1941 in the JSS works of Manggarai, where she served as works shunter. (SNR collection)

returned to The Hague in 1881, where he continued to be involved in East Indian railway matters and even in the project for a railway in the Boer Republic of Transvaal, South Africa, the later Netherlands South African Railway Company. He died in The Hague in 1886, with full honors.

A NOTE ABOUT DUTCH ENGINEERS IN THE INDIES

With very few exceptions, all civil and mechanical engineers working on the railways and tramways of the East Indies up to 1942 were Dutchmen, most of them born and bred in the Netherlands. Quite a few of these men had careers in both countries, following the call for technicians when railways were being developed and built at home or in the colonies. This was why the railways both in the Netherlands and in the East Indies looked alike in many respects despite the difference in gauge, climate, and topography. Despite this essential Dutchness, foreign influences are easily noticeable. Foreign literature—French, German, and English— was available in the Netherlands, and many of these young engineers spoke one or more languages apart from Dutch. New developments in railway or locomotive engineering were closely monitored and used where applicable, and educational inspection tours to foreign countries were not uncommon. We have seen that de Bordes took the trouble to study both Austrian and British Indian mountain railways and Cluysenaer had traveled to Switzerland to see the Riggenbach rack rail system in action. German influence was generally stronger than English, as Germany, the close neighbor of the Netherlands and the most important trade partner as well, was generally better known to Dutch students than England.[9]

As noted above, Maarschalk, himself a military engineer, preferred military engineers as his assistants for the building of the first state lines. The Koninklijke Militaire Akademie (KMA, Royal Military Academy) at Breda had been founded in 1829 as a successor to several smaller military schools in the country. It was a military establishment, and the cadets were disciplined as soldiers and taught a kind of esprit de corps, in addition to the usual courses in civil and hydraulic engineering, mechanics, and such.

For enterprising young men another road to become engineers was offered by the Koninklijke Akademie (KA, Royal Academy) of Delft, founded in 1842, which provided a four-year course in the same subjects as the KMA but without the military parts. In 1864 the KA was converted into the Polytechnische School (Polytechnic School), offering courses in civil, mechanical, constructional, shipbuilding, and mining engineering. In 1905 this Polytechnic School was elevated to the ranks of the universities as the Technische Hoogeschool (TH, Technical High School), now known worldwide as Technische Universiteit Delft (Technical University Delft). The term *high school* in Dutch context should not be confused with the American high school; in Dutch the hogeschool was at the same level as a university but without the *ius promovendum*. The Polytechnic School soon became a serious competitor of the KMA, and in 1879 a total of ninety-five Delft engineers were serving in the East Indies, most of them in water management and irrigation but already six with the young railways. Toward the end of the century, these Delft engineers would almost completely eclipse the military colleagues in civilian works as water management and railways.[10]

A good example of a versatile Dutch engineer with a varied career is Jacobus L. Cluysenaer (1843–1932). He graduated as a civil engineer from the Delft Academy in 1863 and, as many colleagues, participated in the great work of those years, the construction of a railway network in the Netherlands by the state. His major activity in that role was his work on the building of the mile-long bridge across the Hollands Diep, at the time the longest bridge in Europe. An intermezzo were his years as a mathematics teacher at a school in Breda until he was asked in 1873 to survey a railway from the Sumatra Ombilin mines to a harbor on the Indian Ocean. His report was ready in 1876 and the results will be outlined in chapter 7. After returning to the Netherlands, he served two years as a teacher of civil engineering at the Royal Military Academy in Breda but continued his interest in the Ombilin railway, now focusing on the use of the rack system for traction on the steep grades. In 1878 he changed over to the Dutch State Railway Company as chief of Permanent Way and in 1882 became secretary of the CEO of that organization. Then in 1886 adventure tempted again and he was one of the incorporators of the Netherlands South African Railway Company, set up to construct a line in the Boer Republic of Transvaal from Pretoria to Portuguese Lourenço Marques on the Indian Ocean to make Transvaal independent of the railways of British South Africa. He remained some years in Transvaal until in 1890 the State Railways in the home country called him back as CEO of the company. Until his retirement in 1900, he acted in this capacity but never lost interest in the Dutch East Indies as member of the board of the NIS and of a commission to study alternatives for the Ombilin railway.[11]

Serving in Cluysenaer's survey party for the Ombilin coal railway was Jan Willem IJzerman (1851–1932), lieutenant-engineer fresh from the Royal Military Academy of Breda. Like many of his colleagues from this survey, he stayed in the Indies and was hired by Maarschalk as engineer for the construction of the state lines on Java, among them the difficult Buitenzorg–Bandoeng–Tjitjalenka line. In the Netherlands on extended leave since 1886, he was asked by Minister for the Colonies J. P. Sprenger van Eyk to take charge of the construction of the Ombilin coal railway as designed by Cluysenaer. Headquartered in Padang from 1887, he pushed the line inland and in 1892 coal transportation by rail started. Meanwhile, he had undertaken an adventurous exploration of the uncharted central jungle of Sumatra to the east coast of that island to establish the possibility or impossibility of a railway along that route. Pensioned off in 1896, he returned to the Netherlands and started a new career in oil exploration on Sumatra as director of the Petroleum Maatschappij Moera Enim, later absorbed by Royal Dutch Shell.

While working on Java, IJzerman became interested in the ancient Buddhist and Hindu-Javanese monuments on the island; through his influence the restoration of the now-famous Borobudur Buddhist stupa, dating back to circa 850 AD, was begun. As president of the Royal Netherlands Geographic Society since 1899, he organized many expeditions to explore the last white areas on the maps of the Indies, especially in New Guinea, then, apart from the coasts, still largely uncharted. Technical education in the Indies was also something that had his undivided attention, and in 1920 he founded the Technical High School at Bandoeng, today a great technical university. A versatile engineer, historian, and geographer and at the same time a great organizer, he possessed different qualities unique to a single person.[12]

A latecomer was Frans den Hollander (1893–1982), who studied at Delft Technical High School and earned his degree in mechanical engineering in 1916. One of his teachers in Delft was Professor I. Franco, who was working with Werkspoor-Amsterdam on the design of a new large express locomotive for the Java State Railways (JSS), with Den Hollander as his assistant. The young engineer was so impressed by "his" locomotive that he applied for a position with JSS, but because of the ongoing war, he arrived in Batavia only early in 1918 after a complicated journey by way of New York, San Francisco, and Japan. His career on Java was meteoric and by 1937 he had advanced to the position of chief of exploitation of the western lines of JSS. The following year he was allowed to go home for the customary extended leave with the promise that he would be appointed as chief of Java State Railways upon his return. This did not work out as planned because the Dutch government needed him for other work in the national munitions industry. During World War II he played an important role in the national resistance movement against the German occupation forces and earned much praise for this work. Appointed acting CEO of Netherlands Railways in 1946, he advanced to the top position on January 1, 1947. As such he capably organized the rebuilding of the Dutch network, which was seriously damaged during the war, and was also active in seeking close cooperation with other European railway executives.[13]

THE INDIAN ECONOMY OF THE 1870S

With the slow death of the Cultivation System and its mandatory growing of agricultural products for the European market, a new system had to be found to attract more European entrepreneurs and capital to develop the cultures of sugar, coffee, and other staple products. First of all, to clarify the legal foundations of ownership of land to attract Dutch or foreign capital for agricultural purposes, a new and simpler system of land ownership had to be implemented. Several ministers for the colonies had tried to develop such a system, but it was only in 1870 that the liberal minister E. de Waal managed to guide a bill through Parliament. The forced growth of sugarcane was to be slowly abolished, and it became possible for Europeans to acquire land in long lease, up to a maximum of seventy-five years. This opened the way for obtaining capital from banks to establish sugar mills and other agricultural industries. To protect the native population, it was from then on prohibited for Europeans, Chinese, and other "foreign Easterners," as Arabs and British Indian traders were known, to buy land from natives (leasing remained the only possible way). Government was not allowed to expropriate land owned by indigenous individuals or villages, except for public purposes—a great advantage in the carrying out of public works such as roads or railways. All land not legally owned by private persons, native or not, became the property of the government and could be given out to Dutchmen or foreigners resident in the Dutch East Indies in long lease to establish an agricultural or other business. And as the forced system of cultivation was gradually being abolished, private business could again compete with the government cultures. Yet, notwithstanding these measures that promised to push the Indies up into the mainstream of world trade, it took some years before new entrepreneurs arrived in sufficient numbers to develop the sugar business and other cultures as well. Despite this slow start, in the decade 1870–1880 the European segment of the population grew from 44,000 to 56,600 and almost doubled to 90,800 in 1900. At the same time the simple villager in his desa slowly became acquainted with an economy based on money, and the influence of the old feudal aristocracy gradually eroded. The arrival of better ways of communication advanced this trend in no small measure.[14]

NOTES

1. Veenendaal, "Locomotive of Modernity," 101–03. Bruin (de), *Het Indische spoor in oorlogstijd*, 16–18; Reitsma, *Korte geschiedenis*, 24–33.

2. About Isaäc D. Fransen van de Putte (1822–1902), see the recent biography by Paul Consten.

3. Willem, Baron van Goltstein (1831–1901), conservative member of the Second Chamber of Parliament, after 1871 until 1874 member of the Senate, 1874–1876 minister for the colonies and again 1879–1882, Dutch envoy in London 1894–1899. Molhuysen and Blok, eds., *Nieuw Nederlandsch Biografisch Woordenboek*, I, 953.

4. For the construction of the railway network in the Netherlands by the state, see Veenendaal, *Spoorwegen in Nederland*, 102–16.

5. Herwerden (van), *Een spoorwegnet over Java*.

6. Thorner, "Pattern of Railway Development in India," 84–86; also Hurd, "Railways," 148–53.

7. About David Maarschalk (1829–1889), see Molhuysen and Blok, eds., *Nieuw Nederlandsch Biografisch Woordenboek*, V, 327–29; also Reitsma, *Gedenkboek der Staatsspoor- en Tramwegen*, 19–30.

8. Bakker, "Free Extending over the Bandjir," 144–46.

9. Veenendaal, "De kennisoverdracht," 54, 69.

10. Lintsen, *Ingenieurs in Nederland*, 76, 151, 171, 202–04, 347. Also Schippers, *Van Tusschenlieden tot Ingenieurs*, for the lower technical schools.

11. Charité, ed., *Biografisch Woordenboek van Nederland*, 2, 94–95.

12. Ibid., 2, 637–38.

13. About Franciscus Q. den Hollander, ibid., 4, 193–95.

14. Zwaag (van der), *Verloren tropische zaken*, 28–30. Jong (de), *De Waaier van het Fortuin*, 286–88. About Minister Engelbertus de Waal (1821–1905), see Molhuysen and Blok, eds., *Nieuw Nederlandsch Biografisch Woordenboek*, IX, 1267–70. A civil servant in Batavia until 1858, he returned to the mother country and was minister for the colonies from 1868 until 1870, a liberal in his political outlooks.

Maarschalk himself was in charge of the construction of the Soerabaja–Pasoeroean–Malang line (112 km), while Meyners was responsible for the survey of the line to Bandoeng from a junction somewhere on the Batavia–Buitenzorg line of the NIS. There was no discussion anymore about the rail gauge. Indian standard gauge (1,067 mm or 3 ft 6 in) was to be used exclusively, a fortunate decision as European standard gauge (1,435 mm) was not necessary for the present and future needs and clearly too expensive in a mountainous country such as Java. Headquarters of the state system were established in a rented house in Malang and later moved to the station building there, while Meyners operated from Soekaboemi, on the proposed line to Bandoeng.

The first section Soerabaja–Pasoeroean was fairly level, and grading and tracklaying went smoothly; the line was opened by Governor-General J. W. van Lansberge on May 16, 1878, amid great festivities. Maarschalk was not present, as he had left for Holland in March of that year, but Derx deputized for him. The section from Bangil, west of Pasoeroean, to Malang was hillier and hence more difficult to construct. Malang, an important military base and a town with a pleasant climate resulting from its altitude of 380 m above sea level, was a popular spot for Soerabajans—only Europeans or affluent Chinese and Javanese, of course—to escape from the humidity and stifling heat of their city. The line reached the town in July 1879, well inside the schedule, and, more importantly, inside the agreed budget of 10 million guilders, as Maarschalk did not hesitate to mention proudly in his annual report that was included in the Colonial Reports. He considered this clear proof that the government was able to execute large public works with commendable speed and economy, better and cheaper than shown by the long agony of the slow finishing of the privately owned Semarang–Principalities line by the NIS.

It had been Maarschalk's intention to put the construction of the line out to tender, but no big contractors had come forward, so the state had to undertake everything, although certain parts of the line, such as small bridges, station buildings, and cuttings or landfills were contracted out to smaller firms of Chinese, Arab, or Javanese entrepreneurs. For the subsequent building of new lines, this would become the favored way of construction, with the state as chief contractor and smaller sections being parceled out to local or regional businessmen, with European construction firms responsible for the larger bridges and technically difficult parts. In this way a group of entrepreneurs, mostly indigenous, slowly developed; they followed construction all over the island and later even branched out to neighboring Sumatra. In Soerabaja the end of the line was located near the business section of the town, easily reached by land or river, but some parts of the ancient ramparts had to be moved or demolished, including a munitions depot. For seagoing ships this location was unfortunate, so it was decided to continue the railway to the mouth of the Kali Mas River and the roadstead as soon as the planned jetty on screw piles was constructed there. However, this would take another eight years, being finished only in 1886.

As mentioned in the preceding chapter, in the law ordering the construction of the Soerabaja–Malang line, the way of working the line was deliberately left open for a later decision to appease some opponents in Parliament. However, in the annual budgets since 1875 for the construction of the lines, certain sums had been included for the acquisition of rolling stock and locomotives, apparently without anyone in Parliament noticing or objecting to these details. With the opening of the first section by a train composed of Java State Railways rolling stock and engines, it became clear that working by the state was now somehow being established, although some members complained that this feature had been "smuggled in." When the minister objected to the word *smuggled*, the complaining M. P. changed his words in "that exploitation by the state had been tolerated as an unwanted corollary." In actual practice this did nothing to change the decision and the state continued to work the new line and others to be finished in the near future.[1]

MORE CONSTRUCTION BY THE STATE

Maarschalk had already submitted plans for new lines even before the Soerabaja–Malang railway had been opened. One was for a line from Buitenzorg, the terminus of the NIS line from Batavia, to Bandoeng, and the other was a line from Sidoardjo, south of Soerabaja, southwest to Madioen and Solo, with a branch from Kertosono to Blitar by way of Kediri through one of the most promising sugar regions. Negotiations

Excavating a deep cutting with hand tools only took time. Here in the neighborhood of Tjiandjoer between Buitenzorg and Bandoeng in 1879, hundreds of workers are busy with small baskets to carry off the soil. (KITLV collection)

with the NIS had already been opened in 1875 about an extension of the existing NIS line from Solo to Madioen and the simultaneous narrowing of the existing broad-gauge Solo–Semarang line to 1,067 mm. Included in these plans was a concession for the NIS for a line from Djokja to the port of Tjilatjap on the southern coast of Java. Many objections against these agreements were voiced, both in the Indies and in The Hague, with the result that Minister van Goltstein split the proposals into four sections, the first of which was the purchase by the state of the Batavia–Buitenzorg line for 5 million guilders. The other sections covered the narrowing of the gauge on the existing NIS line and some new extensions of that company. Van Goltstein was not really happy with the agreements and his successor as minister, F. Alting Mees, was of the same opinion, but he nevertheless signed the contracts with the NIS in June 1877. A bill for approval was then submitted to Parliament and a storm of protest went up. De Bordes was flatly against the agreement, as he feared that the "unnecessary" new lines would diminish the possibility of dividends of "his" NIS, while an opposing group in the company directorate saw the transactions as necessary for the public good and for the company as well. During these acrimonious

When building the line between Buitenzorg and Bandoeng in the late 1870s, the Dutch engineers had to bore the first tunnel ever on Java at Lampegan, between Soekaboemi and Bandoeng. Here a JSS 2-8-0 engine of the 900 series is about to enter the single track bore on July 27, 1939, with a passenger train. Photo by L. J. Biezeveld. (SNR collection)

discussions, Alting Mees stepped down in November 1877, and his successor, Van den Bosse, no friend of the contracts either, proposed to the NIS to annul the contracts, which, despite the objections of de Bordes and others, was flatly refused by the company's board. The minister then advised Parliament simply not to accept the proposed bill, whereupon the proposals were unanimously voted down on May 24, 1878.[2]

Meanwhile the bill for the construction by the state of Buitenzorg–Bandoeng–Tjitjalengka and Sidoardjo–Madioen with the branch from Kertosono to Blitar was submitted to Parliament on May 14, 1878, ten days before the voting down of the agreements with the NIS. While negotiations with that company were ongoing, the section Madioen–Solo, as surveyed by Maarschalk, was omitted from the new bill, as it was seen as highly possible that the NIS would build this connection. The Second Chamber passed the law with a large majority, and in July 1878 the Senate did likewise with an even greater majority; Maarschalk could start immediately. Madioen was reached in July 1882. The branch to Blitar was opened in June 1884, a good example of fast and solid work. However, with the NIS contracts annulled in the meantime, the now-missing link Madioen–Solo had to be built by the state as well. A bill for construction of that line was submitted to Parliament in 1880 and passed with a large majority by the Second Chamber and even unanimously by the Senate; in 1884 Solo was reached. An eastern extension from Pasoeroean to Probolinggo had been surveyed by Maarschalk before his retirement in November 1880, and that relatively short line was opened in 1884.

For the line to Bandoeng, several options for the junction with the NIS were considered initially, but in the end it was decided to begin the new state line at Buitenzorg at the end of the existing NIS line and go south as far as Tjibadak, then east toward Soekaboemi and from there farther east. Tjibadak was reached in 1881, Soekaboemi in the next year, and Padalarang in 1884. By then the line had entered the Preanger Highlands, necessitating numerous bridges across deep ravines and severe curves and steep gradients as much as 40‰ through the mountains. Even a tunnel of 650 m was needed between Soekaboemi and Bandoeng, something Dutch engineers had never encountered before in the home country. Ironwork for bridges and trestles came from Dutch, Belgian, or German firms who also supervised the erection of the structures in place. Despite the difficult terrain and the tropical climate, Bandoeng was reached late in 1884 and the line was even extended eastward to Tjitjalenka in the same year. Then construction stopped for a time as a result of the bad economic circumstances and the renewed discussion about the advantage or disadvantage of the state working the new lines.

CONSTRUCTION AND EQUIPMENT

All new construction was in the Indian standard gauge of 1,067 mm and single track was considered sufficient for the expected traffic, with passing loops at most stations. Iron rails were 6.80 m (21 ft) long, weighing 27 kg per meter and imported from Belgium and Germany. All other ironwork also had to be brought from overseas, again chiefly from Belgium and Germany. Steel rails would come later. Djati (teak, also called ironwood) sleepers were preferred, but iron and even impregnated pine were also tried. Djati lasted longer than both iron and pine and was cheap, as it grew abundantly in the Javanese highlands, while other woods and iron had to be imported. The flatbottom rail was spiked directly to the wooden ties without any metal underlay. Big coach screws—tirefonds as these were called in the Netherlands, using a French word—to hold down the rail came much later. Most of the lines from Soerabaja were relatively level, but the section between Bangil and Malang was constructed through mountainous country and knew gradients of between 45‰ and 50‰. The branch from Kertosono to Blitar had some of the same nasty inclines that would tax the first steam locomotives to the limit. Lineside equipment was kept to a minimum, with plain station buildings and halts constructed chiefly of wood without embellishments and unnecessary frills.[3]

The relatively unknown English locomotive works of Fox Walker & Co., Atlas Engine Works, Bristol, founded in 1864, was chosen to supply

The JSS line between Malang and Blitar, opened in 1897, needed some spectacular bridges to span the many ravines. This very American-looking bridge was thrown across the deep gorge of the Kali Lawor. A lot of the early bridges such as this one later had to be reinforced to allow heavier locomotives and higher speeds. (Author's collection)

the locomotives for the first lines of the Java State Railways (JSS, Java Staats Spoorwegen). Fox Walker was almost unknown in the Netherlands, apart from a few engines for shunting and light duties on one of the smaller railway companies and also with some big contracting firms. Why this unpretentious factory was chosen is unclear, as Fox had no experience with narrow-gauge railways in tropical countries and it had never supplied engines to the many railway companies operating on the meter gauge in British India. The price offered by the Bristol firm must have decided the issue, but no further orders were ever placed with Fox.[4]

For the more or less level Soerabaja–Pasoeroean line, seven small 2-4-0 side tank engines were supplied, with outside cylinders and a large cab with an overall roof and large openings in the sides for ventilation, something sorely needed in the humid tropical climate. During the monsoon season these openings could be closed with shutters, keeping the rain out but allowing for some movement of air. Numbered 6–12, their total weight was 26 tons, with an adhesive weight of less than 20 tons, 10 tons per axle being the absolute limit for the light tracks of the time. With driving wheels of 1,400 mm, an overall length of almost 8 m and a permitted maximum speed of 60 km per hour, they were sprightly little machines,

not very powerful but adequate for the light trains of the first years. All engines and rolling stock were equipped with the central automatic coupler invented by the Norwegian engineer Pihl. In ever-heavier versions it was used by the State Railways until the very end.

For the mountain line to Malang, the Bristol firm supplied five six-coupled side tank machines, also with two outside cylinders and the same big cab. They carried the numbers 1–5 and had a total weight of almost 25 tons. Driving wheel diameter was only 890 mm, with a permitted maximum speed of just 30 km per hour. These 0-6-0s had cowcatchers front and aft, while the 2-4-0s had them only up front. Lines were generally unfenced, and as the tropical jungle was full of wild animals, large and small, that wandered on the tracks, night traffic was prohibited for that reason. These diminutive engines had to tackle the fierce gradients of the line to Malang with train weights of about 30 tons, and they managed.

Soon after the arrival of the Fox Walker engines in 1878–1879, more engines followed for the new lines that were opened in the early 1880s, but not from the Bristol firm anymore. Hartmann of Chemnitz, Saxony, delivered the first 2-6-0 side tanks in December 1879, and as this new type answered all expectations, many more followed until 1891, when

One of the ubiquitous 2-6-0 tanks as supplied by Hartmann between 1879 and 1891 is waiting for departure with her train in the old Batavia South station, opened by the Batavia Ooster Spoorweg in 1887 and later transferred to the JSS. Nr. 55, after 1912 Nr. 310, was one of the first batches of 1879 and is still a coal burner. (SNR collection)

The Early State Railways 73

forty-eight of these useful tanks were in service. Initially, they were meant for the mountain line in West Java and had a total weight of 30 tons and a maximum permitted speed of 45 km per hour. The two outside cylinders drove the middle coupled axle, and the last coupled axle was constructed with flexible axle boxes as invented by the British engineer Cortazzi, with a play of 12 mm left and right. The front carrying axle was constructed to the 1858 patents of the American engineer Levi Bissel. These two-wheeled pony trucks were widely used—not only in America—and gave a better running on lines with numerous severe curves as was the case in Java. Later numbered in the 300 series, they were for many years the mainstay of traffic on the mountain lines until the arrival of larger and more powerful engines. Hartmann exposed one of these 2-6-0 tanks in 1883 at the International Colonial and Trade Exposition of Amsterdam, his Works Nr. 1220, where it was awarded a gold medal.[5]

Apart from small series of light 2-4-0 and 0-6-0 tanks from Sharp Stewart of Manchester, chiefly intended for light work trains and shunting duties, that firm also designed an express engine for the level lines. The word *express* may be an exaggeration here, as speeds were not greater than 60 km per hour, but the new engines were quite successful for the fast-growing passenger traffic. They were 2-4-0 engines with separate four-wheeled tenders, outside cylinders, and a curious long wheelbase with the Bissel pony truck giving 50 mm play far out in front. Sharp Stewart supplied the first one in 1880, and sixty-four more were to follow over the years until 1896. Total weight of the engine was 20 tons, with 13 tons for a fully loaded tender. Driving wheels were 1,427 mm, giving a good turn of speed. They must have been quality products, as some of them had extremely long lives. One was still in steam in 1979, almost a century later! All locomotives burned coal that was now imported from Australia, Japan, Bengal, or even South Africa, cheaper than fuel from England. Simple workshops were established in Soerabaja for the eastern lines and in Buitenzorg for the western sections.[6]

For the new lines no less than fifteen mixed first-second class carriages were deemed necessary, plus forty-five third-class coaches and fifteen guards vans, all four-wheeled. For the expected freight traffic, sixty open and thirty closed wagons were ordered plus forty open wagons with sheets and twenty wagons for ballast and sand and six ventilated ones for cattle. Everything had to be ordered from Europe, as an indigenous industry did not exist. In 1877 the Haarlem factory of Beijnes delivered forty-nine iron frames with wheels, axles, and draw gear for third-class carriages to the JSS to be used on the new lines. All woodwork and fittings were added in the works of the JSS itself. These first coaches were soon, in 1881, followed by larger and roomier carriages with six-wheel underframes after the Cleminson patent, of which the outer axles were mounted in a

radial truck, and the middle axle could move laterally. Maximum permitted speed of these six-wheelers was only 60 km per hour, no problem as this speed was also the maximum permitted on all lines.

Passenger traffic at first was thought to be of limited importance because the Javanese population was not expected to travel. The first tariff structure as designed by Maarschalk was based on that of the NIS, with a tariff of 10 cents per kilometer for first class, 6 cents for second class, but 2 cents for third instead of 1 cent with the NIS. For most Javanese travelers this was too high and only after Derx, Maarschalk's successor, reduced the tariff in 1881 to 6, 4, and 2 cents, respectively, the number of passengers increased somewhat but still not enough. Hence a new rate was introduced for distances of over 300 km for third-class passengers of only 1.25 cents per kilometer, but even that did not really help to get the Javanese in large numbers in the trains. They simply did not have the need to travel that far. Only in 1900 was the 1-cent tariff introduced on a large scale, at first only from one station to the next, but later it was extended to two or three stations, a measure that the private companies had already taken years ago. The Javanese population then came in droves and was happy to travel by train to sell their wares and animals on market days in the neighboring towns or villages.[7]

Freight wagons, also chiefly of the four-wheeled variety, came from Beijnes, at first only the ironwork but later also as complete wagons. Bogie

Java State Railways Nr. 101, an 0-6-0 tank, supplied by Hartmann in 1898 at an unknown location. The rolling stock consists of simple four-wheeled carriages, adequate for the traffic. The wooden shutters in the windows were meant for keeping out sun and rain, while letting in some fresh air. (Gerard de Graaf collection) freight trucks came in 1895 and were soon used in large numbers. Dutch firms such as Beijnes-Haarlem complained of the import duties on iron parts for carriages and wagons, but not on complete rolling stock, giving foreign industry, Belgian and German foremost, a major advantage in supplying Dutch railways with finished wagons and carriages. Apparently, the government listened to these complaints and in 1886 introduced a tariff on complete coaches similar to that on iron and steel parts.[8]

Hartmann was to become the chief supplier of steam locomotives to the State Railways on Java and to the Netherlands East Indies in general. For all railways and tramways in the Netherlands East Indies, the Chemnitz firm constructed no less than 458 steam locomotives, large and small, from tiny 0-4-0 tanks to truly enormous Mallets of 2-8-8-0 wheel arrangement. Hartmann's share was 26.6 percent of the total of 1,721 units delivered to Java and Sumatra by twenty-four factories worldwide over the years up to 1942. The hundreds of engines for industries and agricultural purposes are not included in these totals. Werkspoor of Amsterdam came second with 240 engines altogether, or 13.9 percent, and Beyer Peacock of Manchester came third with 181 units.[9]

Richard Hartmann had founded a factory in Chemnitz, Saxony, for the making of textile machines. He soon extended his field of business to steam locomotives for the railways in Saxony and delivered his first engine in 1848. More followed and he also entered the export business; in time Hartmann engines came to be known all over the world, especially in Russia, where in 1896 a daughter enterprise was set up in Lugansk in present-day Ukraine. In 1870 the company became known under the name of Sächsische Maschinenfabrik vormals Richard Hartmann Aktiengesellschaft in Chemnitz and it built up a sizable customer base outside Saxony. For Hartmann the JSS became one of the best overseas customers, while, strange to say, the firm only ever supplied five locomotives to the railways of the Netherlands.[10]

Sharp Roberts, Atlas Works, Manchester, was founded in 1828 also for the manufacture of machinery for the textile industry, and its first steam locomotive was constructed in 1833. More followed, including for the Dutch Rhenish Railway in the early 1840s. The name was changed to Sharp Bros. in 1843 and again to Sharp Stewart & Company in 1852. As such it became one of the bigger firms in the locomotive trade and was known all over the world. In 1889 the company moved to Glasgow and expanded even more. In 1903, with two other Scottish locomotive builders, it became part of the newly founded giant North British Locomotive Company Ltd. Apart from the sixty-five express engines described before, Sharp Stewart constructed only eight other engines for the Java State Railways.[11]

1. Reitsma, *Gedenkboek der Staatsspoor- en Tramwegen*, 19–33; Reitsma, *Korte geschiedenis*, 34–35. About Johan Wilhelm van Lansberge (1830–1905), see Molhuysen and Blok, eds., *Nieuw Nederlandsch Biografisch Woordenboek*, III, 739–41. After a distinguished career as a diplomat, he was governor-general of the Netherlands East Indies 1874–1881.

2. About Fokko Alting Mees (1819–1900), see ibid., VIII, 1140. He had a distinguished career as a lawyer in the Indies before he was minister for the colonies for just over a year, September 1876 to November 1877.

3. *Gedenkboek Koninklijk Instituut van Ingenieurs*, 291–97.

4. Lowe, *British Steam Locomotive Builders*, 183.

5. Reiche, *Richard Hartmann*, 48.

6. Oegema, *De stoomtractie*, 66–70.

7. Reitsma, *Gedenkboek der Staatsspoor- en Tramwegen*, 169–72.

8. Asselberghs, *Beijnes*, 146, 151, 221. Oegema, *De stoomtractie*, 111–14. Reitsma, *Gedenkboek der Staatsspoor- en Tramwegen*, 26.

9. Figures from Reiche, *Richard Hartmann*, 50.

10. Messerschmidt, *Taschenbuch Deutsche Lokomotivfabriken*, 174–79.

11. Lowe, *British Steam Locomotive Builders*, 576–80.

SLOWING DOWN 6
AND REORGANIZATION

THE SUGAR CRISIS OF 1884

As already obvious from the previous chapter, the Indian economy showed alarming signs of overheating in the early 1880s. After the gradual abolishing of the Cultivation System, European entrepreneurs assumed that riches were now for the taking in the sugar industry. Overly optimistic dreamers started plantations without any solid knowledge of the growing of sugarcane (or its inherent problems) and without secure financial backing. In 1884 the slump suddenly started with sugar prices halved in a single year. One of the chief causes was the overproduction of beet sugar in Europe, helped in no small way by subsidies from several governments such as France and Germany. The international sugar market collapsed completely, and many plantation owners went broke and had to close their mills and discharge their personnel. Because of the easy credits that had been extended by East Indies banks, some of these institutions also encountered severe problems when debtors were unable to pay up. Only the timely intervention of a consortium of Amsterdam banks and solid trading houses helped the East Indies banks to survive, and from then on they were more careful in extending credit to sugar planters and other businessmen. Only after solid information about the prospective client, his backers, and his business experience were new credits and loans made available. New organizations and solid firms, mostly from Amsterdam, entered the market in these days, of which Handels Vereeniging Amsterdam (HVA, Trading Company Amsterdam) became the most influential, not only by providing financial support and technical knowledge for privately owned sugar mills but also by setting up many sugar estates on Java itself.

An added severe complication was the sereh disease that broke out in these years. This previously unknown plant disease attacked the sugarcane in the fields and destroyed harvests completely. Initially, there was no known remedy, but as a countermeasure Proefstations, experimental stations, were set up where biologists, botanists, and other scientists experimented with the growing of new strains of a cane resistant to the sereh disease. Most of these Proefstations were set up and funded by the sugar industry itself, often with financial help from the Batavian government. It took some time but gradually the disease was mastered. Over the years these Proefstations acquired an international stature, as proven by the well-known American travel writer Paul Theroux's remark. During his rambles through the American Deep South in the 1950s, he encountered an old man who had worked in the sugar industry in Alabama in the 1920s, who told him that the introduction of a new variety of cane, marked POJ, had saved the dying sugar business there. Of course, Theroux then asked what POJ meant and the answer was "Proefstation Oost Java."[1]

An unexpected favorable result of the sugar crisis was the better diversification of the cultures. From then on cocoa, tea, and especially cinchona, the basic plant for the production of quinine, were the new crops that also promised good harvests and profitable results. Cinchona was a special case, as it was known as an antidote against tropical fevers, but it was only available in small quantities from South America. On order of the Batavian government, a botanist had been sent to Peru back in 1853 to smuggle out cinchona plants that only grew there. His secret mission had been considered so important that he had been brought back with his plants and seeds from Peru to the Indies on a Dutch warship. Only after many years of experimentation with different soils, rainfall, and climates, the growth of cinchona on Java had become successful, even to such an extent that toward the end of the nineteenth century, the Dutch East Indies supplied 96 percent of the total production of quinine in the world.[2]

PUBLIC WORKS OTHER THAN RAILWAYS

With the successful construction and working of railways, the Batavian government began to consider itself able to undertake other public works. As noted in earlier chapters, the department of Burgerlijke Openbare Werken in Batavia (BOW, Department of Civilian Public Works) did not have a very good name in the first half of the nineteenth century. It was considered slow, without the necessary expertise in infrastructural matters and lacking the power of decision, so its record was generally negative. By the 1850s Java's road system was mediocre at best, and the BOW had not executed works of any importance since Daendels's Great Post Road. Only after 1860 a gradual improvement is noticeable, with some new roads on Java being constructed, often with forced labor, the Heerendiensten, whereby the local population was obliged to contribute labor for public works in its region, often without pay or at best with modest financial compensation. Spurred on by The Hague, the Batavian

government slowly abolished this system of Heerendiensten. Money for road construction, however, was hard to find, as most public funds now went into the construction of the railway system. Only in the late 1880s and 1890s did the BOW at long last manage to materially improve the road system in the East Indies.

By 1893 on Java alone there was a system of about 3,300 km of post roads, generally hard surfaced, supplemented by 6,660 km of main inland roads, sometimes hard surfaced but more often than not only with gravel and without a substantial, solid base. Then there were some 10,000 km of minor inland roads that served only local or at best regional interests, and their condition was often deplorable. Although not really sufficiently reinforced, even in bad weather the main roads could be used with some difficulties, but bridges over the numerous rivers were often lacking, and travelers had to make use of the usually rickety locally operated ferries. Even where bridges did exist this did not guarantee an easy and safe

Where no bridge existed, primitive ferries had to be used to cross rivers. The two-wheeled carriage of a civilian officer is already on board; horses are following. Image from before 1880. (KITLV collection)

crossing. In 1863 the Dutch painter Frans Lebret in his travels on Java encountered many places where a bridge had been swept away by a *band-jir*, one of the common sudden flash floods. No other way of crossing the river was available: "It appeared that the former bridge was being rebuilt and many workers were around. By them our carriage was lowered from the shore to the river with a long rope—but the way was so steep that our carriage almost keeled over before being let down into the water, strewn with many large boulders. Eight bullocks were then used to draw the coach across and up the less steep opposite bank that had been covered with planks and branches. In the meantime we had been carried across in a large canoe and were happy to take our places in the coach again." Not an easy crossing this, and it should be remembered that Lebret was traveling in style with his brother Jan Hendrik, who was a well-to-do sugar planter in East Java. Lesser subjects suffered more hardships and could summon less help than the Lebret brothers.[3]

With the harbors it was more or less the same. The few natural harbors were hardly improved and generally ships still had to load and unload out in the roadstead, as BOW had done little to improve matters. The port of Batavia silted up continually and measures taken against this were insufficient. In 1861 matters came to a head when the ship carrying a distinguished visitor, the new viceroy of British India, Lord Elgin, got stuck in the mud and became immovable. The exalted guest had to be brought ashore with great difficulties while the helpless reception committee was waiting on the quay. In this same year the vessel carrying Governor-General Sloet van de Beele suffered a similar ignominious fate, and only then things began slowly moving. Parliament in The Hague intervened and made money available for the purchase of powerful steam dredgers in England; these were brought into use to clear the harbor channel, with great success. But even this was only a temporary expedient, and three years after Lord Elgin had suffered this glaring misfortune, not much had improved. Frans Lebret left a vivid description of the trials and tribulations to get ashore in Batavia from his ship with dry feet: "The little proa that would bring us ashore was rocking so much on the waves that the broad gangplank connecting it with the shore was shattered and we had to use a narrow plank as best as we could with only the light of torches to guide us."

Complaints from shipowners, traders, and passengers about the primitive conditions multiplied and became more vociferous, and many companies transferred their business from Batavia to Singapore, where facilities were better. The importance of Batavia gradually diminished when compared to the British emporium. That something really had to be done became clear in 1871 when the first regular twice-weekly Dutch steamship line Amsterdam–Batavia was opened. Maatschappij Nederland, the

Amsterdam firm that operated this line, complained repeatedly about the lack of adequate port facilities for large mail steamers, and a discussion both in the Netherlands and in the Indies began about how to solve the problem. Several plans were ventilated, among others by the NIS, the company that owned and worked the Batavia–Buitenzorg railway. It supported a plan for a new harbor close to the existing Batavia port, by which the company hoped to bolster its still rather precarious financial position by extending its railway line to the proposed new harbor. Opponents claimed that this new facility would silt up as bad or even worse than the old one and put forward the idea of constructing a new port farther east of the town but still on the wide Bay of Batavia. Discussion took years but in the end it was decided that the plan for constructing a complete new harbor with all necessary facilities and equipment was preferred. The well-known and experienced Dutch civil engineer J. Waldorp was asked to design the port, complete with all facilities and equipment. Without ever having been in the Indies but with good maps and figures at hand, Waldorp came forward with an eminent plan for a deep-water harbor, fit for the liners that were getting bigger and bigger every decade. Construction was put out to tender in 1876 but no takers came forward, apart from an unknown English consortium that turned out to be a complete swindle.[4]

A view of Tandjong Priok, Batavia's new harbor, around 1890. The foremost ship is a small steamer of the Gouvernements Marine, the government's navy. Behind is a vessel of the Rotterdamsche Lloyd with its black funnel. (KITLV collection)

With no interest from powerful contractors, the government decided to undertake this major work itself. Civil engineer J. A. de Gelder, who had assisted Waldorp in finishing his plans, was sent out to take charge of the works. He did a marvelous job, changing the plans where necessary when circumstances were different than Waldorp had assumed. Under his expert guidance the works were finished between 1883 and 1885. A major setback was the eruption of the Krakatau volcano in Strait Soenda in 1883. The resulting tsunami killed more than thirty-six thousand people on the neighboring islands and also destroyed the quarry at Merak in Java's western extremity, from where the stone for the harbor works was brought in. The quarry and all its equipment was swept from the face of the earth and all personnel, several hundred altogether, European, Chinese, and Javanese, were killed. Their bodies were never found.

Despite this misfortune the works proceeded and Batavia could finally boast having a modern port and could try to win back part of the traffic and trade lost to Singapore. Unexpectedly, the works at Tandjong Priok turned out to cost more than originally planned, and so Semarang and Soerabaja had to wait many more years for the modernization of their harbors, as the money available for public works was always limited. A simple railway connection between the new harbor installations and Batavia was provided by the Harbor Works, the company responsible for constructing and operating the new facilities.[5]

One of the regular users of the new Tandjong Priok harbor was the Koninklijke Paketvaart Maatschappij (KPM, Royal Packet Company). As described in the first chapter, the Batavian government had contracted with the Nederlandsch-Indische Stoomvaart Maatschappij (NISM), a British company despite the Dutch name, for the regular interinsular traffic. The chief objection against this company was that it directed most of the traffic as far as possible to Singapore and that all outfitting and repairs and such had to be done there. Moreover a serious question was voiced: In case of war, where would the NISM as a British-owned company stand?

Finally, in 1888, with the end of the contract with the NISM imminent, the Batavian government decided not to renew the existing agreement but opened negotiations with a newcomer, the KPM. This shipping business was incorporated by a consortium of dependable Amsterdam and Rotterdam maritime interests and offered to provide all necessary seaborne transport for the government, civilian and military passengers, mail, and money, but at the same time also for private persons and business. In 1891 the KPM started its first lines with a couple of ships taken over from the NISM, and soon this well-run company with dependable connections and services turned out to be a great success. Consequently, in 1899 the KPM obtained a complete monopoly of the interinsular traffic apart from small Chinese and Indonesian operators who cared mostly for

regional and local traffic needs. As a monopolist the KPM also became a most useful tool for expanding and establishing Dutch rule in the far outposts all over the archipelago. With all military expeditions of the late nineteenth and early twentieth centuries, the KPM rendered invaluable services in transporting men and equipment to places where revolts had broken out. However, the KPM worked certainly not only for the government, but also for the development of trade and commerce in the whole area, directing its services not so much to Singapore but concentrating on Batavia and Soerabaja. The steamers of the KPM with their yellow funnels became a familiar sight in even the smallest harbors in outlying districts, giving a dependable regular service for officials and civilians alike. The arrival of a KPM ship often was the only connection with the outside world for many government officers, European business agents, and missionaries. Large, comfortable, even luxurious passenger vessels were soon also built and used on the longer lines to Australia, China, Japan, Ceylon, Malaya, and the Philippines.[6]

The steamships of the Koninklijke Paketvaart KPM came to the farthest corners of the vast archipelago. Here the SS *Bontekoe*, named after a famous VOC captain of the seventeenth century, is anchored in the bay of Gorontalo on the east coast of Celebes. Every two weeks a KPM steamer arrived from Java bringing passengers, freight, and mail, including news of the world, to the 9,466 inhabitants of the little town, of which 207 were Europeans (1928 figures). (Author's collection)

MORE RAILWAY CONSTRUCTION

The precarious financial situation of the Batavian government and the continuing Atjeh war that swallowed millions caused many of the

By far the largest series of engines of Java State Railways were the Nrs. 201–265, 2-4-0 locomotives with separate tender, supplied by Sharp Stewart in several batches between 1880 and 1896. Nr. 240, originally Nr. 80 from 1884, is seen here in a state of undress in the Manggarai Works in 1940. She was repaired and survived the war. Photo by L. J. Biezeveld. (SNR collection)

proposed lines included in the railway plans to be postponed until better times. Despite this slowing some construction continued, albeit on a very small scale. On the annual colonial budget for 1884 the Jogjakarta (Djokja)–Tjilatjap line, 176 km, was proposed and accepted by Parliament with construction starting immediately. The opening of the line to this harbor town on the south coast of Java followed in 1887. Cynics wondered why the State Railways wanted to reach Tjilatjap at all, as it was a "dead town and a deadly town at the same time."[7]

From Soerabaja a line now existed west to Tjilatjap, but with a change of gauge between Solo and Djokja with the broad-gauge NIS line. All freight had to be transferred to broad-gauge trucks at Solo and reloaded again in standard-gauge wagons at Djokja, a cumbersome, time-consuming, and expensive arrangement. Passengers simply had to change trains twice. Nobody was happy with the situation, but it would last until 1899 when a third rail was laid inside the existing broad-gauge track to enable JSS locomotives and trains to continue their journey. Passengers could spend the night in the hotel of the State Railways at Maos, but this lodging soon acquired a bad name because of its sloppy service.

The Chemnitz works of Richard Hartmann continued the construction of the popular and successful 2-6-0 tanks until the final ones of this type arrived in 1891. By then forty-eight of these handsome tanks were in use on both the western and eastern lines of the JSS. The 2-4-0 engines with separate tender for express and passenger traffic, first delivered by Sharp Stewart in 1880, also fulfilled expectations and were reordered in several batches from 1884 with slightly changed dimensions until 1896. The freight and passenger rolling stock was also slowly expanded but still

after the original designs. By 1884 the total number of employees of Java State Railways had slowly risen from about two hundred in 1878 to the still-small number of some eight hundred, including the Javanese personnel on daily wages. European and Indo-European staff was paid by the month. The length of the network in exploitation was 580 km in 1884.[8]

A much more modern engine was Java State Railways Nr. 317, a 4-4-0 with a six-wheel tender, delivered by Hartmann in 1905. The photo dates from before 1912, when these engines were renumbered in the 600 series. The fireman is sitting at ease on top of the firewood in the huge crate while the Javanese gentleman in a white uniform is probably an inspector, as white uniforms were generally not worn by the locomotive engineers. (SNR collection)

TOWARD A NEW ORGANIZATION

When Maarschalk accepted the position of inspector-general, chief of the Java State Railways, he was only nominally subordinate to the director of the Burgerlijke Openbare Werken (BOW) in Batavia. Directors of the BOW were usually recruited from the ranks of civil engineers of the Waterstaat, responsible for rivers, canals, irrigation works, and harbors, but not necessarily real experts in railway working. Maarschalk had obtained a large degree of independence from BOW, so much so that a kind of state within the state had grown, as he did not have to report to the director of BOW at all but straight to the minister for the colonies. In Batavian government circles this caused many problems, and complaints about the irregularity of the relations between BOW and the leader of the railway were numerous, but as long as the forceful Maarschalk remained in charge no one dared to intervene and propose new ideas and plans.

This changed in 1880 after Maarschalk's retirement and especially after H. L. Jansen van Raay's accession to the directorate of BOW in 1886. Van Raay had the support of the Batavian government and also of Minister for the Colonies Sprenger van Eyk in The Hague, and in 1888 a new organization was worked out. Derx, successor to Maarschalk, was to retain the—now meaningless—title of inspector-general but was made subordinate to the director of BOW. The State Railways were no longer an independent entity but became a section of BOW, and from then on the department chiefs of the JSS reported directly to the director of BOW, not to the inspector-general. Derx was furious and it affected his health to such an extent that he stepped down in the next year and returned to Europe to seek recovery. He died in 1890 in a hospital in Germany. His successor, J. K. Kempees, an eminent engineer who had worked under Maarschalk and Derx, became chief of BOW's Section of Railways and Tramways, subordinate to the director of that body and no longer independent as Maarschalk and Derx had been.

Although converted into a more normal organization in Batavia, the Java State Railways now clearly lacked the strong direction of a chief, of a real expert in railway matters who knew the field and its possibilities and impossibilities. Discipline became slack and initiatives from below were disregarded and ignored. Public complaints about the worsening service became numerous, and both in Batavia and The Hague a tsunami of letters and brochures *pro et contra* was published. The Indian daily press, always vociferous and often even nasty, filled its columns with these letters, mostly attacking the Batavian authorities. As usual government was slow in its reaction and only after many years of official reports and recommendations a new organization was developed in 1906 (more about this in a later chapter).[9]

PRIVATE VERSUS STATE RAILWAYS AGAIN

Despite the apparent success of the first few railway lines constructed by and worked by the state, there were still many influential groups of entrepreneurs and government officials who doubted the need for and the ability of the state to develop a railway network on the island of Java. Now that the annual budgets of the Batavian government had to be slimmed down as a result of the current economic slump, many thought that private enterprise would be better able to continue the construction of new lines and to improve the services on the existing ones. In Parliament in The Hague, strong opponents claimed again and again that the state had no role in the construction of railways and that private enterprise would be much more efficient and more profitable. In the Indies the same ideas were ventilated but were also strongly attacked by other groups, official or not, who found that the state was doing a good job in railway matters despite the straightened financial position.

In 1883 two different business consortia offered to buy the Oosterlijnen, the lines east of Solo centering on Soerabaja. One of these applicants was the Nederlandsche Handel Maatschappij (NHM), the former monopolist trading company, now a banking and trading company without any government support. The NHM wanted the eastern lines, possibly with an interest guarantee and with a share of the profits above a certain level for the government, and a company was to be set up to work the lines when the NHM should become owner. The other applicant was a combine of two East Indian railway experts, Johannes Groll, involved in the NIS, and perhaps unexpected, David Maarschalk, who was now a private citizen in the Netherlands after his retirement from the Java State Railways. Their combine aimed to acquire both the eastern and western lines, again with a certain interest guarantee for the western lines, which were supposed to be generally unremunerative. Minister for the Colonies Van Bloemen Waanders dismissed both applications as being too onerous for the government, whereupon Groll and Maarschalk adapted their proposals with financial clauses more advantageous for the state. Opposition was strong, however, not only as to be expected from Derx and Kempees and other Java railway officials but also from trading and mercantile groups in Soerabaja and Batavia, who were not unhappy with the existing state of things.

Van Bloemen Waanders's successor as minister, J. P. Sprenger van Eyk, was certainly not against a transfer of the State Railways to a limited private company, but only when the financial interests of the state were duly guaranteed. In 1887 he sent a bill to that respect to Parliament, but its reception there was lukewarm at best now that the financial situation of the East Indies was improving sufficiently. In the same bill the minister also reserved a sum for the construction by the state of the Tjitjalengka–Tjilatjap line to close the gap between the eastern and western state lines. When Parliament seemed to be no longer interested in a transfer of the state lines, Sprenger van Eyk withdrew his bill and the idea petered out quietly. Moreover, both Groll and Maarschalk were dead by then and no one had replaced them in taking up the cause of private enterprise with the same vigor. In 1889 Sprenger van Eyk's successor, L. W. Keuchenius, included the Tjitjalengka–Tjilatjap line again in his budget and this passed without much opposition; in 1894 the last stretch of this railway was opened.[10]

This was to be all in the field of railway construction by the state for the time being, but as soon as the financial horizon brightened, new lines would be taken in hand and the existing network would be upgraded and improved. In the meantime, despite the lull in new construction and the financial setbacks, a new phenomenon, the steam tram, had become the topic of the day.

1. Theroux, *Deep South*, 276.

2. Gonggrijp, *Schets ener economische geschiedenis van Indonesië*, 127–28, 132–33. Jong (de), *De Waaier van het Fortuin*, 285, 308, 315–16.

3. Horn-van Nispen, "Road to a New Empire," 78–79. For the quotation from Lebret's diary, see Leusink and Sybesma, eds., *Op Reis met Pen en Penseel*, 279.

4. Jan Abel Adriaan Waldorp (1824–1893), engineer with the Dutch National Waterboard, charged with supervising part of the State Railway system in the Netherlands, working with English partners at the North Sea Canal connecting Amsterdam with the sea, designed the Tandjong Priok harbor and served later in Argentina for harbor works. He was one of the outstanding engineers of his time. Molhuysen and Blok, eds., *Nieuw Nederlandsch Biografisch Woordenboek*, III, 1378–82. For the quotation from the journal of Frans Lebret, see Leusink and Sybesma, eds., *Op Reis met Pen en Penseel*, 102.

5. Veering, "Nodes in the Maritime Network," 200–14. J. A. de Gelder was a Dutch hydraulic engineer who had made a name for himself in the Indies. When on leave in the Netherlands he was appointed engineer in charge of the Tandjong Priok harbor works and did an excellent job there. About him and the harbor works, see Berckel (van), "De Zeehaven voor Batavia te Tandjong Priok," 305–7. About the Krakatau eruption and the resulting tsunamis, see Winchester, *Krakatau*; the destruction of the Merak quarry on 247.

6. Jong (de), *De Waaier van het Fortuin*, 321–22, 341–43. About the KPM, see Campo, *Koninklijke Paketvaart Maatschappij*, passim.

7. Reitsma, *Gedenkboek der Staatsspoor- en Tramwegen*, 43.

8. Employment and length of network figures in ibid., 80, 113.

9. Ibid., 37, 44, 94–97.

10. Reitsma, *Korte geschiedenis*, 44–45, and Reitsma, *Gedenkboek der Staatsspoor- en Tramwegen*, 42–44. Johannes Groll (1814–1885), Dutch naval officer and specialist in the electromagnetic telegraph. Under his leadership the first telegraph line Batavia-Soerabaja was opened in 1856 and later more lines on Java and also the undersea cable to Singapore in 1857. After his discharge from the navy he was one of the founders of the NIS railway company Semarang-Vorstenlanden. Molhuysen and Blok, eds., *Nieuw Nederlandsch Biografisch Woordenboek*, VIII, 636. François Gerard van Bloemen Waanders (1825–1892), civil servant in the Indies and specialized in tropical agriculture. Minister for the colonies from April to November 1883; stepped down when his budget was voted down in the Second Chamber. Ibid., IV, 166. Levinus Wilhelmus Christiaan Keuchenius (1822–1893), born in Batavia, studied law at Leyden University and was an active lawyer in the Indies, member of the Council of the Indies, and minister for the colonies 1888–1890; in that capacity he introduced several laws for the improvement of the indigenous population. Ibid., I, 1246–49.

MILITARY RAILS ON SUMATRA

Until now the Buitengewesten, or Outer Possessions, have not played a very conspicuous role in this story. Dutch rule was largely confined to Java, the most populous and economically best developed of the thousands of islands of the Indonesian archipelago. Development of Sumatra, however, was expected to be highly rewarding, and early Dutch governors-general like Van den Bosch had high hopes of the boundless riches of that enormous but largely empty and uncharted island.

It was the sultanate of Atjeh that would prove to be the most troublesome region of Sumatra. Populated by a fierce and warlike Muslim people, Atjeh had never been subjugated by other powers. With the London treaty of 1824, Britain had promised to withdraw all its interests from Sumatra; in return the Netherlands consented to leaving the Atjeh sultanate as an independent power.[1] The Atjehers were not only fierce warriors but also active pirates at sea. They drove a great slave trade despite all prohibition measures from both Britain and Batavia. Nations whose ships had been ransomed lodged many complaints in Batavia; a treaty between Batavia and the sultan of 1857, whereby the latter promised to end piracy and the slave trade, had come to naught. It turned out that the sultan was sultan in name only, with his power confined to just his capital, called Koeta Radja by the Dutch. He was not even a hereditary prince at all but elected by the chiefs of the several inland districts. He could well promise to end piracy, but he had no power in the outlying coastal regions, so piracy continued unabated. Both London and The Hague understood that a new convention about Atjeh was necessary, and in 1871 a new Sumatra treaty was signed: Batavia now got a free hand in Atjeh, and in return all British nationals in Sumatra were guaranteed the same rights as Dutchmen. In addition, the Dutch government finally withdrew from the African Gold Coast and transferred its possessions such as the renowned former slave station St. George d'Elmina and other fortresses, which were losing money after the end of the slave trade anyhow, to Britain. The Dutch government must have found this a positive exchange, as the English were soon in trouble with an aggressive king of the Ashantis, the major tribe of the area, who laid siege to Elmina. A full-scale war was soon fought there with great losses on both sides.[2]

However, all was not well with this exchange. Soon after the signing of this new treaty, Batavia got news that some Atjeh chiefs had contacted Italian and American diplomats in Singapore about a possible treaty. Without orders from Washington, the American consul had indeed signed a preliminary contract with them. This meddling by foreign powers in Dutch territory could, of course, not be tolerated by the Batavian government, and satisfaction was demanded from the sultan. When this was not forthcoming, Batavia declared war in 1873. A first expedition against Koeta Radja miscarried completely, but a second one at the end of the same year managed to take the kraton, the fortified palace of the sultan, who had fled inland. This kraton now became the center of Dutch presence in Atjeh. An endless guerilla war broke out and only in 1879 was some form of Dutch rule established, but largely restricted to the northernmost part of the sultanate. All subversive elements, fanatical Muslims, had disappeared into the unknown hinterland and continued the guerilla war from there. Batavia foolishly thought that a—cheaper—civil government for Atjeh was now possible and the military were withdrawn into a fortified concentrated line around Koeta Radja.[3]

THE FIRST ATJEH RAILWAY

After the establishment of this permanent Dutch fortification in Koeta Radja with a sizable garrison, the problem of provisioning surfaced. The nearby roadstead of Olehleh was unsuitable for larger ships, and everything had to be transferred from ships out at sea by means of small craft to the coast; from there horse-drawn wagons were used on a primitive tramway with a gauge of 3 ft. To improve this complicated and time-consuming transportation, an iron pier was constructed at Olehleh together with a short steam railway into the kraton. This line was some 5 km long and was built to the Indian standard gauge of 1,067 mm (3 ft 6 in). Track materials and rolling stock from Java could now be used, and by the end of 1876 the line was ready for traffic. Two small 0-6-0 saddle tank engines with outside cylinders, open cabs with a roof only, were acquired from Fox Walker & Co. A third still-smaller 0-4-0 tank came two years later from Hohenzollern, but nothing more is known about that one.

To protect the concentrated line, a terrain of about 60 square km around the kraton of Koeta Radja was cleared and stripped of vegetation to give a clear field of fire. The existing railway was extended just inside

the outer border of this terrain with rail access to the several *bentengs*, or fortified outposts. As this was to be a railway only for internal and chiefly military use, it was decided—for financial reasons—to change the gauge to 750 mm (2 ft 5.5 in). The Atjeh war was already a continuous drain on the Dutch government's budget, with millions thrown into a bottomless pit every year, and economy was now sorely needed, hence the choice of the narrower and supposedly cheaper gauge. During the discussions about the most suitable gauge for Java, as noted, the 750-mm gauge had been repeatedly proposed, but fortunately the 1,067-mm gauge had then been chosen. The narrow gauge would have posed too many restrictions for railways on Java, but in Atjeh the capacity of a 750-mm line was considered to be large enough for the intended use.

Despite these safety measures, again and again Atjeh fanatics managed to crawl into this fortified line, damaging the buildings and killing or wounding the soldiers of the Netherlands Indies Army (NIL) and then withdrawing to their hiding places in the jungle. The Dutch garrison was

A view of the first 1,067-millimeter railway entering the kraton of Kota Radja in 1877. A primitive hand-operated switch with a makeshift cabin for the switchman to protect him from sun and rain. (KITLV collection)

A typical Dutch way of patrolling the Atjeh countryside by means of rail bicycles. A reconnaissance patrol of the Netherlands Indies Army on a string of pedal-operated rail vehicles, led by Dutch Marechaussee Lieutenant W. Droogleever, with a few European NCO's and Ambonese fusiliers. Photo from around 1905. (NSM collection)

like a monkey chained to a pole with naughty boys teasing him without fear, as the monkey couldn't reach them. Weak governors couldn't do anything about this hopeless situation, and the Batavian government did not actively support any drastic measures, as they were considered to be too expensive. Working on the tramway was considered dangerous for civilians, so the line was handed over to the military authorities. This stalemate ended only in 1896 with a more active governor-general in Batavia, C. H. A. van der Wijck, and a new regional commander, J. B. van Heutsz, in Koeta Radja. They were advised by the noted orientalist Dr. C. Snouck Hurgronje, who had lived in Mecca for a time, had studied Islam in all its variations, and knew the real power bases in Atjeh. He even spoke the regional languages! Van Heutsz now organized flying columns of *marechaussee*, led by a few European officers and subalterns and consisting of Ambonese and Menadonese—Christian—soldiers, lightly armed with modern repeating carbines and *klewangs*, the deadly Javanese scimitar. They followed the insurgents deep into the jungle of the interior, living off the land and giving no quarter. A dirty guerilla war ensued, with thousands of victims on both sides as the Atjeh fanatics, women and children included, never surrendered but fought to the very end. Slowly, Dutch rule could be extended inland and a semblance of peace restored. The Russo-Japanese war of 1905 saw an upsurge in the resistance, as some leading insurgents tried to interest Japan in assisting the movement, but

An inspection train in the station of Koeta Radja around 1916 with two dignitaries, one European and the other Indonesian, on the rear platform. The station master in white uniform and the train and locomotive personnel are standing at attention. This station, replacing an earlier structure, was built between 1912 and 1917. (Author's collection)

to no avail, and the Dutch authorities easily suppressed this flare up. In 1912 the last guerilla leader was killed in action, and from then on civilian government was introduced again with the intention to develop the country and bolster the regional economy.[4]

On the recommendation of Snouck Hurgronje, the so-called Korte Verklaring (Brief Declaration) was introduced in 1898, to be signed by all sultans, princes, and regional chiefs as proof of their submission to the Dutch government. Around 1910 Dutch rule had been extended into the farthest corners of the Indonesian archipelago, even on the most outlying islands, with the sole exception of the Dutch half of New Guinea, where large areas were still uncharted and virtually unknown.[5]

CONSTRUCTION OF THE ATJEH TRAM

With Dutch authority being pushed inland, the Atjeh Tram could be extended to help in the pacification and the possible development of the country. From Sigli, the garrison town farthest—99 km—from Koeta Radja, the line was built southward to meet construction teams that had begun in Lho Seumaweh, 251 km from Koeta Radja on the coast of Malacca Strait. Idi was reached in 1904 and Besitang at last in 1916. There the Deli Spoorweg Maatschappij (DSM, Deli Railway Company) was met, and a three-rail section to the port of Pangkalan Soesoe was laid in

the next year. The Deli Company used the Indian standard gauge, hence the need for a three-rail section. Freight had to be transferred from one wagon to another, and passengers had to change trains in Besitang. With this extension the Atjeh Tram was one of the longest railways in the world on the 750-mm gauge, 511 km altogether. In parts it was a difficult line to operate, with severe curvature and a maximum gradient of 35‰, many bridges over rivers with unknown hydraulic behavior, simply because no white man had ever been there. Military protection was needed for a long time, and insurgents repeatedly attacked trains and tried to derail them.[6]

Speeds were low and the four-wheel carriages small but well appointed, although seemingly a bit toylike. But it worked and travelers were happy to use it, just as the native population did on market days. A well-heeled Dutch traveler Ernst Sillem left a vivid description how it was to travel in 1889 from Olehleh to the kraton of Koeta Radja, when the concentrated line around the kraton still existed and Dutch presence was confined to that area: "At 9.30 I went by train to Koeta Radja. The railway runs through forest and swamps and past a few friendly kampongs. Through a massive gate we entered the outer limits of Koeta Radja. Outside it is definitely unsafe and even inside the fortifications bullets of Atjeh insurgents fly about at night. The hospital is well equipped and the wards for sufferers from beriberi are well appointed. A railway line connects it with the outlying forts and another line runs to the cemetery to bury the dead." There were indeed many deaths, chiefly from tropical diseases, and the cemetery was sorely needed. It is still there and well maintained.[7]

Later travelers praised the long trek by train from Besitang, where the Deli Spoor ended and the Atjeh Tram began, all the way to Koeta Radja, as a great improvement over the long journey by sea. In 1928 a young Dutch civil servant made the journey and left this vivid description: "From there [Besitang] I traveled the 600 km in the pleasant old fashioned narrow gauge Atjeh Tram in two full days with a night spent in Hotel Nass in Lhoseumawe. . . . I had to protect my new white uniform from the flying sparks and charcoal pieces that were ejected by the locomotive."[8]

The Atjeh Tram, rechristened Atjeh Staats Spoorweg (ASS, Atjeh State Railway) after its transfer in 1916 from the military to the civilian authorities, was in the first place a military line, and economic considerations came to play a larger role only later. It did indeed have a modest part in the development of the region but never became a moneymaker.[9]

BUILDING THE LINE

After the conversion of the existing line to Olehleh to 750 mm, the railway was slowly extended; construction was simple in the extreme, with light flat-bottomed rail and djati ties. Stations were generally built of wood; only Koeta Radja had a more sophisticated building and also workshops for maintenance of the rolling stock. Later the station even sported an overall roof over the tracks and a real water tower. Bridges were numerous, at least fifty with spans of 30 m or more. Most early bridges were constructed with a number of short iron spans resting on cast-iron poles screwed into the soft ground until a stable layer of rock was met. Many bridges were also laid out for ordinary traffic at the same time with wooden planks between the rails for pedestrians and animals. The foundations of these early iron bridges were subject to being washed away when great destructive *bandjirs*—flash floods—swept away everything before them. Therefore later bridges were generally built as steel girder bridges resting on solid stone or brick piers, less liable to be destroyed by *bandjirs*. In the mountain section between Seuleimom and Padang Pidji, many spectacular bridges and viaducts were constructed, commonly with high trestle bridges. The steel supports of these were resting on heavy concrete blocks high enough to prevent elephants reaching the steelwork for rubbing their skin, destroying it in the process. A solid concrete block was more elephant resistant. The largest bridge on the level section was the one over the Tamiang River near Koeala Simpang, 170 m long and constructed as a cantilever bridge, with girder spans on both sides and—with earthen embankments—of a total length of 228 m, easily the longest bridge on Sumatra. It was designed by Dr. J. H. A Haarman, chief engineer in charge of the bridges of the Java State Railways, who would later—in 1921—become professor at the Technical Academy of Bandoeng.[10]

Werkspoor-Amsterdam outshopped this neat 0-6-0 tank with five sisters for the Atjeh Tram in 1901–1902. As wood burners they served well, but a great problem was the limited capacity for firewood, necessitating frequent stops for refueling. Works photo Werkspoor. (NSM collection)

For hauling the miniature four-wheeled carriages and freight wagons at low speeds, only small locomotives were thought necessary. Six 2-4-0 tanks were ordered from Hanomag of Hanover and they entered service in 1887 when the first stretches of 750-mm track were ready. They had side tanks, outside cylinders, and a curious long wheelbase with a Bissel pony truck. Their weight in service was only 10 tons and their maximum speed was 35 km per hour. Three more came from Hanomag in 1894, another one in 1897, and two more were constructed in the Koeta Radja workshops of the Atjeh Tram. Quite an achievement in view of the fairly primitive equipment available there, but no doubt wheels, axles, and probably the boilers also came from outside sources.

With these twelve engines the service could be maintained, but the gradual extension of the line necessitated more and more powerful locomotives. In 1898 Hanomag supplied the first two of a large series of six-coupled tank engines, again with outside cylinders and small driving wheels of only 875 mm. Their weight in service was 12.7 tons, with later ones weighing about 1 ton more. Hanomag supplied more of these little steamers and in 1901 the Dutch factory of Werkspoor-Amsterdam also stepped in and constructed six more, using the drawings and specifications from Hanomag. Five others followed two years later. Altogether there were forty of these versatile engines, but just as the earlier 2-4-0s

they had one big shortcoming: lack of bunker capacity and water tanks that were too small. All AT engines were wood burners, and firewood takes a lot of space, much more than coal for the same amount of work. The AT therefore constructed no less than forty-six four-wheeled tenders for extra water and wood, connected with rubber hoses to the engine for water. Wood was forwarded to the bunker by the fireman at one of the many stops. The engines' huge conical chimneys with spark arresters were clear proof of the wood-burning habit.

As Hanomag would become one of the bigger suppliers to the railways of the Dutch East Indies, some attention should be paid to its history. The factory began on a small scale as a machinery works in Linden near Hanover, founded in 1835 by Georg Egestorff. Production of steam locomotives started in 1846, and in 1868 the firm was converted into a limited company under the name of Hannoversche Maschinenbau-Aktien-Gesellschaft vormals Georg Egestorff in Linden vor Hannover, commonly known as Hanomag. At first production was mostly for German and Russian railways, but the firm soon branched out to other continents. The first locomotive for Java was a small tank engine for the 750-mm gauge for an industrial line in 1879. The factory supplied a total of 202 engines to the several railways in the Dutch East Indies until the production of locomotives was given up in 1931.[11]

The Werkspoor-Amsterdam factory, dating back to the 1830s, was to become one of the chief suppliers of steam locomotives to the railways of the Dutch East Indies. In the 1890s the firm was renamed Nederlandsche Fabriek van Werktuigen en Spoorwegmaterieel (Dutch Factory of Machinery and Railway Rolling Stock, for short Werkspoor), and in 1899 it entered the locomotive business with an order from the Netherlands South African Railway for heavy tank engines. Subsequently, the Dutch and East Indian railway companies ordered large numbers of locomotives from Werkspoor.[12]

For the short—34 km—but severe mountain section with gradients up to 35‰, two of the small tanks had to be used on every train, so something more powerful was sorely needed. In 1904 Esslingen supplied six 0-4-4-0 Mallet tanks with a weight of around 30 tons, very imposing machines for such a narrow gauge. To make room for a wide firebox, the frames of the rear, fixed part of the engine were outside, while the frames of the swiveling front bogie were inside, something commonly found on many of the Mallets for narrow gauges. The four cylinders were all outside. Here again the bunker capacity proved to be too small, so the AT rebuilt the engines with a Bissel rear truck supporting an extension of the cab and bunker, doubling the capacity for wood to 1 ton, converting them into 0-4-4-2 tanks.

So far the AT—by now known as ASS—mostly ran mixed trains at low speeds, but the wish of running passenger trains at higher speeds led to the ordering of two 4-6-0 engines with separate four-wheel tenders from Werkspoor in 1923. They were modern locomotives, equipped with Schmidt superheaters and piston valves and with a total weight for the engines of 19.7 tons, with an axle load for the middle coupled axle of 4.6 tons, rather high for the weak track structure, while the other axles were more lightly loaded. The tender had an even heavier axle load of 5.2 tons, with the result that the locomotives were destructive on the tracks, necessitating continuous repairs. However, more powerful engines were sorely needed and in 1930 six 2-8-0 engines with separate bogie tender arrived from another Dutch factory, Du Croo & Brauns of Weesp, followed by six more of the same dimensions constructed by Hanomag after D&B drawings. Care had been taken that the axle load was more evenly distributed and not higher than 3.7 tons for each of the coupled axles. As a result they ran much better than the two 4-6-0s and caused less damage to the track.[13]

Du Croo & Brauns was a small factory operating in Amsterdam since 1906, making rolling stock and rails for narrow-gauge operations, industrial and agricultural. In 1917 a subsidiary was founded in Weesp, east of Amsterdam, the Machinefabriek Du Croo & Brauns Ltd. for the construction of narrow-gauge locomotives. This company will feature largely later in this book in the chapter on plantation and works railways.[14]

Passenger coaches were no longer only four-wheeled when six-wheelers with Cleminson radial undercarriages were introduced for the more level and straight lines. Comfortable bogie coaches were also acquired, 12 m long and in three variants, mixed first and second class, mixed second and third, and pure third class, the latter having room for as many as forty-two passengers. These bogie coaches were first used on the mountain section only, but later on the rest of the line as well. Freight trucks were mostly four-wheeled with a maximum admissible load of 4 or 5 tons. The few bogie trucks had double that capacity.

SUMATRA'S WEST COAST AND THE OMBILIN COAL FIELDS

More or less against its wishes the Batavian government had become involved in a civil war with religious undertones in western Sumatra, the so-called Padri war of the early 1820s. Foreign Islamic traders had settled there among the local population and were tolerated by the indigenous princes. When well-to-do members of this trading class managed to partake in the annual pilgrimage to Mecca and returned with a strong wish to clean up the local version of Islam with its many older heathen elements, a civil war broke out and some of the princes requested support from the Batavian government. Colonel A. V. Michiels, a veteran of the Napoleonic wars and the Battle of Waterloo of 1815, was sent out with a strong force. He made Padang his headquarters and from there suppressed the Padri movement successfully; Dutch rule was established there and Fort de Kock in the Padang Highlands became the center of Dutch military presence.[15]

In the Padang Highlands along the Ombilin River, good-quality coal had been found in great quantities. And as coal until now had to be imported from far away, engineers and government officials started to think of a way to get this Ombilin coal to the coast for further transport to Java. In a royal decree of 1873, money was made available for a survey of a railway line. Chief of the expedition was J. L. Cluysenaer, and his first report was published in 1875. Other reports followed but the cost of a railway seemed exorbitant in view of the limited funds available. However, in a third report of 1878, Cluysenaer proposed a longer but much cheaper route for the coal trains through the gorge of the Anei River, where rack rail would have to be employed to negotiate the severe gradients. For this line Cluysenaer advocated the use of the system of rack railways as invented and propagated by the Swiss engineer Niklaus Riggenbach, a system that was already in service on a score of short lines in Switzerland and Austria. His system resembled the rack rail used by Sylvester Marsh on the Mount Washington Railway in New Hampshire, opened in 1869. A rack made of two angle irons with pins riveted in between was placed in the center of the track and fixed to the sleepers. A cog wheel on the locomotive engaged in the rack rail drove the engine and train up and braked the train when going down. Most of these early lines were pure rack railways, but on some newer lines in Europe the system was only used on the steepest gradients, while the locomotive operated as a normal adhesion engine on the more level parts of the line. The Ombilin line was to follow this system of mixed rack and adhesion traction. Harbor facilities for this coal line were to be constructed on the Brandywine Bay, south of Padang. Total cost was estimated at ƒ19,400,000, much less than the sum mentioned in Cluysenaer's earlier survey.[16]

ACTION AT LONG LAST

Despite Cluysenaer's positive report, nothing much happened for a time. There simply was no money in the till in Batavia for this kind of action by the government. On the other hand requests from private parties for a concession for the railway and the coalfields were refused straightaway. Apparently the government, although not yet in the position to undertake construction itself, did not want to see the possibly lucrative coalfields fall into the hands of enterprising businessmen, maybe even foreigners. However, as nothing happened through this lack of money, in 1886 a proposal was drawn up by then-minister for the colonies Sprenger van Eyk to open the working of the coalfields to the private interest. In Parliament in The Hague this bill met with such strong opposition that it was withdrawn and the already-announced public tender was never officially put out. Stalemate again and more delays? Thereupon the minister in March 1887 proposed a bill for the construction by the state of a railway of 155 km in length, including the difficult section through the Anei Gorge after Cluysenaer's latest plans, with mixed adhesion and rack propulsion. Gradients of up to 80‰ were to be overcome by means of the rack system, and total length of the several rack sections was estimated at 11 km. The Indian standard gauge of 1,067 mm was chosen. This was to be one of the longest rack railways in the world, quite a rare phenomenon in those days, as most rack railways were only short tourist lines up mountains. Harbor facilities in the Brandywine Bay, soon to be renamed Queen's Bay with the actual port named Emmahaven after Queen Consort Emma, were also part of the proposition.[17]

The bill passed in Parliament without any opposition in July 1887, and J. W. IJzerman was appointed chief of construction. He was a good choice, as he had already participated in the initial survey under Cluysenaer back in the 1870s, so he knew what he was up against: difficult mountain line with severe gradients and heavy curvature through partly uncharted country, intended for heavy traffic of coal trains. The coal was sorely needed in the whole archipelago, both as bunker coal for the growing number of steamships and for the locomotives of the developing railway network. Before IJzerman set out for the Indies he managed

From Padang and Emmahaven, the Staatsspoorweg ter Sumatra's Westkust (SSS) climbed the mountains to reach the Ombilin coal fields. Fort de Kock, the center of Dutch military and civilian power, was reached by a branch in 1891. Photo from 1890/1891. (NSM collection)

to establish for himself an almost inviolable position directly under the governor-general in Batavia, without interference from the authorities of the Burgerlijke Openbare Werken (BOW). And this at the same time that the position of the chief of the Java State Railways was made subordinate to the chief of BOW. IJzerman happened to have the ear of the minister in The Hague and he used it skillfully to his advantage![18]

IJzerman brought a lot of experience with railway construction on Java. He contracted a number of Dutch engineers, some already working on the railways in Java, but also a very limited number of foreign experts, among them the Swiss engineer A. E. Wyss, well versed in the intricacies of the Riggenbach rack system. Construction was split in five sections, some pure adhesion, others with mixed adhesion and rack propulsion. The rail used was the same as laid on Java with a weight of 26 kg per meter, and steel ties with the cast-iron rack rail supports bolted to the ties. On the first of January 1894, the last section to the coalfields, including a tunnel of just under a kilometer in length, was opened and coal traffic could begin. Fort de Kock, the center of Dutch presence in the Padang Highlands, had been reached by a short branch from the mainline; from there an extension to Pajakombo was opened in 1896. The line was single track throughout with passing places at the stations. The section through the gorge of the Anei River was the most troublesome part of the line, with two tunnels and eight steel bridges over the river. *Bandjirs* repeatedly did a lot of damage, closing the line for months on one occasion in

A view of one of the rack sections of the SSS along the Anei River. The heavy rack rail is securely bolted to the steel ties. The work crew with the mandoer (supervisor, in white) is waiting for the photographer to finish his work. Undated photo. (Author's collection)

1892. The railway was internationally praised as a great work of modern technology and was positively described in the international engineering press. It was seen as a wonder of technology, designed and constructed by Dutch engineers who had no expertise in rack railways but who managed to complete the line successfully in a fairly short time. A late praise for this wonder work is the inclusion of the complex of mines and railway in the World Heritage list by Unesco in July 2019. This constitutes a lasting monument for Cluysenaer and IJzerman and their collaborators, and also for the Indonesian staff who operated the mines and railway after the departure of the Dutch until 1998.[19]

On the shores of Brandywine Bay, with the port named Emmahaven, an ultramodern coaling station was laid out, with several quays for the loading of ships by means of a mechanical transporter and an enormous covered storage facility for coal, all protected from storms by a stone breakwater of more than 700 m long. Coal trains were made up of four-wheeled iron hopper wagons that were mechanically unloaded at Emmahaven by means of a modern electric crane. Power came from a power station constructed near the coalfields, its boilers fed with coal waste and smalls. A second power station was opened in 1917 near Padang, all up to date, so IJzerman and his staff could be proud of their achievements. A Dutch traveler who visited Padang in 1889 was full of praise for the quality of the Ombilin coal and expected that it would be easy to compete with the coal available in Singapore as this had to be brought all the way from Wales: "The first coal bed is 8 meters thick and it may well take a hundred years before it is worked out." He was to be proven right![20]

Because the chosen line was roundabout and therefore rather costly to work, ideas for other, possibly shorter lines surfaced again and again. One of these was the idea of building a much more direct line across the Soebang Pass. Cluysenaer in his first report of 1875 had advocated that route, only 96 km long, but later exploration had shown that a line over the pass, 1,041 m in height, if possible at all, would be horribly expensive to build and difficult to operate. An extension of the existing line to Sumatra's east coast with a coal harbor on Malacca Strait was also considered, and IJzerman, to prove that such a line would indeed be possible, did undertake an exploration. In 1891 he set out from Padang with a large party, and after many months of hardship suffered while wandering through the uncharted tropical jungle of the interior of Sumatra he arrived at Siak Sri Indrapoera on a navigable river emptying in Malacca Strait. His conclusion was that a railway would be possible but enormously expensive. His report was shelved and nothing came of it. During World War II, however, the Japanese army ordered such a line to be constructed by Allied prisoners of war and Indonesian forced labor. A line was indeed laid out at the expense of thousands of deaths among the workforce. It was finished to Pakan Baroe on the day of the surrender of all Japanese forces in Asia on August 15, 1945. It was never used, but rusting hulks of steam locomotives are still found in the Sumatra jungle.

In retrospect the construction and operation of the coalfields and the connecting railway was a profitable venture for the government. Despite the high cost of the mountain line through difficult terrain and the extra cost connected with the rack rail operation, the good-quality coal was sold profitably. It materially helped in the success of the Sabang international coaling station on the island Poeloe Weh at the northernmost point of Sumatra on the entrance of Malacca Strait. It also contributed to the ending of importation of coal from Australia and Japan in the 1920s. From then on the Dutch East Indies were self-supporting in this respect.[21]

LOCOMOTIVES AND ROLLING STOCK

For the adhesion sections, the first engines to arrive in 1888 and 1889 from Esslingen were six small 2-4-0 tanks, numbered 1–6 by the

Staats Spoorwegen Sumatra Westkust (SSS, State Railways Sumatra West Coast). They were followed by two more of the same type ten years later, officially also from Esslingen but actually constructed by a subsidiary, the Costruzioni Meccaniche Saronno, founded in 1887 in the vicinity of Milan, with works numbers 31 and 32, SSS Nos. 7 and 8. To keep the Italian daughter busy during slack times, Esslingen sometimes transferred orders to Saronno. Transport of these first products from Saronno was troublesome, as they had to be carried by rail on a low loader all the way to Antwerp or Rotterdam and be shipped from there, an expensive and cumbersome way. Later engines were shipped directly from Italian ports after the facilities there had been upgraded sufficiently with strong cranes and equipment to handle heavy items such as locomotives. Apart from these small tanks, between 1892 and 1904 Esslingen also supplied no less than twenty-four larger engines of the 2-6-0 configuration in several batches. Inside frames, outside cylinders, large side tanks, and a roomy cab characterized these units. With a total weight of 37 tons, they were simple and sturdy and had long lives. All engines were equipped with the automatic air brake, essential when descending the gradients.[22]

The first rack locomotives were of the outside-framed 0-4-2 tank type, with two cylinders driving both adhesion wheels and the toothed rack wheel inside the frames by means of an intermediate axle. Total weight was 28 tons and maximum speed on adhesion stretches was only 15 km per hour, even lower on the rack sections. Between 1888 and 1902 Esslingen supplied no less than twenty-two of these small engines. As the maximum speed of these engines on the long adhesion sections was considered too low for light passenger trains, a single 0-4-0 rack locomotive was acquired from Esslingen, a small tank with direct drive, enabling the little 20-ton machine to reach a speed of 25 km per hour on the adhesion sections. Two more 0-4-0s, somewhat heavier with 23 tons, followed in 1893, later supplemented by three more in 1898, one in 1901, and a final one in 1905. They were also used on ordinary freight trains and had sufficient power and speed for this work.

With these relatively small engines the coal traffic plus other trains were handled. Coal trains predominated, and to enlarge the capacity of the single-track line it became normal practice to couple two down coal trains together on the rack sections, with one engine up front and the other in the middle. With these simple measures the annual total capacity of the line could be doubled to 400,000 tons. In 1906 the SSS had no less than 180 iron coal trucks of 20-ton capacity, sixty smaller of 10 tons, 344 other freight wagons, sixty-four passenger coaches, and four guard's vans. Bogie coal trucks of 24-ton capacity were introduced in the late 1920s.

In view of the growing traffic it would not be long before heavier and more powerful locomotives were needed, but the coming World War

made this problematic. For the adhesion sections, the 2-6-0 tanks were getting too slow; as a stopgap three of the gigantic 2-12-2 Javanic tanks of the Java State Railways were transferred to Sumatra, while two more were ordered from Hanomag and delivered straight to Padang in 1920. For light trains three 2-6-2 tanks of another Java type were taken into service in 1930. More about these engines in chapter 10.

For the rack sections the SSS turned to Esslingen again, now for two 0-8-2 tank engines with a drive as developed by the Schweizerische Lokomotiv Fabrik (SLM) of Winterthur. They were compound engines, with the high-pressure cylinders driving the adhesion section and the low-pressure unit the cog wheel. On adhesion sections the low-pressure unit could be disengaged, with the high-pressure unit exhausting straight into the atmosphere instead of feeding the low-pressure cylinders. Total weight was 50 tons and maximum speed was 50 km per hour. In service in 1913, just before the war, they developed 20 percent more power than the old 0-4-2 machines but still not quite enough. The SSS then went over to the 0-10-0 tank engine, again compounds of the Winterthur system, and these at long last fulfilled all wishes. With their 52-ton weight in working order—with later examples even scaling at 55 tons—they were easily the heaviest rack locomotives on Sumatra's west coast. Because of the war

A loaded coal train on one of the bridges in the gorge of the Anei River descending behind one of the 0-4-2 rack engines. This section of the line was prone to bandjirs, sweeping away bridges and tracks, necessitating extensive repairs. (Author's collection)

A down coal train of 180 tons underway on the Ombilin coal railway. The train is hauled—braked—by one of the 0-8-2 rack engines out-shopped by Esslingen and SLM-Winterthur in 1913 of the series SSS 101–103. Photograph from the early 1920s. (Author's collection)

they arrived in Emmahaven later than planned; the first ones entered service in 1921, with the others following in 1928. Construction was shared between Esslingen and SLM.

After a high point in 1930 when almost 650,000 tons of coal were delivered to Emmahaven, coal production slowly declined. Steamships were gradually being replaced by vessels with diesel engines, and other state mines on Sumatra competed with the Ombilin fields. Yet, until the Japanese attack, the mines remained working and continued to do so even after Indonesian independence. Esslingen supplied ten more of the 0-10-0 tanks between 1963 and 1965, with the last one, works number 5316, being the last steam locomotive built by Esslingen—and the last steam locomotive built in western Europe.[23]

The locomotive factory of Esslingen was the result of an initiative of Emil Kessler, one of the pioneers of the development of the steam locomotive in Germany. He founded the Maschinenfabrik Emil Kessler in Karlsruhe in the Grand Duchy of Baden in 1842 and followed six years later with the Maschinenfabrik Esslingen in the Württemberg town of that name. Esslingen was and is also spelled Eßlingen. Niklaus Riggenbach was for a time connected with the Karlsruhe factory, and that may explain the expertise that Esslingen built up in the construction of rack locomotives.[24]

The Schweizerische Lokomotiv- und Maschinenfabrik was founded in 1873 in the Swiss town of Winterthur. After difficult early years, it became the chief supplier of locomotives to the several Swiss railway companies and also built up a sizable export business. It had a niche business in locomotives for the rack railways worldwide. Later it also supplied some large express engines and Mallets to the Java State Railways.[25]

1. See Reid, *Contest for North Sumatra*, for the complicated relations between Britain, Batavia/The Hague, and Atjeh.

2. See Farwell, *Queen Victoria's Little Wars*, 190–99, about this Ashanti War of 1873–1874.

3. For dates and such, Stapel, *Geschiedenis*, 306–15 is still invaluable. Also Veer (van 't), *De Atjeh-oorlog*, and Goor (van), *De Nederlandse Koloniën*, 260–62.

4. About Christiaan Snouck Hurgronje (1857–1936), see Charité, ed., *Biografisch Woordenboek van Nederland*, 2, 523–26. He was internationally famous as Arabist and expert in the many versions of Islam, lived in Mecca for some time, and advised the governments in The Hague and Batavia about the best ways to handle the Atjeh problem. Also Dröge, *Pelgrim*, for his views about Atjeh. About Joannes Bernardus van Heutsz (1851–1924), see Charité, ed., *Biografisch Woordenboek van Nederland*, 1, 238–40. He was an officer in the Nederlandsch-Indisch Leger (Netherlands Indies Army), and being stationed in Atjeh several times, he developed a theory of how the Atjeh war could be ended sooner. He became acquainted with Snouck Hurgronje and together they developed the system that became the official policy after Van Heutsz was appointed governor of Atjeh in 1898. He left Atjeh for Holland in 1904 and was appointed governor-general of the Netherlands East Indies in the same year. He retired in 1909.

5. Lindblad, "De Opkomst van de Buitengewesten," 5.

6. Ballegoijen (van) de Jong, *Stations en spoorbruggen op Sumatra*, 29–46.

7. Sillem, *De reis om de wereld van Ernst Sillem*, 182.

8. Velde (van), "Uit het leven," 256–86, the quotation on 258.

9. Reitsma, *Korte geschiedenis*, 88–93.

10. Based on Ballegoijen (van) de Jong, *Stations en Spoorbruggen op Sumatra*, 29–98.

11. Spielhoff, *Hanomag Lokomotiven*.

12. About the Werkspoor factory, see Jong (de), *De Locomotieven van Werkspoor*; the two 4-6-0s on 172.

13. The locomotives of the Atjeh Tram in Oegema, *De stoomtractie*, 164–68.

14. Bruin (de), *Du Croo & Brauns Locomotieven*.

15. Jong (de), *De Waaier van het Fortuin*, 231–35. Stapel, *Geschiedenis*, 293–94.

16. Jacobus Leonardus Cluysenaer (1843–1932), engineer from the Delft Polytechnic and in the 1860s employed on the construction of the state railway network in the Netherlands. After his return from Sumatra, he was professor at the Military Academy of Breda and in 1878 chief of the permanent way department of the State Railways in his home country. In 1886 director of the Netherlands South African Railway in Transvaal and in 1888 back to the Netherlands as director-general of the State Railways until 1900. Charité, ed., *Biografisch Woordenboek van Nederland*, 2, 94–95. His reports about the Ombilin coal line in his *Het Hellend Vlak van Agudio en de Stangenbanen*. Niklaus Riggenbach (1817–1899), born in Alsace, France, moved to Olten, Switzerland, where he became master mechanic of the Swiss Central Railway. He built the first rack railway with his system of rack rail in 1871, the Vitznau-Rigi Bahn in Switzerland. Riggenbach, widely seen as the inventor of the rack railway, knew about the earlier rack system as used by Sylvester Marsh in the United States and was clearly inspired by him. His system was soon superseded by other rack systems and he was no successful salesman. In 1880, though, he

undertook to travel to British India to supervise the introduction of his system on the Nilgiri Railway. It is not known if Riggenbach ever visited the Dutch East Indies in view of promoting his patented rack system. Elsasser, *Gnom*, 14–20.

17. Jacobus Petrus Sprenger van Eyk (†1907), financial expert, member of the Council of the Indies and minister for the colonies 1884–1888; minister of finance 1894–1897 and director-general of the (Dutch) State Railway Company 1900–1907. Molhuysen and Blok, eds., *Nieuw Nederlandsch Biografisch Woordenboek*, V, 792. About the history and construction of the coal line, see Reitsma, *De Staatsspoorweg ter Sumatra's Westkust*.

18. Ibid., 28.

19. Jan Willem IJzerman (1851–1932), educated at the Military Academy Breda; in 1874 participated as young lieutenant of the Corps of Engineers in the first survey of a railway on Sumatra's west coast. Section engineer of the Java State Railways under Maarschalk and responsible for the construction of several state lines. On leave in the Netherlands he was appointed chief of construction of the Sumatra coal railway in 1887 and finished this project in 1894. Charité, ed., *Biografisch Woordenboek van Nederland*, 2, 637–38.

20. Sillem, *De reis om de wereld van Ernst Sillem*, 159.

21. Reitsma, *De Staatsspoorweg ter Sumatra's Westkust*.

22. Messerschmidt, *Lokomotiven der Maschinenfabrik Esslingen*, 12–13. Oegema, *De stoomtractie*, 150.

23. Oegema, *De stoomtractie*, 155–60. Works list of all steam locomotives constructed by Esslingen in Messerschmidt, *Lokomotiven der Maschinenfabrik Esslingen*, 186–275.

24. About Esslingen, see Hentschel, *Wirtschaftsgeschichte der Maschinenfabrik Esslingen*, and Messerschmidt, *Lokomotiven der Maschinenfabrik Esslingen*. Also Mayer, *Lokomotiven, Wagen und Bergbahnen*, with a special section on rack locomotives with much attention for the Sumatra locomotives. The Esslingen works were later also involved in the construction of locomotives for the Java State Railways.

25. Moser, *Der Dampfbetrieb*, 11–12. Vogel, *Die Schweizerische Lokomotiv- und Maschinenfabrik*.

SUMATRA'S OTHER RAILWAYS 8

The Sultanate of Deli, on the east coast of Sumatra and a dependency of the more important Sultanate of Siak, was poor, sparsely populated, and almost without any Dutch presence well into the nineteenth century. Only in 1858 did the sultan of Siak acknowledge Dutch overlordship, and in 1865 the Gouvernement Sumatra's Oostkust was set up. The low-lying swampy soil of Deli was found to be very fertile, and so in 1863 a Dutch planter, J. Nienhuys, started the first tobacco plantation there. After some disappointments he was successful, as his tobacco proved to be of superior quality for cigar making and commanded high prices in Europe. He rented more land from the sultan and to get around the problem of the severe shortage of labor, he recruited Chinese workers from nearby Malaya. Nienhuys became rich and together with Amsterdam partners in 1869 he founded the Deli Maatschappij (Deli Company) to start more plantations. In a very short time the young company proved to be a real gold mine. From thirteen plantations owned in 1873, the number grew to sixty-seven in 1881 and to an amazing total of 104 five years later. Others followed, attracting new adventurers, Dutch and foreign, who became rich almost overnight and money flowed freely.[1]

So Deli became the Wild West of Sumatra, where riches were for the taking. Besides tobacco, palm oil also became a golden investment. All these plantations had to be laid out in the jungle and swamps, necessitating an enormous labor force that was simply not to be found locally. The solution was to contract masses of Chinese, first from Malaya, later also from China itself, Klingalese from British India, Thais from Siam, and Javanese from the overcrowded island of Java. The Batavian government reacted by appointing an assistant-resident, who, however, through lack of instructions, money, and personnel, commanded no real power. The result was a rather lawless society with the planters as lords of the realm who could dispose of the lives of the coolies under their command. It

The Deli Hotel in Laboean Deli as it was before 1880, then the center of European presence in the region. (KITLV collection)

took years and a lot of persuasion before the Batavian government had established its authority in Deli and had secured a measure of safety for the laborers, weeding out the most glaring abuses. Courts were opened and law was enforced, but it would be well into the 1930s before the labor situation finally reached a normal quality after the abolition of the hated "coolie ordinances," that had given the planters an almost-unlimited authority over their native workers.

The discovery of oil in 1883 by a tobacco planter in the Sultanate of Langkat, between Deli and Atjeh, caused an unexpected new boom. The usual rush of wildcatters, followed by more solid companies, resulted in a feverish prospecting for oil, reminding visitors of America again. The Koninklijke Maatschappij tot Exploitatie van Petroleumbronnen in Nederlands-Indië (Royal Company for the Exploitation of Petroleum Wells in the Dutch East Indies, generally known as Royal Dutch, after the fusion with Shell Transport & Trading Company in 1907, Royal Dutch Shell), incorporated in 1890, soon managed to establish some order in the region and obtained a near-monopoly in Sumatra oil. The first refinery of Royal Dutch was started in 1892 in Pangkalan Brandan, where the oil from the Langkat fields was distilled and refined into lamp oil, the most important product at the time. The 50 percent gasoline in the crude was used to heat the distilling vessels and retorts and any unused gasoline was burned in an old quarry nearby.[2]

Rubber was the third pillar under the boom on the east coast of Sumatra, especially after 1910. The worldwide demand for rubber, stimulated by the expanding automobile industry, was growing so fast that riches lay again for the picking. In this case it was not so much the large European or American plantation companies that profited from the boom but more the native planters and smaller local businessmen who laid out rubber plantations of moderate size, although the Deli Maatschappij also saw its profits climbing.

After the labor problem was somewhat eased by the importation of coolies from outside Sumatra, the lack of transportation remained as the other well-nigh insurmountable problem. Roads were nonexistent; only footpaths led through the jungle and swamps. The rivers were mostly unnavigable, too shallow, and full of sandbanks and other obstructions. The land was very low lying, with swamps and morasses that had to be drained to make it fit for plantations, so a railway was seen as the only solution to bring in materials, workers, and heavy equipment. A first concession for a short line was applied for by a certain de Guigne in 1881, but his request was refused, as he was not a Dutch national. Next came a new request for a line from J. T. Cremer, director of the Deli Maatschappij. His line, of course strongly supported by the Deli Maatschappij, was to run from Belawan Deli, the roadstead on Malacca Strait, to Medan, the chief town of the area, and from there south to Deli Toewa, altogether 66 km long, to be constructed in 700- or 750-mm gauge (2 ft 3 in or 2 ft 5.5 in). The Dutch government saw no reason to refuse his request, for Cremer was an important person in both the Netherlands and the East Indies; he would even be minister for the colonies from 1897 to 1901. The Deli Maatschappij was the law in Medan and in that company, Cremer was the boss.[3]

The concession was soon changed from a tramway into a real railway in the Indian standard gauge of 1,067 mm, a wise decision, and transferred to the Deli Spoorweg Maatschappij (DSM, Deli Railway Company), incorporated for the purpose in 1883, with Amsterdam as its headquarters and J. T. Cremer as one of the directors. Total share capital was set at ƒ2,600,000, raised in 1897 to ƒ4,000,000 and even higher still later, until in 1937 it was finally fixed at ƒ30,000,000, of which a total of ƒ18,750,000 was actually issued. Finding the first millions was no problem at all, as Deli was seen as a gold mine and investors, Dutch and foreign, came forward in numbers. The DSM now set to work and in 1886 the first line opened, with the rest of the tracks following in 1888. It ran from Belawan to Medan and from there to Timbang Langkat, also known as Bindjei, plus a branch from Medan to Deli Toewa. More lines followed soon, as the plantation owners were clamoring for transportation; in 1890 the DSM had already 103 km in exploitation. New extensions were again needed in 1900, when the line was lengthened southeastward in 1903 to Tebing Tinggi. Northwestward Pangkalan Brandan was reached in the next year and further branches were thrown out during World War I, when the price of oil and rubber was skyrocketing. The junction with the Atjeh Tram at Besitang was opened in 1919 with a three-rail track to the harbor at Pangakalan Soesoe for both ASS and DSM. From Tebing Tinggi southeast the line was continued in 1918 to Teloek Niboeng on the coast, with a line from Tebing Tinggi into

the mountainous interior at Pematang Siantar in 1916. Much later a line
from Kisaran to Rantau Prapat was also added. Altogether in 1937 the
DSM had 554 km of railway line in operation, of which 245 km were listed
as railway first class, the rest as tramway. The section Belawan–Medan was
even double tracked in 1916. Feeder lines with a narrower gauge, generally
600 or 700 mm, were laid in large numbers to give the plantations a direct
means of transportation to the nearest DSM station or halt.[4]

Belawan, situated on an island in the mouth of the Deli River, was
only a port in name, as the river mouth was shallow and constantly silting
up. Oceangoing ships had to anchor far out in the bay and shallow-draft
launches and lighters were employed for loading and unloading. The DSM
carried out extensive works to make the harbor more usable, and in 1913
the company sold the harbor installations and facilities to the Batavian
government for a sum of ƒ500,000. Two large steam dredgers were set to
work, and soon the largest ships of the time with a draft of up to 9.85 m
could enter the port and reach the newly constructed quays. Extensive
new freight sheds and warehouses were put up with the necessary rail
access. In 1928 the works were considered to be finished. Belawan Ocean
Port was the new name with Dutch mail steamers of the Nederland Line
and the Rotterdamsche Lloyd starting to use Belawan as regular port of
call. In 1921 the *Rembrandt* of the Nederland Line was the first liner calling
there, for which the DSM had a special train ready to take the passengers

to Medan in luxury and comfort. By that time Medan had become a modern city with spacious hard-surfaced roads, a number of international banks and offices of all kinds of European and American factories, automobile dealerships, modern hotels providing all amenities and comforts, all thanks to the Deli Maatschappij and the Deli Spoorweg Maatschappij.[5]

CONSTRUCTION OF THE LINE

Construction in the low-lying land, with many rivers and swamps to be crossed, was difficult. Chinese entrepreneurs, many from the Overwal, as the Malayan peninsula was known in Sumatra, were contracted to construct the line with hired Chinese laborers. The usual flatbottom rail as known from Java was used with wooden ties, everything as simple as possible to avoid unnecessary expenses. Reaching Belawan, the port lying on an island in the estuary of the Deli River, proved hard to do. An immense bridge 400 m long and consisting of twenty iron spans of 18 m each, resting on large cast-iron piles screwed into the mud until a hard layer of rock was reached, was finished here after much hard work by the contractor, the Harkort firm of Duisburg, Germany. The bridges constructed by Harkort were built from iron or steel members, not riveted but connected with large bolts and nuts. Riveters were not available in Deli but less skilled workers could screw a nut on a bolt under supervision of a European or Javanese foreman. Harkort constructed most of the bridges needed in the same way until about 1904, when Dutch firms took over. The Belawan bridge remained in service until 1932 when it was replaced by

Belawan was situated on an island, and to reach the mainland the railway had to cross the Deli River by means of an iron bridge on cast-iron piles, 386 meters long. Undated photograph but probably pre–World War I. (NSM collection)

Belawan Oceaanhaven, with the extensive yards of the Deli Spoorweg Maatschappij in the 1920s. A KPM steamer with the yellow funnel is waiting to take the group of well-dressed travelers aboard. (Author's collection)

two single-track bridges next to each other of 60 m each with solid stone causeways at each end. The metal parts came from a Dutch firm, Kloos of Kinderdijk. Other bridges on the later lines were sometimes of imposing dimensions, such as the one near Besitang, where the Atjeh Tram was met, made up of two girder spans of 50 m each. It was opened in 1924, although the railway itself was already crossing the river for four years by means of a temporary wooden bridge. The longest bridge on the whole DSM was on the line to Rantau Prapat, where a bridge over the Asahan River, opened in 1928, was constructed with a span of 75 m.

Apart from wood everything had to be imported, from Java if possible, but chiefly from Europe, always a nuisance causing much delay and expense. Only bricks were available locally after the only existing brick works in the region had been taken over by the Deli Maatschappij. The first simple stations were constructed from galvanized iron imported from England. Later it turned out that when outside temperatures at night were getting lower, condensation dripped from the iron roofs on the goods in the sheds and on the desks in the offices, spoiling everything. Iron was then slowly replaced by more conventional materials. Only Medan was thought worthy of a stone- and brick-built station of some allure. Signaling was simple in the extreme in the earlier period, but when traffic and layouts became more complicated, a true block system was developed with apparatus supplied by the Alkmaarsche IJzergieterij of Alkmaar in the home country, a factory that also supplied sophisticated signal systems to a number of Dutch railway companies.[6]

For the construction of the line two small 0-4-0 tanks were bought from the German factory of Hagans. These two were DSM Nrs. 1 and 2 and were sold again in 1893 and 1896. Hagans of Erfurt, Saxony, was one of the less important German manufacturers, since 1872 specializing in smaller engines and narrower gauges. Apart from these two, it would not supply any other engines to the Dutch East Indies. It is quite possible that these two were bought used, as they had been built back in 1883. A third Hagans engine, DSM Nr. 49, also a small 0-4-0 tank, was bought secondhand from a contractor in 1915. Earlier, in 1902 during the construction of the new lines, the DSM had already bought another 0-4-0 tank, also from a contractor and this time built by Krauss, a German-Austrian factory that specialized in small, mostly four-wheeled locomotives for industries, contractors, and steam tram companies.

The first locomotives ordered for train service were three 0-4-2 and two 0-6-0 tanks; apart from the wheel arrangement, these locomotives were similar engines with outside cylinders and weighing about 30 tons in service. They came from Hohenzollern in the years 1884–1886 and were used for passenger and freight services indiscriminately. These five engines had a fairly long wheelbase for accommodating the large fireboxes burning hardwood as fuel. Apparently, the 0-6-0s were preferred, as Hohenzollern supplied more of them until eleven units were in service in 1891.

The Hohenzollern Aktiengesellschaft für Lokomotivbau was incorporated in 1872 in Düsseldorf-Grafenberg, and after a difficult start became one of the leading German locomotive works. The railways of the Netherlands were good customers and so were the railways and tramways in the Dutch East Indies, including the Deli Spoorweg Maatschappij.[7]

By 1900 more locomotives were needed when the network grew and traffic with it. Hartmann, already well known with earlier deliveries to the Java State Railways, supplied two series of 0-6-4 tanks, the first four in 1900 and five more in 1902. They had outside cylinders, large side tanks, and enough room at the cab end for a large bunker for firewood. The main difference between the two series was the extended wheelbase of the last five, with the bogie placed farther back. Total weight of both series was around 30 tons and maximum speed was 45 km per hour.

In 1903 Hohenzollern supplied six engines of a new type, a 0-4-4 tank, a rare wheel arrangement in the Indies but one liked by the DSM. Total weight was only 30 tons but they were powerful enough for the traffic

A DSM passenger train hauled by a 0-4-2 tank of the series 6–16 at an unknown location. Originally these tanks were constructed as 0-6-0s, but after 1903 the last coupling rod was removed, making them into 0-4-2s. Undated photo. (SNR collection)

and were beautifully steady and quiet. As a result the last or first coupled wheels of all 0-6-0 and 0-6-4 engines were uncoupled by removing the last or first coupling rod, changing them into 0-4-2 and 2-4-4 engines, respectively. The experiment was successful, as they all had long lives in this mode. However, by 1913 traffic had grown again so much that heavier and more powerful locomotives were thought necessary. Hartmann obliged with eight new 2-6-4 tank engines, which were delivered in 1914. They were superheated, the first on the DSM, and weighed no less than 50 tons, with a maximum speed of 68 km per hour and with room for a big load of firewood and the necessary big firebox with a large grate. These new 2-6-4s were most successful and thirteen more followed with small differences in details, this time supplied by Werkspoor of Amsterdam, as Hartmann had problems with timely delivery because of the war and the resulting shortage of parts and materials. The first engines from Werkspoor arrived in 1915 and the last ones in 1920 and 1921. Naturally, the Amsterdam firm also had problems with obtaining the necessary steel and copper parts from Germany during the war years, hence the delay. For the mountain line to Pematang Siantar even more powerful engines were needed and Werkspoor supplied four big 2-8-4 tanks in 1917 for the freight trains on that section. They were a larger version of the earlier 2-6-4 tanks and weighed in at 52 tons, the heaviest of the DSM ever, and despite their relatively

small drivers of 1,000 mm, they had a good turn of speed, 68 km per hour being their official maximum. They were wood burners as all other DSM locomotives and the company acquired forests to grow the necessary firewood, somewhat strange in an area that abounded with oil. The DSM used the automatic vacuum brake for engines and bogie passenger stock, while all freight wagons had handbrakes only. Some of the engines were equipped with turbo generators for electric headlights and also for the lighting of the passenger carriages, quite advanced for the time. The last steam locomotives DSM ordered were ten very modern 2-4-2 tank engines for the passenger services on the main lines. They were supplied by Hanomag in 1928–1929 with an axle load of 10 tons, the maximum allowed by the tracks, and were quite successful on their intended services.[8]

To combat the growing competition of motorbuses, the DSM in 1931 bought a steam rail car from the Sentinel-Wagon Works of London, of a system that was already used with some success in England. It had an oil-fired high-pressure boiler that provided steam for six cylinders driving both axles of the front bogie. It worked quite well, but a drawback was that it was not powerful enough to haul a bogie trailer when traffic was heavy. It was taken off the main line and used with limited success on branch lines with a light four-wheeled trailer. To replace it the DSM acquired some *automotrices*, four-wheeled railcars with Renault internal combustion

motors burning gasoline or kerosene. One of them was equipped with a Swiss Saurer diesel motor, quite advanced for the times. The bodies and undercarriages came from Beijnes in Haarlem.

Freight traffic was always considerable, with tobacco, rubber, palm oil, tea, crude oil, and fibers the most important. Palm oil production continued to grow and reached an all-time high of 260,000 tons in 1941, most of it transported to Belawan by the DSM in tank cars. Of these tank cars the tanks themselves of 10-ton capacity were the property of the big companies such as Royal Dutch Shell, Goodyear, the Deli Maatschappij, or the Handels Vereeniging Amsterdam, while the undercarriages were owned and maintained by the DSM. At the end of the period described, altogether some 1,860 freight trucks were available, with 223 passenger carriages, mostly bogie coaches.

THE SOUTH SUMATRA STATE RAILWAYS

Around 1900 South Sumatra was a vast empty region, supposedly fertile but hardly populated and without any infrastructure—no roads, rails, or telephone lines. The many rivers were the only means of communication, with a small trade center on the banks here and there; farther inland there was nothing and no white man had ever set foot there. Yet there were businessmen who were interested in developing this wilderness and who applied for concessions. The Batavian government slowly became focused on the possibilities of the area. There were a number of highly speculative applications for concessions for rail lines, with or without support from the government, but in view of the sorry state of the government's finances, Minister for the Colonies Cremer did not want to get involved in a railway network there, so all applications were refused. Apparently, he did not think that better means of communication were really necessary, but it is also possible that his motives were more personal, as he may have dreaded a loss of his monopoly in Deli to newcomers in South Sumatra.

Others, however, toyed with the idea of stimulating the migration of people from the overcrowded island of Java to the empty spaces of South Sumatra, where land was plentiful. If Javanese farmers were willing to build up a living there, Batavia was ready to help them with financial incentives and suitable means of communication. In 1904 Governor-General W. Rooseboom initiated a new emigration project for Javanese, and in the next year the first emigrants moved to the other side of Soenda Strait and settled in the Lampong Districts, the southernmost region of Sumatra. By 1911 there were 4,800 Javanese who had made the change, and by 1928 a total 24,300 of them had come over. It turned out to be an expensive project, for emigrants got free passage and also substantial financial help to set up as farmers in the wilds. Emigrants who made the passage without

Facing top, One of the revolutionary *automotrices,* or railcars with a Renault gasoline engine, with its four-wheel trailer. The motor car had room for second-class passengers, while the trailer was only for third-class travelers. Cheaper to run than a full-size steam train, they proved successful for branches with light traffic. (Author's collection, from Pim Waldeck)

Facing bottom, For the Deli Maatschappij, the DSM constructed a 700-millimeter railway between Stabat and Binjei, opened in 1888. It connected several rubber and tobacco plantations and operated regular passenger traffic between the two villages until the late 1920s. Here a train with an 0-4-0 tank at the head is waiting for departure from Binjei in the early 1920s. Two chickens are scratching for food between the rails and a dog sleeps peacefully close by the European supervisor. (Gerard de Graaf collection)

Moeara Enim Station and yard of the Zuid Sumatra Staatsspoorweg (ZSS) on the line between Palembang and Lahat and the Boekit Asam coal mines. Everything simple and cheap but sufficient for the expected traffic. Photo from the early 1920s. (Author's collection)

government aid were few and finally the program was ended. It did not alleviate the problem of the gigantic overpopulation of Java at all, but it did contribute to the slow growth of South Sumatra.[9]

Meanwhile, an official government survey of possible rail routes had been carried out in 1903 and an extensive rail network was optimistically proposed, too extensive probably. Private parties did see possibilities, but only if government would be willing to help. Nothing came of it, as Batavia still hesitated between private and public funding of the railway, the old story. However, in 1908 a new survey of possible railway routes in South Sumatra was ordered by Batavia with engineer P. F. P. Richter being sent out into the jungle with a small party. His report, published in 1911, recommended the construction of a line from Telok Betoeng, opposite Java, to Prabamoelih and on to Palembang on the east coast. From Prabamoelih a branch to Moeara Enim was also proposed. Altogether these lines would be 463 km long at a cost of ƒ37,600,000, which would possibly generate an estimated net revenue of ƒ54.000, or about 0.25 percent of the capital needed for construction. Strong pressure from the Batavian government on then-minister for the colonies J. H. de Waal Malefijt resulted in a law of December 1911 ordering the construction of the lines as surveyed by Richter. Engineer J. van der Waerden, an able man with a lot of experience in railway construction on Java, was appointed chief of construction.[10]

Van der Waerden started construction in two places, at Oosthaven (Pandjang) in the Lampong Districts in the south and at the other end in Palembang. As usual in Sumatra the greatest challenge was finding the labor, as no local workers were available to be contracted, forcing Van der Waerden to open a recruitment center in Java to attract sufficient workers

and tradesmen. All materials and equipment came from Java, and the line was laid in the Indian standard gauge of 1,067 mm, making use of rolling stock and locomotives of the JSS. In 1914 the first sections were ready and three years later the line to Moeara Enim was opened also. Good-quality coal had been located not too far from Moeara Enim and therefore a connection with the Boekit Asam mines, owned and worked by the government, was laid in 1919. Further construction was slow because of lack of materials and the short economic slump of 1921–1922 made money tight, but Lahat was reached in 1924 with the extension to Loeboek Linggau ready for traffic in 1933. At long last, in February 1927, the link between the northern and southern lines was closed, with many festivities and official speeches. By 1933 a total of 643 km had been laid and was in exploitation. The early fairly negative prospects of the rentability of the lines, at the most 0.3 percent of the construction cost, had by then been belied. The growth of the traffic had been such that no less than 3.7 percent was the new figure.[11]

The network was called Zuid-Sumatra Staatsspoorwegen (ZSS, South Sumatra State Railways) and the working of the new lines was simple, because they were initially rated as a tramway with a maximum speed of only 30 km per hour. Signaling was elementary in the extreme and only light rolling stock could be used. Most lines were rather level and easy to work, but the extension to Loeboek Linggau was different, with some real heavy gradients, two tunnels and no less than thirty-four steel bridges. By 1937 a lot of improvement had taken place with heavier rails and more sidings. After the introduction of comfortable bogie coaches, the journey from Kertapati, on the Moesi River opposite Palembang,

The official train decked out with flags and bunting that carried dignitaries to the junction of the Lampong and Palembang networks of the South Sumatra State Railway on February 22, 1927. Two 4-4-0 engines of the 600 class of the Java State Railways are in charge. (Author's collection)

south to Oosthaven, a distance of 400 km, could be done in eight hours, even with a restaurant car for light refreshments. For passengers to and from Palembang the crossing of the Moesi River at Kertapati had to be completed by a ferry ride, as a railway bridge was considered too expensive at the time. From Oosthaven the KPM worked a daily packet service to Merak on Java and twice weekly to Tandjong Priok. In the 1930s the railway had been upgraded to a regular railway of the first class, with a maximum permitted speed of 75 km per hour.[12]

LOCOMOTIVES AND ROLLING STOCK

For locomotives the ZSS leaned heavily on the mother company on Java, and a description of the several classes can be found in the relevant chapters on the JSS; only a short note will suffice here. The first engines sent over from Java in 1913 were four of the 0-6-0 tanks formerly of the Solo Valley Works, followed by one more in the next year and two more of the same in 1920 and 1924. In 1914 the first of the large series of Sharp Stewart 2-4-0s with separate tender arrived in Oosthaven, and until 1923 no less than twenty-two units of this class were dispatched, some to Oosthaven for service on the Lampong lines, and others to Kertapati for service on the Palembang lines. By then Java had more modern 4-4-0 passenger engines available, so the old 2-4-0s were not really missed there. Of the ubiquitous 2-6-0 Hartmann tanks, both the simple and the compound varieties, a total of ten units arrived on the ZSS between 1917 and 1924.

For the mixed trains from Tanjoeng Enim, including heavy coal trucks, more powerful locomotives were needed, so in 1924 five of the 4-4-0 compound engines of the JSS were sent to Sumatra, together with four of the 2-8-0 Consolidations with separate tender. Straight from European factories came eleven more of these powerful freight units, in this case five from Hartmann and six from Hanomag, all delivered in 1925 and 1926. With the closing of the gap between the Palembang and Lampong sections in 1927 and the introduction of through express trains, fast and powerful engines were needed. For this service the ZSS acquired five Pacifics, the impressive 4-6-2 engines of the 700 class of the JSS, constructed in 1910 by SLM. These were the last secondhand engines, and from then on only newly built engines were supplied to the ZSS, but always of the same types already ordered for Java at the same time.

A new universal design had been worked out in the late 1920s jointly by the Java State Railways and Hohenzollern for a 2-6-2 tank, intended for all kinds of services. In 1929 and 1930 Hohenzollern and Borsig supplied twenty-one units to the JSS and Werkspoor and Hanomag added twenty-three of these modern and fast—75 km per hour—engines for the ZSS in the same years. They were equipped with superheaters, piston valves, and other modern fittings, while care had been taken not to exceed the maximum axle load of 10 tons. On the ZSS they were most successful, and they ran all trains apart from the expresses and the heavy coal trains that remained the domain of the 4-6-2s and 2-8-0s, respectively. All engines were coal fired with briquettes from the Boekit Asam mines. Initially, the locomotives were maintained in the works at Tanjoeng Karang, not far from Oosthaven, but after 1930 the newly built works at Lahat took over and Tanjoeng Karang was only used for minor repairs.

In the 1930s bogie carriages had largely supplanted the original four-wheelers for all passenger trains, and even for third-class passengers comfortable welded steel bogie carriages had been introduced, generally after the pattern for Java, but with minor detail differences. Coal traffic was important from the start and special coal trucks had been acquired to a number of 190 bogie units equipped with vacuum brakes with two steel buckets for 6 tons of coal each. At the mines the buckets were filled from above, and at Kertapati they were lifted from the wagon by a crane and when positioned over a ship's hold the sides were opened and the coal dumped. About 400,000 tons of coal were carried annually, but after 1940 the annual output of the Boekit Asam mines rose to 1.4 million tons, which meant 4,000 tons were carried off by train daily, an enormous accomplishment for a single-track railway with a maximum allowed axle load of only 10 tons. Other freight was pepper, rubber, coffee, and crude oil, and for the annual pepper harvest, wagons sometimes had to be borrowed from Java. After 1937, with the revival of the world economy, the pepper harvest was so great that twenty 10-ton wagons had to be brought over from Java for the season. After all, during these years, around 86 percent of the world's pepper came from the Dutch East Indies.[13]

A BRIEF EXCURSION TO CELEBES

Apart from Java plus Madoera and Sumatra, only one other island of the Indonesian archipelago ever had a public railway: Celebes. True, on Borneo there were several rail lines to carry coal from mines to the seaboard, but they did not have a public character and knew only a single kind of traffic. They will be described in chapter 14.

For several other islands, plans had been ventilated, some serious, some less so or highly speculative, and none had come to fruition. Lack of interest from private investors and hesitation on the part of the government were the chief reasons. For Borneo projects were made for a line in the south from Bandjermasin in the direction of Balikpapan, the oil capital of Borneo then still being developed, but it never got beyond the planning stage. The same is true for a line running north from Pontianak on the west coast of that island. In the far northeast of Celebes, lines were envisaged running south and east from Menado, the chief city of that region, but again expectations of traffic turned out to be overly optimistic, and with money getting tighter after the end of World War I, the ideas had to be abandoned. Only in the southwest of the island a short line was constructed and opened for traffic. With the law of December 1919, funds were set aside for the building of a line in Indian standard gauge from Makassar, the chief town and port on the southwest coast, south to Takalar and north to Maros to begin with, but the plans included some 350 more km into the far north of the island. Construction was started from Makassar southward and Takalar—47 km away—was reached in 1922. Traffic was minimal and as a result of the short but general postwar malaise of 1921–1922, the segment to Maros was begun but never finished, and the rest of the planned line was abandoned. Road traffic could easily replace the trains and so in 1930 the short stretch of rail that had been finished was closed again and lifted.[14]

NOTES

1. Jong (de), *De Waaier van het Fortuin*, 302–05.

2. Gerretson, *Geschiedenis der "Koninklijke."* Still useful is Beaton, *Enterprise in Oil*. Beaton also gives the early history of the Koninklijke in Sumatra.

3. Jacob Theodoor Cremer (1847–1923), after working in the Indies for the Nederlandsche Handel Maatschappij became director of the Deli Maatschappij in 1871 despite being only twenty-four years of age. In Medan he worked hard and made the company great, influential, and profitable. After returning to the home country in 1883, he remained active in the mercantile and industrial fields; member of Parliament 1884–1897 and again 1901–1905, minister for the colonies in the progressive liberal cabinet of Pierson-Goeman Borgesius, but without a great impact on colonial society. Charité, ed., *Biografisch Woordenboek van Nederland*, 1, 122–25. Unfortunately, there is no literature about this empire builder in English, but there is a good survey of his workings by Lenstra, in "Jacob Theodoor Cremer." About the Deli Company, see Kommer (van), "De Deli-Maatschappij."

4. The opening of the lines of the DSM in Reitsma, *Korte geschiedenis*, 94–97. Also Ballegoijen (van) de Jong, *Stations en Spoorbruggen op Sumatra*, 99–113. Also Meijer, *De Deli Spoorweg Maatschappij*, and Weisfelt, *De Deli Spoorweg Maatschappij*, passim. The steam locomotives used on the plantation railways in Bergmann, *Die Dampflokomotiven der indonesischen Werkbahnen*, 303–53.

5. Veering, "Nodes in the Maritime Network," 227.

6. Based on Weisfelt, *De Deli Spoorweg Maatschappij*, 41–59; Ballegoijen (van) de Jong, *Stations en Spoorbruggen op Sumatra*, 99–234.

7. Pierson, *Hohenzollern Lokomotiven*, passim.

8. Oegema, *De stoomtractie*, 168–74. About Hagans, see Messerschmidt, *Taschenbuch Deutsche Lokomotivfabriken*, 221–25. For Krauss, see ibid., 89–96. Also Schmeiser, *Krauss-Lokomotiven*, where the engine in question is not to be found.

9. Jong (de), *De Waaier van het Fortuin*, 429–30. Willem Rooseboom (1843–1920) was a career officer of the Corps of Engineers and rose through the ranks until

his retirement as general in 1899. He had no Indian experience but Minister Cremer wanted a governor-general who would be able to reorganize the Indian defense in view of the rise of Japan and the United States as military powers. He was appointed in 1899 and remained as such until 1904. Charité, ed., *Biografisch Woordenboek van Nederland*, 1, 500–01.

10. P. F. P. Richter (1853–1924) was engineer with the Java State Railways between 1895 and 1912 and also involved in the use of waterpower for electric power stations on Java. *De Ingenieur* 39 (1924), 826, 919. J. van der Waerden was a civil engineer with a lot of experience in his home country and later working for Netherlands Railways. Jan Hendrik de Waal Malefijt (1852–1931), from simple descent and without much education, became a successful politician of the Christian Reformed Party, member of Parliament, and governor-general of the Indies 1909–1913 but without much lasting success. Charité, ed., *Biografisch Woordenboek van Nederland*, 3, 644–45.

11. Reitsma, *Korte geschiedenis*, 98–103.

12. Ballegoijen (van) de Jong, *Stations en Spoorbruggen op Sumatra*, 310–406.

13. Oegema, *De stoomtractie*, 161–64.

14. The plans for the outer islands in Reitsma, *Gedenkboek der Staatsspoor- en Tramwegen*, 76. Also Reitsma, *Korte geschiedenis*, 104–05.

THE COMING OF 9
THE STEAM TRAM

THE HORSE TRAMWAY OF BATAVIA

If the Dutch East Indies may have been late with the introduction of steam railways, with the opening of a city tramway with horse traction, Batavia was certainly not lagging. Already in 1869, only five years after the first horse tramway was running in The Hague, Batavia got its city tramway with animal traction. In that year the Bataviasche Tramway-Maatschappij (BTM, Batavia Tramway Company) opened its first line from the old, lower town to Weltevreden, the modern town center where all offices, public buildings, and hotels were located. A curious feature was that this tramway was laid to a gauge of 1,188 mm (ca. 3 ft 10.5 in), a width that was never used anywhere else in the world. The reasons for this are unknown, but it was probably some local or regional measure still in general use there at the time. Horse traction in tropical countries has always been troublesome, as horses generally suffered from the hot climate and often contracted serious diseases. Batavia was no exception. In one exceptionally bad year, the company lost 545 animals—a disaster.

In 1881 the struggling BTM was taken over by a new company, the Nederlandsch-Indische Tramweg-Maatschappij (NITM, Netherlands-Indies Tramway-Company), and the new managers were looking for an alternative form of traction. Regular steam traction was out of the question, as smoke and cinders from the locomotives would be a nuisance for the passengers in the coaches that were open, with a roof and low side panels only. The solution was found in the fireless locomotive. High-pressure steam was generated in two stationary installations, where the boilers of the engines were filled with boiling water and steam, each fill lasting just long enough for a round trip. Between 1882 and 1909 Hohenzollern of Düsseldorf supplied twenty-one of these little teakettles, weighing 9 tons, and their performance in service was found adequate. Hohenzollern, under the guidance of its innovative director Dr. Gustav Lentz,

A pleasant street view of old Batavia in the 1920s. One of the curious fireless locomotives of the Netherlands Indies Tramway-Company in charge of a very mixed consist. Shops advertise in Malay and Chinese, but it is clear that the Moët & Chandon champagne was more intended for European throats. (Gerard de Graaf collection)

had developed a successful type of fireless engine, and over the years the firm built hundreds of them, although usually for industrial services where the fire hazard was great, not for use on public systems. The use of these little fireless monsters by the NITM on a regular city tramway over a long period was somewhat rare and certainly uncommon in the railway or tramway world.[1]

In 1899 the NITM also opened its first electric line, again on the 1,188-mm gauge, soon followed by other lines and extensions. However, the fireless locomotives continued in service on their original line until 1933, no doubt a record. A strange sideline: on double-track stretches of the lines in the middle of the roads, the trams, both steam and electric, were running on the right-hand track, while the road traffic used the left-hand side of the roads. This must have given rise to many unexpected meetings.[2]

THE STEAM TRAM

Operators of tramway systems worldwide were looking for other kinds of traction than the troublesome animal power. Fodder was expensive, especially in times of war when armies used tens of thousands of animals, and sickness of horses or mules could decimate the inhabitants of the tramway stables. The great epizootic of 1872, a kind of influenza among horses, killed thousands of animals in a number of American cities and brought service to a virtual standstill. It's a small wonder that operators were intent on finding an alternative, and in the mid-1870s the steam tram proved to be one of the answers. A small, generally four-wheeled locomotive running on light rails set into the pavement inside cities and on the shoulders of existing roads or even on its own right of way outside the city limits turned out to be a good solution. One or two carriages and a guards' van provided the necessary accommodation to connect the people of outlying villages with the city centers and railroad stations. Batavia had already found an alternative in the fireless locomotive, but for longer runs from the cities into the countryside the steam locomotive was preferred.[3]

In the Netherlands these proceedings were followed closely, and in 1878 trials with steam traction on horse-powered street tramways were held, first in The Hague with a Swiss Winterthur tram engine and later that year in Haarlem with a similar locomotive from Merryweather of London. These trials had no direct results, but a year later a real steam tram was running, laid out and operated by the Dutch Rhenish Railway between its terminus in The Hague and the fashionable beach resort of Scheveningen. Merryweather supplied the small steam locomotives of 0-4-0 wheel arrangement, running on tracks of the European standard gauge. More steam tramway companies followed. After Belgium, the Netherlands became one of the countries most densely covered with steam tramways, in standard gauge or in 1,067-mm and 1,000-mm gauges and even smaller widths, such as the extensive network in the province of Gelderland and neighboring Germany on the 750-mm gauge, the same as used in Atjeh on the northernmost tip of Sumatra.[4]

THE COMING OF THE STEAM TRAM OF THE EAST INDIES

The discussion, as outlined in chapter 6, about the possible role of private enterprise in the railway development of Java may not have resulted in the breaking up of the monopoly of the state in this respect; it did, however, focus the attention of government officials and entrepreneurs on the possible combination of both state and private business. Was it really necessary that the state be the only provider of rail transportation on the island, apart from the broad-gauge NIS, or could other privately owned companies add something to the growing core network of long-distance railway lines built and worked by the state?

The availability of capital was no problem. Capitalists in the Netherlands had invested hundreds of thousands, even millions, of dollars in American railroads, although the financial crisis of 1873 in the United States had caused great losses. Since then Dutch stockbrokers and bankers had been more careful in advising their clients when and where to invest, and besides new American railroads, the possibilities of East Indies railways or tramways had come into focus. The NIS, at first seen as a wild-cat scheme, had developed into a solid company, now making money and becoming a regular source of dividends for the shareholders. Consequently, other railway or tramway projects in the Indies that were to be privately funded were now seriously considered. The backers of these new companies were chiefly Amsterdam businessmen and bankers, well versed in the game of turning the savings of private citizens into these East Indian tramway projects. A few names of Dutch and East Indies government officials on the boards of directors guaranteed the necessary respectability to underwrite these projects.[5]

THE FIRST STEAM TRAM COMPANY

In 1879 three gentlemen applied for a license to build and operate a steam tram between Semarang and Joana, some 50 km to the northeast of Semarang, together with a few local lines in the city of Semarang itself. Although the East Indian railway authorities for no clear reasons advised against these plans, Minister for the Colonies Baron van Goltstein was more positive and gave the green light to Governor-General J. W. van Lansberge to grant the concession. The three concessionaries transferred their rights to the Samarang-Joana Stoomtram-Maatschappij (SJS, Samarang-Joana Steam Tram Company), incorporated in 1881, with headquarters in Amsterdam. In those days the name of the city was generally written as Samarang, hence the *a* in the title of the company. Capital was set at f2,500,000, fully paid in and later raised in stages to f8,000,000, of which at least 6 million was actually sold. At first the gauge to be used was set at 914 mm or 3 ft, an unusual gauge in the Netherlands but already in use in the United States. Dutch bankers must have been familiar with this gauge, as the fledgling Denver & Rio Grande Railroad in Colorado, operating on that gauge, had been initially financed from Amsterdam. Fortunately, in view of later developments, the proposed company changed the width to the Indian standard gauge of 1,067 mm before construction started. Apart from prescribing the use of the standard Indian gauge, the Batavian government also required the rolling stock to be compatible with that of the Java State Railways, to facilitate the running of through trains in the future—a wise decision, as it would turn out.[6]

The iron rails laid were of the same profile as that used by the State Railways, weighing 26–27 kg per meter, too heavy for the expected light traffic but already approved by the authorities in both The Hague and Batavia and readily obtainable from Belgian and German blast furnaces through the Technisch Bureau in The Hague. This way the otherwise-necessary interminable procedures of approbation by the Batavian government could be avoided. The tracks were laid along existing roads with permission of the local and regional authorities, thus avoiding lengthy negotiations for the acquisition of land. Bridges over rivers were generally of wooden construction, to be replaced later by stronger and more lasting iron or steel girder bridges. The layouts of stations and yards were simple in the extreme, too simple and restricted as it soon turned out, later necessitating expensive improvements and enlargements. A village station was no more than a siding with a wooden waiting room and a small office for the agent, in a few cases even with a freight and engine shed. With all later extensions, branches and junctions with other lines, and harbor tracks, the total length of the SJS lines eventually came to 425 km, not bad for a steam tram company.

Passenger carriages were all on bogies, closely resembling the usual Dutch light steam tram stock, but with shutters instead of glass windows. Freight stock was mostly four-wheeled with 6-ton capacity, but it soon became clear that 8 tons could easily be allowed, as the wheels and axles of the JSS pattern were strong enough. Later, 10-ton wagons were introduced and even bogie freight stock was used to a limited extent. The drawgear of engines and rolling stock was nonstandard, more resembling the usual simple Dutch version, but impossible to couple with JSS wagons with the Pihl coupling. When through traffic grew over the years, the engines were equipped with both systems; gradually, all rolling stock followed.[7]

Not surprisingly, the locomotives ordered for the SJS were also of a type similar to the first tram locomotives in the home country: light 0-4-0 tank engines with side panels, an iron roof supported on pillars, and skirts to cover the wheels so as not to scare humans and animals on the road. Total weight in working order was only 12.5 tons, cylinders were inside, and maximum speed was 15 km per hour. Beyer Peacock of Manchester came up with the best offer for the first nine engines and got the order. Dismantled and loaded on several ships, the engines landed in Semarang in 1882. With them arrived James Walker, sent out by Beyer Peacock to supervise the assembly of the engines; he would stay on as locomotive superintendent for three years. Apparently, Dutch technicians were unavailable for this job at the time. Three more of the same type were supplied by BP in 1887, and these twelve small engines were preferred for working the local lines in Semarang. For the long lines to Joana and Rembang, a marginally heavier locomotive was found necessary, and Beyer Peacock delivered the first three of this new pattern in 1884. Apparently, they answered all expectations and the Manchester firm supplied more of both types; in 1905 no less than forty-five of these 0-4-0s were in service.[8]

Initially, all engines burned coke that had to be brought, generally as cheap ballast, by sailing ships from Europe, as there were no coke ovens nearby. Coke was preferred for reasons of smoke abatement. In 1886 a trial

Above, Semarang Central Station, later known as Semarang-Djoernatan, was the terminus of the Samarang-Joana Steam Tram Cy., opened in 1885. It was built in wood but boasted a large overall roof. In 1913, a new and much larger station building was opened in the same location. (Author's collection)

Right, With these small 0-4-0 tanks, the Samarang-Joana Steam Tram started service in 1882. Twelve of these 12.5-ton steam kettles were supplied by Beyer Peacock, and although soon replaced by heavier engines, the veterans served the city lines in Semarang until withdrawal in 1926–1929. Photo of 1907. (Author's collection)

was made with briquettes, which were locally made from coal dust and paraffin and were reasonably cheap. The experiment was successful, and briquettes were used preferably for the local lines in Semarang despite the dirty and smelly smoke the engines produced with this fuel. In 1890

wood firing was tried on the lines running through the djati–ironwood–forests outside the city; the results of these trials were positive despite the need to refuel the locomotives more often than with coke or briquettes. Wood was plentiful along the lines and wood platforms were set up at regular intervals where the engines could be refueled. The operating costs declined dramatically with this change from coal to wood, from 9.1 cents per kilometer to a low of 3.5 cents. And not only the SJS went over to wood burning but also the NIS and even the State Railways started to use cheap wood for their smaller engines on less demanding services in these years.[9]

For the Rembang–Blora–Tjepoe line, under construction since 1899, the SJS needed more powerful locomotives than the Beyer Peacock tram engines. That line, although not running through really mountainous country, had some stiff gradients of one in fifty, and the four-coupled engines could no longer cope. Moreover, the maximum speed had been raised in stages to 45 km per hour and more powerful motive power was required. No longer Beyer Peacock but Hartmann of Chemnitz, the preferred supplier of the JSS, was called upon and in 1898 came up with a design of a 0-6-0 tank engine of more railway-like proportions, weighing 20 tons and with a tractive power almost double that of the old 0-4-0s. The first eight arrived from Chemnitz in 1899, and in 1912 four more were delivered. For the lighter passenger trains, Hartmann also supplied twelve modern 0-4-2 tanks, later supplemented by four more of the same pattern.

Poerwodadie station of the SJS before 1914 when it was replaced by a larger building of the same type as the one at Joana. This station was originally built by the earlier Poerwodadie-Goendih Steam Tram Cy., taken over by the SJS in 1892. The staff in charge is largely Indonesian with one European only, the station master in a white suit and formal hat. (Author's collection)

Under the wooden overall roof of Joana station of the SJS, opened in 1900. A surveyor in a white suit is taking some levels with a man on the platform holding a vertical calibrated stick. One of the early square tramway locomotives is visible in the right distance. (Author's collection)

To cope with the ever-increasing volumes of freight, even the 0-6-0 tanks were not powerful enough and the SJS clearly needed four-coupled engines. However, because of the many short radius curves, an ordinary 0-8-0 engine would probably cause problems when negotiating these. The solution was found in the Klien-Lindner system, invented by two Saxon engineers, Ewald Klien and Robert Lindner, and developed into a practical engine by Hartmann. In this system the front and rear coupled axles each had lateral play of 25 mm on both sides, with articulated coupling rods to allow for this movement. The result was an unusually long engine with a stretched wheelbase, giving a total length of almost 11 m and a weight of 30 tons. In all respects they were modern engines with superheaters, piston valves, and other modern fittings, and despite the rather complicated maintenance they did what they were expected to do. Six of them arrived in 1913 and as late as 1931 the last five with minor modifications were supplied. One of the other tram companies, the Serajoedal, had five of them, also from Hartmann and acquired in 1914 and 1915.[10]

After the success of the SJS, other companies followed suit, the next one being the relatively small Oost-Java Stoomtram-Maatschappij (OJS, East Java Steam Tram Company), launched in 1888 with headquarters in The Hague. Capitalization was set at ƒ3 million, half of which was paid in; the rest followed in 1914. The company started with building two separate networks, one centered on Soerabaja with some local lines in that city, and the other around Modjokerto, southwest of Soerabaja. The two networks were not connected, and in 1889 a deal was closed with the Java State Railways for through running of freight trains, especially in the sugar season, and also for transferring rolling stock from one region to the other. The maintenance works of the OJS were established in Soerabaja, hence the need for exchanging locomotives and rolling stock between the two networks. Total length of the several lines was 79 km, small when compared to the SJS, but during the sugar season traffic surged so much that locomotives and wagons had to be hired from other companies. Construction followed the SJS system closely, with simple light track and plain stations, but rolling stock was equipped with the standard JSS Pihl coupling, as JSS locomotives were used for the run over the metals of the State Company.[11]

In 1889 the OJS started working its first lines with a dozen 0-4-0 tramway engines constructed by the Dutch factory of Backer & Rueb of Breda. Of the familiar square outline, they were smaller than the Beyer Peacock engines of the SJS and at 10.9 tons, about 2 tons lighter, too light in fact for the lines around Modjokerto. Later, they were preferably used on the Soerabaja city lines after heavier and more powerful locomotives became available in 1891 for the rest of both networks. Between 1891 and 1910 Beyer Peacock supplied fifteen of its now-familiar 0-4-0 tram engines of 13-ton weight, the same as those of the SJS.

The factory of Backer & Rueb opened in 1862 in Breda in the southern province of Brabant of the Netherlands, and in 1883 the first steam locomotive left the works. In 1884 the firm was converted into a limited liability company under the name Machinefabriek Breda and from then on it concentrated on the construction of steam tramway locomotives. Its small, square tramway engines were to be found on almost every Dutch steam tram line and also in some foreign countries and in the Dutch colonies.[12]

In 1894 the next steam tramway company was also incorporated in The Hague, the Serajoedal Stoomtram-Maatschappij (SDS, Serajoe Valley Steam Tram-Company). On the board were largely the same officers as with the OJS and the SJS companies, with interlocking directorates. There

was a difference though, as the SDS was more intended for heavy freight traffic. Its sphere of activity—to open the fertile valley of the Serajoe River for agriculture on a commercial scale—was also different, not in the East Java sugar districts but in the middle of the island, from Maos just north of harbor town Tjilatjap to Bandjarnegara by way of Poerwokerto. The JSS had been running from Maos to Tjilatjap since 1887. Capitalization was set at ƒ1.5 million; in 1917 this was raised to ƒ3 million, of which ƒ2,250,000 was then paid in. Altogether, the length of the lines was some 128 km, including a later extension to Wonosobo of 33 km.[13]

The line was built to the same standards as the State Railways, as heavy traffic to the port of Tjilatjap was expected. Because of the gradients in the line, the usual small 0-4-0 tanks were considered insufficient, so the company ordered more powerful six-coupled engines from Beyer Peacock, which by then had become a kind of favored purveyor of locomotives to these tramway companies. The fourteen engines, delivered between 1895 and 1910, with a weight in working order of close to 21 tons, were still classified as tramway engines but without the overall roof and with a more common semi-enclosed cab in the rear. They were coal burners originally but were soon converted to wood burning, and they got a big and ugly crate for firewood behind the cab.[14]

The last of these early companies was the Semarang-Cheribon-Stoomtram-Maatschappij (SCS, Semarang-Cheribon Steam Tram Company), incorporated in 1895, again with the same sponsors as with the earlier SJS and SDS. Headquarters were in The Hague and capitalization was set at ƒ3 million, soon raised to ƒ4 million, to reach eventually ƒ12 million in 1923. The aims stated in the act of incorporation were the building of a 245-km steam tram line from Semarang to Cheribon and the acquisition of the Tegal–Balapoelong line of the Java Spoorweg Maatschappij, adding another 24 km. For the Semarang–Cheribon line, which promised high returns on the investment, many applications for a concession with or without an interest guarantee from the government had already been received, but all had been refused for different reasons. This time it was a serious proposition, with solid financial backing, and after the concession was awarded the company started straightaway with construction, beginning from both terminals and finishing the line in 1899.

There certainly existed a demand for better and cheaper travel between Cheribon and Semarang, as mentioned by Ernst Sillem in his diary of 1889. The journey from Cheribon to Tegal with the mail cart took him seven hours for the 49 paal (a paal is 1,500 m, somewhat less than a mile), and the cost was a reasonable 25 cents per paal. But from Tegal to

SDS engine Nr. 4, an 0-6-0 tank of the series 1–14 outshopped by Beyer Peacock between 1895 and 1910. Originally, the first eight engines had side skirts covering wheels and motion, but these were soon removed. (Author's collection)

Above, Semarang-Cheribon Steam Tram engine Nr. 40 with a long and very mixed train at an unknown location, photographed before 1914. This locomotive was built by Werkspoor-Amsterdam. (SNR collection)

Right, In the early years the SCS ran its trains with these simple 0-4-0 tank engines, series 5–47, and apart from five from Werkspoor, all were constructed by Beyer Peacock between 1895 and 1907. All SCS engines were equipped with the standard Pihl coupler of the Java State Railways. Photo from 1907. (Author's collection)

Semarang the road was more severely graded, and the mail cart needed four horses, would cost 90 guilders, and would take between eight and nine hours. Sillem thought this excessive and contracted with a Chinese operator for a small cart with two horses for ƒ25, still a lot of money in 1889![15]

One of the neat Hartmann 0-4-0 engines of series 101–127 in a ceremonial role at the opening of the new station at Cheribon. The four-wheeled inspection vehicle of the SCS is waiting for the white-uniformed party to embark. Photograph from around 1920. (SNR collection)

From the first the line of the SCS was built to the standards of the State Railways, through generally level country along the north coast of Java. All rolling stock was fitted with the Pihl coupler as used by the JSS to make through traffic possible. For the rest everything was kept as simple as possible, without frills. Sugar was the main freight; no less than twenty-seven sugar mills were located along the line. Rolling stock was the usual tramway stock, with 8-ton freight wagons and bogie carriages for passengers. Speeds were low, as by law only 15 km per hour was then allowed on tramways, although this was raised in several stages to 45 km per hour and even much higher later in the twentieth century.[16]

Locomotives were the usual 0-4-0 tramway engines, forty-three in all, of which were thirty-eight from Beyer Peacock, delivered between 1895 and 1907, and five from Werkspoor-Amsterdam in 1902/1903. Until 1907 this fleet sufficed, but for the longer distances the tramway locomotives did not have enough fuel and water capacity, so a 0-4-0 with separate four-wheel tender was developed by Hartmann and supplied between 1908 and 1913 in twenty-seven units. These were extremely neat-looking machines, with outside cylinders, a long wheelbase, and a graceful tender cab that closely followed the lines of the engine cab, providing good protection against sun and rain for the engine crew. Their maximum speed was 45 km per hour and at that velocity their running was quiet and stable.

The Samarang-Joana, the Oost-Java, the Serajoedal, and the Semarang-Cheribon were jokingly called the Zustertrammen, the Sister

Above, Another Hartmann engine of the series 101–127 in a more familiar role, at the station near the Gempol sugar mill with a heavy mixed train of four passenger carriages and a large number of freight wagons. Photo from before 1914. (Gerard de Graaf collection)

Right, An idyllic view of the track of the Semarang-Cheribon Steam Tram, 59 kilometers west of Semarang, running through the tropical forest along the Java Sea. Later this light track would be substantially upgraded and straightened, permitting speeds of 75 kilometers per hour and even higher in places. Photo from before 1907. (Author's collection)

Tramways, because of their interconnected directorates and their easy exchange of rolling stock and even locomotives. Their European joint headquarters were in The Hague and they often acted as one unit in negotiations with the Batavian government. Although they were all conceived as tramways with limited speed and simple equipment, several of them were converted in the 1920s and 1930s into fully fledged railways with much higher speeds, mainline locomotives, and more comfortable rolling stock.

The first of these other, generally smaller tramway companies were two units operating in East Java, both incorporated in 1895 and with the same directorate, the Passoeroean Stoomtram-Maatschappij (PsSM) and the Probolingo Stoomtram-Maatschappij (PbSM), opening their first lines in 1896 and 1897, respectively, and by the end of 1912 having reached a length of some 140 km and 45 km. The Passoeroean started with five of the usual Backer & Rueb square 0-4-0 tram engines but supplemented these with twelve 0-4-0 tanks from Hohenzollern with more railway-like looks. The Probolinggo, with heavy sugar traffic, began with three Backer & Rueb engines and soon went over to six of the same Hohenzollern 0-4-0 tanks. The Backer & Rueb engines were generally seen as too light, not only here but also with the other tramway companies. For the really heavy freight trains, five 0-6-0 tanks were acquired from Hanomag in 1913.[17]

Next came the Kediri Stoomtrammaatschappij (KSM) of 1895, launched to operate tram lines in the residencies of Soerabaja and Kediri, southwest of the city of Soerabaja. The first lines were opened in 1897 and by 1900 a total of 122 km had been laid. Many sugar mills were located along the lines, which provided heavy traffic in season. The company began with fifteen of the Hohenzollern 0-4-0 tanks of the familiar square outline, and Henschel supplied two other 0-4-0 tanks, a factory standard, in 1900 and 1908. When the sugar traffic continued to grow, just before the outbreak of war in 1914, the Kediri managed to obtain from Henschel the first of ten heavier 0-6-0 tanks of a more railway-like type with outside

Arrival of a long train of the Probolinggo Steam Tram Cy. in Djati, between Probolinggo and Kraksaän. The engine is one of three 0-6-0 tanks, delivered by Hanomag of Hanover in 1913 as PbSM Nrs. 11–13. Three more of the same type arrived in 1921 but it is unknown which of the six this engine is. Photo from the 1920s. (Author's collection)

A train of two bogie car-
riages and a van, hauled
by an 0-4-0 tank of the
Malang Stoomtram
Series 1–12 (Hohen-
zollern, 1897–1902)
arrives at the end of the
line at Toempang, 1914.
(Author's collection)

cylinders and a cab at the rear end. Because of the war the last two of these
successful engines arrived only as late as 1926.

The Malang Stoomtrammaatschappij (MS) was incorporated in 1896
with the same sponsors and the same directors as the Kediri, with the
intention of developing a network of tram lines around Malang in the East
Java hill country, serving a number of sugar mills and other plantations.
In 1908 the largest extent of the network was reached with a total of 85 km.
Service was opened in 1897 with 0-4-0 tram engines from Hohenzollern;
thirteen of these were available by 1911. For the heavy freight trains, more
powerful locomotives were needed and Hohenzollern obliged in 1913 with
a heavy 0-8-0 tank engine, of which eleven units were supplied until 1924.

Operating in the same area as the Kediri tram was another of the
smaller companies, the Modjokerto Stoomtrammaatschappij (MSM).
Modjokerto had been the center of the great Modjopahit Empire of the
fourteenth century, but few remains of these golden years had been preserved. The tramway company in this historic region was incorporated in
1896 with headquarters in The Hague but not with the same directors as
the Zustertrammen. It opened its first line in 1897 and until 1907 about 77
km of steam tram line were laid to serve the villages and the sugar mills
in the area. Backer & Rueb supplied six 0-4-0 tram engines of the familiar
outline for the first services but soon they had to be supplemented by four
Krauss 0-4-0 tanks of a more modern type. More powerful 0-6-0 tanks
were ordered, again from Krauss, in 1907, 1912, and 1926; in 1922 Hanomag
supplied two more 0-6-0s for the sugar traffic.

Georg Krauss, another of the chief suppliers of steam locomotives
to the East Indies, founded his locomotive factory in München in 1866
under the name of Locomotivfabrik Krauss & Comp. He specialized in
small engines for industrial purposes and business was good. In 1872 he
opened a second works in München-Sendling; this one became the chief

factory for the production of narrow-gauge locomotives. The first Krauss engines for an East Indies tramway, the Babat-Djombang, came from Sendling in 1899. The Amsterdam firm of Figee & De Kruijff was the official representative of Krauss in the Netherlands and the Dutch colonies, and in the works lists this name crops up again and again, so it must have exported quite a number of engines to Java and Sumatra for plantation railways and industries.[18]

A latecomer was the Madoera Stoomtram Maatschappij (MT), incorporated in Amsterdam in 1897. The island of Madoera lies close to Java's eastern end and was important for its salt workings, a government monopoly. Because of this proximity, Madoera was generally included in all statistics of Java. It was a well-populated island with a large number of villages; traffic to Java was handled by ferries and small craft. There was no rail connection between the two islands, although plans for train ferries were brought forward again and again. As usual the first lines were short—18 km opened in 1898 between Kamal and Bengkalan—but until 1913 more than 221 km of tram line were constructed, raising the Madoera Steam Tram to one of the largest of such undertakings of the twin islands of Java and Madoera. The first traffic was handled by two Hohenzollern 0-4-0 tramway engines, but already in 1898 Hartmann supplied twelve 0-6-0 tanks, soon joined by eight more of the same type. As one of the first on Java these engines were equipped for burning petroleum residue. The firebox was lined with firebricks, and the fuel was carried in the left-hand side tank; success in service was limited. Traffic was surging again in the 1910s, so more powerful engines were sorely needed. In 1912 Borsig-Berlin built four heavy 0-8-0 tanks, with six more arriving the following years. They bore the brunt of the salt traffic until the arrival in 1922 of two more of the same wheel arrangement, now superheated and constructed by Hartmann.

The last of these independent steam tram companies was the small Babat-Djombang Stoomtram-Maatschappij (BDS), incorporated in 1897 to construct a line between the two towns of its name. Djombang is located on the Soerabaja–Madioen line of the JSS and Babat is on the NIS line between Soerabaja and Semarang that was opened in 1900–1902. The BDS remained small and never had more than 70.5 km of line. Two of the ubiquitous Backer & Rueb 0-4-0 tramway engines were used in the first year, when only a short section of the line was open, soon supplemented by six Krauss 0-4-0s between 1899 and 1901. Two more powerful 0-6-0 tanks, again from Krauss, arrived in 1903 and 1913, but they could not improve the worsening financial situation of the company. Traffic did not meet expectations and revenues were insufficient. In 1916 the Babat-Djombang was sold to the Batavian government and incorporated into the Java State Railways, thus ending its independent existence.[19]

All of these steam tram companies were financed privately and exclusively from the Netherlands, capital never being in short supply. The possibilities of a profitable investment in East Indies enterprises in plantations, insurance companies, construction workshops, or steam tram companies had become clear to Dutch entrepreneurs and capitalists, making it easy to raise the necessary capital for such ventures. Loans secured by a mortgage on the property or parts of it were generally floated to acquire additional funds for expansion, betterments, or new rolling stock and engines, and these loans too were easily placed. Interest rates were generally 4 percent with some lows of 3 or even 2.5 percent and highs of 5 or 5.5 percent for less promising companies.

REGULATIONS FOR RAILWAY AND TRAMWAY OPERATIONS

In 1866, when the first railway line on Java was opened, a set of regulations for the new mode of transportation was published by the Batavian government. It contained mostly articles meant to ensure public safety and order, but at the time of the opening of the first state-operated lines, a new set of regulations was deemed necessary. So in 1885 the new Algemeen Reglement voor de Spoorwegdiensten (General Regulations for Railway Services) was published. It was strongly influenced by the Dutch Railway Law of 1875, which in turn was a Dutch version of the current German laws. These German laws contained rather elaborate and stringent rules for freight traffic, which were not really sufficiently adapted to the situation in the Indies. At the time of publication steam tramways did not yet exist and consequently they were not covered in the 1875 law. For this reason the Samarang-Joana, having obtained its concession in 1881, was free of these restricting measures.

This changed in 1883, when a fairly stringent set of rules for the steam tramways was published; though modified in 1885, these rules seriously hindered the incorporation of new tramway companies. This was recognized by the authorities in Batavia and gradually the need for a new set of rules was acknowledged. The result of these ideas was a new general and more liberal Algemeen Reglement for steam tramways, published in 1893, containing many articles that made the organization of traffic on the tramway lines chiefly a matter for the companies themselves, subject only to general rules about safety and such. For instance, the maximum speed permitted was raised from 15 to 25 km per hour with the possibility of even 40 km per hour when circumstances allowed. Local differences could lead to even higher speeds, longer trains, and double heading, to name but a few of the issues, and on behalf of the tramway companies the regional government officials could deviate from the general rules. This fairly loosely worded set of regulations partly explains the sudden explosion of new tramway companies in the late 1890s. The other factor was the enormous growth of sugar production at the end of the nineteenth century, with sugar mills clamoring for better and cheaper transportation.[20]

TWO PRIVATE RAILWAY COMPANIES

Apart from the State Railways and the steam tram companies there were private interests that were cautiously feeling their way into the complicated Javanese railway world. This time these parties were not interested in steam trams but in real railways. The Java Spoorweg-Maatschappij (JSM, Java Railway Company) was the first to be incorporated in 1884, with headquarters in The Hague and with Dutch and British capital amounting to ƒ1,440,000, fully paid in. Share certificates were printed in Dutch and English, and the British interest was also clear from the presence of James Staats Forbes on the board of directors. Forbes was a well-known figure in the Dutch and British railway worlds, being director of both the Dutch Rhenish Railway and the London, Chatham & Dover Railway Company. Another Britisher among the incorporators was Alexander Fraser, one of the triumvirate that founded the NIS back in 1863. The aim of the JSM was to build a line from Tegal, a busy port and commercial town on the north coast of Java, to Balapoelang, more inland and important for the sugar industry. A branch from Balapoelang to Pangka was also included in the plans. The mainline, if one could call it that, was finished in 1886 on the standard Indian gauge of 1,067 mm, but the financial results were meager and the JSM was only too happy to sell the railway plus rolling stock to the Semarang-Cheribon Stoomtram in 1895. The branch to Pangka, now extended to Proepoek to meet the state line from Cheribon to Poerwokerto and Tjilatjap, was opened by the SCS only in 1918. The four locomotives ordered by the JSM, 0-4-0 tanks of 18.6 tons supplied by Hohenzollern-Düsseldorf, all bore names of the English incorporators, among them James Staats Forbes and the duke of Sutherland; the duke's name was spelled on the engine nameplate in Dutch as Hertog van Sutherland! George Granville William Sutherland Leveson-Gower (1828–1892), third duke of Sutherland, was a liberal Scottish nobleman with a vast fortune and as a landowner second only to the queen of Great Britain. He was interested in railways as a means to develop his holdings and had built his own railway in Scotland from Dunrobin, where his castle was located, to Helmsdale, since 1884 part of the Highland Railway to the far north of Scotland. His role in the OJS was more financial than managerial, apparently, as he had no seat on the board of directors.[21]

Another newcomer was the Bataviasche Oosterspoorweg-Maatschappij (BOS, Batavian Eastern Railway Company), incorporated in 1884 by mostly Amsterdam businessmen and bankers with the intention

The Java Spoorweg Maatschappij began its services with four small but neat 0-4-0 tanks from Hohenzollern-Düsseldorf, of which Nr. 1 was named Hertog van Sutherland after one of the capitalists behind the venture. After the sale of the company to the Semarang-Cheribon in 1895, it became SCS Nr. 1 and lost its name. Hohenzollern Works photo. (SNR collection)

of constructing a railway line from Batavia by way of Meester Cornelis eastward to Bekassi and beyond. Share capital was set at ƒ1,700,000 and fully paid up, no doubt as a result of the guarantee given by the Nederlandsche Handel Maatschappij (NHM) of a 4.5 percent dividend for the first three years. The NHM itself took shares amounting to ƒ0.5 million. The first part of the line—in 1,067-mm gauge and 27 km long—was opened to Bekassi in 1887; from there it was slowly extended until Krawang, 36 km from Bekassi, was reached in 1898. Financial results were disappointing, however, and later that same year the company, with all its rolling stock, was sold to the Batavian government and incorporated into the JSS. In the following years the JSS extended the line eastward to Tjikampek and from there south to Padalarang by way of Poerwakarta, thus forming a shorter connection between Batavia and Bandoeng and going over lines wholly owned by the JSS, but at the cost of 56 km of difficult mountain line through the Preanger Highlands. For the first services the BOS obtained eight small 2-4-0 tank engines from Beyer Peacock of Manchester. They were extremely light at just 14 tons, with outside cylinders, a short wheelbase, and a maximum speed of only 30 km per hour, but they were sufficient for the first years. After the takeover by the JSS, they were used all over the system for menial duties on level lines.[22]

NOTES

1. Gladwin, *History of the British Steam Tram*, 108; Pierson, *Hohenzollern Lokomotiven*, 69, 71.

2. Duparc, *De Elektrische Stadstrams op Java*, 9–12. Oegema, *De stoomtractie*, 137–38. Reitsma, *Korte geschiedenis*, 37–39. Puffert, *Tracks across Continents*, doesn't

mention this unusual gauge. A possible explanation may be the following: a gauge of 1,188 mm when measured between the railheads results in a width of 1,219 mm, or 4 ft, when measured in the usual way between the centers of the railhead. A 4-ft gauge was now and then used in England and British India. With early street railways it was not uncommon to use this more unusual way of measuring the rail gauge.

3. For American tramways and such, see Miller, *Fares Please*; Hilton and Due, *Electric Interurban Railways in America*; also Middleton, *Time of the Trolley*. For Europe, see Baddeley, *Continental Steam Tram*.

4. Overbosch, De *Stoomlocomotieven*, 9–10, 40, 208.

5. About the investments of Dutchmen in American railroads, see Veenendaal, *Slow Train to Paradise*.

6. Reitsma, *Korte geschiedenis*, 39–40; *Gedenkboek Samarang-Joana*; Oegema, *De stoomtractie*, 122–24. About the Dutch interest in the Denver & Rio Grande, see Veenendaal, *Slow Train to Paradise*, 63–65.

7. *Gedenkboek Samarang-Joana*, 49–58.

8. Gladwin, *History of the British Steam Tram*, 45; Oegema, *De stoomtractie*, 123–25; Hills, *Beyer Peacock Locomotive Order List*.

9. Oegema, *De stoomtractie*, 56–57.

10. Ibid., 126–27.

11. Duparc, *De Elektrische Stadstrams op Java*, 56–63; Reitsma, *Korte geschiedenis*, 55.

12. About the firm of Backer & Rueb/Machinefabriek Breda, see Pater (de), *Locomotives Built by "Machinefabriek Breda."* The OJS engines on 19–20. Also Oegema, *De stoomtractie*, 123.

13. Reitsma, *Korte geschiedenis*, 56.

14. Oegema, *De stoomtractie*, 125.

15. Sillem, *De reis om de wereld van Ernst Sillem*, 113–14.

16. Reitsma, *Korte geschiedenis*, 56–57. Oegema, *De stoomtractie*, 123.

17. It will be noticed that the spelling of *Stoomtram-Maatschappij* in Dutch varied at the time. Sometimes it was spelled in two words with a hyphen; others used it as one word: *Stoomtrammaatschappij*. The spelling *Passoeroean* with two *ss* is probably a printer's error, as the common spelling at the time was *Pasoeroean* with a single *s*.

18. A short history and complete works lists in Schmeisser, *Krauss-Lokomotiven*.

19. The description of the several tramway companies is based on Reitsma, *Korte geschiedenis*, and *Gedenkboek Samarang-Joana*. The motive power in Oegema, *De stoomtractie*, 122–38.

20. A good survey of the regulations concerning railway and tramway traffic in *Gedenkboek Samarang-Joana*, 29–39.

21. The JSM locomotives 1–4 were taken over by the SCS in 1895 and kept their original numbers with the new owner. Oegema, *De stoomtractie*, 124, 216. About the third duke of Sutherland and his railway interests, see Ross, *Highland Railway*, 47–48.

22. The role of the NHM in Graaf (de), *Voor Handel en Maatschappij*, 106. Oegema, *De stoomtractie*, 74; Reitsma, *Korte geschiedenis*, 40–41, 47–49.

THE BOOMING ECONOMY

It has been said that in the ten to fourteen years before World War I, which broke out in August 1914, the Netherlands East Indies changed more than in the three centuries before. The first signs of that great change were already apparent in the late 1880s and 1890s. The disastrous Sugar Crisis of 1884 had resulted in a new and better organization of the sugar industry, followed by the introduction of new and more disease-resistant varieties of sugar cane. Early Dutch banks such as the Nederlandsch-Indische Handelsbank (NIH, Netherlands-Indies Commercial Bank) of Amsterdam had rashly advanced capital to amateur entrepreneurs in the sugar business without any knowledge of the matter. As a result of this lack of information, the NIH found itself unable to satisfy its creditors. Too many sugar mills had to close down without any hope of repayment of loans; apart from the NIH, several other banks suffered too. Only an intervention of a few great Amsterdam bankers and big mercantile houses had brought relief; afterward, the banks were more careful in advancing credits for agricultural purposes. Another effect of this devastating sugar crisis was that the banks perforce became owners of sugar lands and mills that had defaulted, at first somewhat reluctantly and forced by circumstances, but gradually these banks started to play an active role, not only in the sugar industry but also in other cultures. Big trading companies such as the Handels Vereeniging Amsterdam (HVA) also entered the field and acquired and worked extensive plantations on Java and Sumatra. Modern equipment was brought in and real agronomists were hired and put in charge; in this way the large-scale Dutch and foreign-owned plantation became the prevalent agricultural system in the Dutch colonies.[1]

Before 1904 sugar was the East Indies' most important export product, representing 32 percent of total exports. At 25 percent coffee came next, followed by tobacco (13 percent) and tin (5 percent). Exports of less important products totaled 23 percent, and so-called new products such

Soerabaja Kotta freight station of the Java State Railways on the bank of the Kali Mas, with a city line of the Oost Java Steam tram crossing the river on its own bridge, in the 1920s. (Author's collection)

as oil, rubber, and copra represented a poor 2 percent. The total value of all exports together grew with leaps and bounds from 175.3 million guilders in 1880 to 289.1 million in 1904 (in current prices).

After 1904 the so-called new products slowly grew in importance with ups and downs to reach an average percentage of 32 of the combined exports over the period 1904–1939, followed by sugar with 24, tobacco with 8, tin with 6, and coffee now with only 4 percent. Other, less important products made up the total with 26 percent. In value the difference with earlier years is less impressive, largely as a result of the falling prices of sugar and coffee on the world market. From the 289.1 million guilders of 1904, the value had climbed to 674.1 million by 1914, not bad of course, but fluctuations of prices on the world market outside the influence of either the Dutch or East Indies governments played an important role. World War I caused a short stagnation in exports as a number of formerly good customers for sugar, coffee, and tobacco such as Germany or France had fallen away as export markets, but prices of strategic products such as oil, rubber, and tin soon pushed the total value of exports up to a high of 2,152 million guilders in current prices in 1919.[2]

CONSEQUENCES OF THE GROWTH OF THE ECONOMY

Simultaneous with the booming economy the authority of the Batavian government was now firmly established in even the most outlying islands of the archipelago, peacefully when possible, forcibly if necessary. Of course, both phenomena were interrelated. When serious businessmen or even adventurers discovered new fields of enterprise, Batavia was quick in following these entrepreneurs with governmental structures, judicial systems, and police to make these areas safe for development. Both European settlers and the indigenous population profited from the more secure surroundings and the opportunities for obtaining a better life. Schools were set up to teach the population the basics of reading and writing in order to prepare people for jobs in the new environment. For the white or mixed-blood children, schools were founded to educate them for working in the new organizations, such as big commercial enterprises, railroad companies, insurance, and banking firms. In short, all the implements of a western civilization were either eagerly awaited by or forced on most segments of the population.

This development may well be called a form of modern imperialism, visible in other parts of the globe as well with Britain, France, and Germany participating. Compared to these three, the Netherlands was only a small country but with a gigantic colonial empire. The old Batavian policy of abstaining from interfering in regional conflicts while ruling only through contracts and treaties with regional rulers had been definitely left behind. The Korte Verklaring (Brief Declaration) was the visible sign of the new policy, and all local rulers were required to sign this declaration that ended their relative independence. If need be military force was used to persuade them, as the Lombok expedition of 1894 and the final end of the Atjeh war had clearly demonstrated. An important element in these policies of "pacification" was the KPM, the (since 1891) contracted privately owned Dutch shipping company that had acquired an absolute monopoly in 1899 for the carrying of government officials and supplies, monies, and other vital cargoes. Though the KPM became the connecting and unifying service for the whole archipelago, the Java State Railways and the private railway and tramway companies came to fulfill the same role for Java.[3]

The modernization of the economy did not go easily everywhere. The gradual transfer to the modern system of wage labor was not readily accepted in all regions, and small free farmers felt themselves degraded to coolies; on the other hand, the old feudal society was slowly disappearing, replaced by a western and European system of government and taxation. Messianistic movements surfaced from time to time and occasional regional revolts had to be suppressed with military force. The dip in the economy in the 1880s was seen as the chief cause for these revolts, while at the same time Java's population had exploded from 16.2 million in 1870 to 28.3 million thirty years later. Famines occurred in certain areas where rice and other foodstuffs had to be brought in from elsewhere.

The role of the Binnenlands Bestuur (Internal Civil Government) was changing too. The Dutch *residenten* had always seen themselves as kings of sorts, enlightened despots in their jurisdictions, but around 1900 younger officers wanted changes: less centralization and more support for economic development instead of the old-but-still-prevailing laissez faire mentality. Another moving force was the ethical policy as advocated by journalists like P. Brooshooft and the member of Parliament C. Th. van Deventer. This lawyer, after a career on Java, wrote a controversial article under the title "Een Eereschuld" ("A Debt of Honor") wherein he advocated that the government should stop to see the Indies as a colony suitable only for extracting money, as had been done for centuries. From then on this debt should be repaid in the shape of creating more favorable living circumstances for the indigenous population. Better education, less oppressive taxation, more irrigation projects, and emigration from the overpopulated Java to other islands were some of the ideas ventilated by Van Deventer. It is remarkable to see how soon these ideas took root in Batavian government circles and in the home country—and were even going to be implemented. Minister for the Colonies and Governor-General A. W. F. Idenburg, a member of Abraham Kuyper's antirevolutionary Christian Party that was a power in Parliament, was the moving force behind this new policy that gradually transformed the old colony into a modern state.[4]

THE JAVA STATE RAILWAYS TAKE OFF AGAIN

The straightened financial circumstances of the Batavian government and the hesitation of the Dutch government to invest more in the colonies at the time that the Atjeh war was still swallowing millions are reflected in the growth of the network of the Java State Railways. For the eastern lines, the last section to be opened in 1886 was Soerabaja–Kalimas, planned long before and only 5 km long, serving the port of Soerabaja. This would be the last state line opened until 1895. For the western lines, west of Djokja several lines had already been ordered before the Sugar Crisis of 1884; they were finished between 1884 and 1889. The section of Djokja–Tjilatjap, 176 km long and opened in 1887, was easily the most important. Yet, the eastern and western state lines were not yet connected, as there was still a gap between Maos and Tjitjalengka of some 180 km, a serious flaw in the state system.

As usual a lot of words were used and often wasted to emphasize the advantages or disadvantages of several projects ventilated by both private parties and State Railways officials such as Kempees. Minister for the Colonies Van Dedem at last decided that a general plan should be drawn

Construction of the new railway through the Preanger Highlands was difficult and necessitated a large number of cuts and fills and many spectacular bridges. In this photograph, taken around 1905, workers are filling small four-wheeled dump trucks by hand. No steam excavators yet. (Gerard de Graaf collection)

up indicating which lines were needed, which of them were to be constructed as railways of the first class, and which could be started as simpler tramways. In 1893 the Batavian government issued this plan for new railway construction that included lines to open up some still underdeveloped regions such as Bantam, the former sultanate in the extreme west of Java. Other projects were for a Cheribon–Semarang line, but this was left to private parties who incorporated the Semarang-Cheribon Tramway Company as described in chapter 9. The Bantam line was begun in 1896 and Anjer was reached in 1900; a branch to Laboean followed in 1906. More important was the state's purchase of Batavia Ooster Spoorweg (BOS) in 1898. New construction by the state was now taken in hand with fresh impetus. Krawang–Tjikampek–Poerwakarta was opened in 1902 and Poerwakarta–Padalarang in 1906, making connection with the Buitenzorg–Bandoeng line. The latter town, growing fast because of its pleasant climate, could now be reached over two different lines. The line to Padalarang through the Preanger Highlands was a difficult one, with severe gradients, much curvature, and even a tunnel at Sasaksaät just north of Padalarang. As such it was a triumph of Dutch engineering and technology. The engineers of JSS could be proud of their work, and foreign travelers did not restrain themselves in their praise.

The railway through the Preanger Highlands was one of the highlights of railway travel on Java. It was a spectacular piece of engineering, crossing valleys on spindly trestle bridges. Here a stretch of the line near Sasak-saät with one of the trestles in the distance. Photo from around 1920. (Author's collection)

Building east from Tjikampek, the JSS construction forces reached Cheribon, 137 km, in 1912, making connection there with the steam tramway of the SCS. Important too was the decision, taken in 1912, to build a line from Cheribon southeast by way of Proepoek to Kroja—158 km—on the JSS southern east–west mainline, giving a shorter connection between Batavia and Soerabaja, but this long and partly mountainous line was not finished until 1917.

THE REORGANIZATION OF 1906

As outlined in chapter 6, the independent position of the State Railways organization had been terminated in 1888 and the whole had been brought directly under the director of Burgerlijke Openbare Werken (BOW) in Batavia. The departmental chiefs of traction, permanent way, and such were no longer responsible to the *hoofdinspecteur* (inspector in chief) but to the head of the two divisions of Westerlijnen and Oosterlijnen (Western and Eastern lines), who in turn were responsible to the director of BOW directly. The *hoofdinspecteur* was chief in name only. He had no

real grip on the day-to-day business on the railways, which led to a lack of discipline of the staff and general decline of service. Despite many complaints from the traveling public and shippers, fanned by critical newspapers in the Indies, it took years before the responsible government officials came to realize that a new reorganization was necessary to guarantee adequate service on the now-greatly-expanded network. In 1906 the new *hoofdinspecteur*, H. F. van Stipriaan Luiscius, managed to restore the independence of the JSS system to a large degree. From then on all department chiefs reported only to him, and he in turn to the director of BOW, no longer called BOW but renamed *Gouvernements-bedrijven* (government businesses). With some later improvements, this new system of organization remained largely in place until the Japanese occupation in 1942.[5]

THE BATAVIA–SOERABAJA CONNECTION

Between the government center Batavia and the mercantile center Soerabaja, the two most important cities on Java, traffic was always heavy. Roads were bad and most traffic had gone by sea, but this was slow. Railways had

The halt at Lebakdjero, east of Bandoeng, with a passenger train from Djokja to Bandoeng. The halt was opened in 1906 in the middle of the gorgeous tropical mountain scenery. Photo from around 1920. (Author's collection)

changed the picture profoundly and since 1894, with the opening of the last sections of the Tjitjalengka–Djokja line, the JSS could offer through passengers a reasonable traveling time, although Batavia–Buitenzorg was still in the hands of the NIS. Real express trains were unknown, and travelers had to endure many stops at wayside stations and halts when underway from Buitenzorg to Djokja. A first overnight stop was in Tasikmalaja, east of Tjitjalengka, where the traveler had to spend the night. Next day another JSS train took him to Djokja for another night in a hotel. The NIS then forwarded the weary traveler over its broad-gauge line to Solo, where another JSS train was ready to take him to Soerabaja by way of Madioen. Two nights in hotels and 32.5 hours of actual railway travel were necessary to cover the distance of about 850 km in some measure of comfort.

In 1896 a new schedule was introduced with only twenty-four hours of real travel time and with a single overnight stop in Maos, where the JSS hotel unfortunately soon acquired a bad name. Still, the transfer from standard to broad gauge at Djokja remained with all the nuisance and expenses involved. In 1895 a deal was concluded in The Hague between the NIS and JSS whereby the JSS was allowed to lay a third rail inside the broad-gauge track between Djokja and Solo. In 1899 these works were ready but still in an unsatisfactory shape, with too many awkward connections at the stations. The result was that they were little used and then chiefly only for freight traffic. Finally, by 1905 the tracks had been strengthened and straightened out sufficiently to allow through JSS passenger trains to use this section but still at reduced speed. Night traffic was generally prohibited because of the dangers of wild animals on the unfenced tracks and so all trains stopped for the night at 18:00 (6 p.m.).

In 1906 the opening of the Batavia–Krawang–Padalarang state line provided the JSS with a shorter line of its own between Batavia and Djokja, without the NIS-owned Batavia–Buitenzorg section. The schedule could now be shortened, but still included an overnight stop in the unsatisfactory hotel at Maos. In 1909 the first express trains were introduced on this service, which meant that total travel time with the new Oost Java Expres from Bandoeng to Soerabaja and vice versa could be reduced to thirty-six hours. Travelers to Batavia had to spend the night in Bandoeng; it was much cooler there than Maos. In the other direction the West Java Expres offered the same facilities, now with a hotel stop at Djokja. Matters stood there for a long time until in 1917 the new Cheribon–Kroja line was opened, but still the broad-gauge section Djokja–Solo remained a bottleneck, and total travel time for Batavia-Soerabaja could be reduced only by 2.5 hours.[6]

SOME FIGURES FOR JAVA STATE RAILWAYS[7]

Staff, European and Indonesian

1890	2,000
1900	5,600
1910	17,000
1914	23,000

Number of passengers in all four classes

1890	6,000,000
1900	12,000,000
1910	26,500,000
1914	40,000,000 (of which about 35,000,000 in third class)

Freight in tons/kilometers

1890	65,000,000
1900	160,000,000
1910	245,000,000
1914	370,000,000

Totals of receipts and surplus after deduction of exploitation costs and other expenses

1890	6,000,000	surplus 1,000,000
1900	15,000,000	surplus 5,000,000
1910	26,500,000	surplus 11,000,000
1914	38,000,000	surplus 16,000,000

Kilometers in exploitation on Java, 1,067-mm gauge only

1890	890
1900	1,590
1910	1,980
1914	2,100

Locomotives and Rolling Stock in 1914

Steam locomotives	450
Passenger carriages	1,320
Freight wagons	~8,000

WORKSHOPS, DEPOTS, AND ROLLING STOCK

For the maintenance of the steam locomotives two works had been set up, one for each of the two networks. For the eastern section Madioen was chosen and a small but comprehensive workshop was established there. From 1910 it was extensively rebuilt and reequipped with modern tools and such. The works were even electrified, using hydroelectric power from a power station on the Tjatoer River nearby. Bandoeng was chosen for the maintenance works for the western lines, also modernized over the years but gradually replaced by a completely new complex in the Batavia agglomeration at Manggarai, near Meester Cornelis, under construction since 1915 and finished only in 1920. This up-to-date plant was laid out by W. F. Staargaard, then CME of the State Railways, after he returned from an extensive European tour. The new works were extremely modern and equipped with everything that could be wished for. Total workforce was around two thousand men, European and Indonesian. In East Java Soerabaja-Goebeng had replaced the insufficient Soerabaja-Kota in 1910, but this works catered only for carriages and freight wagons. Smaller works were located in Djember, East Java.

Engine depots were situated at all stations where locomotives were regularly changed, equipped with the necessary facilities for watering and fueling the engines, and also for small repairs. Gradually these original

Above, Two of the popular 2-6-6-0 Mallet tanks are being readied at the new engine shed of Bangil, south of Soerabaja, around 1920. (Author's collection)

Facing, The 2-6-6-0 Mallet tanks of 1904 were meant for the line through the Preanger Highlands, but traffic grew so fast that they had to be used in pairs as seen in this publicity photograph of a long express on the spectacular bridge near Melangbong north of Padalarang. (Author's collection)

simple depots were rebuilt and modernized and adapted to service the heavier and more complicated locomotives. Poerwakarta was one of the more important depots, being heavily rebuilt in the early years of the century. Soerabaja-Sidotopo was reconstructed in 1923; during the busy sugar season it housed some seventy-five engines, serviced by a workforce of more than one thousand men. During the slack years of the 1930s, many depots were closed. Of the twenty-four original engine depots, only thirteen remained in 1934.

All original passenger coaches were four-wheeled, but already in 1881 the need was felt for longer vehicles and so six-wheelers were introduced, with Cleminson radial underframes to adapt them to the sometimes-severe curves. The first bogie carriage came in 1891, a saloon for the governor-general, and from 1895 more bogie carriages followed, steel framed and with wooden bodies. Windows could be closed with glass panes, frames with wire mesh or wooden shutters, adaptable to every kind of weather. Their length was around 13 m and they still had the Norwegian Pihl coupling system without side buffers. For the higher speeds envisaged in the 1920s, longer—18.5 m—steel bogie carriages were imported, with wooden paneling inside, as the steel parts could become too hot to touch in the tropical sun. To give the coaches more stability at high speeds they were equipped with side buffers and heavy central couplers. Over the years lighting evolved from simple candles to kerosene or acetylene lamps, with electric lamps being introduced in 1917, using English Stone equipment or the Swiss system as developed by Brown Boveri of Baden. The wooden coaches were varnished and the steel ones painted in a light brown, until in the 1930s green for the parts below the windows was used with cream upper parts. All trains had the automatic vacuum brake of the Hardy system.

Freight wagons were all four-wheeled with a capacity of 8 tons, raised to 10 tons after heavier axles had been mounted in 1904. During the war years, when little or no new rolling stock could be obtained, capacity of the four-wheelers was again raised, now to 12 tons, at first temporarily but when still-heavier axles had been fitted after 1918, the 12-ton limit could be maintained. In 1920 a new and larger wagon type was successfully tested, now with 15-ton capacity. Bogie freight wagons with a capacity of 20, later raised to 24 tons, were introduced in 1895 and the fleet was gradually expanded, also with steel coal trucks of 30-ton capacity. Private owner wagons were first introduced in 1925 by the Pure Cane Molasses Company of Java Ltd., in the shape of 15-ton tank wagons, eventually in 311 units. These were constructed in the Indies by the Nederlandsch-Indische Industrie of Soerabaja, one of the few privately owned mechanical works in the Indies. Other private firms followed the lead of the Pure Cane Cy. and so freight trains could present a colorful ensemble.[8]

Despite the lull in the construction and opening of new railway lines by the Java State Railways in the 1880s, additional locomotives were still necessary, as traffic on existing lines grew and the few new lines opened needed motive power too. The well-liked 2-6-0 tanks of the 300 Series, supplied by Hartmann-Chemnitz, were continued, with three more arriving in 1886, followed by no less than sixteen more from 1887 until 1891. Later in 1891 six more arrived in two lots, making a grand total of forty-eight of these versatile engines available for service on both eastern and western lines. The equally successful 2-4-0 tender engines of Sharp Stewart, of which the first had arrived on the premises in 1880, were also continued during the 1880s. From 1884 until 1896 twenty-five of the same arrived, although with slightly enlarged dimensions, making sixty-five in all. Several were transferred to South Sumatra between 1913 and 1923, where they performed sterling services. On Java some of them, a century or more old, were still in service into the 1970s. Sharp Stewart built for eternity!

One remark should be made here: in 1912 the Java State Railways introduced a general renumbering of all locomotives. Initially, numbers had been given in the order of arrival of the engines on the premises, independent of the class of the locomotives, making for a poorly organized and hard-to-use locomotive list. In 1912 this was changed and locomotives were from then on listed by class, making the lists more clear and easy to use for the staff and also for later historians. As far as possible the post-1912 numbers have been used in this book. All steam engines of the JSS were painted black, while some newer engines had boiler jackets of what was called "Russian" iron, which had a metallic bluish hue and gave a nice touch of color in the tropical sun.

In Europe compounding had been introduced in the 1880s to reduce the fuel consumption of locomotives. Several systems were tried whereby the high-pressure steam was first used in one or two small cylinders and then again at a lower pressure in one or two larger cylinders, before being exhausted into the atmosphere. Different inventors favored their own patented methods, but in Germany the system as developed by August von Borries of the Prussian Railways was the most used and became fairly successful. He opted for one high and one low pressure cylinder, outside or inside, and the Java State Railways decided in 1892 to order a compound version of the well-proven 2-6-0 tanks after the Von Borries system, the series JSS 401–483, delivered by Hartmann making a grand total of no less than eighty-three units between 1892 and 1902. They had two outside cylinders, the high-pressure one on the left and the larger low-pressure cylinder on the right of the engine. The total weight was just over 31 tons, with the later ones weighing 1 ton more; adhesion weight was 24.4 tons, and a bit more for the later somewhat heavier units. Maximum speed was set at 45 km per hour. Initially, they were chiefly used on the mountain lines in West Java until superseded there by the later Mallet locomotives. Then they found further employment on more level lines and most of them had long lives, several still running well into the 1970s.

Other tank engines, also two-cylinder compounds but now built as 0-6-0 tank locomotives, meant for the mountain lines in West Java were supplied by Hartmann in 1892–1893 in sixteen units. However, these were found to be too slow and too light for these services, so their life on the mountain lines was extremely short and they were all scrapped in the 1930s. Ten heavier (26.8 against 18.2 tons) 0-6-0 tanks were constructed by Hartmann from 1898 until 1912, and Werkspoor-Amsterdam delivered another ten of these during the same years, also with the same low maximum speed of only 30 km per hour; they were soon superseded by larger and heavier Mallets. For the more easily graded Djokja–Tjilatjap section, eleven 2-4-0 side tanks were supplied by Hanomag in 1886 for passenger trains, JSS 74–84 after the renumbering of 1912. They were very German looking, with outside cylinders, and were simples, not compound engines, with a maximum speed of 60 km per hour, enough for the then-still-low speeds even on lines of the first class.

Other locomotives were taken over by the JSS in small lots during these years. The largest number came from the Solo Valley Irrigation Works, a large and most ambitious irrigation project in the valley of the Solo River in mid-Java, begun by the government in 1895. The Ministry for the Colonies had ordered twenty-four small 0-6-0 tank engines for the transport of the enormous quantities of soil involved, and Cockerill of Seraing, near Liège, Belgium, delivered these in that same year. However, the project turned out to be too ambitious, as the regular flow of the Solo River was too small for the large volume of water needed for the vast irrigation works, so the project had to be stopped in 1898, temporarily at first. The locomotives were transferred to the JSS between 1901 and 1908 where they, then as JSS 501–524, were used for work trains and shunting duties. Some were later transferred to South Sumatra and two were shipped to the short-lived tramway on Celebes.[9]

Until about 1900 the passenger trains on the lines with only minor gradients had been worked by the 2-4-0s of Sharp Stewart, but it slowly dawned on the management of JSS that higher speeds than 60 km per hour and heavier trains would soon become the norm. As elsewhere in the world, the choice fell on the 4-4-0 with separate tender, driving wheels of 1,500 mm, and a maximum speed of 80 km per hour. Hanomag of Hannover, not Hartmann this time, offered the best conditions and suggested a two-cylinder compound engine, a smaller and lighter version of the then-current P4 machine of the Royal Prussian Railways. The first eight units arrived in 1900. Their weight of 31.2 tons with 20 tons more for the six-wheel tender was no problem, as the maximum axle load was still only 9 tons, and within the limits then in force. They looked definitely Prussian, not surprising considering their origins. Why Hartmann, the favored supplier of the JSS, did not get this order is unknown, but financial considerations would have played a major role here. They came equipped with the automatic vacuum brake of the Hardy system that had been introduced by the JSS some years before. In 1902 Hanomag delivered five more, followed by seven more in 1903. Another six came in 1904, now from Hartmann, and in the next year the Hannover factory again constructed six more. Then Werkspoor-Amsterdam stepped in with four of the 4-4-0s in 1907, Hartmann again with two units in 1908, and Werkspoor completed the series with four more in 1910. In the renumbering scheme of 1912 they became JSS Nrs. 601–644 and all had long lives.

By 1910 the introduction of the superheater, as developed by Dr. Wilhelm Schmidt of Kassel, Germany, brought about a revolution in steam technology. With this new device, major savings in both fuel and water could be reached, more than with the complicated compound propulsion, and the JSS decided to start a trial with this new equipment despite the fairly high patent fees of some 100 guilders per engine demanded by Schmidt's firm. Hartmann-Chemnitz supplied the first seven of these new 4-4-0s in 1912, and apart from the absence of compounding, they resembled their earlier sisters closely. Total weight was up 3 tons and their maximum speed of 80 km per hour was the same as of the earlier 4-4-0s. Werkspoor delivered four more of them in 1914, but by that time they were clearly outmoded and not powerful enough for the greatly increased traffic. They formed the series 651–661 of the JSS, but after these eleven no more were ordered, as by 1910 the first 4-6-2 Pacifics had already arrived on the premises and were better able to handle the express trains of the time.

THE MALLETS

In the 1890s traffic on the mountain lines in West Java had grown almost 50 percent and the faithful 2-6-0 tanks had great difficulty in hauling the trains over the severe gradients combined with sharp curves. On some sections with 40‰ gradients they were limited to 42 tons train weight, but as trains regularly weighed more than that, double-heading had become standard practice. An eight-coupled engine was clearly necessary, but because of the severe curvature of the lines, the JSS authorities hesitated. The solution was thought to be the Mallet locomotive, with two groups of four driving wheels each and a carrying axle under the cab and bunker. For these services Hartmann designed a 0-4-4-2 tank engine with a total weight of 42 tons and delivered the first of eight units in 1900. Four more followed in 1907 and again four more in 1908, now constructed by Schwartzkopff of Berlin. In 1912 they were renumbered 501–516. In these Mallet engines the rear group of powered axles was fixed in the frame, with the two forward axles in a swiveling group. High-pressure steam powered the rear group, while the forward axles were driven by low-pressure steam from the hp cylinders. For lines with severe curvature, these engines were ideal although at the cost of perennial problems with keeping the joints in the steam pipes from the high- to the low-pressure units steam tight, a problem with most Mallet engines all over the world. Initially, they burned coal or briquettes, but later some were equipped for wood burning, with a big crate on top of the firebox.

Although these 0-4-4-2 Mallets proved equal to the duties expected of them, traffic on the mountain lines continued to grow fast, especially for the section Poerwakarta–Padalarang; with its severe gradients and curvature, something more powerful was necessary. As the Mallet principle with its divided drive had given reasonable satisfaction, Hartmann was asked to design a heavier locomotive. In 1904 the first of these new machines was ready in the shape of a 2-6-6-0 tank engine. Total weight had grown to 58 tons, but the maximum axle load was still just 8.5 tons, well inside the permitted maximum. The earlier 0-4-4-2 tanks scored over 9 tons here! Between 1904 and 1909 a total of twenty-three of these bigger Mallets were delivered, most of them by Hartmann but also six from Schwartzkopff-Berlin. They were numbered JSS 521–543. One unique feature of these Mallets was the construction of the long side tanks. Outwardly, they looked just that, extremely long side tanks, but in reality they consisted of two separate articulated sections. The rear section was, as usual, constructed in a fixed position on the footplate, but the front part was resting on the frames of the forward driving unit on both sides and swung out with the frames when negotiating curves. When on a curve, there was just enough room between the forward part of the boiler and smokebox to allow for this movement of the side tanks without touching the boiler.[10]

By 1910 traffic on the mountain lines had grown again to such an extent that more locomotives were needed. And although the two classes of Mallets were generally fulfilling expectations, they did have their limitations. The problem of steam leaking from the connections between high- and low-pressure cylinders was never truly solved, and maintenance remained troublesome. Moreover, because of inequality of loading between the two units, the forward units of the engines were prone to slipping. In 1911 Werkspoor delivered eleven more of the 2-6-6-0 tanks (JSS 551–561), now with a bigger boiler and weighing 63.6 tons. They proved to be better steamers but the other problems remained. And still traffic continued to grow and speeds increased gradually, so the JSS authorities had to think hard again what to do next. And thus making a bold step in 1912, JSS suddenly found itself in the forefront of locomotive development worldwide with a unique twelve-coupler.[11]

THE JAVANICS

Karl Gölsdorf, the eminent Austrian locomotive engineer in charge of the locomotive department of the Imperial and Royal Austrian State Railways from 1893 until 1916, had to cope with several limitations that severely restricted his possibilities and scope. Austria at the time included large portions of what is now the Czech Republic, Slovakia, parts of Poland, Romania, and large tracts of former Yugoslavia. Hungary, also part of the empire, had its own railway system. Generally, the mountainous Austrian mainlines had a severely restricted maximum axle load, in combination with heavy gradients and much curvature. In 1900 Gölsdorf designed the first ten-coupler with sideplay for the first-, third-, and fifth-coupled axle, enabling the unit to negotiate the curves on the mountain lines without problems. Other locomotive designers followed his example and ten-couplers soon proliferated in Europe. In 1911, with train weights continually increasing, Gölsdorf went one step further with his system and designed the first twelve-coupler, a giant 2-12-0 freight locomotive with an axle loading just below the permitted maximum of 14 tons. Several ingenious devices and measures had been taken that made it possible for such a giant to negotiate the severe curves of the Tauern railway, one of the most exacting lines.[12]

Apparently, the technical staff of the JSS and the Technisch Bureau in The Hague were well informed about developments in Europe's locomotive world, probably by the regular perusal of English and German technical journals. And although the Mallets were generally liked and up to their work, making the joints in the steam pipes really steam tight remained a nuisance and involved a lot of maintenance. An engine without these problems but with six coupled axles now seemed possible after Gölsdorf's 2-12-0 locomotive had been successfully tested. Early in 1912 the JSS and the Technisch Bureau approached Hanomag and asked the company to design a twelve-coupled tank engine of sufficient power and flexibility for the Preanger mountain lines. Hanomag worked fast and still in 1912 the first of the (twenty-eight) truly enormous 2-12-2 tank engines arrived. With a total weight of 78.80 tons, of which 62.63 tons were available for adhesion, they were true giants on the 1,067-mm tracks. The front and rear

To supplant the 2-6-6-0 tanks, JSS ordered the Javanics of the rare 2-12-2 wheel arrangement. Although not the hoped-for solution for the heavy trains on the Preanger line, the Javanics were a success. Here Nr. 319, delivered by Werkspoor in 1913, at rest at Malang in 1936; the fireman is checking something on the running plate. Photo W. R. G. van den Broek. (SNR collection)

carrying axles were constructed after Adams, while Gölsdorf's system of giving some of the coupled axles limited sideplay had been adopted to make them suitable for curves of 150-m radius, a real challenge. A modern boiler with superheater provided enough steam, and other modern fittings and appliances, such as dependable sanding gear, materially helped adhesion. A large well tank partly between the frames and partly above the footplate gave them good stability, but maximum speed was set at only 55 km per hour, although later in their lives they were allowed 75 km per hour when running on less tortuous lines. The Javanics, as they were named after the American custom, did what they were supposed to do, but at the cost of abnormal wear of the front driving wheel tires, which needed replacement after only 6,000 km despite the Gölsdorf axle construction. Consequently, they were moved to other mountain lines with less severe curvature, where they were indeed most successful. The first ten came from Hanomag in 1912–1913, followed by six more in 1914–1915. Another six came from Werkspoor in 1915 and four more again from the Amsterdam works in 1917, although World War I meant delays and problems in obtaining fittings and other materials. Hanomag finally completed

the total number with two more in 1920. The JSS numbered them 801–823 and the five others were serving on Sumatra's west coast on the coal line near Padang. It had been a bold venture that did not quite solve the traction problems on the Preanger line, although the engines themselves were quite a success and served well into the 1970s. On the mountain lines the faithful 2-6-6-0 tanks were retained for some more years, often out of necessity double-heading the heaviest trains.[13]

THE PACIFICS

With the introduction of modern bogie carriages for the express trains and the higher speeds now required, the two classes of 4-4-0 engines, both simples and compounds, were not powerful enough for the work anymore. Six coupled wheels were clearly necessary, and in 1908 tenders were invited from several European locomotive works for six-coupled engines with the required power and speed. The Schweizerische Lokomotiv- und Maschinenfabrik (SLM) of Winterthur came up with the best design and price and got the order for five Pacifics, 4-6-2 machines, superheated with two outside cylinders only and a large tender on bogies. The complicated compound system had already been discarded by JSS, as superheating was expected to give at least the same savings in fuel and water with less complications. The first five arrived in 1910 and Hartmann-Chemnitz supplied five more in 1911, with two more coming from SLM in 1912. Hartmann then completed the order with four more in 1914, making a grand total of sixteen, numbered JSS 701–716. These sleek and elegant Pacifics gave great satisfaction, having no problem at all with the express trains on the more level lines. In 1914, between Maos and Djokja, their regular haunt, service speeds of more than 120 km per hour were reached, and even then the machines ran steadily and quietly. At the time this was seen as an absolute speed record on the 1,067-mm gauge anywhere in the world—hard to prove or disprove, but certainly plausible.[14]

The first Pacific locomotive of the JSS was Nr. 377, delivered by SLM-Winterthur in 1911 and intended for heavy express trains on less hilly lines. In 1912, with the general renumbering, she became JSS Nr. 701. She and her four sisters proved to be an excellent investment, and more were to follow until in 1914 fourteen of these elegant machines were in service. (Author's collection)

1. Gonggrijp, *Schets ener economische geschiedenis*, 132–33, 139.

2. Figures based on Lindblad, "De Handel tussen Nederland en Nederlands-Indië," 262, 267, and Bijlage II, 278.

3. Jong (de), *De Waaier van het Fortuin*, 319–45.

4. Ibid., 353–61.

5. Reitsma, *Gedenkboek der Staatsspoor- en Tramwegen*, 92–105.

6. Oegema, *De stoomtractie*, 178–80.

7. Figures from Reitsma, *Gedenkboek der Staatsspoor- en Tramwegen*.

8. Reitsma, *Gedenkboek der Staatsspoor- en Tramwegen*, 139–45; Oegema, *De stoomtractie*, 110–14.

9. About the Solo Valley Works, see Ravesteijn, *De Zegenrijke Heeren der Wateren*, 173–206. The steam locomotives of the JSS in Oegema, *De stoomtractie*, 66–74.

10. I have to thank my good friend Remmo Statius Muller for the explanation of this feature. Schwartzkopff had been incorporated in 1870 as the Berliner Maschinenbau-Actien-Gesellschaft vormals L. Schwartzkopff and catered for German railways in the first place, but also built up a customer base in foreign countries such as Russia. The firm became a great supplier for narrow-gauge plantation and industrial lines in the Indies.

11. About Mallet locomotives in general, see Durrant, *Mallet Locomotive*. Also Vilain, *Les locomotives articulées du système Mallet dans le monde*. Vilain does not mention Werkspoor-Amsterdam as constructor of Mallet locomotives.

12. Gölsdorf, *Lokomotivbau*, 115–16.

13. Oegema, *De stoomtractie*, 81–85.

14. Ibid., 182–86.

THE NEDERLANDSCH-INDISCHE
SPOORWEG-MAATSCHAPPIJ OF THE
1890S AND EARLY 1900S

In the early 1890s the NIS could at long last begin to think of expanding its network. The government loans dating back to the first years had been paid off, and the financial situation of the company had been substantially improved by more traffic and more revenues, from sugar first and foremost. Apart from a short—1 km—section in Djokja, no new lines had been opened since 1873, while during the same period the State Railways had grown enormously. The improved financial situation and the need to modernize and expand the network enabled the NIS to issue a new 2.5

A new NIS share of ƒ250 as issued in 1920. Of the 125 dividend coupons, 119 have been cut off and paid; only the last six have never been paid. (Author's collection)

percent loan of no less than ƒ30 million in 1896. However, it is not clear if this issue was fully taken up. More loans followed and there was little problem in getting them placed. In 1901 a 4 percent issue of ƒ15 million was floated, and the next year ƒ5 million more at 3.5 percent. Still more money was needed for new construction and improved rolling stock, so in 1913–1914, later extended to 1915–1918, a ƒ14 million loan was issued at 5 percent and fully taken up. Apart from the 3.5 percent issue, all these loans had been redeemed by 1938.[1]

In 1893 the NIS obtained concession for a steam tram line in broad gauge from Djokja southwest to Brossot. The Batavian government at first objected to the choice of gauge but eventually gave in; the 23.4-km line was opened in 1895. There was no connection with any standard-gauge line, so the gauge difference could never become a problem. Next came the tramway Djokja–Magelang—this one in Indian standard gauge—which was later extended to Willem I. A branch from Setjang to Parakan was also included in this concession. Willem I—the military establishment near the village of Ambarawa—was already at the end of a broad-gauge line from Kedoeng Djati since 1873. Magelang was reached in 1898, Setjang in 1903, and Willem I finally in 1905. The section between Setjang and Willem I was steeply graded, so steep in fact that part of the line had to be built as a rack railway. Total length of the line from Djokja to Willem I was 87 kilometers, with the branch to Parakan adding another 27 km.[2]

Much more important was the Soerabaja–Goendih line; at the latter place it met the broad-gauge main line of the NIS for the rest of the journey to Semarang. With this line—in Indian standard gauge—the company hoped to provide a better connection between Soerabaja and Semarang than the roundabout way over Solo and Madioen. Moreover, the new line would bring all traffic over NIS lines and not over those of the State Railways between Solo and Soerabaja. Concession for Soerabaja–Goendih was granted in 1896, with construction starting straightaway. The first section could be opened in 1900, while the whole line, 182 km long, was ready for traffic in 1903. Initially, the new line was worked as a tramway with a maximum permitted speed of only 25 km per hour. From Soerabaja one daily *sneltram* (express tram) took ten hours with sixteen stops to Goendih; from there the broad-gauge section to Semarang took another two hours, giving a total traveling time between Soerabaja and Semarang of twelve hours, with one change of trains. A 13.5-km-long branch to the ancient harbor town of Grissee, north of Soerabaja, was opened in 1902.

NEW LOCOMOTIVES AND ROLLING STOCK OF THE NIS

For the short tramway line Djokja–Brossot in broad gauge, the NIS bought four Backer & Rueb 0-4-0 tramway locomotives of the familiar

B&R pattern. However, just as elsewhere, they turned out to be not powerful enough for the mixed passenger and freight trains over this route. They had been constructed as convertibles, with the possibility of a change to Indian standard gauge, but only one of them ever underwent this drastic operation. The other three were chiefly used as switchers at the Djokja works of the NIS. For this tramway line, seven bogie tramway carriages were ordered; these were rebuilt to 1,067-mm gauge in 1911 and used on other NIS lines.

For the broad-gauge branch Kedoeng Djati–Willem I/Ambarawa, three large 2-6-2 tanks arrived from Werkspoor-Amsterdam in 1901, followed by four more in 1906. They had large driving wheels of 1,557 mm, as they were also intended to work the trains all the way to and from Semarang. However, this never happened, as their driving wheels were too big for the mountainous branch to Willem I and they were hardly used at all. Maintenance and oiling of the inside cylinders and motion was difficult because of the outside water tanks under the footplate without large enough access openings.

Shortly after 1900 traffic on the broad-gauge Semarang–Solo–Djokja main line was booming and the old-fashioned Beyer Peacock 0-6-0 and 0-4-2 tender engines, of which the last ones had only been delivered in 1901, could now no longer cope. Modeled after an earlier 4-6-0 tender engine for Norway, Hartmann-Chemnitz constructed six near copies for the NIS in 1902. They were four-cylinder compound engines, a system the NIS had only experimented with shortly before on other engines. The only differences with the Norwegians were a shorter tender because of the limited length of the NIS turntables; they had a large double roof to keep out the tropical sun and rain, and they were wood burners instead of coal burners. Apparently, the compounding was something that the company did not really appreciate, as the next two to the same general design arrived in 1906 as two-cylinder simples, with only minor modifications for the rest. In 1910 Hartmann supplied two more and in 1914 it delivered the last six to the same pattern. Some of the later ones were equipped with superheaters, piston valves, and other modern fittings. These engines hauled the twice-daily mixed trains on the main line, 166 km, in both directions in three hours, fifteen minutes, with a maximum speed of 75 km per hour and with nine or ten stops for fuel and switching. No real speed merchants, but adequate for the times.

For the heavy sugar trains in season, often consisting of about forty wagons with a total weight of 1,000 tons, even the 4-6-0 machines were not powerful enough, so the NIS ordered from Hartmann four 2-8-0 Consolidations with separate tenders, each weighing 60 tons in working order. They proved to be a godsend for this traffic, and four more were delivered by Hartmann in 1922. Until then, old main line engines had been

Looking very much like its 0-4-2 sisters, NIS Nr. 251, an 0-6-0 tank, was one of a series intended for hilly lines such as Djokja–Magelang. Photograph taken in Poerwosari in 1938. (Author's collection)

used for switching duties at harbors and sugar factories, but as this was uneconomic, Werkspoor in 1910 supplied a 0-6-0 switcher for this work, a handsome tank engine with two outside cylinders, a high-pitched boiler, and side tanks, weighing 40 tons. Four more arrived in 1912 and these had, apart from the hand brake, a steam brake, as they were also used for freight trains on the tramlines south of Djokja.[3]

For the new lines in 1,067-mm gauge the NIS needed a completely new fleet of locomotives and rolling stock, the equipment running on the Batavia–Buitenzorg line being absolutely outdated and insufficient. For Djokja–Magelang, also worked as a tramway, Hartmann in 1899 supplied two 0-6-0 tank engines with inside cylinders and outside water tanks below the footplate. They were handsome, almost elegant machines with the characteristic overhanging double roof as used by the NIS. They had a top speed of 50 km per hour, more than enough for a tramway where only 25 km per hour was allowed initially. The first eight locomotives came with an installation for burning petroleum residue as an additive to coal, but apparently this was not an unqualified success, as the later ones arrived without this feature. Some were later superheated and rebuilt with piston valves.

For generally level lines, a three-coupled engine was not deemed necessary, so for Goendih–Soerabaja Hartmann also supplied twenty 0-4-2 tanks between 1898 and 1901. They were two-cylinder compound engines, the first of this system for the NIS. Their exterior was almost the same as that of the 0-6-0 tanks, but their interior was much different: again, inside

cylinders but now with different bores, outside water tanks below the footplate, and the familiar double roof over the cab. Weight was around 25 tons, of which 17 tons were available for adhesion. Maximum speed was set at 55 km per hour, and they all came with the equipment for burning petroleum together with coal. Trial runs with this novel fuel had been held since 1896 with some success, but after 1902 the price of this waste oil increased so much that the company abandoned the system and went over to cheaper wood for fuel. For heavier freight trains on Goendih–Soerabaja, the 0-4-2 tanks were too light, and in 1902 Hartmann delivered the first of ten 0-6-2 tank engines, outwardly the same as the earlier smaller 0-4-2 and 0-6-0s but longer and heavier, 33 tons, of which 25 tons were available for adhesion.

For passenger trains on the Djokja–Magelang tramway line—extended to Willem I/Ambarawa in 1905, with the branch to Parakan opened in 1907—the NIS ordered from Werkspoor-Amsterdam ten 2-6-2 tank engines of a novel design, developed by Werkspoor. They were meant for trains on the hilly lines and also on the rack section between Setjang and Willem I, but on that section with a reduced load of only two

NIS Nr. 317, an 0-4-2 tank supplied by Hartmann in 1901, one of a series of twenty. They were two-cylinder compounds and equipped for burning petroleum residue in addition to coal. The large tank on top of the firebox held the petroleum. The photograph must have been taken before 1914, as the mixed coal/petroleum system was discarded by then. (SNR collection)

For its relatively level Soerabaja–Goendih line in Indian standard gauge, the NIS ordered nine 0-4-2 tanks from Hartmann-Chemnitz in 1898, supplemented by eleven more in 1900–1901. These engines were constructed as two-cylinder compounds with inside cylinders of different bores, 280 and 415 millimeters, respectively. The low-slung water reservoirs lowered the center of gravity and improved stability. When L. J. Biezeveld took this photograph of Nr. 321 on July 6, 1938, in Malang, she had been relegated to shunting and other menial duties. (SNR collection)

carriages. As they turned out to be a great success, fast and powerful, five more arrived in 1911. Superheated and with piston valves, they had all modern devices that were available at the time. Like almost all other NIS engines by that time, they were wood burners, as djati was plentiful along the lines. Water was a problem, though, as during the dry season rivers used for watering purposes tended to run dry. To be certain of a dependable water supply, an artificial lake was dug out near Goendih, and special water wagons were constructed to deliver this boiler water to stations along the line when needed. Most tank engines, with their limited water and fuel capacity, had to run with homemade tenders attached that could hold 10 m³ of water and 5 m³ of firewood, materially increasing their range.

By 1912 travel time on the important Soerabaja–Goendih connection had been substantially reduced from the abominable twelve hours of the first years to a creditable seven hours thirty-five minutes, including eleven stops. New comfortable bogie stock was introduced about the same time, even with real restaurant or buffet carriages. For these popular trains, new traction was needed, and the NIS decided to stop hauling these trains with the generally undersized tank engines and switch over to modern 4-6-0 engines with separate tenders. In 1912 Beyer Peacock constructed ten of these up-to-date superheated locomotives, followed by more units in the years after World War I, until altogether thirty of these handsome machines were in service. The post–WW I units were built by Werkspoor, Beyer Peacock, and Henschel with unimportant detail differences. Their total weight was 35 tons, adhesive weight 25 tons, and a fully loaded tender was good for another 22 tons. Maximum speed was initially set at 60 km per hour, but after several improvements and better balancing 75 km per hour was allowed. Occasionally, much higher speeds were recorded, even up to 105 km per hour, with the engines still running quietly and stable. With the opening of the standard-gauge line between Goendih (Gambringan) and Semarang in 1923, avoiding the change of trains at Goendih, real through trains could now be introduced. After upgrading the rest of the line to a railway of the first class, Soerabaja–Semarang then took only four and a half hours, a marked improvement.[4]

For the rack section of 8 km between Setjang and Willem I, special engines were needed for trains of more than two carriages. As rack locomotives were already successfully in use on the coal line on Sumatra's west coast, it was only to be expected that the NIS also ordered the necessary engines from the Maschinenfabrik Esslingen that specialized in this kind of traction. They were of the familiar 0-4-2 outline, compounds with four cylinders. On the adhesion section only the two high-pressure cylinders were used for driving the wheels, but on the rack section they worked as compounds, with the low-pressure cylinders powering the rack machinery. The three engines ordered were delivered in 1903 and two more followed in 1906, also supplied by Esslingen. All five had long lives and survived World War II.

With these new additions the NIS network consisted of two Indian standard gauge groups, separated by the broad-gauge line between Goendih and Solo, making the maintenance of the engines and rolling stock problematic. The first works of the company were located in Semarang; since 1897 the standard-gauge locomotives and stock were brought to that facility on a broad-gauge transporter wagon. For Goendih–Soerabaja a maintenance facility was built at Tjepoe, about halfway. A second transporter wagon, now on six wheels and with a carrying capacity of 35 tons, was placed in service in 1907 for the heavier engines then in use.

This all changed when an up-to-date maintenance facility was constructed in Djokja between 1911 and 1917, complete with all modern equipment and facilities. Even a village of two hundred houses for the European and Javanese staff was added. This new housing development had a state-of-the-art sewer system and an installation for burning household refuse. Semarang works was then closed and Tjepoe followed in 1930, leaving Djokja as the only maintenance works, although the nuisance of bringing standard-gauge stock on special broad-gauge transporter wagons to Djokja remained.[5]

The Batavia–Buitenzorg railway line had been opened by the NIS in stages between 1871 and 1873 and had proved to be a good investment for the company's shareholders. After all, Buitenzorg was the seat of the governors-general and Batavia the center of Dutch rule and administration. Traffic between the two cities was brisk and the existing road in horrible shape, making the railway indispensable. However, for the NIS it remained the only property in the western part of Java and at the time the only one in the Indian standard gauge of 1,067 mm. With the state itself stepping into the railway business with construction of a line from a junction with the Batavia–Buitenzorg line south and east to Bandoeng, the NIS line became the only connection of the state system with the capital Batavia, a most unwanted situation. As mentioned before, back in 1875 negotiations had been opened with the NIS for a possible sale of the line to the state and a sum of 5 million guilders had been offered, plus some favorable conditions and opportunities for new lines for the NIS, but the company had hesitated to accept.

The situation became more complicated when the Tandjong Priok harbor line was opened in 1877. This short railway was owned by the Bataviasche Havenwerken (Batavia Harbor Works), the company that was at the time constructing the new harbor at Tandjong Priok. It was operated with leased motive power and rolling stock from the NIS, and a physical connection with the NIS in Batavia opened in 1879. New movement became visible in 1878 when the NIS offered to lease the B–B line to the state, but the minister for the colonies refused this offer, as he wanted to buy the line outright, not on long-term lease. He introduced a bill in Parliament for the purchase of the contested railway for 6 million guilders. The Second Chamber narrowly agreed but the Senate threw the bill out and the problem remained unresolved, with the diminutive 2-4-0 tanks of the NIS continuing the service. A small improvement for travelers was the opening of a JSS-NIS joint station in Buitenzorg in 1881. Passengers could now change trains in one and the same station, but change from train to train remained necessary. To alleviate this, in the 1890s experiments were conducted with through JSS carriages Batavia–Bandoeng for first- and second-class passengers only.

Even more complicated became the situation in 1884, when the first mail steamers from Holland arrived in the new harbor of Priok and discharged their passengers at the small terminus of the Bataviasche Havenwerken (BH). There the travelers had to board the little train of the BH and were carried to downtown Batavia. So far so good, but when they wanted to get to Weltevreden or other more fashionable parts of the city, as most travelers did, they had to change to an NIS train to get there, or use the city tramway. And passengers wanting to continue their journey to Bandoeng or beyond had to change trains again at Buitenzorg for the JSS train to Bandoeng. To ease matters somewhat the harbor line was transferred from the Havenwerken to the State Railways, but the nuisance of changing trains at least once, but often enough twice, remained. The NIS had refused to work the harbor line when the state put in a proposal for such a deal in 1885, yet the next year the company recanted its decision and declared itself willing to operate the line in connection with its own line to Buitenzorg. Now it was the turn of Minister Sprenger van Eyk to decide and he seemed willing to grant the request, but strong opposition from the State Railway authorities on Java forced him to refuse. Stalemate again. Three years later the NIS offered to sell the B–B line outright for 6 million guilders. The laying of a third rail on the broad-gauge Solo–Djokja line to make JSS through traffic possible was included in the proposal. In return the NIS requested a 3.5 percent interest guarantee for the proposed Djokja–Magelang tramway line. Discussions about this offer led nowhere and in 1892 Minister Van Dedem finally declared that he had no funds available for the purchase of the B–B line. The impasse was complete.[6]

To offer a better service, the NIS then decided to introduce express trains between Batavia and Buitenzorg, but in order to raise the speed of these trains, heavier and faster locomotives were needed. Beyer Peacock, one of the favored suppliers of engines to the NIS, came up with two smart outside-cylindered 2-4-2 tank engines in 1893. They looked nice but apparently they were not an unqualified success, as they were never reordered and the two units remained the only ones of their kind.[7]

These simple improvements could not hide the fact that the continuing presence of the NIS in a complete State Railways regime around Batavia was a considerable source of friction, leading to inconvenience for travelers and shippers alike. Both sides recognized this and were now willing to compromise. The NIS wanted to be rid of this outlying property, and the state wanted to be sole master in and around Batavia. In 1910 both parties agreed to a deal: the state offered ƒ10,600,000 for the line, but Parliament in The Hague, which had to provide the money, was hesitating. A bill for this sum was narrowly passed by the Second Chamber but thrown out by the Senate as the senators opined that the price was too high. Three years later a new arrangement was reached with the NIS. This time a sum of only ƒ8.5 million was agreed on, plus, as compensation to silence troublesome shareholders, more relaxed and favorable conditions for some proposed new tramway lines of the NIS. This time Parliament agreed and so on July 20, 1913, the Batavia–Buitenzorg line at long last passed into the fold of Java State Railways. The primitive maintenance works in Meester Cornelis, near Batavia, were included in the deal. The NIS company withdrew its rolling stock and JSS trains took over. A feud that had lasted almost forty years had finally been settled. The winners were the traveling public and shippers.

The success of the several private steam tramway companies did not go unnoticed at JSS headquarters in Bandoeng. In 1907 the JSS opened the first section of a tramway network based on Madioen, a line to Ponorogo, 31 km long. Later extensions farther south increased the length with some 24 km more. On the western lines a short tramway was extended south from Tasikmalaja to Singaparna, 17 km long and opened in 1911. When the mainline Tjikampek–Djatibarang–Cheribon was under construction, a branch from Djatibarang to Indramajoe on the north coast of Java was included and opened in 1912. More important were a couple of lines originating in Bandoeng and extending south to a total of some 100 km, opened between 1921 and 1924. In 1916 the state took over the failing private tramway company Babat-Djombang, operating west of Soerabaja, and integrated it into the JSS network, adding 70 km more. Another line was built from Bandjar west of Kroja—on the east-west mainline—south to Kalipoetjang, 43 km long and opened in 1916. A 39-km extension to the south coast of the island was opened in 1921. When traffic was heavier than initially expected, some of these tramways were upgraded to second-class

This flimsy bridge carried the Babat-Djombang Steamtram over the Kali Brantas west of Soerabaja. Opened in sections between 1899 and 1902, the line was not an economic success. Its locomotives were small, the largest being Nrs. 9–10, with a total weight of 18 tons. (NSM collection)

railways, with higher speeds and greater axle loading permitted. All these lines were built in the Indian standard gauge.

For a time the JSS authorities thought that by using a narrower gauge than the Indian standard, economies in construction and exploitation could be obtained. A first line in 600-mm (1 ft 11.6 in) gauge was opened between Tjikampek and Tjilamaja, 28 km long, in 1909, followed by similar lines in 1919 and 1920 in the same area on the north coast. In the east a line of 40 km was opened in 1913 between Rambipoedji and Poeger, but in the end it turned out that the presumed advantages were not as great as envisaged, and the 600-mm gauge lines never amounted to more than 120 km.[8]

For the 1,067-mm tramway lines, small and old tank engines, made superfluous by the influx of new and more powerful engines, could be used, but for the 600-mm gauge new engines had to be found. First motive power consisted of two small and light—7 tons—tank engines from the Solo Valley Works. Next came five 0-4-2 tanks from Arthur Koppel, bought new in 1909. When these were found too slow and feeble for the services, three 0-8-0 tanks of 17 tons built by Hartmann were acquired. Three more of these arrived in 1926 and all gave good service. Just before 1914 Hartmann supplied six superheated 0-6-0 tank engines that turned out to be eminently suited to the 600-mm lines, followed by more after 1918, making a total of fifteen of these versatile units. Working of these lines was simple in the extreme, with open-sided bogie coaches for passenger services and light freight stock. Maximum speed was only 15 km per hour.[9]

THE PRIVATE STEAM TRAMWAY COMPANIES

The Semarang-Cheribon Steam Tram did well in the early 1900s. Its main-line of 243 km served no less than twenty-seven sugar mills, which were all dependent on rail transport for bringing the finished sugar to ports for export. A continuous upgrading of the tracks and other installations was necessary to keep abreast of the growing traffic, and the twenty-seven 0-4-0 locomotives with separate tender, delivered by Hartmann between 1908 and 1913, were needed to handle the heavy sugar trains. In 1909 the SCS decided that it wanted to convert its existing tram line into a railway and requested permission to build two deviations to shorten the distance between Semarang and Cheribon to 223 km. The line between Kaliwo-engoe and Kalibodri, 15 km long, avoiding the minor port of Kendal on the north coast, was opened in 1914. Another straightening took place on the western end near Cheribon with a 28 km section between Losari and Moendoe. The now-abandoned former mainline portions remained in service as connections to sugar mills.

Above, A proof of the
exchanges of rolling
stock between the
Zustertrammen: one
of the neat 0-4-0
tender engines of the
Semarang-Cheribon
with a very mixed train
of the Samarang-Joana
at the Stopplaats (Halt)
of Kedjaksaän. Was she
on trial with the SJS to
see if these engines
were suitable there too?
Photograph from before
1914. (SNR collection)

Right, Most unusual
engines were the six
0-8-0 tanks as delivered
by Hartmann to the
Samarang-Joana com-
pany in 1913–1914. They
were extremely long
machines with the two
outer axles constructed
after the Klien-Lindner
patents, allowing lateral
movement. SJS Nr. 305
is seen in Tjepoe on
December 6, 1938. (SNR
collection)

From January 1, 1914, the SCS offered trains that covered the distance
between Semarang and Cheribon and vice versa in a single day. Night traffic was still prohibited but the overnight stop in Tegal was now no longer
needed. The discussions with the Batavian authorities about the conversion of the tramway concession into one for a railway continued but did
not lead to a solution during these years. In Semarang the station of the
SJS, called Semarang-Djoernatan, was used, and it was reached from the
west over the city tramway tracks. In 1914 the SCS opened its own station,
called Semarang-West or Pontjol, with an extra-long overall roof, always

For the steadily growing sugar traffic, the Probolinggo company (PbSM) needed heavier engines than the first small engines. In 1913 Hanomag supplied three heavy—21 tons—machines of the usual tram outline as shown by PbSM Nr. 13. They were used for the heavy sugar trains and came equipped with the standard Pihl coupler of the State Railways. Undated photograph, pre-1914. (SNR collection)

Below, Kediri Stoomtram Nr. 23, an 0-6-0 tank from Henschel delivered in 1920, one of a series of ten similar engines. They were wood burners, and firewood was stored in the side tanks and on top of the firebox, with water in a well tank between the frames. The apparatus on the running plate was a steam pump with a kind of purifier to separate mud from water. The KSM had few water stations along the line and water had to be taken from rivers and brooks on the way. (SNR collection)

highly appreciated by the public during the monsoon. A gigantic and imposing office building was erected in Tegal in 1913, serving as headquarters of the company. Maintenance works were also established at Tegal and a new station building there was finished in 1918. Tegal became the center of operations of the SCS, complete with houses for the staff and an elementary school for the children.[10]

The Passoeroean Company also served many sugar factories in its district, and for these heavy trains two ex–Solo Valley Works were acquired of the same 0-6-0 arrangement as those of the JSS. In 1905 the first one

A broad-gauge tramway of the NIS under construction circa 1895, probably Djokja–Brossot, with a "square" locomotive from Backer & Rueb in charge. (NSM collection)

entered service with the PsSM and the second one followed in 1908. In Pasoeroean the PsSM also brought heavy freight trucks of the State Railways over the harbor line to the port, hence the need for powerful locomotives. The Serajoedal Company (SDS) constructed an extension of its line from Bandjarnegara to Wonosobo, 23 km long and opened in 1917. Other steam tram companies extended their networks too, but only with small sections of 1,067-mm track.

NOTES

1. A survey of the stock and bond issues of all privately owned railway and tramway companies in the Dutch East Indies was compiled by P. Baas and H. B. Roos in 2017. It is only available on the internet and has not been printed.

2. Reitsma, *Korte geschiedenis*, 62.

3. Oegema, *De stoomtractie*, 43–47.

4. Ibid., 51–61.

5. Ibid., 61–65.

6. This section based on Reitsma, *Korte geschiedenis*, and Reitsma, *Gedenkboek der Staatsspoor- en Tramwegen*. Willem Karel Baron van Dedem (1839–1895), civil servant in the Indies and the Netherlands, member of Parliament, and minister for the colonies from 1891–1894. He was a strong advocate of more influence of the state in public transportation and mining companies. Molhuysen and Blok, eds., *Nieuw Nederlandsch Biografisch Woordenboek*, I, 694.

7. Oegema, *De stoomtractie*, 50–51.

8. Reitsma, *Korte geschiedenis*, 71–73.

9. Oegema, *De stoomtractie*, 138–40.

10. Reitsma, *Korte geschiedenis*, 77–78. Amstel (van), "Historie van een stoomtrammaatschappij," 563.

WORLD WAR I AND ITS 12
GOLDEN AFTERMATH

12

NEUTRALITY

During the nineteenth century, the Kingdom of the Netherlands had maintained a policy of strict neutrality and had indeed managed to stay outside all partnerships and alliances in Europe. That did not mean that the country would be safe from invasions from the East, as proved by the original German Schlieffen plan of the early 1900s for an attack on France that had included an advance through Dutch Limburg. When this German attack finally came in August 1914, it turned out that the plans no longer implied an advance through Limburg and so Dutch neutrality was respected. The neutral Netherlands were seen by the Germans as a kind of lifeline or breathing tube when their own harbors were going to be closed by a British blockade. On the other hand, Great Britain had entered the war as a guarantor of Belgium's neutrality, now violated by Germany, and could not well violate the neutrality of the Netherlands that Britain had guaranteed at the same time. Thus the Dutch government managed to remain neutral in the midst of all European belligerents, more or less thanks to this attitude of Germans and Brits, but the country was completely surrounded by warring parties. The Netherlands mobilized its armed forces on July 31, 1914, the first country in western Europe to do so, to impress the great powers of the strong will to defend its neutrality. This neutrality was severely tried during the war years. From the first months of the war, more than thirty thousand Belgian and two thousand British soldiers crossed the border into the Netherlands to avoid being made prisoners of war by the Germans. All these soldiers had to be disarmed, interned, housed, and fed, and they caused a multitude of problems. This was aggravated by the more than 1.1 million Belgian civilians who sought refuge in the Netherlands during the siege of Antwerp in October 1914. They all had to be housed and fed for at least six months, while several hundred thousands of them remained for the duration of the conflict.

With the mother country remaining neutral, the colonies in the east and west had to be declared neutral too; as a consequence of this policy, mercantile ships of all belligerents were freely admitted in the Indian harbors without too much fuss. Refueling and repairs were permitted. Warships were a different matter, of course; international treaties and agreements regulated the coaling and refitting of such vessels in times of war. This was important for the Sabang coaling station on the northernmost point of Sumatra, where coal from the Ombilin mines was readily available. A fairly large number of German merchantmen sought refuge in East Indian harbors where they awaited an opportunity to slip home if possible without meeting British warships. Quite a few of these ships stayed there for many years or even for the duration of the war. Some of these German vessels were handed over to the Dutch authorities as compensation for Dutch merchantmen torpedoed "by mistake" by German submarines in the North Sea or Atlantic.

The defense of the Indies was chiefly the duty of the Royal Netherlands Navy, not surprising in view of the enormous number of islands, large and small, of the archipelago. The main naval base was Soerabaja with dry docks, fuel, and munitions magazines and stores of all kinds. A number of smaller depots were located on other islands, and the telegraph connected most of the bases with headquarters, but certainly not all of them. In 1914 the Dutch naval force in the Indies consisted of a number of rather small but fairly modern armored cruisers, gunboats, torpedo boats, minelayers, and even a few submarines. The Gouvernements Marine (Netherlands Indies Government Navy), had a large number of ships, old and new, but they were only lightly armed and intended for police duties in the first place, though they were also useful for supporting services.

The Nederlandsch-Indisch Leger (NIL, Netherlands Indies Army) had been set up in 1832 and was initially composed of Europeans, professional soldiers contracting for long terms of service. Between 1816 and 1900 no less than eighty-four thousand men and five thousand officers were sent out to the Indies. Many foreigners served in this NIL for different, chiefly private reasons, just as in the French Foreign Legion, and it was never a problem to find enough suitable candidates for filling the ranks of officers and noncommissioned officers. Even in the upper ranks above major, foreigners were admitted without any misgivings. The brother of the German WW I general Erich von Ludendorff served in the NIL! On the other hand, for the lower ranks, finding enough of the right men in Europe became an ever-greater problem during the second half of the nineteenth century. To fill the ranks, more and more indigenous men had to be contracted. Ambonese and Menadonese were clear favorites as fighters, the more so because they generally were Protestant Christians. Later, Javanese and Madoerese took service in larger numbers, also being valued as good fighters and proving their mettle in the Atjeh War of the early twentieth century. The governor-general in Batavia was the supreme commander of all armed forces in the East Indies. In 1914 no real danger was presented by the few German settlements in China and in the Pacific, but Japan was thought to cast an envious eye on the East Indies with their abundance of strategic materials for modern warfare. Japan was already active in China and Korea and was readily supposed to be willing to stimulate local unrest in Malaya and the Dutch East Indies for its own purposes. In the end the safety of the Indies was never challenged by any foreign power during World War I, but the problems of equipping and manning the fleet and the army, with the mother country at the other end of the globe and almost out of reach, grew by leaps and bounds.[1]

After the mobilization the Dutch mercantile marine was held back in home waters, and it took some time before ships were again venturing out into the now-unfriendly seas. In the first year of the war the sea lanes to the Indies remained relatively open, although stray mines did cause loss of ships and crews. However, the British gradually imposed all kinds of checks and controls to make sure that their blockade of Germany was not evaded by way of the neutral Netherlands with its large mercantile marine. The unlimited submarine warfare as announced by the Germans later in 1917 meant an almost-complete stop for the mercantile marines of all neutral powers.

The telegraph connection between the mother country and the colony was either in British or German-American hands, but the latter cable—running from Menado (Celebes) to Yap Island (a German possession since 1899) and from there to Guam (originally Spanish, American since 1898) and thence to Hawaii and San Francisco—was cut by the British at the beginning of the hostilities. The British cables remained open for Dutch messages, but the cable authorities forbade the use of secret codes and British messages, of course, had priority. And all neutral messages passing through the British cables were sure to be read by the British authorities! Already in 1913 the first plans for a connection with Batavia by radiotelephony had been ventilated, making use of three intermediate stations between Amsterdam and Batavia, but nothing came of it. The war changed this, of course, and steps were taken to establish such a connection. However, it took many years before the line could be opened, too late for war service but a noble experiment.[2]

A WARTIME ECONOMY

An export-oriented country such as the Dutch East Indies was severely hit by the outbreak of war in 1914. Some good markets for tobacco and coffee like Germany and central Europe became hard to reach as a result of the British blockade of German—Hamburg and Bremen—and Austrian—Triëst—ports. And different and often-conflicting divergence of views between British and Dutch authorities of what constituted contraband severely hampered the transit traffic between the colony and Germany by way of the neutral Netherlands. Quinine, for instance, could be peacefully used as a medicine against malaria in the first place but could also serve the German armies in the waterlogged trenches and fields of Flanders against this sickness. And 96 percent of the world's quinine came from the factory in Bandoeng, causing many problems between the Indian supplier, the Dutch government, and British authorities. Shipping charges multiplied as insurance rates shot up, and losses of neutral shipping to mines and German submarines also contributed to the mounting problems of getting exports from the Indies to the traditional markets in Europe. Fortunately, new markets could be opened, first and foremost in the United States. Shipping to the American West Coast was not liable to be ruptured by warfare after the German cruiser *Emden*, operating in the Indian Ocean and the Pacific, had been destroyed by British forces. The Java-China-Japan Lijn, the daughter company of the two largest Dutch shipping companies and operating in the Pacific, opened a direct weekly line from the East Indies to San Francisco in 1915, a sure sign of the shift to other markets.

Every war will be accompanied by an artificially enlarged supply of money, resulting in serious inflation and less buying power for a given amount of money. In the Indies a certain panic was visible when imported goods were getting scarce or were stockpiled in the hope for better prices, while export goods had to be stored in the ports when shipping was unavailable. Factories in Java and Sumatra had to lower their production as a result of the scarcity of imported hardware and raw materials and consequently had to reduce their labor force. Real wages declined and widespread poverty was visible among the indigenous population without monetary reserves. However, the upper echelons of society, the banks and big industry, did make exorbitant profits with the high prices that could be asked for imported goods, while wages of the laborers remained low. The state budget was inflated too, showing a growing deficit that could only be eliminated to some extent by a new income tax that was shifting the main burden away from the Javanese to the European population. New loans had to make up the deficits, enlarging the state debt, but could easily be serviced when exports really exploded in the 1920s. New products such as rubber and oil were in great demand with the automobile industry, so exports to the United States expanded. Though before WW I these freights to America amounted to only 4 percent of the total exports of the Dutch East Indies, in 1925 they were good for 14 percent and still growing.[3]

The late 1920s were to be the golden years of the Dutch East Indies. Just as had happened during the years 1901–1914, sugar production doubled again between 1914 and 1928 to a maximum of 3 million tons, good for about 10 percent of the world production. On the other hand, the export of coffee declined after the government cultures had been abolished, although new markets were opened in the United States, France, and Denmark. A boom in rubber developed in the 1920s, culminating in the years 1925–1927, when almost one-third of the total value of exports from the Dutch East Indies was the result of sales of rubber. Total value of exports from the Indies in current prices was still growing despite the war, but only slowly from 674.1 million guilders in 1914 to 676.1 million in 1918, with an intermediate high of 865.4 million in 1916. The first postwar year (1919) showed a virtual explosion to 2,152 million guilders, and the level remained high until 1930, when the value of exports (in current prices) was still 1,160.5 million, with a high of 1,801.5 million in 1925. For comparison, figures in 1913 prices may be more illuminating: from 641.9 million guilders in 1914 down to 447.7 million in 1918 with an intermediate high of 779.3 million in 1916. The first postwar year also showed a sudden rise to 1,138.6 million; again the level remained high, at 1,511.7 million guilders, until 1930.[4]

Rubber (*Hevea Brasiliensis*) was a special case, as contrary to other exports more than half of the total rubber production did not originate from large European or American-owned plantations. In 1925, for instance, 242,000 tons of rubber were exported, of which 19 percent came from Java, 25 percent from large European-owned plantations on Sumatra, and 56 percent from smaller plantations and gardens on Sumatra, owned by small Indonesian or Chinese entrepreneurs. Total value of rubber exports amounted to 582 million guilders.[5]

All through the 1920s the bubble continued. Import prices were high but exports kept growing in tonnage and value. Money was abundant, although the native population did not share equally in the wealth. Since 1900 the European group of the population had grown steadily from 90,800 souls to 240,000 in 1930, and as they tended to fill the better-paid positions in society, this gradual shift came at the expense of the indigenous and Chinese sections of the population. New was the gradual appearance of an Indonesian intelligentsia, having studied at universities in the Netherlands or at the Bandoeng Technical College, who became the center of a movement toward emancipation for Indonesians and Indo-Europeans at the same time. Yet, despite their education and their knowledge of how society should work for them too, access to the upper level of Indian society remained restricted. On the other hand, in the more remote areas of the country, there was dissatisfaction with the breaking up of traditional society as a result of the economic changes and the move toward the construction of a westernized society. The dialogue between the several groups and the government was difficult, slow, and unrewarding. Hardliners on the right wing of the European groups reacted with suppression (and force, if need be), and this led to social unrest, not only in the big cities but also in the countryside where communist agitators were active. In 1920 and 1922 strikes of government employees and railway workers occurred in several places and had to be stamped out with force.

To give an outlet to these movements the Volksraad (People's Council) was set up in 1918, with European, Indo-European, and Indonesian members appointed by the governor-general, but as a body without any real power. Advice could be given and petitions submitted, but no decisive power was granted to the Volksraad. By 1928 it became clear that the more right-wing parties were gaining ground and that associatie (association), as it was called, meaning the collaboration of the several population groups toward a more multiracial form of government, had not been accomplished despite attempts of several more liberal governors-general. The majority of the European group leaned more and more to a strict separation between their group and the still-small body of Indonesian nationalists, who were now starting to work toward an Indonesia without any European influence. Yet apartheid was not officially allowed and hardly visible in Indian society, which was a mixed society without a real color bar, where everybody black, brown, yellow, or white could be a member of the same association or club. "Totoks," who were imported Europeans, mixed blood Indo-Europeans, who were born in the Indies, and educated, well-to-do Chinese and Indonesians could and did get on in daily life very well together. Only one exclusive club in Soerabaja was open to whites only.[6]

THE JAVA STATE RAILWAYS DURING THE WAR

Railway construction on Java had slowed during the war because of lack of materials. Until then, steel rails had been imported chiefly from Belgium and Germany, and as the heavy industry of the southern neighbor was now under German occupation, supplies from factories such as Cockerill of Liège had dried up. German works were still delivering rails to the Netherlands, but war orders for the German armies always had precedence. On the other hand, the Netherlands held a trump card, as Germany was very much dependent on the supply of foodstuffs from its small western neighbor now that the British blockade became stricter and more strangling. Meat, butter, potatoes, and produce could be exchanged for steam locomotives, steel rails, and other hardware. All locomotives constructed for the Dutch East Indian railways by Hartmann and Hanomag during the war had to be sent overland by rail or river boat, dismantled into many parts and shipped in Dutch vessels from Rotterdam or Amsterdam, as the German ports were now unavailable. Werkspoor-Amsterdam, although a Dutch factory, was highly dependent on the German industry for the supply of parts such as wheels and axles, but despite trouble in getting these materials regularly the company was able to deliver some steam locomotives to the JSS and the SSS lines. Apparently, the British authorities did not consider these cargoes as contraband, or was it that they could find no use for these at the front as being all on the 1,067-mm gauge? A giant 2-12-2 tank engine of the Javanic class was not easy to use anywhere else than on its intended rails in Java. Not so lucky were the State Railways in the Netherlands in 1915 when fourteen large 4-6-4 tanks, constructed by Beyer Peacock and standing ready in Hull to be shipped to Rotterdam, were requisitioned by the British government and sent to the front in France to help the Railway Operating Division with the transport of men and materials. After the end of the war they remained in France and had long lives there.[7]

AMERICAN INDUSTRY GETS A CHANCE

The Javanics, the giant 2-12-2 tanks of the Java State Railways, although powerful enough for the intended services, had not proven to be ideal for the severe curves of the Preanger line in West Java and had to be transferred to other lines. And as traffic continued to grow on the lines to Bandoeng despite the war circumstances, the 2-6-6-0 tanks were still needed for the heavy trains, often in pairs. The JSS authorities had no other choice than going back to the articulated Mallet system to be able to have eight driven axles with the necessary ability to negotiate curves of 150 m radius, despite the continuing problems with the tightness of the steam pipes between high- and low-pressure cylinders. As all traditional European locomotive works were somehow affected by the war and unable to promise delivery on accepted new orders, the United States, still neutral at the time, came to the rescue as a possible supplier. The American Locomotive Company (ALCO) of Schenectady, New York, was approached and it offered a big 2-8-8-0 Mallet engine with separate tender on two bogies, a typical American locomotive with bar frames, a big boiler with superheater, and piston valves for the high-pressure cylinders only. Total weight was over 92 tons, the maximum permissible on the mountain lines, with another 41 tons for a fully loaded tender. Their maximum speed was set at a low 40 km per hour, no problem as they were chiefly meant for slogging heavy freights over the gradients between Poerwakarta and Padalarang. The order for eight of these monsters was placed early in 1916 and six

months later all were in service. They had some mechanical problems at
first, especially fractures in the frames, but in general they did what was
expected of them. Twelve more, with some modifications and a weight of
96.6 tons, were ordered in 1919 and delivered by ALCO in the next year.
Two firemen were needed to feed the grates of these giants and so two of
the Mallets were equipped with an American Duplex mechanical stoker,
but with no great success. These 2-8-8-0s were the largest and heaviest
locomotives that could be accommodated within the strict limits of the
loading gauge of the Javanese 1,067-mm lines.

In general the American Mallets were satisfactory but too slow to
be used for passenger trains, so in 1923 JSS ordered from Hanomag three
more of the same type but with many modifications and improvements,
among them plate frames instead of the troublesome bar frames, and they
could indeed be used for faster trains on the mountains. Hartmann followed with three in the next year, and finally Werkspoor-Amsterdam
completed the order with four more in 1925, the biggest and heaviest steam

locomotives ever constructed by this relatively small Dutch factory. All big Mallets were coal burners, although some experiments were done with oil firing, but without success, as the copper fireboxes easily corroded. During the war the JSS switched almost completely to Ombilin coal, as imports—coal brought in as ballast—were scarce due to a lack of shipping. Later, the Boekit Asam mines of South Sumatra also supplied fuel, but its coal proved to be somewhat inferior to the Ombilin product and was mostly used for the production of briquettes. In 1925 a factory was opened in Tandjong Priok where small coal and coal dust from Boekit Asam was compressed with tar and waste oil into briquettes.[8]

STILL MORE NEW ENGINES

For freight trains on the more level lines the trusted 2-6-0 tanks were getting too slow and feeble and double heading had to be used, making traction expensive. Thoughts went out to a Consolidation, a 2-8-0 engine with separate tender, and Hanomag was charged with the design in 1913. The first six were delivered just before the outbreak of war in 1914, and they proved able to haul trains of 550 tons with ease on moderate gradients. They had superheaters and large grates high over the driving wheels to be able to use the coal from the Ombilin mines and briquettes. Total weight of the engine was around 48 tons. Hartmann constructed other engines of the same design, and in 1915 SLM-Winterthur and Werkspoor-Amsterdam supplied seventeen more. As these engines fitted the bill exactly, thirteen more from Hanomag and Werkspoor followed in 1921 after the end of the war, making a grand total of forty-two of these versatile units.

With these Consolidations the buying spree of the JSS was not over yet: for switching duties in the classification yards of Batavia and Soerabaja twelve 2-8-2 tanks, JSS 1401–1424, weighing 68.6 tons, were ordered in 1921 from Hanomag, based on the successful Consolidations. Werkspoor also built twelve of the same, one of them, JSS 1414, being its five hundredth engine that left the Amsterdam works with some pomp and circumstance in 1922. Back in 1916 the JSS had ordered from SLM-Winterthur fourteen 4-6-4 superheated tank engines, weighing 63 tons, for suburban traffic around the big cities of Java. Maximum speed was 80 km per hour and they were quite successful in these services. Just as Werkspoor in Amsterdam, SLM in neutral Switzerland also had great troubles in obtaining the necessary materials and so delivery of the first fourteen engines had to be postponed until 1918. More engines of this JSS Series 1101–1139 were supplied by Werkspoor in 1920. The last five came from an unusual source, the British firm of Armstrong Whitworth & Company, in 1921. This company was better known for its war material, guns, munitions, armor plate, and such, but in 1919 the firm converted a former shell factory at Scotswood near Newcastle into a locomotive works. So far it had never supplied steam locomotives to either the Netherlands or its Asian colony, but now the war was over it had to look for new fields of business. And to keep the new locomotive department going in a world of overproduction, it was willing to offer a very competitive price, hence the order from JSS.[9]

Even when the 4-6-4 tanks of the 1100 class were still being delivered, JSS was already ordering thirty heavier—79 against 63 tons—tank engines with the same wheel arrangement from Henschel of Kassel. They were thoroughly modern engines with a good turn of speed—90 km per hour—and enough space for water and coal, but at the expense of a fairly high axle loading of 12 tons. After the thirty engines from Henschel, the firms of Hartmann and Esslingen enlarged this JSS Series 1300 to fifty-eight locomotives. Werkspoor complained that this large order went to German works, which could offer extremely low prices because of the current overproduction in Germany and the problems with the devaluation of the German mark. This deflated prices so much that Werkspoor simply couldn't compete. All these Indian tanks had long lives and many of them served well into the 1970s.

An unexpected windfall for JSS was an offer from Hartmann in 1920. That firm was left with ten 2-8-2 Mikado engines of 53 tons with separate bogie tenders on its hands, ordered by the Hedjaz Railway Damascus–Medina in the Ottoman (Turkish) Empire in the Middle East. At the end of World War I, that empire had disintegrated and the line was almost completely wrecked by the activities of British-Arab guerilla groups, among whom T. E. Lawrence and his Camel Corps are possibly the best known. These units had been built to a gauge of 1,050 mm (3 ft 5.3 in), a gauge only used on this and some other lines in Syria, but the small difference with the Indian standard gauge made conversion to 1,067 mm fairly simple. Most other vital dimensions were already in accordance with JSS specifications so they, JSS 1501–1510, performed well on Java and were long-lasting. The JSS was happy with a good bargain.

Even with all these new and thoroughly modern and advanced engines, JSS still needed more specialized traction for the mountain lines in West Java. The American and European 2-8-8-0 Mallets were able to cope with the traffic but were slow, and moreover their axle loading of between 12 and 13 tons was on the high side for some bridges and viaducts where only 11 tons could be allowed. Bridge strengthening was in progress but would take some time and so JSS decided to go for a 2-6-6-0 Mallet engine, more powerful than the tanks of the same axle arrangement and with separate tender to lower the weight of the engine. In 1927 SLM-Winterthur turned out the first of sixteen very modern 2-6-6-0 Mallets, and in 1928 Werkspoor supplied another fourteen to the same designs. Their total weight was 72.6 tons with an axle loading of 11.7 tons, still a bit high but low enough to be tolerated. They all came with the characteristic tender with rounded undersides as developed by Werkspoor to prevent accumulation of dirt and rust in the square corners of the older tenders. The locomotives of JSS Series 1601–1630 were chiefly intended for heavy freights but were also used for passenger trains, although their maximum speed of 55 km per hour was in reality too low for those services. Moreover, at that speed their running was very unpleasant but despite this handicap they served a long time. Much later, one of the Werkspoor units was returned to the home country and is now exhibited in the Railway Museum in Utrecht.

HIGHER SPEED MEANS NEW LOCOMOTIVES

With the opening of the JSS line Cheribon–Kroja in 1917, the direct connection between Batavia and Soerabaja came one step nearer. However, the section Djokja–Solo, although now also with a third rail in Indian standard gauge inside the broad-gauge NIS tracks, remained a bottleneck, as all stations and halts had to be passed with a speed of no more than 40 km per hour. After lengthy negotiations with the NIS, a solution was reached. That company was to construct a standard-gauge line between the two cities next to its existing broad-gauge line but without any actual physical connection, permitting higher speeds. The NIS leased the line to the state and in 1929 it became operational. For many years already the ideal of the JSS had been to provide a train that could cover the distance (821 km after the Cheribon–Kroja line was opened) between Java's two

Werkspoor-Amsterdam was rightly proud of the impressive Pacifics of the 1000 class constructed for the JSS. Here Nr. 1015 is readied in the yards of the company's works in Amsterdam. Photo by L. Derens, 1921. (Author's collection)

most important cities in one day, the Eendaagsche (Single Day Express). The new separate standard-gauge line along the NIS tracks was intended for that service, but some curves elsewhere on the lines had to be straightened to permit higher speeds. From 1929 travel time between Batavia and Soerabaja was thirteen and a half hours, in 1934 shortened to twelve hours, and finally in 1939 it was eleven and a half hours, making the Eendaagsche the world's fastest train on the 1,067-mm gauge, with speeds of more than 100 km per hour on some sections.

With the future coming of the Eendaagsche in mind, the JSS technical staff in 1916–1917 designed a Super Pacific, a heavier edition of the Swiss 4-6-2s of Series 700. Together with Professor I. Franco of Delft Technical University and Werkspoor-Amsterdam, this design was worked out, which resulted in a four-cylinder compound 4-6-2 with 1,600-mm diameter driving wheels, an axle load of 12.2 tons, and total weight of 65.3 tons, of which 36.7 were available for adhesion. Modern features were a superheater and feedwater heater plus a bogie tender with a capacity of 5 tons of coal and 20 m^3 of water. They were meant to be the showpiece for JSS and Werkspoor, but in daily traffic they turned out to be a bit disappointing, as their running at high speeds was somewhat unstable. However, small improvements in balancing obviated most of these problems and the twenty engines of the JSS Series 1000 became the mainstay of heavy passenger services of the company. They hauled trains of 300–400

Pacific Nr. 1020 of Java State Railways at Kroja in 1926. The boiler cladding of "Russian iron" is gleaming in the sunlight. (SNR collection)

tons on level lines at 100 km per hour, with ease, and were regularly used for the Eendaagsche between Soerabaja and Poerwokerto via Kroja and Proepoek, where a 700 Pacific took over for the last leg of the journey from Proepoek to Batavia by way of Cheribon.[10]

THE QUEST FOR A UNIVERSAL LOCOMOTIVE

At the very end of the period covered in this chapter a new universal locomotive for passenger and freight services was found necessary, with an axle loading of no more than 10 tons to ensure that the engines could be used all over the Java network. Older engines that were nearing the end of their lives could be replaced by these new and up-to-date machines. The result of these thoughts were the units of the JSS 1700 Series, 2-6-2 tanks, of which the first five came from Hohenzollern in 1929, followed by seven more in 1930 from the same works and eight more from Borsig. For the Zuid-Sumatra Spoorwegen (South Sumatra Railways), twenty-three of the same 1700 class were turned out by Werkspoor—eleven engines— and Hanomag—twelve units—in 1929 and 1930, respectively. Three others went to the SSW on Sumatra's West Coast, the coal railway. These 2-6-2 tanks were the last new steam engines built for the State Railways of the Dutch East Indies. The worldwide crisis that began in 1929 made new acquisitions unnecessary, and many of the newer engines were

One of the "universal" 2-6-2 tanks of Java State Railways Nr. 1711, constructed by Hohenzollern and delivered in 1930, one of the last new engines for the JSS. She was photographed in Tjimahi, near Bandoeng in the spring of 1931. Other members of this class were constructed by Borsig and Werkspoor. (Remmo Statius Muller collection)

mothballed in the hope of a brighter future. In the next chapter it will be seen whether this ever happened.

SURVEY OF STEAM LOCOMOTIVES OF THE DUTCH EAST INDIES

By 1942, altogether 1,504 steam locomotives, large and small, had been supplied to public railways and tramways of the Dutch East Indies, of which the Chemnitz firm Hartmann constructed almost one-third: 458 engines, or 30.4 percent of the total. Werkspoor-Amsterdam came in second with 240 units, or 15.9 percent, a good score as its first delivery to the Indies dated from 1899 only. The two other Dutch factories, Backer & Rueb and Du Croo & Brauns were good for thirty-four and six engines, respectively, but Du Croo & Brauns will figure strongly as a more important supplier in the chapter on industrial and plantation locomotives. Beyer Peacock of Manchester came third with 181 engines, or 12 percent, closely followed by Hanomag-Hannover with 175 locomotives, or 11.6 percent. Hohenzollern-Düsseldorf supplied 107 engines—7.1 percent—and deliveries by Esslingen totaled 101 units, or 6.7 percent. Of the many German works only Hartmann, Hanomag, and Hohenzollern outshopped substantial numbers of engines for the Indies, with Maffei of München conspicuously absent, while other big firms such as Henschel and Schwartzkopff each had a minor share only. Curious also is that of the numerous big Belgian factories, only Cockerill was charged with construction of small engines for the Solo Valley Works and nothing more. French factories were completely absent. It should also be noted that from

Britain only Sharp Stewart and Beyer Peacock were big in business in the Indies. Apart from Fox Walker, smaller British firms do not figure at all and larger ones—such as Neilson and Dübs, both of Glasgow, or Robert Stephenson & Co. of Newcastle—are almost totally absent. Apparently, once the Java State Railways and the Technisch Bureau of the Ministry for the Colonies in The Hague were happy with a supplier, they clung to the choice and did not venture into unknown worlds. Only in the twentieth century we see that terms of delivery and prices begin to play a more important role in the choice of a factory, and then orders are often split between several firms.[11]

THE JAVA STATE RAILWAYS IN FIGURES

The growth of the network and the corresponding services is closely reflected in the numbers of staff. In 1914 total staff, European and Indonesian, on Java and Sumatra, counted close to 22,000 men and a few women. During the war years still more lines were opened and services extended, and in 1919 personnel stood at 31,000 but grew to no less than 45,000 in 1921. The crisis of the early 1920s meant a reduction to 38,000, but in 1928 the total number had climbed again to around 40,000, which made the JSS one of the greatest employers of Java and Sumatra. Since 1912 the lower—mostly indigenous—ranks of the staff had been organized in groups according to the kind of work—for example, traction and maintenance, train services, and such—and representatives of these groups served as spokesmen for the members in the contacts with the directorate. In the later 1920s, reflecting the movement of the Indonesian population toward more influence and greater responsibilities, several independent labor unions had been started and they had gradually taken over the duties of the earlier group representatives. A real labor union was the Spoorbond (Rail Union) of the intermediate ranks of the staff, while the higher echelons of the staff—chiefly Europeans—were represented by four unions grouped after the sort of work: administration, track and bridges, traction-rolling stock and maintenance, and movement, the running of the trains. Headquarters of JSS were located in Bandoeng since 1924, housed in a never-finished hotel with several additions, forming a real rabbit warren for the newcomer and occasional visitor. Houses for staff were built where nothing was available commercially and rented out at reasonable rates. In the bigger cities and at the chief workshops and stations doctors were appointed to provide medical care to the staff free of charge, and a company hospital was set up in Bandoeng.

Passenger traffic had become more important in the early 1900s and had reached a high of 40 million passengers in 1914. During the war it had grown to some 51 million in 1918 and after the end of the war it surged to

The vast Soerabaja Sidotopo freight yard in the 1920s. A train of empty ballast wagons is standing close by with an ancient Sharp Stewart 2-4-0 at the head. The high rack for firewood is conspicuous on the short tender. (Author's collection)

around 71 million in 1920, an all-time high. After that year the number of passengers declined somewhat to 47 million but remained at that level for many years to come. In 1920, a record year, more than 66 million passengers traveled third class, 2.5 million in second, and only a half million in first, bringing in total revenues of more than 26 million guilders.

The figures for freight did not really follow those of passenger traffic. Just over 6 million tons of freight were carried in 1918; this number grew to near 7 million in 1921 but declined to 6.5 million tons in 1924. Total revenue from all kinds of freight stood at just over 43.6 million guilders; after a high of almost 70 million guilders, it declined to 59 million in 1924.[12]

In the 1920s it became clear that the existing regulations for railways and tramways no longer covered the actual situation. Some tramways, still listed as such, had assumed a more railway-like identity and indeed were operated as railways. New regulations were clearly necessary, and with the railway law of 1928, a new set of rules was published. Three categories were now distinguished: city tramways, railways of the second class, and railways of the first class. City tramways were few and existed only in the larger towns. The former country tramways, sometimes hundreds of kilometers long, were now classified as railways of the second class, together with a fairly large number of light railways, formerly worked as tramways. Railways of the first class were all mainlines plus, in due course, some former tramway lines such as the Semarang-Cheribon after its substantial upgrading. For city tramways the maximum speed was set at 20 km per hour, and municipal administrations were allowed to add other regulations. For second-class railways the speeds were more than 20 and less than 60 km per hour and were subject to other regulations for freight traffic, too much to elaborate here. On railways of the first class the maximum permitted speed was 60 km per hour, soon raised to 75 and in practice even more. The governor-general could give permission for higher speeds where possible and necessary. All existing lines of the JSS, so far worked as tramways, now became railways of the second class, and of the private companies the lines were now listed as second class with speeds set between 20 and 60 km per hour, depending on the quality of the tracks. The higher speeds were only allowed on lines that had already been upgraded with heavier rails and better alignments. Some of these, such as the SCS mainline and also Soerabaja–Goendih of the NIS, were still later uprated to first class with maximum speeds in the region of 100 km per hour.[13]

A heavy mixed train of the Semarang-Cheribon near Gempol on its long—originally 243 kilometer—mainline. The engine is one of the twenty-seven powerful 0-4-0 engines with separate tender, supplied by Hartmann between 1908 and 1913. Photo from the 1920s. (Author's collection)

THE PRIVATE RAILWAYS AND TRAMWAYS

With traffic booming all over Java, not only were the Java State Railways doing well but also the private railways and tramways saw their revenues increasing. Though most of these companies' networks were in place in 1914, with only small additions during the war, they continued the

Though other compa-
nies ordered new and
heavier locomotives, the
Samarang-Joana still val-
ued its small 0-6-0 tanks,
of which Hartmann
supplied twelve units
between 1898 and 1902.
(Author's collection)

upgrading to higher standards with heavier steel rails, bridge strengthening, and extension of yards and stations. As most of the lines had been
built to the same loading gauge as the State Railways to make through
freight traffic possible, the cooperation between JSS and the tramway
companies grew apace. The Semarang-Cheribon (SCS) was one of the
best examples of the new cooperation.

Traffic surged and in 1927 the NIS carried almost 3.5 million passengers on both broad- and standard-gauge lines, maybe not too much when
compared to the 45.5 million carried by the JSS, but more than enough to
make a profit. Compared to the NIS the private tramways did even better, with the SCS at almost 7 million and the SJS still higher at 13 million
passengers carried in that same year. Freight presented the same picture:
NIS transported about 1.5 million tons of various freight in 1927, the SCS
only a fraction less at 1.2 million tons. Other private tramways carried less
but enough to make a profit from their limited length of track.

For its headquarters the NIS built a large and well-equipped building
in Semarang during the 1920s, executed in the popular "colonial style"
with whitewashed walls, generous windows, and large overhangs to close
out the sun as much as possible in an era when air-conditioning was not
yet known. Other companies followed, as has been noted in the case of
the SCS with its new headquarters in Tegal.

Generous dividends made shareholders happy and willing to invest
more if necessary. Between 1922 and 1928 the NIS owners got an annual

average dividend of 11 percent with a high of 17 percent in 1928. The Semarang-Cheribon was a bit less exuberant with dividends ranging from 7 to 12.5 percent in 1928, and most of the private companies gave about the same results. Some fared worse, however, such as the Oost Java Steam Tram that did not average more than 5 percent and the Madoera company that came out with an average of about 4 percent. Still, even these companies at the lower end of the scale paid out.

The Semarang-Cheribon was originally a simple steam tram company but generally with tracks on its own right of way, not along existing roads, and the company was soon busy with strengthening its mainline to be able to accommodate heavier sugar trains. Passenger traffic was improved too, and in 1914, together with JSS, through trains Batavia–Cheribon–Semarang had been introduced with comfortable bogie coaches of both JSS and SCS. Engines were changed at Cheribon. New rolling stock was introduced after the end of World War I and for these trains heavier and more powerful locomotives were needed, as the ubiquitous Hartmann 0-4-0s with separate tenders were too slow. Hartmann supplied modern 4-6-0 engines with separate tenders for these services, the first of thirteen units arriving in 1922; Beyer Peacock of Manchester added six more in the same year. These were thoroughly modern locomotives, with outside cylinders, superheaters, and feedwater heaters, weighing 38.6 tons with 26.6 tons available for adhesion. Maximum speed was set at 75 km per hour but in service they proved able to reach much higher speeds. By then the

For the through traffic with the State Railways between Batavia and Semarang by way of Cheribon, the SCS needed more powerful locomotives and in 1922 ordered nineteen 4-6-0 units from Hartmann and Beyer Peacock, Nr. 214 being one of the English engines. These elegant engines were preferred for the passenger traffic and were most satisfactory. These would be the last engines ordered by the SCS. (Author's collection)

SCS line had acquired the status of a railway of the second class, allowing a service speed of 60 km per hour, and further upgrading made it possible to obtain the status of railway first class in 1935, with a maximum speed of 75 km per hour. Until the Japanese invasion, these 4-6-0s bore the brunt of the passenger traffic of the SCS.[14]

In the years after World War I the NIS also started a process of upgrading its broad-gauge mainline Semarang–Solo–Djokja. For the heavier and faster trains the existing 4-6-0 engines Nrs. 81–94, dating back to 1902, were slowly improved with new superheated boilers, piston valves, and other modern appliances to bring them up to date. Apparently, more powerful locomotives were needed, and in 1923 Hartmann supplied four modernized and faster units of the existing 4-6-0 type. They were meant for the express trains Semarang–Solo–Djokja and had a maximum speed of 90 km per hour. Semarang–Solo (108 km) took one hour and forty-five minutes, not bad but open for improvement later.

For the heavy sugar trains, the four 2-8-0 engines of 1912 were no longer enough, so the NIS ordered four more from Hartmann in 1922, all four arriving in Semarang just in time for the annual cane harvest. Trains of ninety-three four-wheeled freight cars could be handled by these Consolidations, the last four being equipped with electric headlights for night operations.[15]

For the Indian standard gauge (1,067-mm) lines, especially for the long Soerabaja–Goendih–(Semarang) line, the NIS company had already ten 4-6-0 engines with separate tenders from Beyer Peacock in service. After 1919 their numbers were strengthened with five units from Werkspoor and in 1921 with two more from Henschel and five more from Beyer Peacock. Still not enough, Henschel supplied three more of the same in 1922 followed by five more from Werkspoor in 1923. These thirty engines sufficed for these services until the end of the existence of the company in 1942.

NOTES

1. About the defense of the Indies, see Teitler, "Dutch East Indies." Also the history of the Government Marine in Wijn, *Tot in de verste uithoeken*.

2. Brink (ten) and Schell, *Geschiedenis van de Rijkstelegraaf*, 192–202.

3. Gonggrijp, *Schets ener economische geschiedenis*, 153–70.

4. Figures from Lindblad, "De Handel tussen Nederland en Nederlands-Indië," 279.

5. Figures from Gonggrijp, *Schets ener economische geschiedenis*, 169–70.

6. Jong (de), *De Waaier van het Fortuin*, 410–11, 447–506. Immigration figures from Bosma and Mandemakers, "Indiëgangers."

7. Statius Muller and Veenendaal, *De Nederlandse Stoomlocomotieven*, 214–15.

8. Oegema, *De stoomtractie*, 84–91. About the briquette factory, see Touwen, "Palembang en Djambi," 148. About ALCO, see Davies, *North American Steam Locomotive Builders*, 22–26.

9. About the locomotive side of Armstrong Whitworth & Company, see Lowe, *British Steam Locomotive Builders*, 27–30.

10. Oegema, *De stoomtractie*, 178–92.

11. Figures adapted from Oegema, *De stoomtractie*, 221.

12. Figures from Reitsma, *Gedenkboek der Staatsspoor- en Tramwegen*, 169–87.

13. Beyen, "De nieuwe Spoor- en Tramwegwetgeving voor Nederlandsch-Indië."

14. Oegema, *De stoomtractie*, 128.

15. Ibid., 47.

This is how many people will remember traveling on a slow train through Java. At every halt, local women went along the train peddling their wares, drinks, and food. No glass in the windows and only shutters to keep out rain and sun. (SNR collection)

TRAVEL IN THE TROPICS— 13
ELECTRIFICATION

13

EXPERIENCES OF TRAVELERS

Many travelers have left sometimes-vivid descriptions of train rides on Java and Sumatra, both positive and negative. To be expected, most of these stories were written by European travelers, not by the thousands of indigenous train riders. Most stories describe travel in first or second class; only very few are from third-class passengers. In the early days, even first-class travel could be hot and uncomfortable, although the shutters in the window did allow some draft in, mixed with smoke and cinders. Only in the late 1920s and 1930s were coaches in the upper classes completely closed and equipped with fans and even a primitive form of air-conditioning (cooling by ice blocks). Restaurant and buffet cars were then carried in the more important trains as well, making long-distance traffic more pleasant.

An exalted visitor in 1893 was Archduke Franz Ferdinand of Austria, the one who was murdered in Sarajevo in June 1914, who came for a prolonged hunting tour on Java. After being received ceremonially by the directors of the Java State Railways on his arrival in Tandjong Priok, he traveled by train over the island in the official directors' carriage—built by J. J. Beijnes of Haarlem in 1891—with several first-class carriages for his retinue and a couple of vans for his armory. He shot at least eight crocodiles near Batavia and later in the Preanger Highlands five monkeys, five deer, and some birds. He regretted that he had not been able to bag a couple of tigers! At the end of his visit before boarding the Austrian armored cruiser *Kaiserin Elisabeth* that was to bring him to Pola, the Austrian naval base near Triëst, the august visitor expressed his satisfaction with the arrangements provided for him by the Java State Railways. His equerry Prince de Wurmbrand Stuffarth presented a purse with 500 guilders (equal to $200 then and $5.650 in today's money) to be distributed over the crews of locomotives and trains that had served him. The head of the Java State Railways at the time, Dirk R. J. Baron van Lynden (1850–1930), was elevated to knight of the Austrian Leopold Order.[1]

Of course, Austrian archdukes were no ordinary travelers, and the common man was not wont to expect luxuries as provided for Franz Ferdinand, but in the early twentieth century the first-class carriages of the JSS were comfortable enough, as described by Dutch world traveler François van Hoogstraten in February 1914. On the sixth of that month he rode from Batavia to Bandoeng via Buitenzorg, where he visited the world-famous botanical garden, and commented: "Beautiful train ride. I was sitting at the best side of the train and enjoyed the gorgeous views of the land of the Preanger, the panorama of the Leles plain with straight ahead the black Goentoer mountain with its top in the clouds. [February 9, from Bandoeng] By train to Djokja. Between Tjibatoe and Tasikmalaja the line is winding in continuous curves down the Preanger Mountains, one of the most beautiful sections of the line.... To Maos the train crossed the plain at high speed."[2]

There were other opinions, though. When Dominique Berretty, a colorful journalist and founder of the press agency Aneta in Batavia, was obliged to travel between Batavia and Soerabaja in the 1920s, he much preferred going by boat if he had time. In the trains there was "only nasi goreng [fried rice] and cinders," while on the KPM ships the kitchen was better and there were card tables. Later travelers in first class were more positive about the trains. J. J. Hangelbroek, a civil servant on his way to his post in 1937, commented: "The journey over Java from Batavia to Soerabaja was done by train, comfortably in the sleeping car cooled with ice blocks."[3]

On June 17, 1914, an anonymous traveler wrote about his experiences in a third-class wagon somewhere on Java in the *Algemeen Handelsblad*, the well-known Amsterdam newspaper: "In a small mostly enclosed compartment three apparently distinguished indigenous persons were seated. Here it was relatively clean and the occupants were behaving very respectably. In the other part of the same wagon, where some Chinese with native women, children and an immense number of packages, baggage, fruits and smelly eatables were nestling down, it was, to speak plainly, a pigsty."[4]

A different sort of third-class train travel was undertaken—forcibly—by well-known Dutch author Willem Walraven. He was living near Malang at the time but had to serve a prison term of one month on a trumped-up charge. In 1941 he was taken by train, in this case the Eendaagsche express, from Soerabaja to the prison near Bandoeng: "Seats had been reserved for us in a third-class carriage. It should really have been fourth class but as the Eendaagsche has only three classes, it was third class. The whole journey I remained seated at my window seat. I bought a loaf at the Solo stop and that was enough for the whole journey.

The train attendant brought iced coffee and ice water." Not bad for a pris-
oner traveling third class![5]

THE GROWTH OF TOURISM

It will come as no surprise that tourists started to flock to Java in the 1920s
and even in the 1930s despite the worldwide Depression. It was no longer
big-game hunters like Archduke Franz Ferdinand but rather well-heeled
Dutch, British, American, and Japanese tourists who wanted to see the
tropical splendors of Java, its active volcanoes, and the colorful village life
in the interior with the traditional quaint but pleasant gamelan music. Not
only Java was attracting these wealthy customers but also Sumatra, where
the Padang Highlands saw many visitors as well. The Batavian government saw possibilities here and actively supported a Travellers Official
Information Bureau in Weltevreden, the fashionable suburb of Batavia,
where all the better hotels were located. It was a not-for-profit organization with agencies in Soerabaja, Medan, and Bali, where all information
about hotels, railways, and other services was to be had free of charge. The
KPM, the packet navigation company with offices in practically all ports
of the archipelago, played much the same role, but, of course, primarily
to sell tickets for its own shipping lines.

This tramway line is
laid in elegant curves
through the Javanese
farmland, where local
farmers grow rice and
tobacco. Progress may
have been slow, but the
carriages were comfort-
able and adapted to the
tropical climate. The
inspection trolley of the
photographer is stand-
ing close to the track.
(SNR collection)

A steam tram of the Serajoe Valley Steam Tram is approaching somewhere in central Java along the Serajoe River. This—arranged—image gives a good impression of what train travel in Java in the early days really meant: not too fast but in a gorgeous landscape full of tropical wonders. Pre–World War I photo. (SNR collection)

Commercial travel agencies also smelled business here, and in 1930 the Nederlandsch-Indisch Reisbureau Lissone-Lindeman Ltd was founded with headquarters again in Weltevreden. This was a joint venture of two established travel agencies in the Netherlands—Lissone & Sons in Amsterdam, dating back to 1876, and the somewhat-younger agency of A. J. Lindeman of The Hague—who had merged in the late 1920s. Apart from Batavia-Weltevreden and Soerabaja, they had agencies in all major cities in the Netherlands and also in New York and San Francisco to cater for the American clientele. They offered the usual services: tickets and reservations for trains, buses, hotels, local tourist attractions, in short everything that a tourist might need in an unfamiliar country. Hotels in the bigger towns of Java were generally on the European plan and quite comfortable, with running water and electric lights, serving the needs of the often-demanding tourists. On Sumatra only Medan and Fort de Kock could offer similar luxuries. Elsewhere cheaper hotels, run by Chinese or Indonesian entrepreneurs, were available, offering simpler but cheaper accommodation.[6]

Java State Railways also recognized the need for catering to these affluent new customers, who were promising a new source of much-needed revenue. All kinds of folders and booklets in many languages were issued, extolling the attractions of Java that could be reached by train. Special tourist tickets for certain well-traveled routes were made available, giving a client the opportunity to stay some days at a place from where sights such as the Borobudur or one of the many active volcanoes could be reached. After his visit the traveler could continue his journey on the same ticket.

A new genus of tourist was the cruise passenger. In the 1930s the world tour became a new mode of seeing things, and between four and six international liners, chiefly British and American, provided tours to the East Indies every year, including road and rail tours over Java. A famous one was the worldwide cruise of an affluent British group with the Cunard liner *Franconia* in 1939. On arriving in Tandjong Priok on April 8, 1939, the eighty-six passengers disembarked for a trip over Java. In automobiles they went to Bandoeng and from there by train to Djokja. Two 4-4-0 locomotives of the 900 class hauled the luxury train consisting of a luggage van, a couple of first- and second-class carriages, two diners, the directors' carriage, and two open saloons. Quite a cavalcade![7]

STATIONS

For all travelers, young and old, rich and poor, their first sight of the railway was the station, but, different from Europe and the United States, even the early terminal stations in the Indies were plain and unimposing. The first NIS stations were simple in the extreme. Apart from Semarang, which got a solid but dull brick building, almost all others were cheap and only just enough to be able to function as a halt for the trains. Stations were clearly at the bottom of the list of necessary expenditures. Most buildings at halts were constructed with a wooden framework with bamboo fillings and only the more important ones sometimes boasted an awning to keep waiting passengers dry during the monsoon season and shaded the rest of the year. Most stations and the more important halts also had an office for the stationmaster, a telegraph room, a baggage room, sometimes a small post office, and in exceptional cases even waiting rooms with a buffet. No architects were involved in the designs of these buildings and generally the section engineer was responsible, but the director of the BOW had to approve the plans. Living quarters for the station master were sometimes provided in the station, or a house was built for him and his family when nothing was available locally.

Solo had a more substantial brick building—Solo-Balapan station— that was rebuilt in 1884; with the coming of the standard-gauge rails of

the JSS, it was remodeled again and adapted for the new user, but with an awkward layout so that JSS trains had to change direction here. That nuisance was eliminated in 1921 with a new layout, and in 1927 a striking new headhouse was added. The JSS also had its own station for trains from Soerabaja that went no farther than Solo, known as Solo-Djebres, where the soesoehoenan of Soerakarta used his own luxurious waiting room while waiting for the train. He had donated land for the construction of the railway line and the station, hence his preferential treatment.[8]

Djokjakarta had two stations, Toegoe for the JSS trains and Lempoe-jangan for the NIS, but since 1887 Djokja-Toegoe was the joint station for both companies. It had an island layout with a very wide platform, with all offices and services concentrated there and everything covered by a large iron overall roof resting on forty-four cast iron columns supplied by the Pletterij Enthoven of The Hague. In 1927 it was remodeled with a new Art-Deco frontage but the overall roof was left in place, even extended.[9]

Semarang started in 1867 with a terminus with two open platform tracks, situated in what was known as the swamp, not readily accessible from town. It served until 1914 when it was replaced by a new and more convenient edifice, Semarang-Tawang, closer by the city center. It was

designed and decorated by Dutch engineers and craftsmen. The roofs were covered with pantiles from Dutch-Limburg, while Werkspoor-Amsterdam supplied the iron roofs over the platforms. The Samarang-Joana had its own station, Semarang-Djoernatan, and the Semarang-Cheribon built Semarang-West, later called Semarang-Pontjol. Steam trams of both companies used the Djoernatan station. Travelers arriving from the West were advised to tell the guard of their Semarang-Cheribon train that they needed a sado—two-wheeled horse carriage—or a taxi to catch their connecting train of one of the other companies.[10]

In Batavia the first station, later known as Batavia-North, was opened by the NIS in the old town for the line that would eventually end in Buitenzorg. The line from the harbor of Tandjong Priok of the Bataviasche Havenwerken, later worked by the JSS, terminated in the town just south of this NIS station in a small edifice originally constructed for the Batavia Ooster Spoorweg, taken over by the JSS in 1898. This became known as Batavia-South. Slowly, more halts were opened following the gradual movement southward of the population of the capital, and by 1913, after the line to Buitenzorg had come into the hands of the JSS, everybody agreed that something had to be done to simplify

The new station of Cheribon of the Java State Railways, also used by the Semarang-Cheribon company for through traffic, although the SCS had a modest station of its own in the town. The JSS station was designed by the architect P. A. J. Moojen, one of the founders of the pleasant Dutch-Indian style of the early twentieth century. The building was opened in 1912 and is still in use. (Author's collection) and streamline railway operations in Batavia. In 1929 a large new station, called Batavia-Benedenstad (Lower Town), was opened to replace the old North and South stations. It was a terminus with twelve platform tracks for the electrified lines to Buitenzorg and Tandjong Priok, and for the steam-worked lines to Bandoeng and Soerabaja east and also to Merak on the western point of Java, where the ferry to South Sumatra berthed. Again, the design came from Dutch architects, the reinforced concrete piles rammed into the swampy ground on which the whole construction was resting came from the Netherlands, and all ironwork was supplied by the Pletterij Enthoven, which by then had moved to Delft.[11]

Generally, the State Railways followed the NIS in regard to station building: as simple and cheap as possible. Only much later, when traffic and revenues had grown sufficiently, bigger and more imposing buildings were erected. The same is true for the various steam tram companies that blossomed in the 1890s. Batavia is a special case: with the gradual extension of the built-up area of the city, new stations were laid out in subdivisions such as Weltevreden and Meester Cornelis, but it would take too much space to mention them all and they are indicated on the map. However, one exception might be made, the station of Tandjong Priok, the place where travelers arriving with the mail steamers of the Nederland and Rotterdamsche Lloyd companies had their first glimpse of Java.

Tandjong Priok got its first extremely simple station in 1885 with the opening of the port for traffic. It was brick-built and had a long iron roof over the two platforms for protection of arriving passengers. In the early twentieth century it was described by travelers as inconvenient, dirty, and flea-ridden, not fit as the first meeting place for Europeans with the Indies. In 1925 a grandiose new edifice was opened, a bit farther from the landing stage of the ships, but imposing with its gigantic overall roof and the clean white lines of the head house. The building was designed by the chief architect of JSS, C. W. Koch, constructed by the Hollandsche Beton Maatschappij, and rested on hundreds of reinforced concrete piles. The iron roof, spanning eight tracks, came from the Machinefabriek Braat of Soerabaja, a subsidiary of Braat of Delft. It was the largest overall roof ever constructed in the East Indies. The building boasted waiting rooms and buffets for "natives" or fourth-class passengers, another for third-class passengers, and one for first- and second-class travelers, with dining rooms for all three classes. Separate waiting rooms for ladies were also provided. Opening of the station was simultaneous with the opening of the first electric railway of the Indies between Meester Cornelis and Tandjong Priok, an occasion for great festivities.

Buitenzorg, as seat of the governor-general and the location of the world-famous Plantentuin (Botanical Garden), needed a more imposing building, but the impecunious NIS in 1873 provided only a simple construction. With the extension by the JSS of the line in the direction of Bandoeng, a new joint building became necessary, to be paid for by the JSS but erected on land ceded by the NIS. This new edifice of 1881 was brick and stone built and quite imposing, with a separate waiting room for the governor-general and a long iron roof over three tracks. The proprietor of the fashionable Hotel du Chemin de Fer nearby ran the station buffet to the satisfaction of the general public. In 1873, when the line opened, there were a meager two trains, but in 1929 electrification had reached Buitenzorg, with trains to Batavia every thirty minutes.

Bandoeng is a prime example of the way the State Railways extended, improved, and rebuilt a station when traffic warranted the financial outlay. In 1884, the year the station opened, Bandoeng was still a small and relatively unimportant town. After 1900 the town, helped in no small way by its pleasant climate, started on the road to national importance with the coming of all kinds of government offices and institutions, the Ministry of Verkeer en Waterstaat (Department of Traffic and Water Board), the headquarters of the State Railways, various industries, and last but not least the Technical College, later known as the Technical University. The population virtually exploded from 90,000 in 1920 to 157,000 nine years later, of which 18,000 were Europeans. The station followed this expansion with several additions to the original structure over the years, culminating in an extensive enlargement in 1909 after the opening of the new, shorter connection with Batavia via Padalarang in 1906. In 1929, as a result of the ongoing population explosion, a new and more radical rebuilding took place, including a modern front in Art Deco style with all sections featuring electric lights, reportedly the best of the Indies. Plans for a still more radical expansion were ready by 1939, but the coming war precluded execution. Altogether, the JSS had 357 stations and halts on Java in 1928, and sixty-six locomotive sheds. Comparable figures for the NIS were thirty-six stations and halts and twelve engine sheds.[12]

Of the Outer Possessions Sumatra followed the lead of Java closely. Stations there were simple in the extreme and the Deli Spoorweg Maatschappij (DSM) excelled in the use of galvanized iron imported from Britain for its stations. Other halts were constructed of wood with atap—palm leaf—roofs. Only toward the end of the nineteenth century some simple brick-built stations were erected and the old structures gradually removed or put to other uses. Only Medan had a more imposing building of stone and brick, with an iron overall roof. Originally, it was a kind of large two-story house, part station, part offices of the DSM; it was substantially enlarged in 1892 and again in 1910 when a second platform was laid out, connected to the main building by a pedestrian tunnel, the first in the Indies. In 1938 a last and more drastic rebuilding was undertaken, giving the station a completely different and strikingly modern frontage

with a clock tower, all in white brick and concrete—very impressive and fitting for a modern town such as Medan had become.[13]

The other railway companies operating in Sumatra generally all began their services with plain wooden stations and only upgraded these when warranted by the traffic. In many cases this upgrading never happened and the original constructions were used right until the end of the Dutch operation of the lines in 1942.

BRIDGES

An aspect of the railways of Java and Sumatra that travelers never failed to mention were the many spectacular bridges. Engineers in the Netherlands had been erecting fabulous bridges over the many branches of the Rhine and Meuse rivers and had become leaders of bridge construction in Europe. The bridge over the Lek, a branch of the Rhine, near Culemborg and opened in 1866, was for many years the longest span—155 m—in the world, while the one across the Hollands Diep, the estuary of the Meuse, opened in 1872, was the longest bridge in Europe with its fifteen spans of 100 m plus two drawbridges. In the East Indies, however, conditions were different. There were no problems with masses of ice that could completely block a river with huge ice dams as in the home country, but here *bandjirs*, the sudden disastrous flash floods after heavy rainstorms, had to

be reckoned with. A *bandjir* could flood a valley in a short time, destroying everything in its path, sweeping away bridges, roads, and buildings. Many bridges had to be rebuilt after such a disaster, some even more than once, and each time the bridge had to be lengthened to make more room for sudden floods, even when the water was not more than a trickle for most of the year. Another problem was the lack of skilled personnel, riveters and metal workers especially, in the early years. De Bordes had used his bridge wagon to obviate this lack of skilled workers with some success during the construction of the first railway in the East Indies in the 1860s. To solve this problem the railways soon started to educate indigenous workers and train them in the use of western tools and machinery.

On Java alone about 5,100 railway bridges were built over the years for the Java State Railways, with a total length together of 50 km, impossible to describe them all. On top of this the NIS had another 924 bridges with a combined length of 9.4 km. Until about 1900 the JSS had its own bridge department, where the designs for the necessary bridges were made. Through the Technisch Bureau in The Hague, the best and cheapest Dutch, Belgian, or German firms were selected and the ironwork ordered. Most bridges had to be fully erected in the works first and then shipped in large sections to Java, where they were reassembled in situ. Around 1900 a change was made in the way bridges were ordered. German factories were asked to design and erect them for the Krawang–Padalarang line, with its

The line though the Preanger Highlands between Krawang and Padalarang was known for its spectacular bridges and viaducts. Here an aerial photograph from the 1930s of the trestle bridge over the valley of the Tjipoda River. (SNR collection)

many spectacular crossings of the ravines in the Preanger Highlands. The trestle bridge across the deep Tjisomang ravine, with its three spans of 60 m with two steel supports, more than 60 m high, on armored concrete foundations, was constructed by a German firm. Other trestle bridges, very American looking, were necessary on this and other lines, making for a most spectacular mountain railroad.

In more level terrain, the bridge over the Serajoe River on the Cheribon–Kroja line was designed and constructed by the JSS in-house again, consisting of a central span of 90 m, flanked on both sides by spans of 60 m each, with smaller spans of 15 m at both ends. Pletterij Enthoven of Delft did not submit the lowest bid but got the job, as the lowest bid was from a foreign firm and the home industry had to be supported. All steel and iron came from Europe, the actual erection being done by JSS and Pletterij Enthoven staff. The steel sections were shipped from the Netherlands and landed at Tjilatjap on the south coast of Java, the closest port, at the end of September 1915. The Serajoedal Steam Tram Company, co-user of the new bridge, took care of the transport of the steel to the site by steam tram. A cable lift across the river was installed to get the heavy sections to the other side and pneumatic riveting was used, powered by an air compressor working on kerosene. Javanese workers were instructed in the art of riveting by a few Indo-European experts and were quick in learning the job. At the end of December 1915 the bridge was ready for traffic, a most commendable achievement. Dr. J. H. A. Haarman, chief of the bridge

Above, To construct bridges across deep ravines without the need for elaborate and costly falsework, a new technique was developed in the 1920s by J. H. A. Haarman, the chief of the bridge department of the JSS. In the valley of the Tjipamottan River, the concrete foundations have been laid, on which the steel uprights will be erected. The steel girders will be installed one by one with the aid of a traveler moving over the completed spans. (Author's collection)

Facing, Not only in West Java were high bridges to be found. Also, in the mountainous eastern part of the island, high trestle viaducts were necessary to cross ravines, such as here in the Kalisat–Banjoewangi line over the Kali Rampe, opened in 1903. (Author's collection)

department of the JSS and later professor at the Bandoeng Technical College, designed this and many other bridges and also developed a system of constructing bridges without falsework, which was always vulnerable for *bandjirs*.[14]

On Sumatra for the Atjeh Tram a couple of spectacular high trestle bridges had to be constructed to cross the deep ravines carved out by rivers in the mountain section of the line. Most were constructed by German firms in the early years of the twentieth century, with novel methods used to span the valleys without the use of falsework, often impossible because of the depth of the ravine. The danger of *bandjirs* is graphically illustrated by the bridge over the Blang Mé River in Atjeh during the building of the line of the Atjeh Tram to Lohkseumawe. A first bridge over that river was a simple one on piles screwed into the riverbed into stable layers of soil or rock. Even before it could be used it was destroyed by a *bandjir* in 1902. A second bridge, consisting of a 49-m steel girder on solid concrete piers resting on concrete piles was opened in 1904, but as the opening for the floodwaters was still too small, a second span of 49 m was added in 1916, plus three of 8 m each. This bridge was swept away in its turn by a *bandjir* in 1926 and then it was decided to bridge this unruly river with a single span of 100 m, the longest span in the East Indies, resting on solid concrete foundations. The design was made at the JSS Bridge Dept. in Bandoeng, and Werkspoor-Amsterdam supplied the steel work and supervised the erection. That bridge is still standing.[15]

ELECTRIFICATION

As a source of energy the steam locomotive is a very inefficient user of fuel—coal, wood, or oil—with a thermal efficiency of only 10 to 12 percent at best. To supplant these inefficient monsters, engineers all over the world were experimenting with electricity, and in the last years of the nineteenth century electric street tramways had become a common sight everywhere. Even Batavia had an early electric tramway as described in chapter 9. Most of these systems worldwide used direct current (DC) at low tension, 600 to 900 volts generally. In Germany and Switzerland experiments were conducted with high-tension alternating current (AC) for mainline railways, these trials being followed with great attention everywhere. In 1908 in the Netherlands a first mainline electrification was installed with 10,000 volts AC, for a line between Rotterdam, The Hague, and Scheveningen, also known as The Hague Beach; despite some growing pains, the line was a great success. In the United States the electric interurban had a meteoric but short-lived career: a heavy electric tramway, running on its own right-of-way mostly and connecting small wayside communities left out by the steam railways serving the nearby cities. Most of these interurbans used DC at voltages of 1,200 at the most, and they enjoyed a short-lived popularity in rural states such as Ohio and Indiana and also in California around Los Angeles. Automobile competition killed most interurbans in the 1930s.

All these developments were followed closely by engineers of Netherlands Railways (NS) and of Java State Railways as well. In 1919 an NS commission had advocated the use of 10,000 volts AC for the electrification of the Amsterdam–Rotterdam railway line, choked with traffic and impossibly expensive to quadruple because of the built-up area it traversed. However, the commission had not been able to look at the more recent electrifications in Europe and America because of the war, and foremost of these new ventures was the recent electrification of two long mountain sections of the Chicago, Milwaukee & St. Paul Railroad with 3,000 volts DC. The Dutch government was then advised by a new commission to try DC electrification at 1,500 volts. These proposals were implemented and the first section between Leiden and The Hague was brought under catenary in 1924. The system was gradually extended and after World War II, all important lines were brought under the wires. Despite the drawback of heavy overhead wires because of the relatively low tension, the system still works adequately.[16]

Naturally, electrotechnical engineers in the East Indies followed these developments at home closely. After all, they knew each other quite well personally, as 99 percent of them had graduated from Delft Technical University. Since 1911 studies had been ordered for possible electrification of selected lines on Java, and in a final report of 1917 electrification of some sections of the network was recommended. First of all it was necessary to inquire into the possibility of using waterpower to generate the electric power needed. The answer was positive and already in that same year the construction of two hydroelectric power stations in the hills south of Buitenzorg was started. Two rivers, the Tji Tjatih and the Tji Anten, were dammed, the resulting lakes expected to hold enough water for powering the turbines; in cases of extreme droughts, the coal-fired power station for the electric trams in Batavia was supposed to act as a standby. Dutch engineer Dr. G. de Gelder, a well-known expert in railway electrification with great experience, was sent out in 1920 to take charge.[17]

Until then it was not quite clear what would be the targets of the coming electrification, while only the complex of lines in and around Batavia had been mentioned. At the time Batavia had a population of about 378,000, of which some 35,000 were Europeans (figures of 1928). Traffic in the widely built-out town with its extensive suburbs was getting difficult and complaints were voiced. Clearly something had to be done, but not everyone saw this as the most important part of the electrification plans. Some engineers thought that several mainlines had to be included as well

One of the new electric trains of a motor car with a semipermanently coupled trailer is standing ready for departure in Passar Senen station in the outskirts of Batavia. The first station of Passar Senen dated back to 1886 and was built by the short-lived Batavia Ooster Spoorweg. In 1925, it was replaced by this modern building with a wide central platform and overall roof. (SNR collection)

and wanted to electrify the fairly level northern line to Soerabaja. Others, de Gelder among them, preferred the electrification of the mountain lines to Bandoeng, and rightly so, as steam traction for the mountain lines was always a problem, just as in other mountainous countries worldwide. In their vision Batavia–Buitenzorg would be the first step for the extension of the electrification as far as Bandoeng. A lot of opposition was generated by these proposals and, as money was tight, it was decided to finish only the hydroelectric power station on the Tji Tjatih, later named the Oebroeg station, and wait on the other, named Kratjak. Initially, only the Meester Cornelis–Tandjong Priok line was to be electrified.

Early reports and studies had advocated the use of high-tension AC, but for the suburban lines around Batavia, de Gelder preferred DC. He managed to push his choice through and 1,500 volts DC was decided upon. De Gelder also opted for motor trains instead of electric locomotives, as they had better acceleration after the many stops, just as in his home country. Orders for the necessary materials and equipment could now be placed, chiefly with German firms: Siemens Schuckert and Allgemeine Elektrizitäts Gesellschaft (AEG) of Berlin for all electrical components, catenary masts from Pletterij Enthoven of Delft, and rolling stock from Beijnes of Haarlem with electrical gear from General Electric. Werkspoor-Amsterdam supplied some carriages with Westinghouse equipment. The motor trains consisted of two units each, one motorized car and one trailer, semi-permanently coupled together and connected

SLM-Winterthur and Brown Boveri-Baden supplied four electric locomotives for the Electrische Staatsspoorwegen (ESS, Electric State Railways) in 1924 for the through trains on the Tandjong Priok–Batavia–Buitenzorg–Bandoeng line, of which the section to Buitenzorg was electrified. Here ESS 3001 on a trial trip leaving the old station of Passar Senen. Brown Boveri publicity photo. (SNR collection)

by means of American automatic couplers with harmonicas for easy passenger movements between cars. The seats in all three classes were of the flipover model, as used in most American interurbans. Outside they looked American too, a solid and heavy version of an interurban.

The first line, Meester Cornelis–Tandjong Priok, together with the new harbor station in Priok, opened on March 1, 1925, amid celebrations and festivities for the Batavian population. A year before the green light had also been given for the extension of the electrification to Buitenzorg and the finishing of the Kratjak power station. The other lines of the Batavian complex were opened in 1927 and the line to Buitenzorg in 1930, but further extensions had to be postponed when the worldwide Depression gained momentum. For through trains Tandjong Priok–Batavia–Buitenzorg–Bandoeng, the multiple-unit trains were not considered suitable, as passengers would have had to change trains at Buitenzorg, something the JSS wished to avoid at all cost. For these through trains of bogie carriages, no less than four classes of electric locomotives were ordered for trial purposes. The Swiss firms of SLM-Winterthur for the mechanical part and Brown Boveri of Baden for the electric side supplied two 2-B+B-2 locomotives of 1,500 HP for fast passenger trains on level lines. They had the Swiss-patented Büchli drive with a motor for each driven axle and were good for 90 km per hour with trains of 300 tons. These two were numbered in the ESS 3000 series. ESS stood for Electrische Staats Spoorwegen (Electric State Railways). Two others, numbered in the ESS 3100

One of the two heavy 1-B+B-1 locomotives from AEG-Berlin is waiting to leave Buitenzorg station with a fast train for Batavia. These two, numbered ESS 3101 and 3102, were meant for the fast and heavy passenger trains on the electrified section Batavia–Buitenzorg. (SNR collection)

series and also of the 2-B+B-2 wheel arrangement, were delivered by AEG of Berlin. These were equipped with a single large motor for each group of drivers with outside connecting rods. On paper they were more powerful, 1,570 against 1,500 HP, and were meant for express and slower passenger trains for lines with more gradients. Total weight of these two was 80 tons.

Two units of a third type, series 3200, also of 2-B+B-2 arrangement, had four motors driving each axle through gear wheels directly. They developed 1,200 HP, weighed 70 tons, and were meant for mixed service. Based on a design of Baldwin-Philadelphia, they were built by Werkspoor-Amsterdam for the mechanical part and Heemaf of Hengelo for the electrical equipment, using Westinghouse products and patents. Heemaf, not known for locomotives so far, even installed a 1,067-mm trial track on its factory grounds at Hengelo to be able to test the engines in practice. The first two were shipped to Batavia in 1925, and as they turned out to be most reliable in service, four more of the same class were supplied in 1928, being used for all trains, passenger and freight. For fast passenger trains, two more of the 3000 class were ordered. All new rolling stock and locomotives were equipped with the continuous Westinghouse air brake, which meant that some existing rolling stock had to be rebuilt with a dual system, as JSS until then only had used the automatic Hardy vacuum brake.[18]

ESS Nr. 104, a two-unit motor train, approaches a guarded level crossing in Meester Cornelis in 1927. (Gerard de Graaf collection)

Although the planned electrification of the mountain lines in the Preanger Highlands was never implemented because of the Great Depression, de Gelder and his staff could well be proud of their achievement. In only nine years a complete electric system had been installed on some hundreds of kilometers of existing railway lines, while steam service had to continue during the reconstruction. All equipment was imported from Europe; two hydroelectric power stations were developed in the mountains of West Java; and rolling stock was designed, ordered, tested, and placed in service. Indonesian staff had to be taught the use of high-tension electricity, something new to most of them, and everyone was to be warned about the intrinsic dangers of electricity. Despite some teething troubles, a reliable level of service was soon reached, and to do this in less than ten years was indeed something to be rightly proud of.

SIGNALING

In the early years of railways on Java signaling was simple. With only a few daily trains, sometimes not more than two or three, only signals protecting the entry into a station were deemed necessary. They came in the form of a red disc that could turn on a vertical axis. Red meant stop, and when the disc was invisible, entry was permitted. The signal was weighted to allow it to return to the red aspect. A simple improvement on this system was the introduction of safety bars on switches that allowed the disc to be rotated only when the appropriate switch was lined in the correct direction. The so-called Krian installation, named after the halt where it was first introduced in 1906, made it impossible to allow a train on a track that was already occupied by another train. Signals on both sides of the station could not be pulled off to the safe mode simultaneously.

With the gradual extension of station yards and junctions, a new system was introduced around 1915 with greater safety precautions, based on the system generally used in the home country. The switches and signals, coupled together, were operated by fairly heavy handles in the signal boxes, and some measures had to be taken to make the use of these apparatus possible for the generally less-muscled Indonesian operators. The absolute block system, where only one train is allowed in a certain section of a railway, was introduced in the 1920s on certain mainlines where traffic density required it.

Semaphore signals were introduced gradually, often with two arms, the upper one for the through line, and the shorter one indicating access to a siding or branch line. Some were also equipped with arms showing the position of the next signal. A caution indication here meant an absolute stop at the next signal. Signal bridges spanning several tracks came into use in large yards. As in the mother country, many of these systems were produced by the German firm of Siemens & Halske or by the Alkmaarsche IJzergieterij (Alkmaar Iron Foundry) with the result that in the 1920s and 1930s most East Indies railways were very much looking like a Dutch railway in tropical surroundings. Color light signals were introduced by the Deli Railway Company when its line Belawan Harbor–Medan was doubled in the 1930s. Most lines on Java were and remained single track with the exception of lines in and around Batavia, with the line to the port of Tandjong Priok even quadrupled and electrified.[19]

NOTES

1. Ido, *Indië in de goede oude tijd*, 47–51. *Spoor- en Tramwegen* 3 (1930), 368. About Archduke of Austria Franz Ferdinand, nephew of Emperor Franz Joseph and designated heir to the throne, and his ideas of modernization of the Austrian-Hungarian Dual Monarchy, see Clark, *Sleepwalkers*, 105–11.

2. Hoogstraten (van), *Gloria Mundi*, 60, 63.

3. Termorshuizen and Veer, *Een groots en meeslepend leven*, 98.

4. Text quoted and translated from Pieterse, *Sporen van Smaragd*, 94.

5. Walraven, *Een maand in het boevenpak*, 44.

6. *De Koloniale Roeping van Nederland/Holland's Colonial Call*, A 2–3; also Reitsma, *Van Stockum's Travellers' Handbook*, 8–18.

7. Wal (van der), *Besturen Overzee*, 132. The *Franconia* trip in Pieterse, *Sporen van Smaragd*, 98–99. Figures about cruise ships in annual reports of the State Railways.

8. The complete encyclopedia of all railway stations past and present on Java is given by Ballegoijen (van) de Jong, *Spoorwegstations op Java*, 65–68.

9. Ibid., 145–47.

10. Ibid., 164–76. The advice about sados and taxis in Reitsma, *Van Stockum's Travellers' Handbook*, 265–66.

11. Ballegoijen (van) de Jong, *Stations en Spoorbruggen op Java*, 78–88.

12. For Tandjong Priok, see ibid., 94–100; for Buitenzorg, 111–13; for Bandoeng, 129–32. About Bandoeng, also Reitsma, *Van Stockum's Travellers' Handbook*, 192–98.

13. Ballegoijen (van) de Jong, *Stations en Spoorbruggen op Sumatra*, 126–42.

14. Reitsma, *Gedenkboek Staatsspoor- en Tramwegen*, 119–26. About the Serajoe River bridge, see Bakker, "Free Extending over the Bandjir," 142–43.

15. Ballegoijen (van) de Jong, *Stations en Spoorbruggen op Sumatra*, 61–62, 78–80.

16. Veenendaal, *Railways in the Netherlands*, 155–60.

17. The description of the development of the electrification on Java is chiefly based on Gelder (de), "The Electric State Railways" in *De Koloniale Roeping van Nederland/Holland's Colonial Call*, 71–95.

18. For the Werkspoor-built locomotives, see Jong (de), *De Locomotieven van Werkspoor*, 179, 182–83.

19. There is no general survey of the signaling system of the Indian railways. This section based on Reitsma, *Gedenkboek Staatsspoor- en Tramwegen*, 126–30, and Brugman, "Beveiliging van het Treinverkeer."

THE NONPUBLIC RAILWAYS 14

14

SEMIPUBLIC RAILWAYS

So far this book has been covering railways and tramways with a public character, operating in accordance with governmental laws and regulations, with their services published in timetables. But besides these public lines there were many more kilometers of railway laid to smaller gauges and built to serve a single plantation company or industry. These operated only in the interests of that company, with only the most elementary form of governmental supervision and without public timetables. However, besides these numerous strictly nonpublic railways there were a few companies offering a kind of public service besides their main aim of catering to agricultural or industrial interests. One of these will be described first.

An unusual mix of private and public exploitation of this kind was offered by the Landbouw Maatschappij Madjenang (Agricultural Company Madjenang) on the NIS mainline Goendih–Solo. As a sugar mill the firm opened in 1913, and in 1917 the Batavian government granted it a concession for working a tramway with steam traction for the general public from Madjenang to Meloewoeng. The schedule of this 700-mm line, 18 km long, was published in the official railway and tramway guides until 1924, when the line—together with the sugar mills—was closed. For this public service four 0-8-0 steam engines were available with four passenger coaches and some freight trucks. Tickets could be had from the conductor of the train. For a time the service was profitable, with about 138,000 passengers carried in 1921, but after that year traffic dried up and service was suspended and the rails removed. It was a rather unique mix of private and public service.[1]

Most of these nonpublic railways and tramways were privately owned, generally by the large agricultural corporations headquartered in Europe or America. A few were state owned, as was the case with the many hundreds of rail lines in 600- or 1,067-mm gauge of the state Boschwezen

(Forest Service) to serve the vast government-owned forests of Java and the other islands. In 1930, at a rough count of all these nonpublic railways and tramways, there were no less than 12,682 km of light railways of sugar mills and other agricultural enterprises, mining companies, and industries, mostly on a large-scale and generally, with few exceptions, European or American owned. These railways were laid and operated in no less than twenty-one different gauges, of which 700 mm (2 ft 3 in) was the most important, with 141 networks large and small, followed by 600 mm (1 ft 11.6 in) with fifty-nine, and 750 mm (2 ft 5.5 in) with sixteen networks.[2]

FORESTRY OPERATIONS

The Dienst van het Boschwezen, the forestry department of the Batavian government, was an operator of gigantic proportions. It owned and exploited djati (Java teak) forests with an area of 2.5 million hectares on Java alone, and in the Outer Possessions, Sumatra and Borneo foremost, even 121 million hectares of other tropical hardwoods. The iron-hard djati wood was—and is—used for house building, for furniture, for railway ties, and as firewood. The Boschwezen owned extensive forests of these valuable trees around Tjepoe, East Java, which were first worked

Most unusual was the forest railway on the outlying island Si Maloer off the west coast of Sumatra. It was the only industrial or plantation line in 1,435-millimeter gauge and one of only two that used American Climax locomotives. Here *Wilhelmina*, a Climax B-type of 1911, Works Nr. 1117, is shifting cars under an impressive crane, probably in the 1930s. (Gerard de Graaf collection)

with elephants to get the felled trees to a railhead. But in 1907 already 100 km of 1,067-mm gauge tracks were in place, supplemented by easily transportable Decauville track of smaller gauges. In 1929, the peak year, about 1,970 km of Indian standard gauge (1,067 mm) were in use, without counting the many hundreds of kilometers of often temporary Decauville tracks. Besides hundreds of log trucks the Boschwezen also had one or two coaches for passengers, mostly bought secondhand from one of the steam tram companies, used to bring children of the staff to school.

Besides these government-owned forestry railways, other, privately owned forestry companies, too many to list here, were also laying rails to transport the products of their operations. One rare logging operation, however, merits a short description. This was certainly the most unusual of all, the forestry line on Si Maloer–Simeuluë, the northernmost island of the Mentawei chain off the west coast of Sumatra. This rather short line was used for the transportation of logs to a small port, but, strange to relate, it was laid to the European standard gauge of 1,435 mm. Why such an expensive layout? Was secondhand rail and equipment used here or had the initiators, the Bosch Exploitatie Maatschappij of Amsterdam, greater visions? At this time the use of this broad gauge was distinctly unpopular with government officials and private operators alike. Only three locomotives were ever used on this distant island and one of them was an American Climax 0-4-4-0 of that firm's B-type of 1911, named *Wilhelmina* after the Dutch queen. A rarity in the East Indies, although Boschwezen also operated some Climaxes in narrower gauges around Tjepoe; again why?[3]

AGRICULTURAL RAILWAYS: SUGAR

When considering the importance of the sugar industry for Java, it will not come as a surprise that the circa 210 sugar mills on Java produced 2.9 million tons of sugar in the peak year 1929. After that year production declined and many factories and mills were closed until in the mid-1930s about half of them had been stopped, at least temporarily, some of them to reopen again after 1935 or 1936. Every year the sugar season ran generally from May, when the cane was cut, to September when the refined sugar was ready for shipment, with natural fluctuations caused by irregularities in the monsoon season.

In the olden days sugar cane was harvested by hand and transported to the early mills on bullock carts. With the end of the Cultivation System in the 1870s, private entrepreneurs again became more interested in sugar production, and after the sereh disease had been successfully brought under control, new sugar mills were established, in East Java first, but later also along the lines of the steam trams of Central and

During the construction of the Djatiroto Sugar Mill work trains were already used for bringing workers to the construction sites. An Orenstein & Koppel 0-4-2 tank is in charge of such a work train with European and Javanese personnel. The rolling stock looks a bit homemade. Photo from February 2, 1908. (Gerard de Graaf collection)

West Java. Since the early 1890s these modern mills, generally financed from Europe and equipped with modern installations developed by Werkspoor-Amsterdam; Stork-Hengelo; and by firms from Germany, Belgium, and France, blossomed. The sugar plantations were operated on a large scale and bullock carts no longer sufficed for the transportation of cane to the mills. Rail transportation was the answer, and so these mills with their vast cane fields developed extensive networks of narrow-gauge railways. Systems of 100 km or more of 600- or 700-mm rails were no exception, sometimes even with substantial brick-built roundhouses and real workshops for the stabling and maintenance of the steam locomotives and other rolling stock. Solid steel bridges of spans of 40 m or more were common to cross ravines or rivers, and these railways were often so well constructed and equipped that they came close to or even surpassed a modern and up-to-date light railway in Europe. The sugar factory Redjosari, east of Madioen, East Java, for instance, with over 100 km of 700-mm track, had numerous steel bridges to cross some deep ravines, one of them having a main span of 40 m with several smaller spans all in steel on substantial concrete supports. Even European light railways often could not show comparable structures. The pressed and dried cane called bagasse or *ampas* was used as fertilizer and also as a cheap fuel for the steam locomotives and the steam-driven machinery in the mills. Practically all sugar mills and plantations, large or small, used steam traction on their networks of 600- or 700-mm lines.[4]

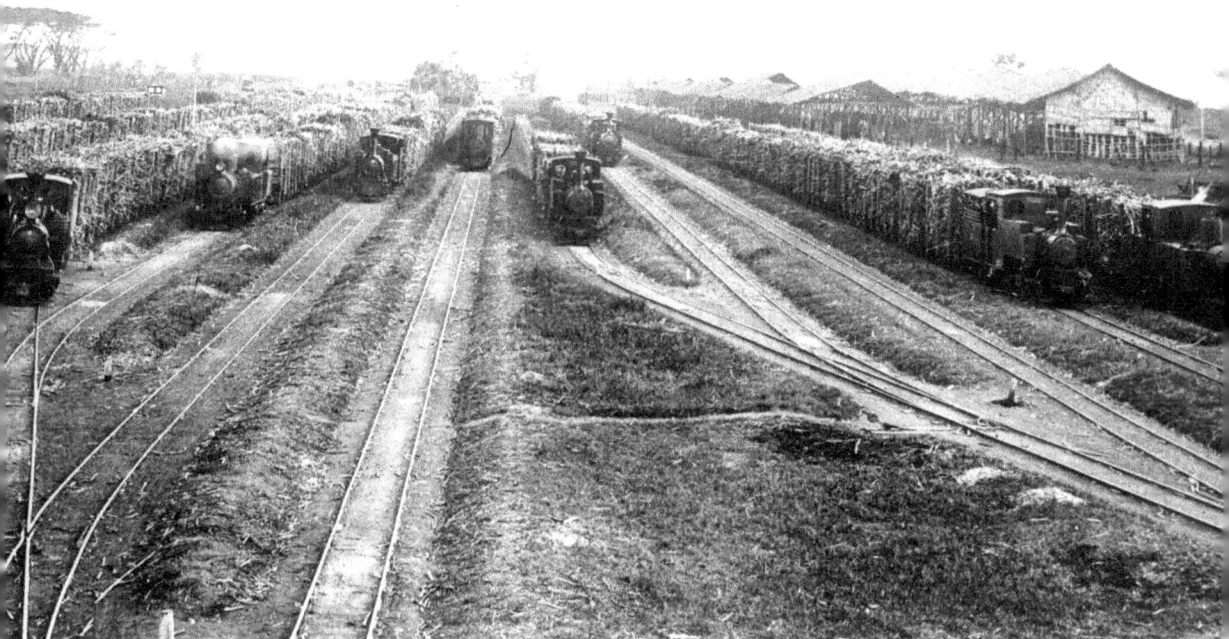

The Suiker Fabriek Djatiroto, located west of Djember in East Java and owned by the Handels Vereeniging Amsterdam (HVA), was easily the sugar mill with the largest rail network. It boasted a network of no less than 448 km of 700-mm railway, serviced by some fifty steam locomotives. Many a steam tram company in the East Indies or even in Europe could well be jealous of such a network and its equipment. Of course, most of the seasonal traffic was sugar cane to the mills and bagged sugar and molasses in barrels to the station of the public railways, in this case the State Railways. But a regular train was provided to take the children of the workers to school every workday and a company hospital was set up by the railway to take care of injured or sick workers, European or Javanese, who were taken there by rail in a dedicated hospital motor lorry.[5]

A latecomer among the sugar mills, also owned by the HVA, was the Suikerfabriek Semboro, opened only in 1926. It was located near Tanggoel in East Java and boasted a rail network of 133 km in 700-mm gauge, plus a connecting line to Tanggoel station of the State Railways in 1,067-mm gauge of another 6 km. More than thirty small steam engines were in use, but it also had a four-wheel gasoline-powered railcar plus trailer in 1,067-mm gauge, built by Beijnes of Haarlem, to bring children of the European staff and those from neighboring Javanese villages to school. It could also be rented for excursions and parties, quite exceptional.[6]

At the other end of the scale, different from the plantations and mills with European capital and management, was the fairly small sugar factory

Most of the sugar mills on Java had some form of rail traffic, generally at a narrow gauge with some form of steam traction. The mill with the largest network was the Suiker Fabriek (sugar factory) Djatiroto, opened in 1909 southeast of Probolinggo; with its 448 kilometers of track, it easily surpassed all other mills. On this photograph from the 1920s, no fewer than eight fully loaded cane trains with steam traction are visible, surely a record. The factory is still operating and is Java's largest and still has a rail network. (Gerard de Graaf collection)

The Sugar Mill Gemoe, about halfway between Solo and Djokja, was one of the few that operated with American-built engines. In this photograph, two of its 600-millimeter locomotives built by Dickson in 1899 and 1901 are visible, together with the Dutch and Javanese staff. The size and solidity of the mill building is also remarkable. Photo before 1914. (Gerard de Graaf collection)

owned by Pangeran–Prince–Ario Prabo Prang Wedana, member of the Soerakarta royal house. His plantation was situated 9 km east of Solo and it operated a single four-coupled tank engine, constructed by Couillet in 1885 for 750-mm track. An almost royal engine?[7]

AGRICULTURAL RAILWAYS: RUBBER AND PALM OIL

Next to the sugar plantations, other "cultures," large-scale agricultural companies mostly owned by Dutch Cultuur Maatschappijen (Agricultural Companies), were opened on Java and Sumatra toward the end of the nineteenth century. Tobacco, tea, rubber, and sisal came first, and oil palm trees were grown on a small scale since the 1860s; however, production of palm oil really took off in the 1920s and 1930s, first and foremost on Sumatra. On that vast island grew a great number of these new plantations, large and small, too many to list them all but a few deserve to be mentioned here. The Deli Spoorweg Maatschappij (DSM) laid quite a number of short 700-mm light railways from smaller plantations to the nearest railhead of the DSM for the transport of the products, which relatively short lines were mostly operated with animal traction and a few also with steam locomotives. Other, bigger plantations laid their own light railways when

traffic grew and when the extent of the area planted was really so extensive that the use of steam locomotives was warranted. One such was the Hollandsch-Amerikaansche Plantage Maatschappij (Dutch-American Plantation Company), generally known as the U.S. Rubber Plantation near Boenoet, Deli. Its lines, many kilometers long, were laid to a gauge of 610 mm (2 ft), a gauge little used for plantation lines. American influence perhaps? The famous Maine two-footers were laid to the same gauge and quite a number of the steam engines used on Sumatra were supplied by Baldwin and Davenport. Another extensive rubber plantation was the Wingfoot Estate, owned by the Goodyear Corporation of Akron, Ohio, near Rantau Prapat, South Sumatra. Again, this plantation worked with many steam locomotives with a track gauge of the more usual 700 mm. There was also a passenger coach, a kind of "Galloping Goose," with a gasoline automobile engine mounted in front on a four-wheel bogie and a fixed driven axle behind under the primitive passenger compartment. All these plantation networks were connected with the DSM lines of the Indian standard gauge.[8]

The production of palm oil may have shown a slow start, but in the 1920s the culture of oil palms was undertaken on a grand scale by European and American consortia and by smaller regional companies. One of

The Wingfoot Estate, operated by the Goodyear Rubber Corporation, near Rantau Prapat at the end of a long branch line of the Deli Spoorweg in North Sumatra, had a rail network in 700-millimeter gauge, worked with steam locomotives. For the few passenger movements, it also had a Galloping Goose railcar, with a four-wheel truck up front under the automobile-type engine and a single axle behind. It looks homemade but it worked. The new bridge on steel piling, apparently replacing an earlier wooden one, seems substantial enough. Photo from the 1930s. (Gerard de Graaf collection) the biggest of these European organizations was the HVA, incorporated in 1878, with most of its plantations located in Deli or the nearby part of North Sumatra. Some of these HVA plantations had been started for growing fiber palms for the production of sisal, but when profits in the oil palm business skyrocketed, they changed over to oil palms. One of the largest was the Sisal Plantation Deli near Pematang Siantar, Deli. It had many kilometers of 700-mm track connecting the several plantations with the DSM line. More than twenty steam locomotives were used for the internal transportation of sisal and later palm oil, plus machinery and equipment. Another big operation of the HVA was the Vezelpalm Cultuur Dolok Ilir near Tebing Tinggi, Deli, again begun as a sisal plantation but changed over to oil palms. Here both 600- and 700-mm tracks were used, the narrower gauge for the internal transport in the actual mills, with much longer 700-mm tracks to connect the fields with the mill. Over the years some thirty steam locomotives were used here. The third of the bigger companies, also owned by the HVA, was the Dolok Silumbah plantation, 25 km from Pematang Siantar, Deli, with a network of 700-mm lines and some twenty steam locomotives. A specialty here was the operation of trains of 700-mm transporter wagons each loaded with a standard 1,067-mm tank wagon. At the transfer station of the DSM, the tank wagons were rolled off the transporters and taken on to the port on their own wheels by the DSM.[9]

COAL AND OIL

In the chapter on the railways on the west coast of Sumatra, the Ombilin coal mines were described as being the reason for the construction of the state-owned mountain railroad to the coal harbor of Emmahaven. The first coal was mined in 1892 and as it was found to be good steam coal, although inferior to the more expensive imported Welsh coal, production soared. The coal mined at the government-owned Ombilin Steenkolen-mijnen (Ombilin Coal Mines) at Sawah Loento, West Sumatra, was transported down to the coast on the 1,067-mm line with rack sections, but for the mine tunnel a 600-mm line was laid out in 1892. That first line was 3.6 km long, and even more exceptional was that in 1902 it was electrified with 220 volts DC, power being generated at a mine-owned power station burning waste coal from the mines. A second tunnel was opened in 1921, again with a 600-m railway of some 3 km long. An electric rack railway was opened in 1907 between the several mines high in the mountains and the coal screens at Sawah Loento. The modern Abt system of rack railway was used here, not that of Riggenbach as in use on the public state line to Emmahaven. The Allgemeine Elektrizitäts Gesellschaft of Berlin (AEG) supplied seven electric rack locomotives for this line and also between

The Boekit Asam government coal mines in South Sumatra had a network of lines in 600-millimeter gauge around the mine and its adjacent installations and connection with the 1,067-millimeter South Sumatra Railways. Two Orenstein & Koppel steam locomotives with their crews and visiting officials pose for the photographer sometime in the 1930s. (Gerard de Graaf collection)

1902 and 1930 no less than forty-two small electric engines for the mine galleries and tunnels, equipped with a trolley pole to contact the overhead catenary. A fairly intricate and vulnerable system, and it worked after a fashion.[10]

The other government-owned coal mines on Sumatra were situated farther south, and these Boekit Asam mines became productive in 1919. The coal was inferior to the Ombilin product but could well be used for the production of briquettes as practiced on the Java State Railways. Kertapati, on the Moesi River opposite Palembang, was the favored harbor for shipping the coal to Java. At the mines 600-mm gauge tracks were used to bring coal from the mines to the 1,067-mm tracks of the Zuid Sumatra Spoorweg (ZSS) and several locomotives of the standard Indian gauge were owned by the BA mines. At Kertapati the company also had some 1,067-mm engines for working the tracks to the transporter, where the coal was loaded in seagoing ships.[11]

On Borneo there were other, generally smaller and less elaborate mining ventures, among them a coal mine operated by the Koninklijke Paketvaart Maatschappij (KPM) for its large fleet of steamships. These KPM mines were situated near Rantau Padjang in northeast Borneo and operated by the Parapattan Steenkolen Maatschappij (Parapattan Coal Company) to provide the fuel for the circa hundred steamers of the KPM. A 600-mm line was opened from the mine to the landing stage on the nearby river; as there was no road between the two ends of the 4.5-km line, a regular passenger service was also operated. At least ten simple four-wheel passenger coaches were available plus some 170 coal trucks. At both terminals regular platforms were constructed for the passengers, an exception among these industrial and mining railways. Other coal mines were worked in different places on Borneo and most if not all had some rail network in narrow gauge in operation to get the coal from mine to river or sea wharf for shipment.[12]

The first concessions for oil refineries and tank parks on Borneo were issued by the Batavian government in 1889–1890. The Bataafsche Petroleum Maatschappij, (BPM) later part of Royal Dutch Shell, drilled its first wells in 1892 near Balikpapan on the coast of East Borneo. This grew into an enormous complex of oil wells; tank parks; refineries; paraffin and sulphuric acid works; villages for the staff, both European and indigenous; shopping centers; churches; hospitals; and harbor installations, all connected by an extensive 1,000-mm (3 ft 3.4 in) network and served by steam locomotives burning heavy waste oil. Even a daily (except Sunday) shopping train was run regularly, with a closed carriage—one of three—for European ladies and an open one with a roof only for Indonesian women. Apparently, the Batavian government never objected to this rather haphazard semipublic operation without any legal status. Smaller networks of 600- and 700-mm lines were laid around the several oil wells, but the connection between all different centers was by the meter gauge railway. The BPM also operated around Palembang on Sumatra, here on a big scale too, but the rail network there was smaller than the operations on Borneo.[13]

OTHER MINERALS

Tin mining on the island of Billiton, southeast of Sumatra, went back a long time, with the Dutch-owned Billiton Maatschappij being set up in 1851 to work the tin mines. First operations were mostly simple open pits, but later, when these were becoming exhausted, more elaborate deep shafts were constructed to open up underground layers of tin ore. On the neighboring island of Banka, government-owned tin mines were opened that soon eclipsed the Billiton production in tonnage and revenues. The Dienst der Tinwinning Banka began operations in 1896 and soon the tin ore produced there amounted to twice the tonnage from Billiton. Both Billiton and Banka were most profitable undertakings, as tin was a strategic material much used by industry worldwide.

The Billiton Company opened its first rail network on the island in 1886, eventually measuring a good 67 km. A second smaller complex came later, and both were laid with a gauge of 721 mm (2 ft 3.3 in), a rare gauge and hardly ever used elsewhere. About fifteen steam engines were in use and the company also provided regular passenger traffic, as there was no road between mines and the refining center. The Batavian government frowned upon this "illegal" passenger traffic and in 1917 sent two JSS officials to inspect the premises; although they condemned the practice, nothing much changed.[14]

The Dienst der Tinwinning on Banka eventually operated three separate rail networks, two operating on the 600-mm gauge with lengths of 44 and 23 km, respectively, and one of 33 km with the 700-mm gauge. Roads on the island were nonexistent, hence the need for rail transportation. Some of the steam locomotives for the 600-mm gauge were transferred to Banka from the abandoned Solo Valley on Java.

Gold and Silver mines had been operating in Benkoelen, southwest Sumatra, since early days and some foreign-owned private companies were set up to work the diggings, some of them operating narrow-gauge railways for the transportation of ores, materials, and equipment. Most were short-lived and of little importance.[15]

Although the Batavian government did not have a complete monopoly in the field of coal and tin, it did operate the winning and sale of salt to the exclusion of all others. On the island of Madoera, just off the coast of northeast Java, salt had been produced since olden times, but in the nineteenth century the government had established its absolute monopoly there. Seawater was let into shallow artificial pools, and after the water had evaporated in the hot sun, the remaining salt crystals were harvested and pressed into bricks for easy transport. Rail lines of 600 mm served the salt lakes and the storage facilities and brought the salt to transfer yards of the Madoera steam tram.[16]

A short-lived shortline was used for the operation of the stone quarries at Anjer Kidoel on the western point of Java, where the stone for the Tandjong Priok harbor works was quarried. Two steam locomotives operated on the 1,067-mm line until the disastrous tsunami caused by the eruption—*explosion* would be a better word—of the Krakatau volcano in Soenda Strait in 1883 ended it all. The quarry and all equipment were completely destroyed with great loss of life, and the two locomotives were severely damaged. They could be repaired, however, and served honorably at the Tandjong Priok harbor works.[17]

A MULTITUDE OF STEAM LOCOMOTIVES

For all these light railways and industrial tracks—sometimes hard to reach and hidden in the dense tropical jungle, sometimes out in the open on tracks running in the village streets or on landings along the rivers— literally hundreds of small and big steam locomotives were in use in a bewildering variety. Light rail, uneven track, weak bridges, sharp curves, and occasional severe gradients necessitated light but powerful locomotives with as many coupled axles as possible to reduce the axle load without losing tractive force, hence the many systems of movable driven axles to accommodate severe curvature. Maintenance had to be simple in the extreme to make it possible for the less schooled maintenance staff with sometimes primitive equipment to keep everything running. Breakdowns during the busy sugar season had to be avoided at all cost as they could paralyze the whole organization, resulting in big losses.

Before 1900 narrow-gauge steam locomotives for plantation or industrial duties were rare in the East Indies. The Belgian firm of Société de Couillet was the first to deliver some small 0-4-0 tank engines, among others to the only "royal" sugar factory of a member of the house of the soesoehoenan of Soerakarta, as noted. The French firm of Decauville, known for its agricultural equipment, portable rail sections, and light engines, was the next with some small units for rubber plantations in Sumatra and for the Billiton Maatschappij. Orenstein & Koppel supplied its first steam locomotive to a sugar factory on Java in 1894; this pioneer O&K engine would be the first of a total of at least 635 narrow-gauge locomotives from the Berlin firm for the Indies.

Altogether more than a thousand industrial steam locomotives were supplied by at least thirty-five locomotive works in Germany, the Netherlands, Belgium, Great Britain, France, and the United States of America. Some suppliers are present with only one or two engines and it is remarkable that Hartmann, with its hundreds of engines constructed for the Java State Railways and NIS, is listed here with only nine narrow-gauge engines. With other famous firms such as Maffei or Henschel it is just the other way around. They delivered only a handful of mainline engines to Java State or the NIS, but are present here with seventy-three units from Henschel and sixty-four from Maffei. The American works with the largest number of locomotives supplied to the East Indies is the Vulcan Iron Works of Wilkes Barre, Pennsylvania, with twenty-nine units. Of the other US factories Baldwin came close with twenty engines, followed by Dickson with eleven; Climax with three; and Cooke, Davenport, and Porter with two each. Apart from the twenty mainline 2-8-8-0 Mallets for the Java State Railways, ALCO never constructed steam locomotives for East Indian industrial or plantation railways under its own name, although before the amalgamation individual constituent companies such as Dickson did.[18]

Many of the German locomotive firms had their agents or representatives in the Netherlands or in the East Indies or even had a subsidiary company of their own there. It is sometimes unclear who constructed what and when, and moreover there was a lot of swapping of engines between the plantations owned, for instance, by the HVA and other big operators with more than one rail system. However, it is clear that German firms, directly or through agents in the Netherlands and the Indies, controlled the market almost completely, with Orenstein & Koppel as the leader. This firm had a most complicated corporate life. From several earlier firms and factories headed by Max Orenstein and Arthur Koppel, respectively, all specializing in equipment, rails, and locomotives for industrial and works railways, a kind of cooperation was set up as Orenstein & Koppel in 1897, not yet as a limited company, for the construction of equipment and locomotives for industrial railways. To tidy up the corporate structure, Orenstein & Koppel merged in 1909 with Arthur Koppel AG as a limited company. This new Aktien Gesellschaft (Limited Company) had branches and factories all over Germany and in other European countries, and even a factory in Koppel, Pennsylvania. In Amsterdam the former O&K agency was transformed into an incorporated daughter company trading under the name of NV Fabrieken van Spoorwegmaterieel voorheen Orenstein & Koppel (Factories of Railway Equipment, formerly O&K, Ltd). In the Netherlands they had secured a large share of the market of industrial and contractor's locomotives and equipment. In the East Indies the main agency under the name of O&K was in Soerabaja with branches in Semarang, Batavia, and Medan, indicating the scope of its activities in the Dutch East Indies.[19]

Du Croo & Brauns has already been mentioned in passing in chapter 7 with its engines for the Atjeh Tram, but here the firm should get some more attention as it was only second to O&K, with deliveries of at least 205 narrow-gauge locomotives to the East Indies. The Dutch firm originated from earlier factories that supplied narrow-gauge railway equipment for contractors, industrial lines, and such. In 1917 they became official representative of the German Maffei works in the Netherlands and five years later the firm, by then a limited company trading under the name Machinefabriek Du Croo & Brauns with a factory at Weesp, east of Amsterdam, built its first narrow-gauge locomotive. They also had several engineering works at Soerabaja, where complete installations for sugar mills were produced, and agencies in Medan, New Delhi, and, surprisingly, Buenos Aires, Argentina. In 1936 the locomotive department was moved to Amsterdam. Altogether the company constructed 398 steam locomotives, a number of diesels, and hundreds or even thousands of lorries, dump trucks, rail cranes, and other railway equipment for both narrow and standard gauges.[20]

Most early plantation, mine, and works locomotives in the Dutch East Indies were of the 0-4-0 or 0-6-0 tank types with outside cylinders. Inside cylinders were practically impossible because of lack of room between the frames outside or inside. Driving wheels were usually between 600 and 700 mm in diameter, while pilot wheels, if present, were generally

450 mm. Tank engines of the 0-4-2 axle arrangement were also used in the early years. Most numerous, with over 350 examples, was the 0-8-0 tank, often with movable outer axles after the Klien-Lindner, Gölsdorf, or Lüttermöller patented systems. The latter system worked with gear wheels for the two end axles, and even 0-10-0 tanks with this gear were supplied to some clients by, among others, Du Croo & Brauns, Henschel, and Schwartzkopff.

Surprisingly, after the 0-8-0 tanks, the 0-4-4-0 Mallet tank engine was the most popular class in the East Indies with no less than 203 units, the most numerous Mallets on the narrow gauge anywhere in the world. In view of the light rails and often-sharp curvature of the tracks, combined with the need for high adhesion for hauling the heavy cane trains, their large number may be not so surprising after all. They were all true Mallets with compound propulsion, the high-pressure cylinders on the fixed rear unit, and low pressure on the swiveling front unit. Only three Climax locomotives were ever supplied to the East Indies, where their ability to negotiate uneven track and severe curves must have been an advantage. Other American logging types have never been used there.

All locomotives used on these plantation and works rails had to be sturdy, simple machines without frills, as workshop equipment was often severely limited and skills of the staff only basic. Yet a lot of tinkering was done by the generally Indonesian workers when the hectic sugar season was over. When wood-burning engines were adapted for burning bagasse, simple tenders were often fashioned with a wooden or steel bin on a lorry underframe, to be able to store enough of the voluminous pressed bagasse blocks for a long run when tank engines had too-restricted fuel storage. Originally, almost every engine was equipped for wood burning, with only a few coal burners at the several coal mine operations. Bagasse or *ampas* came later to be used on a large scale, as it was practically free at the mills. Some palm oil plantations used the dried pressed nuts as fuel, again almost free of charge. Steam pumps and injectors for filling the boilers were both used and often changed between engines at times when spare parts were difficult to obtain. Superheaters were well-nigh unknown as being too complicated. Weights in service varied enormously, from the 9.3 tons of a diminutive 600-mm gauge Krauss 0-4-0 tank, as delivered to the Solo Valley Water Works in 1899, to the 19.6 tons of a 700-mm Du Croo & Brauns 0-4-4-0 Mallet of 1929, built for a sugar mill on Java, or the 23 tons of a 750-mm D&B 0-10-0 tank of 1927.[21]

Locomotives with internal combustion engines, mostly running on gasoline, were still rare but were introduced slowly on the more sophisticated networks. Mechanically they were more complicated than steam locomotives and the often-primitive maintenance facilities generally had trouble keeping them going. Du Croo & Brauns, well known for its steam engines, began early with experimenting and delivered three small four-wheel diesel engines of 700-mm gauge to the Corps of Engineers of the Koninklijk Nederlandsch-Indisch Leger (Royal Netherlands Indies Army) in 1924 and 1925. They were used at the Engineers depot of Soerabaja, but for what purpose is uncertain, and nothing is known about their later fate.[22]

NOTES

1. Bergmann, *Die Dampflokomotiven*, 267.

2. A most comprehensive and exhaustive study of all privately owned plantation and works railways and their locomotives in the Dutch East Indies and later Indonesia is Bergmann, *Die Dampflokomotiven*, written in German, but with a translation of the introduction into English by Keith Chester. The information in this chapter is mostly based on this book. More concise but useful is Oegema, *De stoomtractie*, 141–48. Also Heijst (van), "Means of Transportation," 147–49.

3. For the Climax Manufacturing Company of Corry, Pennsylvania, see Davies, *North American Steam Locomotive Builders*, 142–45, and White, *Short History of American Locomotive Builders*, 37.

4. Bergmann, *Die Dampflokomotiven*, 182–85.

5. Ibid., 95–101.

6. Ibid., 188–94.

7. Ibid., 270.

8. Ibid., 310–14.

9. Ibid., 318–28.

10. With thanks to Gerard de Graaf, who is working on a book covering all coal mines in the Indonesian archipelago, to be published in 2021.

11. Bergmann, *Die Dampflokomotiven*, 392–95.

12. Ibid., 380–82.

13. Ibid., 405–10.

14. Puffert, *Tracks across Continents*, 318, doesn't mention this 721-mm gauge, nor the most popular—in the East Indies—700-mm gauge.

15. Bergmann, *Die Dampflokomotiven*, 370–80.

16. Amstel (van), "Madoera Stoomtram Maatschappij."

17. Bergmann, *Die Dampflokomotiven*, 411–13.

18. About Vulcan Iron Works, see White, *Short History of American Locomotive Builders*, 101. The firm began construction of industrial steam locomotives in the 1870s and built up a sizable customer base at home but also entered foreign markets, as shown by their entry into the East Indian market. Baldwin Locomotive Works of Philadelphia, Pennsylvania, needs little explanation here, as it is well known. The Dickson Manufacturing Company of Scranton, Pennsylvania, constructed its first locomotives in the 1860s and was one of the more productive firms in the USA. It was taken over by ALCO in 1901 and locomotive construction ceased in 1909. Cooke Locomotive and Machine Works of Paterson, New Jersey, was also merged into ALCO in 1901 and afterward specialized in small industrial locomotives until production was ended in 1926. Davenport Locomotive Works, of Davenport, Iowa,

started the production of industrial locomotives only in 1901 and built up a good customer base in the USA and overseas but never got a real foothold in the East Indies. After being reorganized several times, the firm of H. K. Porter & Company started business under this name in 1878 and soon concentrated on the construction of industrial, logging, and other locomotives for special purposes. Ibid., 27–29, 38, 41, 43–45, 77–79. About Baldwin, see Brown, *Baldwin Locomotive Works*.

19. The complicated corporate history of Orenstein & Koppel in Bude et al., *O&K Dampflokomotiven*.

20. For Du Croo & Brauns, see Bruin (de), *Du Croo & Brauns Locomotieven*.

21. Bergmann, *Die Dampflokomotiven*, 20–28, 467.

22. Bruin (de), *Du Croo & Brauns Locomotieven*, 85.

The year 1929 was a peak year worldwide. The economies of the western world were booming; investment in new factories, novel industries, and consumer goods was solid; and all lights were seemingly showing green, until October 24 of that year, when the Wall Street stock market suddenly collapsed, precipitating a worldwide crash. At first it was thought that the crisis would only be temporary and would blow over quickly, as had happened so many times before. But on the contrary, it deepened and worsened until an absolute bottom was reached in 1932–1933. Factories and offices closed and mass unemployment and poverty on an unprecedented scale resulted. About 25 percent of American workers were unemployed in 1933, while in some industrial cities the jobless reached 50 percent or more of the total of workers. And not only the United States were hit; the Depression soon spread to other countries and continents.[1]

The Kingdom of the Netherlands was no exception in this worldwide crisis, and the economy of the home country and its colonies was severely hurt. As a positive countermeasure, Great Britain devaluated its pound sterling in 1931, but the Netherlands government unwisely clung to the gold standard until as late as 1936 and only then devaluated the guilder by about 20 percent, causing an almost immediate although only partial recovery.

The Dutch East Indies were extremely vulnerable for fluctuations of world trade and rates of exchange because of the preponderance of agricultural products and raw materials in the total export. Volume and prices of the traditional Indian export products declined alarmingly. Sugar production on Java fluctuated between 2.3 and 2.9 million tons between 1927 and 1930 but was down to 1.5 million tons in 1931. In 1934 the sugar export was still lower at just over 1 million tons and of the 179 sugar mills on Java many were inoperative. The next season saw 132 mills closed and only forty-seven still working. With rubber the figures were about the same and the value of rubber exports had fallen from a total of 83 million guilders in 1929 to just over 16 million in 1931. The result was widespread unemployment, not only among the Indonesian employees but also for the European staff. In 1931 already 2,180 Europeans were officially registered as unemployed; a year later this figure had grown to four thousand, reaching a high of around ten thousand in the next years. It was not unknown for a European to drive a taxi and wait in line for a customer outside railway stations together with Indonesian and Chinese colleagues.

For workers still employed, salaries and wages were reduced, sometimes as much as 75 percent, with widespread poverty as a result. Government income in the Indies declined substantially as revenues from taxes were drying up: for instance, corporation taxes declined from over 59 million in 1928 to a paltry 7.8 million guilders in 1934. On the other hand, government could not cut expenses everywhere, although salaries and wages were severely reduced where possible. The annual budget of the Batavian government had shown a surplus of 41 million guilders in 1928, but by 1930 this had turned into a deficit of 85 million and even 142 million two years later.

Despite the long-standing inclination of the Batavian government toward free trade, some measures were taken to protect the Indian economy by introducing a quota system for imports of articles and materials that were also produced in the East Indies. For instance, the Goodyear tire factory on Sumatra was protected by a quota system against cheap Japanese automobile tires, and other Indian producers were likewise helped to survive. With some other countries, such as British Malaya and Ceylon, agreements were reached for the export quota of certain products such as rubber for each country. Together with Sumatra these two British colonies were the three most important producers in the world. Stimulated also was the opening of modern foreign industries on Java and Sumatra, such as General Motors, Goodyear, and British-American Tobacco, to name the big three. All these measures had a certain positive influence, but the most effective was the devaluation of the Dutch and East Indian guilder in 1936. It was better late than never and the result was almost immediate.[2]

Total value of all East Indian exports in 1928—in current prices—was a staggering 1,580 million guilders, and although lower than the boom year of 1925, still a most respectable figure. The year 1930 again showed a fairly healthy 1,160 million guilders, but from there the fall was deep to 448.9 million in 1935, the lowest in decades. From that disastrous year the total exports slowly rose again and in 1937 showed a doubling to 953.4 million guilders. Still, the value of exports during all those years always exceeded that of imports by an ample margin, as imports of foreign-made articles and consumer goods had fallen even more steeply since the peak years of the late 1920s.[3]

The political relations between Dutch and Indonesians suffered from the widespread poverty and the rise of Indonesian nationalism. Indonesian nationalist leaders such as Tjokroaminoto and Soekarno, often Dutch educated, called for more influence in matters of internal politics. They struck a chord in indigenous society, not the least because of an expanding Malay press, but met with little success with the colonial establishment, due to growing repression. On the other end, right-wing white groups active at the same time were bent on excluding Indonesians from governmental functions. Communist disturbances and strikes were something new in 1926 and 1927 and were also an indication of the widening gap between Indonesian nationalists and Dutch authorities. Caught between these two extremes, the Batavian government increasingly followed a course of repression, with press control, more grip on political parties, and even the exiling of Indonesian leaders to outlying parts of the archipelago. Of course, there were also far-seeing and vociferous opponents of this shortsighted policy among the European group, but they were not strong enough to really alter governmental attitudes. With growing anxiety these well-informed groups noticed the increase of antagonism and the widening gap between the European and Indonesian segments of the population. The war made an end to this development but the seeds for the establishment of a state dominated by Indonesians had been sown.[4]

THE JAVA STATE RAILWAYS IN LEAN TIMES

Just as other government services and enterprises, the Java State Railways had to tighten its belt when the worldwide Depression made itself more and more felt in the East Indies. The electrification of the line to Buitenzorg could be finished and the necessary rolling stock and locomotives were delivered, but the plan for extending electric service all the way to Bandoeng had to be shelved, temporarily it was hoped, but definitively as it turned out.

One way to combat the losses of the railways was to close unremunerative sections of the network, as was done in the home country, where hundreds of kilometers of country branches were closed. This did not happen on a large scale on Java and only very few of the JSS and NIS lines were closed permanently; on Madoera this did indeed happen, where some branches were closed and even lifted. This, however, did remain the exception. What was done on a large scale was reduction of frequencies of trains on lightly used lines. Three instead of four trains a day became the norm, first of all on lightly traveled branches.

Another way to attract more passengers was the reduction of fares and rates. The competition of the motorbus, hardly regulated by government, was killing much of the short-distance rail traffic; lower rates did not really help. Laws to regulate the motorbus were indeed passed after some years but strict compliance with the law was not enforced, and the railways had to continue the struggle with the buses on the more profitable connections. However, the bus operators did not challenge the railways and tramways on the money-losing sections in the countryside, where the railways had to maintain service so as not to lose the concession, wherein an absolute minimum of daily services had been stipulated. The extensive bus lines operated by the ZSS on Sumatra, the Autodiensten Staatsspoorwegen (Motor Services of the ZSS), were severely curtailed because of ruinous competition from the "wilde bussen," the unregulated motorbus operators.

The number of passengers carried by JSS declined substantially by 23.17 percent between 1931 and 1932 and by some 10 percent more in the following years, resulting in a total of only 23 million paying passengers in 1935. Of the three state systems operating in Sumatra only the ZSS had seen a growth of passenger traffic between 1932 and 1933, the result of improved services, but SSS and ASS showed declining numbers. In 1929 the Java State Railways had shown a positive net result of 23 million guilders but by 1935 this had changed into a deficit of almost 2 million. In 1935 both SSS and ASS had deficits of about a half million each, and only ZSS had been able to recover and could show a small net result of 230,000 guilders.[5]

As usual in slack times personnel considered superfluous was discharged all over the railway system and services were abolished or reduced. This happened worldwide of course; the East Indies were no exception. The State Railways on Java and Sumatra discharged more than 15,000 staff members between 1930 and 1935, both Europeans and Indonesians. Cuts in wages were becoming normal too, as for instance with the Malang Steam Tram, hard hit by the competition of "wild" motorbuses. The salaries of the European staff were cut 5 percent in 1934, and 10 percent for the indigenous personnel, who were apparently supposed to be able to live more cheaply. The next year another cut was deemed necessary, now of 10 percent for the Europeans and 15 percent for the Indonesian workforce.

A third way of saving money now that traffic was falling off was the mothballing of steam locomotives no longer needed for the reduced services. Older units were scrapped right away, but the fairly modern 2-8-8-0 Mallets of the JSS were withdrawn and stored. Maintenance of these mastodons had always been heavy, especially on the bar frames and the joints in the steampipes. They were now stored inside sheds and all moving parts were thoroughly lubricated and greased, and boilers filled with water that had been heated to over boiling point to remove all impurities, in the hope that rust formation would be minimal. The modern 2-8-2 tanks of the 1400 Series, acquired in 1921 and 1922 for shunting the hump yards of Batavia and Soerabaja, were no longer needed now that the volume of freight traffic had declined so much; they were placed in storage too.

A clear indication of the almost-unbelievable decline of receipts of the several railway and tramway companies in the East Indies over 1935 compared to 1929 is this survey, devastating by its negative results.[6]

State Rlys. (Java and Sumatra)	minus 68.9 percent
NIS	minus 69.5
SJS	minus 73.4
SDS	minus 80.6
SCS	minus 68.7
DSM (Deli)	minus 55.8
NS (Netherlands)	minus 44.0

More elaborate figures are not necessary; the Dutch East Indies were indeed hit hard by the worldwide Depression, even more so than the home country, and recovery was slow, slower than in the Netherlands.

POSITIVE DEVELOPMENTS

Despite the cutting back of operations to reduce deficits, there were sorely needed positive developments too, most of all designed to attract new traffic by reducing travel time or lowering of rates. The Eendaagsche was described in an earlier chapter and it continued to do well, not in the least because of the continuous upgrading of the service and the speeding up to only 11.3 hours between Batavia-Weltevreden and Soerabaja. Tickets were now cheaper than the 1929 rate of ƒ37.50 for first class and ƒ24.70 for second class—no third class yet—for the whole journey, now reduced to first class ƒ31, second class ƒ21.60, and third class ƒ10.80 in 1939. These reductions were also necessary to combat a new competitor on this route, the airline. The new Douglas DC-2 planes now used by the Koninklijke Nederlandsch-Indische Luchtvaart Maatschappij were faster than the Fokkers of 1929, which did the journey in five hours, and although much more expensive than the trains, the airline attracted the well-to-do travelers and hurried businessmen.

Running trains at night in the East Indies had always been avoided, as tracks were largely unfenced and large animals crossing the tracks in the dark could and did cause derailments. Most stations all over Java were closed at night and not manned. The Javanese population living nearby were wont to use the rail lines as a convenient way for walking, causing

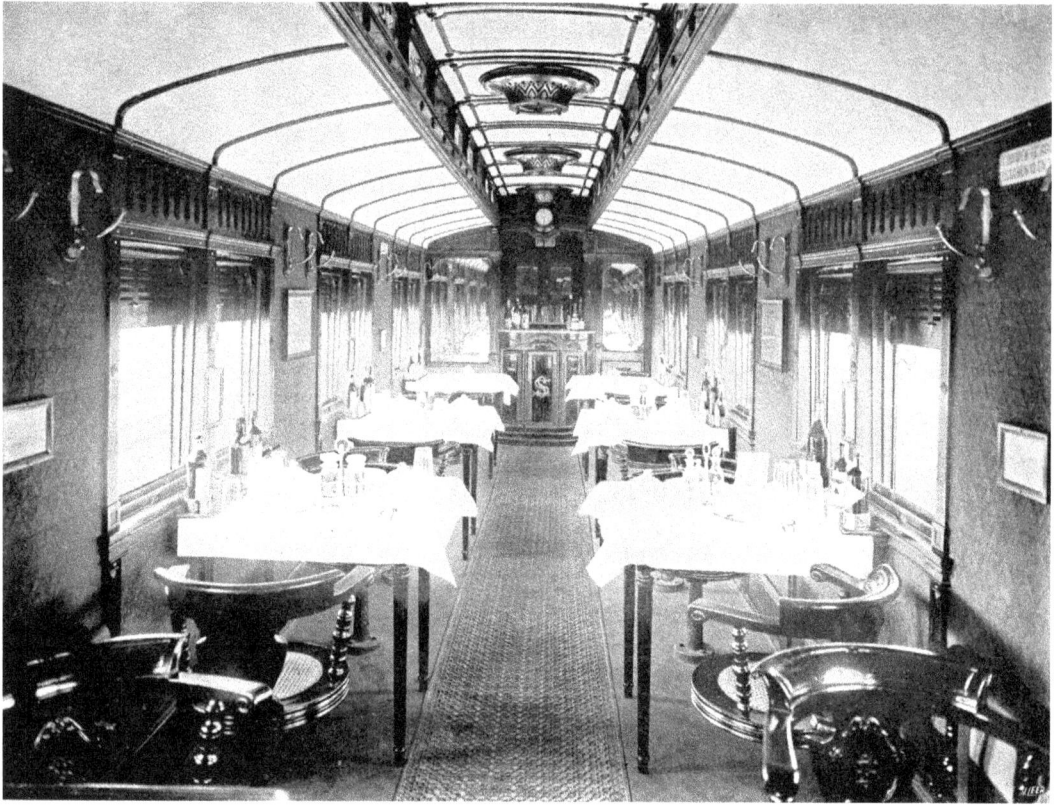

In the 1920s and 1930s, the Java State Railways did not hesitate to advertise their superior service in the press and even in the cinema. Here, a publicity photograph of the interior of a restaurant carriage complete with snow-white tablecloths, porcelain, silver flatware, and glass and crystal of excellent quality. Of course, these luxuries were available only for first- and second-class passengers. (Author's collection)

many often fatal accidents. In 1935 at least ninety-nine people had been killed in accidents on Java only: two passengers, six railway servants, and ninety-one others—the latter mostly trespassers, often at night. Some tramway companies, however, ran nocturnal sugar trains when traffic surged, with extra lookouts stationed on the locomotives to warn the drivers of approaching animals and people.

Yet, despite the dangers involved, the JSS in November 1936 decided to introduce a Nacht Expres (Night Express) between Batavia and Soerabaja and vice versa. It had been found that there was a certain demand for a night train among businessmen who did not want to lose a day's work. The first Nacht Expres ran on November 1, 1936, and was a success right from the start. During daylight hours the average speed was 85 km per hour, by night on the section between Cheribon and Madioen 60 km per hour. The train left Batavia each day at 17:34 (5:34 p.m.) and arrived in Soerabaja the next morning at 7:40. In the other direction the train left Soerabaja-Kota at 18:35 (6:35 p.m.) and arrived in Batavia at 7:40 the next day. The first sleeping carriages were rebuilt by the JSS Manggarai shops from older ordinary coaches, but in 1938 Beijnes of Haarlem supplied new welded all-steel sleepers 20 m long, with a weight of 39 tons. According to contemporary newspapers, they could stand comparison with the best the

Wagons Lits Company could offer in Europe. For traction the JSS chose the older 700 Series of 4-6-2 Pacifics, as they were still giving sterling service. They were upgraded in several ways and equipped with feedwater heaters and much larger tenders taken from other engines. Maximum speed of these night trains could well be raised to 90 km per hour or even more, as the old Pacifics had no trouble at all with keeping the schedules.[7]

THE VLUGGE VIER AND VLUGGE VIJF

Until 1934 the important connection between Batavia and Bandoeng was maintained by two expresses with the powerful 2-8-8-0 Mallets in charge on the heavy mountain section between Poerwakarta and Padalarang. Three hours and forty minutes were needed to cover the distance of 175 km, of which 56 km was mountain line with gradients of 16‰. Locomotives had to be changed twice, which took time; moreover, the Mallets were slow. The JSS now decided to accelerate these trains by splitting them into four lighter—150 tons—trains that could be hauled all the way by one of the 58 modern 4-6-4 tanks of the 1300 series supplied by Henschel and Hartmann in 1921/22. Experiments had shown that one engine

JSS Nr. 1209, delivered by ALCO in 1919, at rest at an unknown depot. This was the first of a series of twelve 2-8-8-0 Mallets supplied by the American works when the first eight units of 1916 had proved satisfactory. During the early 1930s, these engines were mothballed but later put in service again, with small modifications such as the double exhaust to improve their steaming. Photo by L. J. Biezeveld, 1939. (SNR collection)

of this class could handle the train all the way, with speeds of 100 km per hour on the level lines and 55 km per hour on the mountain sections. With three stops at Krawang, Tjikampek, and Poerwakarta, an overall traveling time of two hours and forty-five minutes could be reached, a full hour less than before. The success of these trains was immediate and most trains were regularly sold out. JSS called them the Vlugge Vier (Fast Four) and generated a lot of publicity in the press and the cinema to make sure that everybody knew about the possibilities of the new service. A full restaurant car was included in the first and third trains of the day, and a buffet coach in the other two. On the days that the weekly Dutch mail steamers arrived in Tandjong Priok, one train made the connection there.

Between Soerabaja and Malang in the cool highlands of East Java the situation was different as the distance was only 96 km, with a first level section as far as Bangil and from there 35 km of mountain line with gradients of 21‰. Motorbus competition here was more severe than on Batavia–Bandoeng because of the shorter distance. To counter this competition JSS decided to run five trains a day, each of five carriages weighing 125 tons, with one engine of the 1300 class between Soerabaja and Bangil and with two of the same series from there to Malang. Total traveling time of these Vlugge Vijf (Fast Five) was one hour and thirty minutes, half an hour less than before. Here the success was even greater than with

Batavia–Bandoeng, so in 1935 a sixth train had to be added. Businessmen now looked upon Malang and neighboring Lawang as ideal places for stabling the family in the cooler mountains, while they could keep their daily work in Soerabaja and commute by train. A cool weekend now also became possible to escape the heat and humidity of the city. As noted, the number of passengers of JSS alone had fallen from over 49 million in 1929 to a low of just more than 23 million in 1935, a decline of more than half, but the new services were able to reverse that downward move.[8]

IMPROVING EXISTING LOCOMOTIVES

The great improvement by the introduction of the Vlugge Vier between Batavia and Bandoeng caused JSS to consider acceleration of trains between Buitenzorg and Bandoeng over the original line via Soekaboemi as well, also a mountain line with gradients as severe as 40‰. The 1400 series of 2-8-2 tanks intended for switching duties had been mothballed but were now taken out of retirement and heavily modified. In Europe the work of André Chapelon, chief mechanical engineer of the Paris-Orléans Railway (PO), had become widely known. He had improved existing locomotives of the PO by carefully balancing all mechanical parts, streamlining the internal steam passages (along with a number of other measures) with spectacular results. The driving wheels of the JSS 1400s now were better balanced and other improvements as suggested by Chapelon were carried out with success. As modified the tanks were good for 75 km per

One of JSS's 1400 class 2-8-2 tanks after the upgrading and improvements to make them suitable for passenger trains is seen hauling a short passenger train through the paddy fields of Java around 1938. Most of the coaches are in the new green and white colors. (Gerard de Graaf collection)

hour and even more, so in 1938 a new much faster service could be introduced between Bandoeng and Soekaboemi. The modified 1400s were used for these trains with great success, their only handicap being the limited water capacity of only 9 m³.

With the improvement of the 1400 class, other engines could qualify for similar treatment to upgrade the machinery. Most of the 900 class of 2-8-0 Consolidations from 1914–1921 had also been stored when freight traffic fell off but were hauled into the light and critically examined. Balancing was improved in the same way as with the 1400s and the results were even better. These 2-8-0s, originally intended for freight trains, were now able to run at speeds of over 100 km per hour. With other smaller improvements they became ideally suited for hauling passenger trains on mountain lines, and with tenders good for 16 m³ of water, stops were less frequent. The use of these freight engines for passenger trains did cause a shortage of modern freight engines now that the economy was growing again, so older machines had to be dug out of retirement as well.[9]

THE OUTER POSSESSIONS

The Atjeh Tram, now ASS, always more a military and strategic line than an enterprise with an economic purpose, got into great troubles in the 1930s. Traffic fell off alarmingly, with only 324,000 passengers carried in the whole of 1934, although there was a slight improvement to 336,500 in the next year. Motorbuses continued to siphon off the few remaining travelers and voices were raised to abandon and scrap the whole tramway. After long discussions the decision was taken to keep the line running, chiefly for strategic and social reasons, and so the ASS soldiered on as best as it could. The original 2-4-0 tank engines were withdrawn and scrapped while the lowering of rates helped a bit to attract more passengers and freight. The tram had outlived itself, as it was seen in some quarters, but the ASS management fought back and so a nightly freight train was introduced for taking cattle to market in Medan—of course, still with a change of trains at Besitang. This service was well received and moreover in 1938 a lone passenger carriage was attached to this train in order to give travelers an opportunity for a cheap but slow ride. Plans for rebuilding the line with heavier rails came too late and were never carried out.[10]

The South Sumatra State Railway (ZSS) did better on the whole, particularly after the connection with Kertapati and Palembang was brought into use. At first passengers were few, with 403,000 in 1934 and 332,000 the following year, but in the coming years the situation improved materially. And when finally the Boekit Asam mines began producing the volumes of coal that had been hoped for, coal trains did help to fill the coffers of the company. A total of 384,000 tons of freight was carried in 1934; this

figure grew to over 468,000 tons in the next year, largely the result of the expanding output of the mines. Gradually, this production grew to a high level and in 1941, when European coal could no longer reach the Indies, a peak of 1.4 million tons was reached. It would be an all-time high.[11]

The Ombilin mines in West Sumatra continued into the 1930s with the production of coal and reached a high of 642,212 tons in 1930, only to decline slowly thereafter. However, by 1935 production had grown again and SSS carried more than 600,000 tons that year, mostly coal, but also cement from the Padang Cement Works. Ideas of abandoning the whole system, mines included, had been ventilated again and again, but nothing came of them and the mines continued to produce coal and the railway continued to bring it down to Emmahaven for export. Passenger traffic was always negligible for SSS, with only 133,200 souls transported in 1935.[12]

In Deli the recession was severe, with rubber prices falling from 1 guilder per pound in 1929 to 10 cents in 1934. The Deli Spoorweg (DSM) reacted in the usual way with a wage cut of 10 percent and a reduction of fares and rates, but despite this, freight transported fell from around 1 million tons in 1928 to 560,000 tons in 1934, to climb again to 830,000 in 1938. General rearmament worldwide contributed materially to this growth. Revenue declined from almost 10 million guilders in 1928 to a low of 4

The DSM operated a special luxury train of seven bogie carriages between Belawan and Medan on the days that the liners of the Nederland Line and the Rotterdam Lloyd (once a week) and the Norddeutscher Lloyd (once every two weeks) called at Belawan-Oceaanhaven. The well-maintained permanent way of the DSM is noteworthy. (Author's collection)

Facing top, In 1930, the Probolinggo Steam tram managed to find cheaper ways to operate trains. Petrol railcars, similar to those operated by the Deli railway, were introduced with some success. (Author's collection)

Facing bottom, Despite its financial woes, the Samarang-Joana company was able to introduce new and more comfortable trains for its main line. SJS Nr. 214, an 0-4-2 tank from Hartmann supplied in 1921, came equipped with superheater, piston valves, and an extended bunker behind the cab for firewood. She is in charge of one bogie van and two bogie carriages, well patronized. Probably a publicity photograph of the SJS from the late 1930s. (SNR collection)

million in 1934. From a total of 162 heads in 1929, the European staff was more than halved to seventy-four in 1934, and, of course, as the Europeans were the better-paid personnel, the reduction in money was substantial. Construction of the South Asahan line to Rantau Prapat, where work had been going on since the late 1920s, had been stopped about halfway, with the last 50 km left without rails and bridges, although all land needed for the line had already been leased or purchased. However, by 1936 the financial situation of the company had improved so much that it was decided to finish the line; toward the end of 1937 Rantau Prapat was reached. A healthy traffic soon developed, especially after Goodyear's great Wingfoot plantation started to use the new terminus for transport of its rubber to Belawan. Despite the grave financial problems that beset the DSM during the early and mid-1930s, the company never defaulted on the payment of interest on its outstanding loans, although shareholders had to go without dividends in 1931 and the next few years. Even at the bottom of the Depression in 1931 the company managed to make a small profit of ƒ323,000 that went into the reserve fund, truly a deep fall compared to 1928 when the net profit had been almost 4.5 million guilders. But 1931 did show a profit, a rare phenomenon in those years and better than most companies were showing at the time. In 1936 dividend payments could even be resumed at 2.5 percent, raised to 4 percent in the next year, not bad at all![13]

THE PRIVATE TRAMWAY AND RAILWAY COMPANIES

Most of the steam tram companies were hard hit by the competing privately owned motorbuses that siphoned off most of the short-distance passenger traffic. Freight traffic declined severely when Java's sugar production collapsed and many mills were closed. Only the Malang and Kediri Companies managed to pay off all their outstanding loans before 1940. The Oost-Java Company was the first of the trams in September 1933 to apply for a moratorium of interest payments, initially for eighteen months, but extended three times into 1940, when all communication with the directors in the home country was severed because of the occupation of the Netherlands by Nazi German forces in May 1940. A new 4 percent loan had been issued just before war broke out, but it was never signed by the directors, and bondholders had to accept heavy losses. The next company to default was the Samarang-Joana at the end of 1933, also extended until 1940. In 1933 ƒ100 was paid out on every bond in anticipation of a complete reorganization, which never came.

In the same year 1933 the Semarang-Cheribon stopped the mandatory annual gradual redemption of outstanding loans for seven years, although interest payments could be continued until 1938. Then these

A train similar to the one in the previous illustration but this time of the Semarang-Cheribon. SCS Nr. 122, one of the successful Hartmann 0-4-0s, is posing with three bogie carriages and a van in tow for photographer L. J. Biezeveld. Photograph from the 1930s, probably at the SCS station in Semarang. (SNR collection)

were terminated too, never to be resumed. The Serajoedal Company underwent a reorganization in 1935, when 50 percent of the face value of all outstanding loans was written off and interest on the rest reduced by 25 percent. Again a severe loss for bondholders. Dividends were not paid at all during these years. The Madoera Company converted all its outstanding loans in 1940 into a single new 4 percent loan of ƒ853,750. Existing bondholders had to accept some losses with this conversion.[14]

In view of these financial setbacks, it will not come as a surprise that these companies did not invest in new rolling stock, locomotives, or imposing stations. Schedules of trains were eased to reduce fuel consumption and little-used lines got less trains per day, although a minimum of service was always maintained because of the stipulations laid down in the concessions. Yet, some upgrading of tracks was undertaken, first of all by the Semarang-Cheribon Company in order to accelerate the trains between its two terminals. Competition from motorbuses, run by both Chinese and Indonesian operators, was less severe here because of the greater distance.

As with the State Railways, the old Nederlandsch-Indische Spoorweg (NIS) was hit hard by the wild buses over shorter distances, but the longer-distance trains fared better. First of all the company managed in 1937 to clear up its financial structure by paying off all outstanding loans with a new large 3.5 percent loan, totaling no less than 20 million guilders. This loan, although with a low rate of interest, was easily placed in the Netherlands, simplifying the financial operations of the company. The last dividend paid out was over 1930 at 9 percent; afterward, dividends were

impossible. The ever-larger deficits could be charged to the substantial reserve fund that had wisely been built up during the good years. After the nadir of 1935 with a loss of 638,000 guilders, the first profit could be booked again in 1937, amounting to some 685,000 guilders. Although profits declined again in the later 1930s, the worst years were over.[15]

Upgrading of services was a sure thing to raise revenues, but the NIS had no money in the till for purchase of new rolling stock. So thirty older broad-gauge bogie carriages were rebuilt and modernized in the company shops between 1938 and 1940 with new steel exteriors, electric light, and cooling by means of ice blocks. They were meant for the Vlugge Vijf of the NIS, five daily trains Semarang–Djokja introduced in 1935, an idea and a name stolen from the State Railways. These were scheduled at a higher maximum speed of 90 km per hour with fewer stops and at lower rates, covering the distance in just less than three hours. For these higher speeds better and more powerful locomotives were needed than the existing 4-6-0s, but financial restrictions precluded the ordering of new engines in Europe or America. Netherlands Railways (NS) was approached about a possible sale of four of the popular 3700 series of 4-6-0 locomotives, but NS answered that they could not be missed. Instead, they offered a couple of older 4-6-0s of the 3500 series, but NIS politely declined, as these were notorious for weak frames and consequent trouble and repairs. Ultimately, the NIS was forced to contract for new 4-6-0 engines in 1938 with Werkspoor, but because of the war the order had to be canceled. Pity, as they would have been a godsend with their intended maximum speed of 120 km per hour and beautiful, clean, streamlined exterior.[16]

A heavy express for Cheribon and Batavia is drawing away from Semarang-Pontjol (west) station of the Semarang-Cheribon company. It is hard to believe that this line had started in the last years of the nineteenth century as a simple and slow steam tram. In charge is one of the successful 4-6-0s, and the train consists of one bogie van and at least five bogie carriages, a far cry from the original light tramway stock. Photo by G. Diephuis, August 1, 1941. (Remmo Statius Muller collection)

A posed publicity photograph of an NIS broad-gauge train Semarang–Djokja. The refurbished carriages are hauled by an engine of the 87–91 series, noncompound 4-6-0s, but the number is partly hidden by the headlight. Semarang-Tawang station of the NIS is visible in the right background. (SNR collection)

For the Indian standard gauge lines (1,067 mm) the NIS, although financially strapped, did more. The Soerabaja–Goendih–Semarang tramway was upgraded to a railway second class in 1935, with 60 km per hour maximum speed allowed, and later, with again heavier rails and better curves, even to a railway of the first class with an allowed maximum of 75 km per hour or better. Five through trains Soerabaja–Semarang were run daily, with seven intermediate stops between the two terminals, in five hours and ten minutes and after 1937 in four and a half hours. Quite a good performance. The 4-6-0 engines Nrs. 381–400 used on these services were rebuilt with better balancing, more powerful vacuum brakes, and other new equipment; they were just powerful enough to handle these trains, but with precious little reserve. To speed up these trains even more the NIS then ordered three ultramodern multiple unit diesel-electric train sets from Beijnes-Haarlem in 1938. That firm had made a name for itself by constructing streamlined diesel-electric trains for Netherlands Railways in 1934–1935, and NIS now wanted to acquire something similar. The three steel and aluminum bodies of the first set were indeed erected at Beijnes, but because of the German invasion of the Netherlands in May 1940, they were never finished. The diesel power units—seven, two for each train and one as a spare—were built by Thomassen of De Steeg after a Danish Frichs patent. They were finished during the war but secreted away to keep them out of the hands of the Germans. After the war they were used to re-motor

some of the American Whitcomb Bo-Bo diesel-electric locomotives that NS bought from the US Army.

Despite this apparent knowledge of the advantages of diesel-hydraulic or diesel-electric propulsion, it is somewhat unexpected to note that the Java State Railways (JSS) did not initiate a program of trials of locomotives with the new kind of engines and transmissions. The German Fliegende Hamburger and the Dutch diesel-electric units of 1934 had made a big splash in the international railway world; moreover, the Royal Siam Railways (RSR) nearby, in another tropical and fairly poor country, had made an early start with dieselization. On Java these developments had apparently made no impression on the Dutch engineers in charge. In Siam, now Thailand, the railway company had started experiments with diesel-mechanical switchers in 1928, followed by impressive diesel-electric units for mainline duties in 1931, using Swiss and Danish technology. Sulzer and Oerlikon of Switzerland and Frichs of Denmark, all three world leaders in the field of diesel-electric propulsion, built these generally satisfactory meter-gauge engines. With these locomotives RSR had undoubtedly become a leader in this new technology, but so far without any following in the Dutch East Indies.[17]

As a measure for better defensive possibilities against the threatening Japanese forces, the NIS Goendih–Solo line was rebuilt with a third rail, so as to enable NIS standard-gauge trains to reach the Djokja works

Islamic feast days meant heavy traffic for the railways, as here on the NIS Poerwosari station where masses of humans try to board a train to bring them to Solo for the festivities. Most companies charged lower fares at these occasions. Photo from the 1920s. (SNR collection)

One of the Pacifics of the 1000 Class is seen entering the station of Meester Cornelis in the outskirts of Batavia in the 1920s with a heavy express from Djokja of at least twelve bogie carriages and vans. Heavy railroading at its best! The electrification of the regional lines around Batavia is finished and in use. (Author's collection)

without the use of transporter wagons, and also useful for the military to reach both Semarang and Soerabaja via this shorter route.[18]

THE SITUATION BEFORE THE JAPANESE ATTACK

The image of the 1930s railway as a dependable and modern transportation system in Java, fully able to service the needs of travelers and shippers, may have been exaggerated in the press and contemporary literature by the success of a few trains and connections between a few major cities on Java. In the rest of Java, train service was still largely unchanged and, although regular, very slow and old-fashioned, with antique rolling stock and motive power. And there were warning voices that the system as run in the late 1930s would not be able to continue the present services indefinitely. The most intensive use of engines that had not been designed for really high speeds or heavy work did cause a lot of wear and tear, as was outlined in the last—and never printed—annual report of the State Railways for 1941. G. F. Berg, the chief mechanical engineer, made it only all too clear that maintenance of these mostly elderly locomotives was not adequate and horribly expensive, with spare parts often no longer available. Acquisition of new power units was necessary, even urgent. Service could not be guaranteed with the older units, as most were nearing the end of their useful lives. He strongly advocated the purchase of modern American diesel-electric locomotives of some 1200 horsepower and 75 tons weight, as these would be ideal to take over the services of the steamers. Also most of the antique wooden carriages needed to be replaced as

JSS Nr. 1006, one of the impressive Werkspoor Pacifics is standing in Madioen station with an express made up of modern bogie stock, September 20, 1939. The disks with green or red glass next to the headlight were used for indicating the character of the train. All mainline JSS engines were equipped with this device. Photo by L. J. Biezeveld. (SNR collection)

soon as possible by modern steel stock, as the ancients were creaking in all their joints and distinctly unsuitable for the higher speeds of 1940. Berg stressed that capital had to be invested on a large scale for buying modern engines and rolling stock, probably from the USA, as Europe was inaccessible because of the war. Patching up the old stock would be a waste of money and absolutely insufficient and, if traffic would grow again, the existing fleet was clearly inadequate. Berg also stressed that continuing improvement of tracks and signaling would be unavoidable, with more welded rails, doubling of many sections of track and more electrification. His plan for improving and upgrading the whole system, to begin in 1943, would cost 10 million guilders extra annually for at least ten years, in order to obtain a really modern and up-to-date railway network fully able to serve the country's needs. However, war intervened and Berg's ideas had to be shelved and were never implemented. And what Berg wrote about the State Railways was also true for the private companies. There also too little investment in the infrastructure had been the norm in the 1930s, and rolling stock and locomotives were nearing the end of their lives. Soon a costly upgrade would be urgent there as well.[19]

In 1939, almost at the end of the period covered in this book, there were 7,583 km of public railway and tramway lines on Java and Sumatra, of which 2,218.km were railways first class and 5,365 km railways second class. Of this total only 266 km—3.5 percent—was in Indian broad gauge of 1,435 mm, and 6,644 km—87.4 percent—in Indian standard gauge of 1,067 mm. The 750-mm gauge, only in use on Sumatra, was good for another 520 km—6.9 percent—and 120 km of 600-mm gauge—1.6 percent—made up the remainder. These figures cover only the public railways and tramways, both of the state systems and the private companies. The hundreds of plantation, industrial, and other nonpublic railways are not included in these totals. Readers may protest that these figures do not add up to the full 100 percent. The 33 km—0.4 percent—of the Batavia city tramway, with its odd gauge of 1,188 mm, make up the total.[20]

NOTES

1. Brownlee, *Dynamics of Ascent*, 409–14.

2. The NV General Motors Java (a limited company under Dutch law) had opened a large plant in Tandjong Priok in 1927, where Chevrolet automobiles were assembled from American parts. Soon other GM models such as Oldsmobile, Pontiac, and Buick were added to the production as American automobiles proved to be better suited than European makes to the sometimes-bad roads of the East Indies. The modern factory employed more than one thousand workers, for a large part indigenous. *Holland's Colonial Call*, A15–16.

3. Based on Gonggrijp, *Schets ener economische geschiedenis*, 172–99; Zwaag (van der), *Verloren tropische zaken*, 41–44; Lindblad, "De Handel tussen Nederland en Nederlands-Indië," 240–98. Jong (de), *De Waaier van het Fortuin*, 507–14.

4. Jong (de), *De Waaier van het Fortuin*, 533–44.

5. Figures from Annual Reports of State Railways (Java and Sumatra) over 1930–1935.

6. Figures from Annual Report 1935 of the Semarang-Cheribon Steam Tram Company.

7. Jong (de), *De Waaier van het Fortuin*, 113, 181–86. The accident figures in Annual Report State Railways over 1935.

8. Oegema, *De stoomtractie*, 193–201. Jong (de), *De Waaier van het Fortuin*, 193–201. Passenger numbers from Annual Reports of the State Railways System 1930–1935.

9. About André Chapelon's work, see his book, originally published in French, *La Locomotive à Vapeur*, but also available in English. About the JSS and Chapelon's precepts, see Oegema, *De stoomtractie*, 94–98.

10. Ibid., 168. Passenger numbers from Annual Report 1935 of State Railways.

11. Ibid.

12. Ibid. Also Oegema, *De stoomtractie*, 160–64.

13. Meijer, *De Deli Spoorweg*, 68–72. Figures from Weisfelt, *De Deli Spoorweg Maatschappij*, 180.

14. All financial details based on Baas and Roos, *Catalogue of Issued Stocks and Bonds*.

Facing top, A freight is leaving Djokja behind an ex-Hedjaz Railway 2-8-2 Mikado of the JSS 1500 series. These locomotives, although originally not constructed for the Java State Railways, gave remarkably good service. The high semaphores are looking very Dutch, and the whole scene could easily have been shot in the Netherlands. Photo by L. J. Biezeveld, October 1939. (SNR collection)

Facing bottom, A very different kind of railroading! It was not difficult to feel lonely in the Javanese jungle with its giant trees, unfamiliar and dangerous animals, and other tropical surprises. Here a European track inspector of the Samarang-Joana with two assistants is being wheeled through the impressive forest on a hand-operated trolley. Photo from around 1900. (NSM collection)

15. Figures from Annual Reports of NIS 1935–1939.

16. Bruin (de), *Het Indisch spoor*, 72, 79. Oegema, *De stoomtractie*, 48.

17. Ramaer, *Locomotives of Thailand*, 60–63; Webb, *British Internal-Combustion Locomotive*, 84.

18. Oegema, *De stoomtractie*, 60–61. Bruin (de), *Het Indisch spoor*, 83.

19. Ibid., 73.

20. Figures based on Oegema, *De stoomtractie*, 208. In turn his figures are based on computations by the late S. A. Reitsma, the great authority on railways in the Dutch East Indies.

EPILOGUE 16

The Kingdom of the Netherlands was late building railways in its greatest and most important colony, the Dutch East Indies, nowadays the Republic of Indonesia. Just as in the home country, the discussion about the choice between private initiative and construction by the state was well-nigh endless and inconclusive for many years. All sorts of objections were raised, ranging from the supposed absolute superfluity of railways in the Indies with an economy that could well survive on animal traction, to a supposed danger of use by a foreign enemy of a railway once built. Compared to the other important European colonial power in Asia, Great Britain, the Netherlands were indeed lagging far behind. In British India railways were already being constructed before the Mutiny of 1855–1857 had clearly indicated that they could materially help to establish British power over a multitude of local and regional princes. Railways were pushed ahead there after the end of the bloody conflict, and major cities, fortifications, and ports were soon connected.

Although the British Indian example was closely monitored by Dutch and East Indian authorities, conditions there were very different from the islands of the archipelago, especially Java, the nucleus of Dutch rule and also the center of economic activity. When finally construction of a first railway on Java was undertaken by a private company, the NIS, this firm managed to construct its intended line despite serious technical, managerial, and financial problems, leading to severe financial stringency and dependency on the help of the government in Batavia. Only toward the end of the nineteenth century was the company able to resume construction of new lines and expansion of its services. Its early equipment and rolling stock was simple and cheap, but to a certain extent it fulfilled the expectations of its incorporators and materially stimulated the economic development of the region served by its trains.

Even during the construction of this first line the wisdom of leaving railway building to private interests was already heavily disputed both in Batavia and The Hague, leading to a final decision to entrust the creation of a real railway network on Java to a state organization. These state railways, both on Java and Sumatra, ably filled the void left in the 1870s by the impecunious private company, and they managed to lay out a core network of lines that served well to connect the most important towns and harbors and open up promising regions to large-scale export-oriented agriculture. Toward the end of the nineteenth century, the steam tramways, in these years again mostly privately owned, adequately filled the gaps in the mainline network and catered to the needs of the blossoming agricultural industries and other regional business.

When this first line was constructed to the established Stephensonian railway gauge, as generally used in Europe, the debate about the pros and cons of the chosen gauge of 1,435 mm continued. Was it really the most suitable gauge for Java, where mountains and other geological and natural obstacles abounded? Here the government played a decisive role when Dutch railway experts and specialists were brought in to settle the question. They came to the conclusion that a narrower gauge of 1,067 mm, already successfully used in Norway and in several British colonies, would be cheaper to construct, while on the other hand, it would certainly suffice for the transportation needs of Java and later also of Sumatra.

Meanwhile, the discussion of the best way of constructing and working Java's railways by private interests or the state had not ended. Even after the state had finally decided to undertake the building of some lines with public money, there were still many parties, in Batavia as well as in The Hague, in favor of selling these first state lines to private interests or to find a compromise by allowing construction by the state and working by private commercial interests. In short, these acrimonious discussions were just the same as in the mother country, where they had been going on until 1860, when the state finally stepped in to break the deadlock. In the East Indies these ongoing discussions caused a delay of almost twenty years before the State Railways could open its first lines in the 1870s. And although some of the leading statesmen in the home country and in the Indies still had doubts about the necessity of state construction of railways, the Java State Railways never looked back.

For economic and financial reasons, the pace of new construction was occasionally slowed or interrupted, but with the booming economy toward the end of the nineteenth century railways turned out to be absolutely necessary to serve the growing number of new plantations and connected mills and industries. Although it is hard to compute exactly, for lack of dependable figures and statistics, it is certain that the railways have contributed in no small way to the growth of the economy of the Dutch colonial empire in Asia. For an export-oriented economy such as that of the Dutch East Indies, the availability of all-weather means of transportation of the agricultural and mineral products from the inland sources of production to the ports was paramount. Rivers, often hardly navigable, were no alternative to a railway for the carrying of bulky goods, and only much later hard-surfaced roads were gradually offering other means of transportation. The riches of Java and Sumatra, such as coffee, sugar, tobacco, palm oil, coal, petroleum, rubber, quinine, and hundreds of other products, agricultural or not, were distributed to the world by means of the railways as carriers for the first stretches of the journey. And the other way round, imports from all over the globe could reach the great cities as well as the smallest desa deep in the tropical forests on a freight wagon of one of the many steam trams that stretched into the interior of Java and parts of Sumatra. The railway may not have completely annihilated time and space on Java and certainly not on Sumatra but it did materially contribute to make the vast space of these two islands more manageable.

Apart from serving the economy, railways also played an important role in the pacification of outlying districts of Java and Sumatra and consequently also in the next step, the inclusion of these regions in the world economy. And that was not all. For the first time ever the whole archipelago was governed from one central place by one single government. No longer did aristocratic families, princes, or kings rule distinct areas and regions, often warring with each other to the detriment of the population and often enough also losing life and possessions themselves in the course of these struggles. From now on there was one law for everybody, although still supplemented by local and regional "adat" customs where applicable. The Republic Indonesia is the rightful heir of this unified nation, the development of which took centuries. Without the building up of transportation services, where the railways played the initial and important role, this unification would have been hard to achieve. Here also the contribution of a dependable network of shipping lines in the archipelago to this unifying process should not be forgotten.

Financing the first private railway venture on Java was problematic. The search for capital came at an unfortunate moment, with serious problems for the banks; only government support and an infusion of capital from British investors saved the day. And just in time, for in 1866 the big Overend Gurney bank in London failed with disastrous sequences, not only in Britain but also overseas. For the State Railways this problem did not exist, as they were financed from the annual Colonial Budget as determined by Parliament in The Hague, sometimes liberally, also occasionally stingy, depending on the financial situation in the home country. Later in the nineteenth century and in the early twentieth century, capital for private railways and tramways tended to be abundant again, as expected returns had become most positive. Investors willing to risk some capital in the Indies were now easy to find, and the rewards were generally liberal. Of course, the worldwide Depression of the 1930s disrupted this rosy picture, but even in these troubled years some companies managed to float new low-renting loans to clean up their financial structure. It should be stressed that over all these years almost 95 percent of the necessary capital for railway and tramway construction came from Dutch banks and Dutch investors. Foreign capital played a role in some of the extensive twentieth-century agricultural companies, and only in one short-lived railway company. Of course, the several state railways were publicly owned, but the many private railway and tramway companies, the KPM and the KNILM, were all working with predominantly Dutch capital.

An earlier competitor, the steamship or sailing vessel connecting the many islands, was always a factor to be reckoned with. Transportation by sea between Java's many ports, large and small, both by KPM and smaller Chinese or Javanese operators, was always a serious competitor for freight and passengers not in a hurry. Competition from the air was negligible until the late 1920s, when the Koninklijke Nederlandsch-Indische Luchtvaart Maatschappij (KNILM, a daughter of the Dutch KLM) opened its first regular lines between the major cities of Java and Sumatra. In the period described in this book, air traffic remained limited, although the pioneering regular weekly Holland–Indies airline operated since 1924, first with Fokker Trimotors and later with Douglas DC-2s.

Contrary to British India, there were no great contractors like Brassey or Peto in England interested in building the first railways on Java. The NIS had great trouble in finding a contractor for its first lines and had to resort to construction by its own workforce under the direct supervision of the company engineers. The State Railways encountered the same problem in the decades after the NIS began, but then it was found that there were local or regional smaller contracting firms, Chinese or Javanese, that were willing and able to undertake small sections of a line or one bridge or station building at a time. Gradually, these firms developed and were able to contract for larger sections of a railway line, including more complicated layouts.

Bridges were a special case. Small stone or brick spans could be executed by these small contractors, but large iron or steel spans were a different matter. These bridges were generally designed and erected by Dutch or German works with their own personnel brought in for the purpose. Later, in the twentieth century, the Java State Railways bridge department under Haarman designed the necessary steelwork, but erection was still generally trusted to experienced Dutch and German companies. Werkspoor-Amsterdam built up a sizable customer base in the Indies, but smaller Dutch factories also profited in this respect. Steam locomotives were never built locally but imported from established European works. Despite the high cost of overseas transportation, these firms could work cheaper and more efficient than a local machine shop. British and German works were the most favored, but here again Werkspoor managed to wrest a big part of the orders from these more established firms. The American ALCO was brought in as a kind of stopgap during World War I when the usual European suppliers had problems with shortages of materials and workers.

Originally, it had been thought that the indigenous population of Java would not be interested in travel outside its desa or village, but it soon turned out that, given a really low rate, the population enthusiastically used the trains, especially on market days. Cheap rates for travel to the next village or bigger town on market days enabled the people to sell their wares and produce at better prices than at the local market. The railway also made a contribution to getting the Javanese in the interior of the islands used to an economy based on cash, no longer on barter. Of course, cash, in the shape of the bronze VOC *duiten* had been used for centuries, especially in the many small ports and government centers. But the railways, as employers of tens of thousands of men—and a few women—changed this picture materially by paying their staff, European or indigenous and even in the smallest outpost reached by the rails, in cash, something unknown until then on this scale. Taken all together, for the development of the economy, first of Java and then later in the nineteenth century also that of Sumatra, the railway has been invaluable.

After the end of the Great Depression in the late 1930s, the economy of the Dutch East Indies was only slowly recovering and, until prevented by the outbreak of war, the railways had to make good many arrears in maintenance, modern technology, and services. It is more than certain that if the war had not intervened, the railways on Java and Sumatra would have needed a substantial infusion of capital to finance a thorough modernization of the infrastructure. Acquisition of modern rolling stock and locomotives in large numbers would also have been necessary to enable them to continue to play an important role in the Indonesian economy.

It is worth mentioning that the technology of constructing and operating the railways came from Dutch engineers and technicians. Technology was chiefly imported from the home country, further developed locally, and adapted to the different needs. No strong foreign influence is visible apart from a few isolated cases. Of course, these Dutch engineers, schooled at the Military Academy of Breda or the Delft Technical School, were influenced by developments in Germany, Britain, and France. They were able to adapt these foreign innovations to the peculiar circumstances of Java and Sumatra, with a large but generally uneducated population, an unfavorable climate for Europeans, and a geographical environment that was enormously different from the home situation. Yet they managed to build up and operate a network that was second to none in other colonial territories in the world.

This all ended on March 8, 1942, when the commander of the KNIL (Royal Netherlands Indies Army) surrendered to the Japanese invader. Three and a half years later the Japanese in turn surrendered to the Allies, but the surviving Dutch officials and civilians, after three years in Japanese concentration camps, returned to a very different Indonesia. And for the railways, they had been used by the Japanese for their own military purposes and had suffered a great deal of damage. The post-1945 struggle for independence of Indonesia, to be free from Dutch influence, lasted for years; the railways took part in this fight and suffered still more damage. After the official transfer of sovereignty of December 27, 1949, to the Indonesian government, all railways, except the Deli Spoor, were taken over by the Djawatan Kereta Api, later known as Perusahaan Negara Kereta Api and still later as PT Kereta Api Indonesia, the government-owned company that is still operating the remaining railways in Indonesia.

MAPS

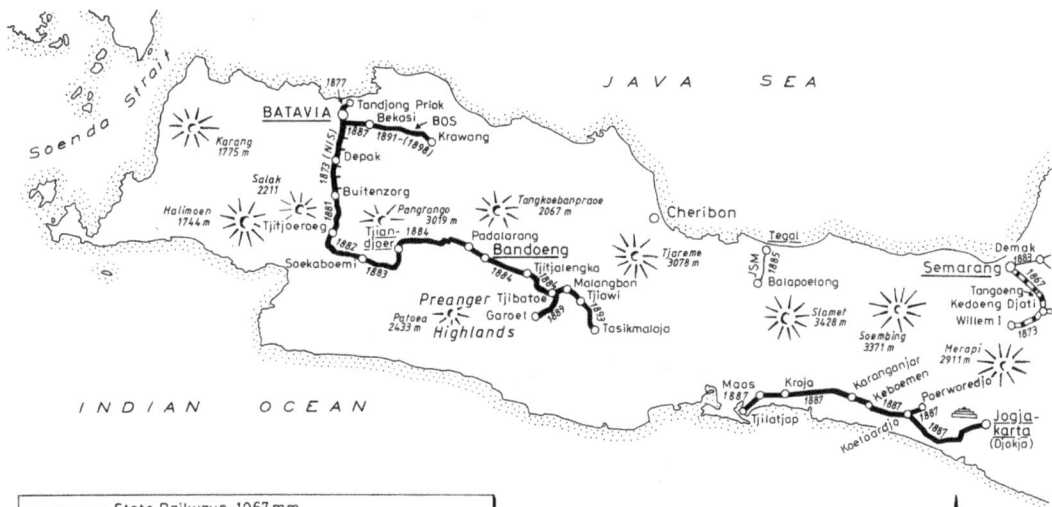

Map legend:
- State Railways 1067 mm
- Dutch East Indian Railway Company 1067 mm
- Dutch East Indian Railway Company 1435 mm
- Tramlines

RAILWAYS AND TRAMWAYS WEST JAVA 1893

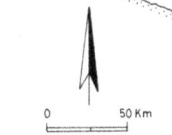

Dick v.d. Spek 1-2019 Th.316

273

RAILWAYS AND TRAMWAYS EAST JAVA 1893

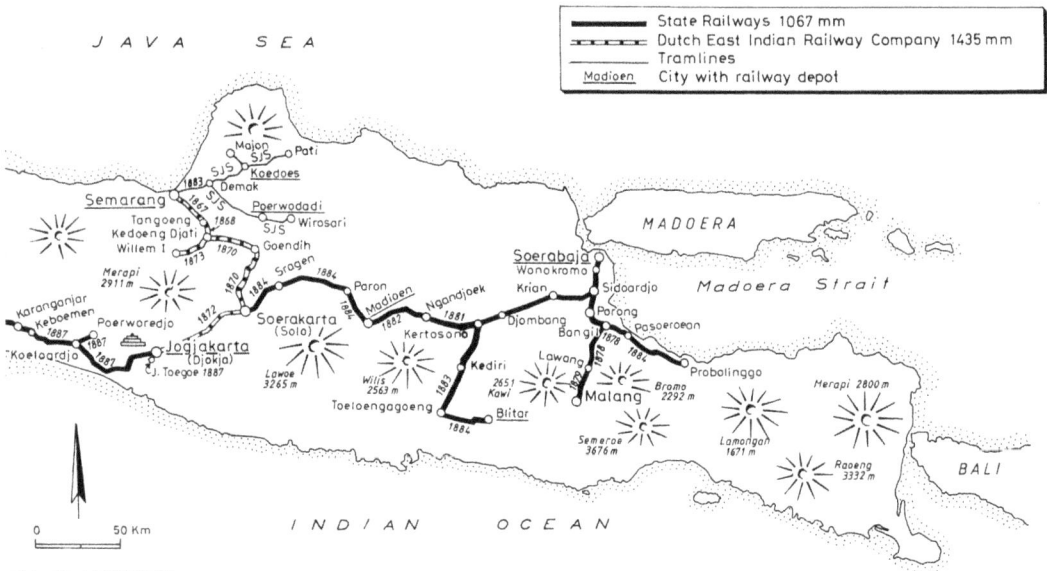

▬▬▬	State Railways 1067 mm
┅┅┅	Dutch East Indian Railway Company 1435 mm
────	Tramlines
Madioen	City with railway depot

J A V A   S E A

M A D O E R A

Madoera Strait

Majon
Pati
SJS
Koedoes
SJS
1883
Demak
Semarang
1867
Poerwodadi
Tangoeng 1868
Kedoeng Djati
Willem I
1873
1870
Goendih
SJS
Wirosari
Soerabaja
Wonokromo
Merapi
2911 m
1872
1884
Sragen
Paron
Madioen
Krian
Sidoardjo
Karanganjar
Keboemen
1887
Poerworedjo
Soerakarta
(Solo)
1882
Ngandjoek
1881
Djombang
Parong
Bangil
1878
pasoeroean
1884
Koeloardjo
1887
1887
Jogjakarta
(Djokja)
J. Taegae 1887
Lawoe
3265 m
Kertosono
Kediri
2651
Kawi
Lawang
Bromo
2292 m
Probalinggo
Merapi 2800 m
Wilis
2563 m
Malang
Toeloengagoeng
1884
Blitar
Semeroe
3676 m
Lamongan
1671 m
Raoeng
3332 m

B A L I

I N D I A N   O C E A N

0   50 Km

Dick v.d. Spek 1-2019 Th.317

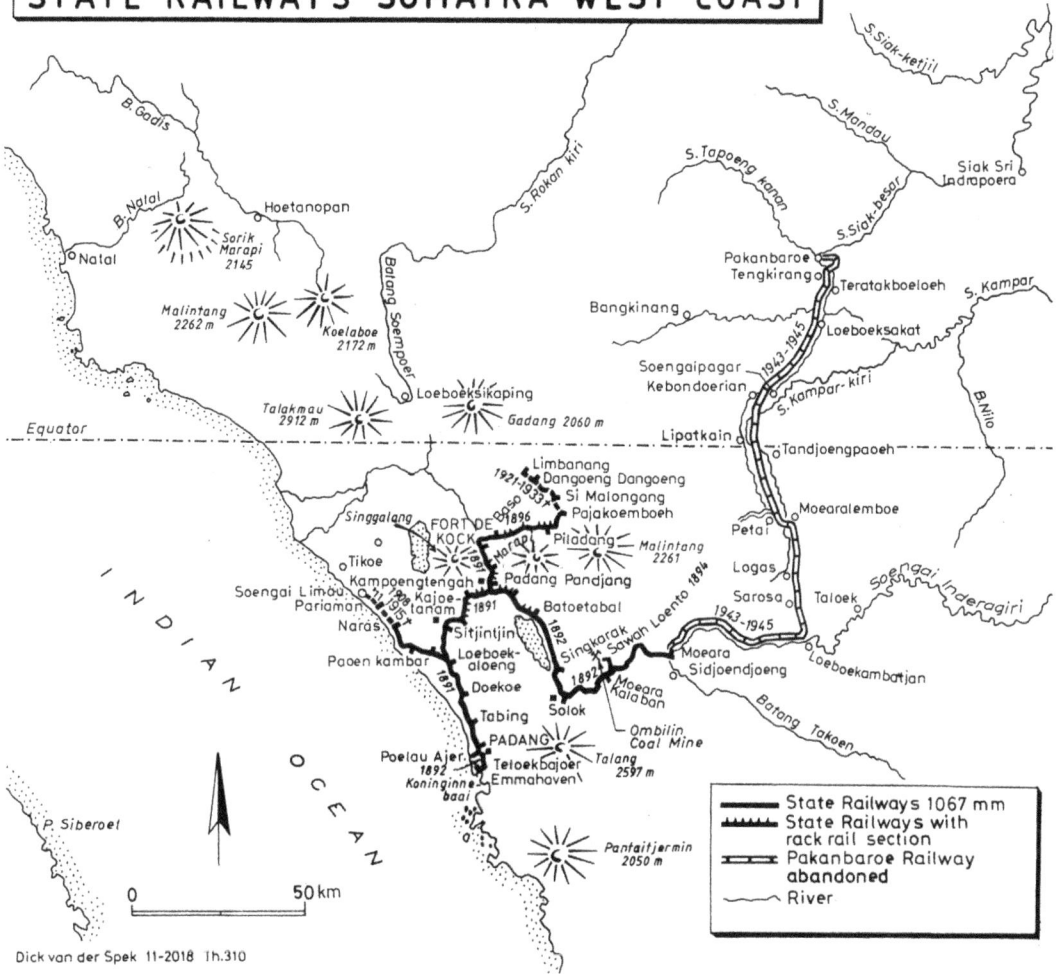

STATE RAILWAYS SUMATRA WEST COAST

B. Gadis

S. Siak-ketjil

S. Mandau

B. Natal

Hoetanopan

Sorik Marapi 2145

S. Tapoeng kanan

S. Siak-besar

Siak Sri Indrapoera

Natal

Malintang 2262 m

Koelaboe 2172 m

Batang Soempoer

Pakanbaroe
Tengkirango

Teratakboeloeh

S. Kampar

Bangkinang

Loeboeksakat

Loeboeksikaping

Talakmau 2912 m

Gadang 2060 m

Soengaipagar
Kebondoerian

S. Kampar-kiri

B. Nilo

Equator

Lipatkain

Tandjoengpaoeh

Limbanang
Dangoeng Dangoeng
Si Malongang
Pajakoemboeh

1921-1933

Soso

1896

Moearalemboe

Singgalang

FORT DE KOCK

Harapi

Piladang

Malintang 2261

Petai

Soengai Inderagiri

Tikoe

Kampoengtengah

Padang Pandjang

Logas

Sarosa

Taloek

Soengai Limau
Pariaman

Kajoe-
tanam

1891

Batoetabal

Singkarak

Sawah Loento 1894

1943-1945

Naras

Sitjintjin

1892

Loeboekambatjan

Paoen kambar

Loeboek-
aloeng

1892

Moeara
Sidjoendjoeng

Doekoe

Moeara
Kala ban

1891

Tabing

Solok

Batang Takoen

PADANG

Ombilin
Coal Mine

Poelau Ajer

1892

Teloekbajoer

Talang 2597 m

Koninginne-
baai

Emmahaven

P. Siberoet

Pantaitjermin 2050 m

State Railways 1067 mm	
State Railways with rack rail section	
Pakanbaroe Railway abandoned	
River	

0   50 km

Dick van der Spek 11-2018 Th.310

SOUTH SUMATRAN STATE RAILWAYS

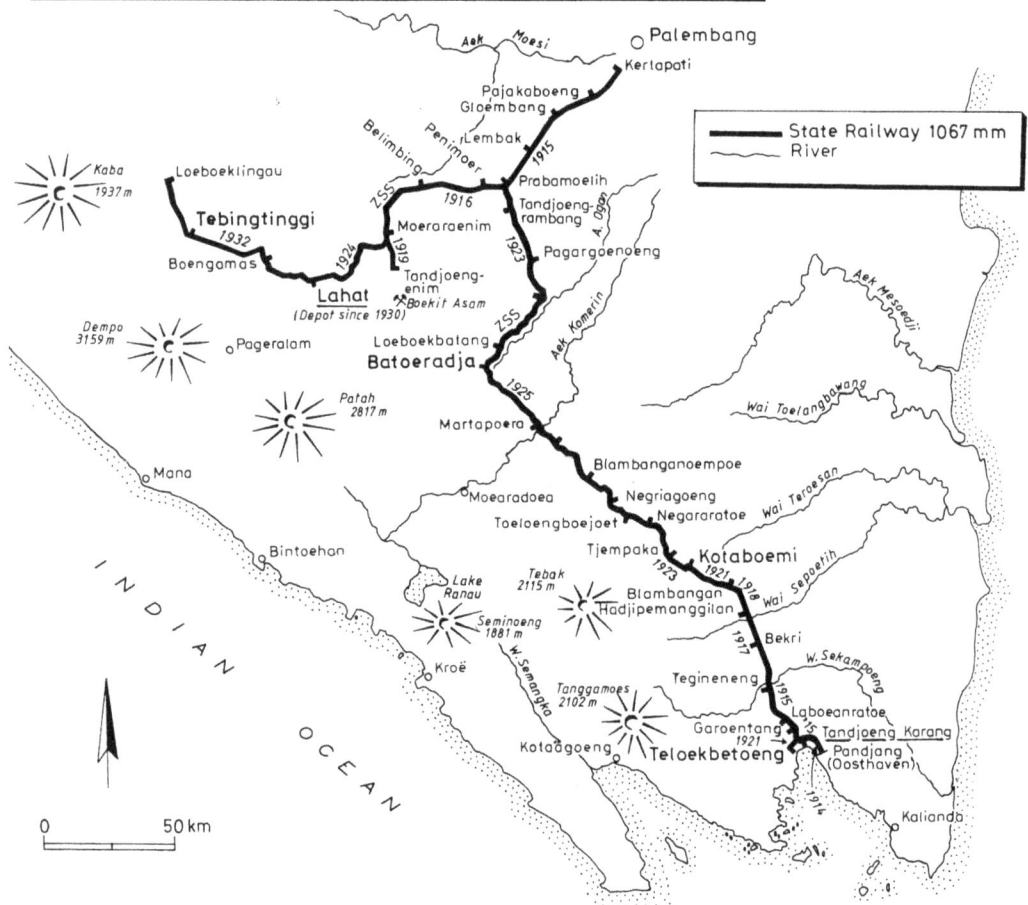

Palembang

Kertapati

Pajakaboeng
Gloembang

Prabamoelih

Tandjoeng-rambang

Pagargoenoeng

State Railway 1067 mm
River

Belimbing
Penimoer
Lembak

Loeboeklinggau

Kaba
1937 m

Tebingtinggi
1932

Boengamas

Moeraraenim

ZSS

1916

1915

1923

1924

1919

Tandjoeng-enim
Boekit Asam

Lahat
(Depot since 1930)

Dempo
3159 m

Pageralam

Loeboekbatang

Batoeradja

ZSS

1925

Aek Komerin

Aek Mesoedji

J A V A   S E A

Wai Toelangbawang

Patah
2817 m

Martapoera

Blambanganoempoe

Mana

Moearadoea

Negriagoeng

Negararatoe

Wai Teraesan

Toeloengboejoet

Bintoehan

Tjempaka

1923

1921 1918

Kotaboemi

Wai Sepoetih

Lake
Ranau

Tebak
2115 m

Blambangan
Hadjipemanggilan

Bekri

1917

Seminoeng
1881 m

W. Sekampoeng

Kroë

Tegineneng

1915

Laboeanratoe

Tandjoeng Karang

W. Semangka

Tanggamoes
2102 m

Garoentang
1921

Pandjang
(Oosthaven)

Kotaagoeng

Teloekbetoeng

1914

Kalianda

I N D I A N   O C E A N

Aek   Moesi

A. Ogan

0   50 km

D.van der Spek 11-2018 Th.311

SUMATRA

MALACCA STRAIT

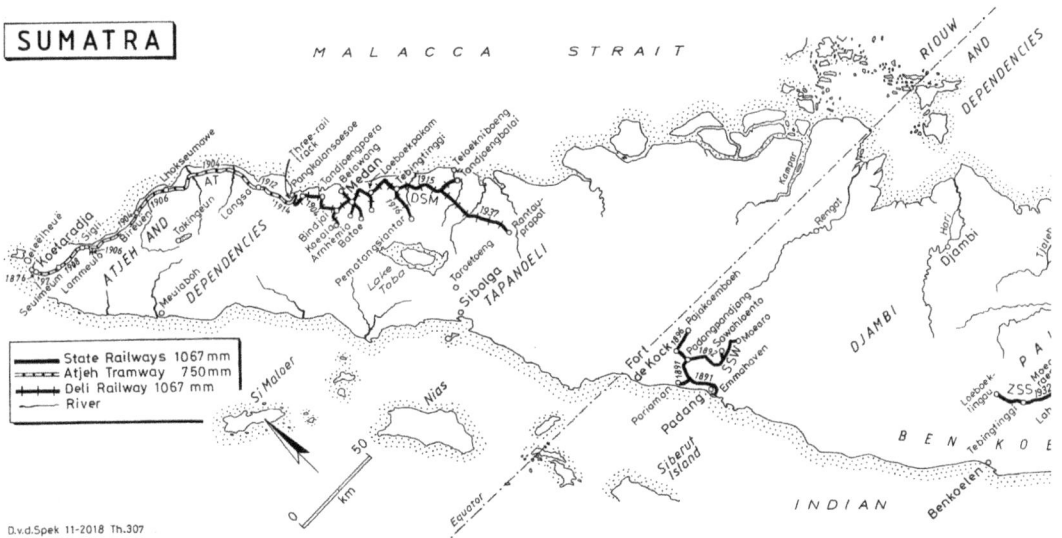

RIOUW AND DEPENDENCIES

Three-rail track

Lhokseumawe
Takingeun
Langsa
Pangkalansoesoe
Tandjoengpoera
Binjai
Belawan
Medan
Loeboekpakam
Tebingtinggi
Teloeknibeng
Tandjoengbalai

Geulieuë
Koetaradja
Sigli
Bireuën
Seulimeum
Lammeulo

ATJEH AND DEPENDENCIES

Karolanden
Armnema
Batoe
DSM
Pematangsiantar
Rantau prapat

Meulaboh

Laut Toba
Taroetoeng
Sibolga

TAPANOELI

State Railways	1067 mm
Atjeh Tramway	750 mm
Deli Railway	1067 mm
River	

Si Maloer

Nias

Siberut Island

Fort de Kock
Priaman
Padang
Padangpandjang
Pajakoemboeh
Sawahloento
Emmahaven

DJAMBI

Djambi

BENKOELEN

INDIAN

Equator

0   km   50

D.v.d.Spek 11-2018 Th.307

ATJEH STATE RAILWAY

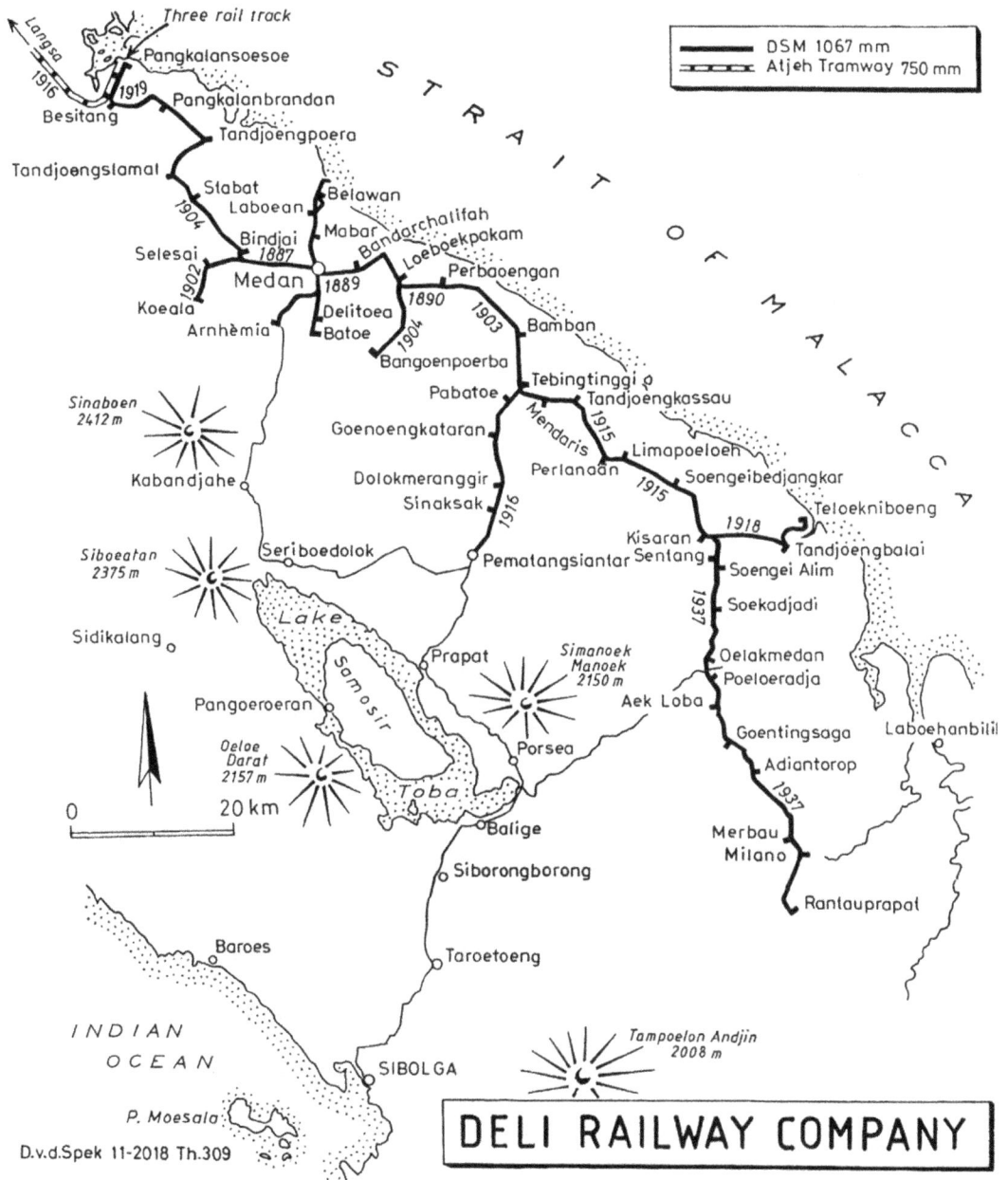

Three rail track

Langsa
1916

Pangkalansoesoe

Pangkalanbrandan
1919
Besitang

Tandjoengpoera

Tandjoengslamat
Stabat
Laboean
Belawan
1904
Bindjai
1887
Mabar
Bandarchalifah
Selesai
1902
Loeboekpakam
Medan
1889
Perbaoengan
Koeala
Delitoea
1890
Arnhèmia
Batoe
1904
Bamban
1903
Bangoenpoerba
Tebingtinggi
Pabatoe
Tandjoengkassau
Goenoengkataran
Mendaris
1915
Limapoeloeh
Dolokmeranggir
Perlanaän
Soengeibedjangkar
Sinaksak
1916
1915
Teloekniboeng
Seriboedolok
Kisaran
1918
Pematangsiantar
Sentang
Tandjoengbalai
Soengei Alim
Soekadjadi
1937
Lake
Prapat
Simanoek
Manoek
Oelakmedan
2150 m
Poeloeradja
Pangoeroeran
Aek Loba
Laboehanbilil
Porsea
Goentingsaga
Oeloe
Darat
Adiantorop
2157 m
Toba
1937
Balige
Merbau
Milano
Siborongborong
Rantauprapat
Baroes
Taroetoeng

INDIAN
OCEAN
Tampoelon Andjin
2008 m
SIBOLGA

P. Moesala

D.v.d.Spek 11-2018 Th.309

Sinaboen
2412 m
Kabandjahe

Siboeatan
2375 m

Sidikalang

Samosir

STRAIT OF MALACCA

0   20 km

DSM 1067 mm
Atjeh Tramway 750 mm

DELI RAILWAY COMPANY

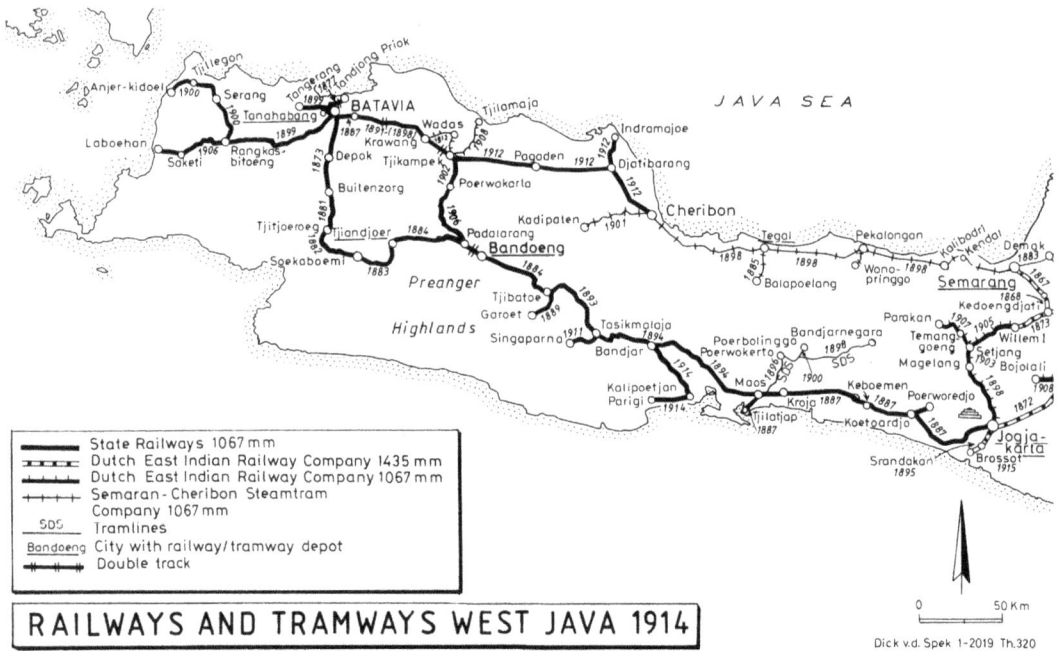

State Railways 1067 mm
Dutch East Indian Railway Company 1435 mm
Dutch East Indian Railway Company 1067 mm
Semaran-Cheribon Steamtram
Company 1067 mm
SDS   Tramlines
Bandoeng   City with railway/tramway depot
Double track

RAILWAYS AND TRAMWAYS WEST JAVA 1914

0   50 Km

Dick v.d. Spek 1-2019 Th.320

RAILWAYS AND TRAMWAYS EAST JAVA 1914

━━━━━	State Railways 1067 mm
┅┅┅┅	Dutch East Indian Railway Company 1435 mm
━┿━┿━	Dutch East Indian Railway Company 1067 mm
┼┼┼┼┼	Semarang – Cheribon Steamtram Compagny 1067 mm
─·─·─	East-Java Steamtram Company 1067
┼┼┼┼┼	State Railways 600 mm ──SJS── Other tramlines
○	City with railway/tramway depot
━╫━╫━	Double track

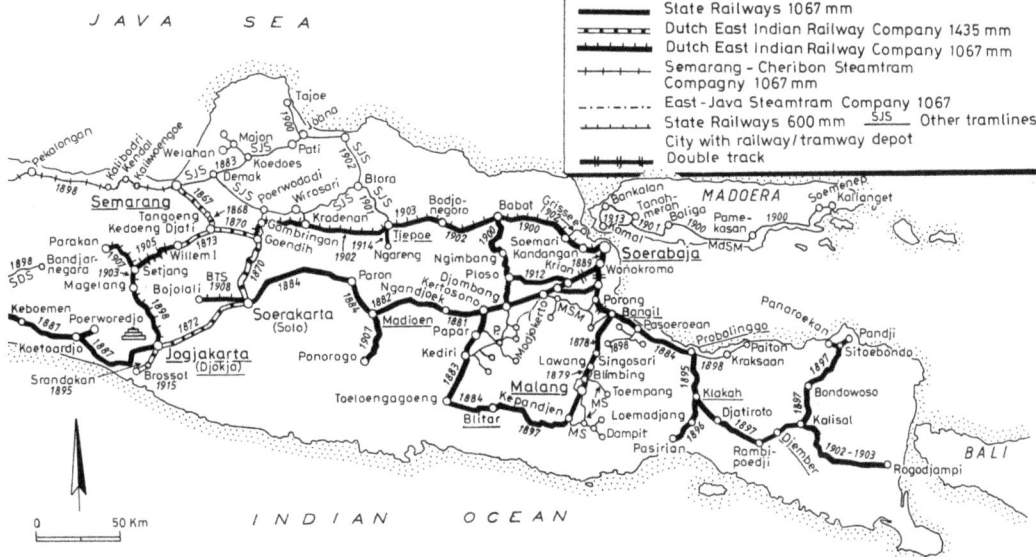

JAVA SEA

MADOERA

INDIAN OCEAN

BALI

Semarang
Soerabaja
Soerakarta (Solo)
Jogjakarta (Djokja)
Malang
Madioen

0   50 Km

Dick v.d. Spek 1-2019 Th.321

RAILWAYS AND TRAMWAYS WEST JAVA
1931

Tjilegon
Anjer-kidoel
Bantam
Serang
1900
1900
T. Priok
1877
Rengasdengklok
1899
Tanahabang
Batavia
Indramajoe
Karangompel
Cheribon
Karang
1899
Wadas
Tjiiamaja
Laboehan
Menes
1906
Rankasbitoeng
Mr. Cornelis
Krawang
1912
1912
1908
Saketi
1873
Depok
Tjikampek
1902
Pagaden
1912
Djatibarang
1912
1916
Buitenzorg
Poerwakarta
1912
1881
Tjitjoeroeg
Tjiandjoer
1884
1906
Padalarang
Bandoeng
SCS
1901
1858
G.Giwoer
1882
Tandjoengsari
Kadipaten
Soekaboemi
1883
Kiaratjondong
Tjitjalenka
1916
K.Soewoeng
Dajeuhkolot
1884
Tjibatoe
Tjiwidej
1922
1889
1893
Goentoer
1921
Garoet
Tasikmalaja
1894
1930
1894
Tjikadjang
Singaparna
1911
Bandjar
1914
Parigi
1914
INDIAN OCEAN
Tjidjoelang
1921

State Railways 1067 mm	
Dutch East Indian Railway Company 1435 mm	
Dutch East Indian Railway Company 1067mm	
Semarang-Cheribon Steamtram Company 1067 mm	
Soerakarta – Jogjakarta 1435 + 1067 mm twined track with (seperate) 1067	
East-Java Steamtram Company 1067 mm	
State Railways 600 mm	
SJS Other tramlines	
Blora City with railway/tramway depot	
Double track	

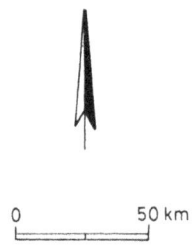

0   50 km

D.v.d.S. 1-2019 Th. 313

RAILWAYS AND TRAMWAYS CENTRAL JAVA 1931

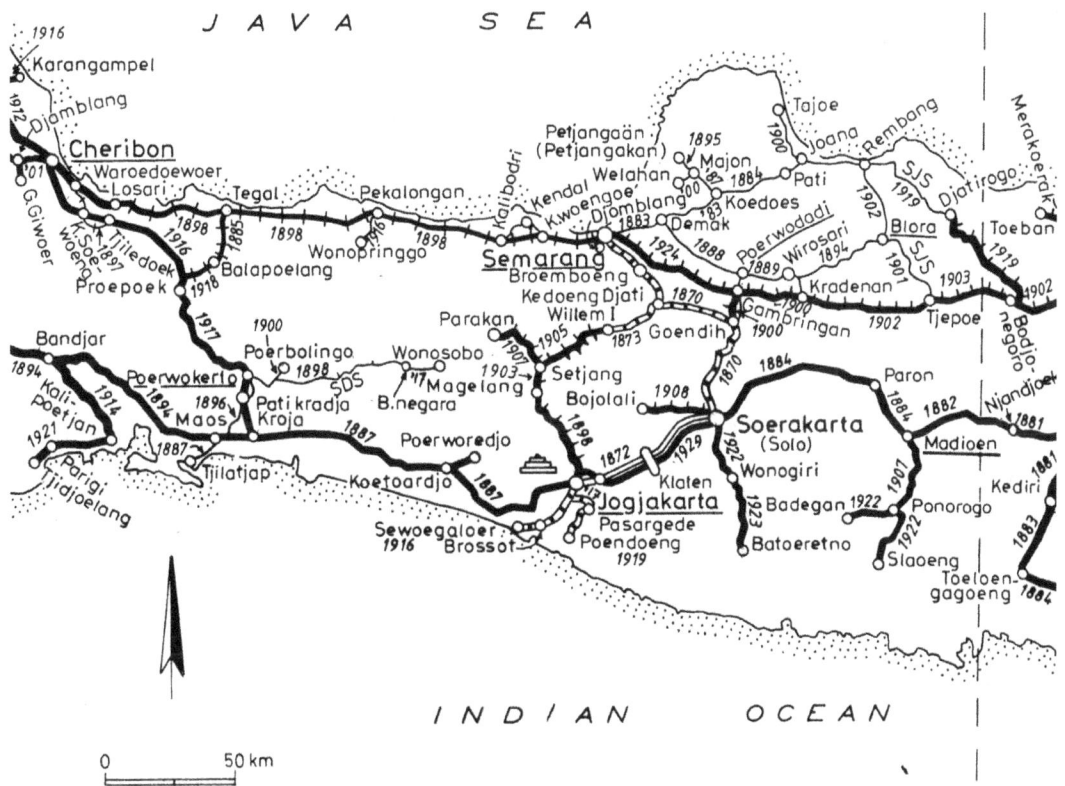

JAVA   SEA

1916

Karangampel

Djomblang

1912

Cheribon

1901   Waroedoewoer

Losari

Tegal

Pekalongan

Petjangaän
(Petjangakan)

1895

Kalibodri

Kendal   Welahan

K.woengoe

Majon

1884

1900

Tajoe

Joana

Rembang

Pati

Koedoes

Djomblang

Demak

1883

Poerwodadi

Wirosari

1889

Blora

SJS

1902   1919

Djatirogo

Toeban

1919

1898   1885   1898

1896

Wonopringgo

1898

Tiledoek   G.Giwoer

1897

Proepoek   S.

woer

1918

Balapoelang

Semarang

Broemboeng

Kedoeng Djati

Willem I

1924

1888

Kradenan

1889   1894

SJS

1901   1903

1902

Tjepoe

Bodjo-
negoro

1902

Bandjar

Kali-
Poetjan   1894

1921

1914   1896   Maos

Parigi   Tjidjoelang

1887

Tjilatjap

Poerwokerto

1900

1898

1896   Pati kradja

1901

Poerbolingo

SDS

Wonosobo

B.negara

1917   Magelang

Kroja

1887

Poerworedjo

Koetoardjo

Parakan

1905   1907   1903

Kedoeng Djati

1870

Goendih

1873

1900

Gambringan

1870

1900

1908

Setjang

Bojolali

1898

1872

1887

Sewoegaloer   Brossot
1916

Pasargede
Poendoeng
1919

1884

Gambringan   1902

Soerakarta
(Solo)

Paron

1884

1882

Njandjoer

1881

Madioen

Kediri

1883

Wonogiri

1929   1922   1923

Jogjakarta

Klaten

Badegan   1922

Ponorogo

1907

1922

Slaoeng

Batoeretno

Toeloen-
gagoeng   1884

INDIAN   OCEAN

0   50 km

D.v.d.S. 1-2019 Th.314

Maps   283

RAILWAYS AND TRAMWAYS EAST JAVA

1931

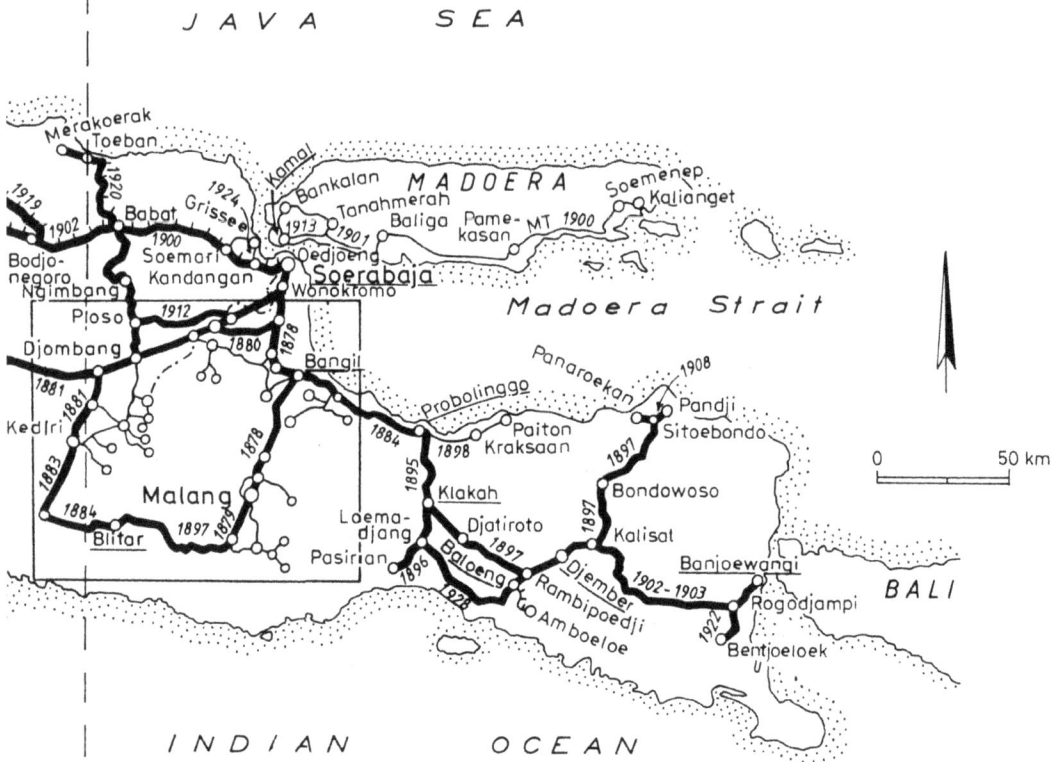

Map legend labels (as printed on the map):

J A V A   S E A

Merakoerak
Toeban
1919 1902 1920
Babat
Grissee 1924
Bodjo- 1900
negoro
Ngimbang
Soemari
Kandangan
Ploso 1912
Djombang
1881
1881
1883
Kediri
Malang
1884
Blitar 1897 1879
1878
1880
1878
Bangil
Wonokromo
Soerabaja
Oedjoeng
1901
1913
Tanahmerah
Bankalan
Kamal
M A D O E R A
Baliga
Pame-
kasan
MT 1900
Soemenep
Kalianget
Madoera Strait
Panaroekan 1908
Probolinggo
Paiton
Kraksaan
1884
1898
1895
Klakah
Loema-
djang
Pasirian
Djatiroto
1897
1896
Baloeng
928
Amboeloe
Rambipoedji
Djember
1897
Kalisat
1902 - 1903
Bondowoso
1897
Sitoebondo
Pandji
Banjoewangi
Rogodjampi
1922
Bentjoeloek
U
B A L I

0   50 km

I N D I A N   O C E A N

D.v.d.S. 1▲2019 Th. 315

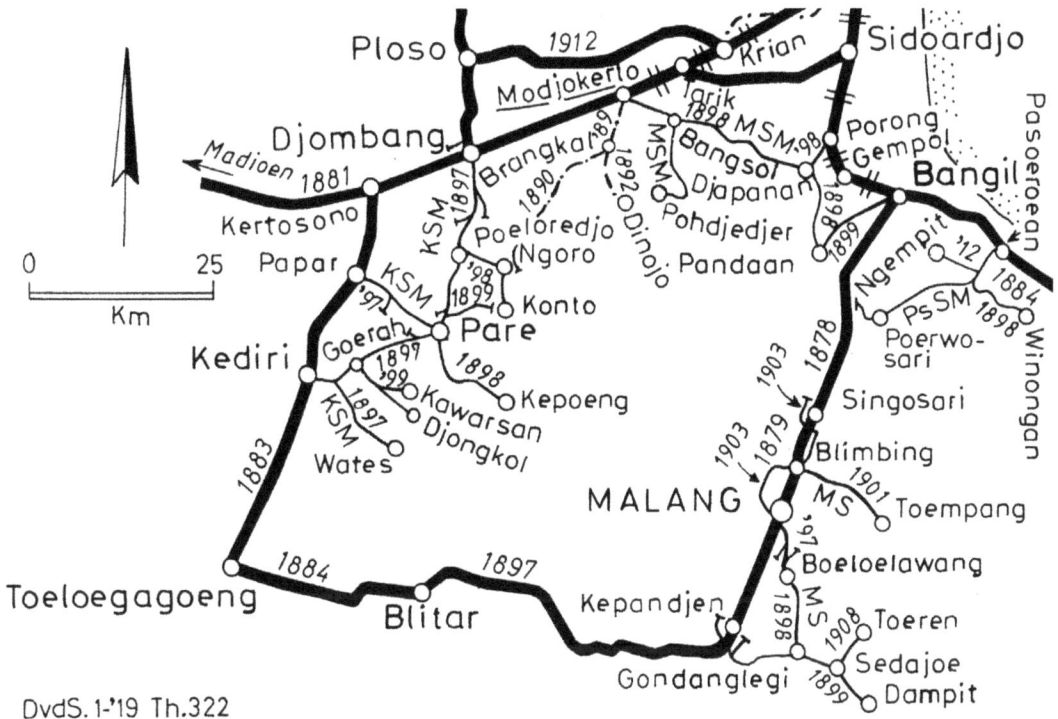

Ploso — 1912 — Krian — Sidoardjo

Modjokerto

Djombang — Brangkar — Tarik 1898 MSM '98 — Porong Gempol — Bangil

Madioen 1881

Kertosono

Papar — KSM 1897 — Poeloredjo (Ngoro) — 1890 — 1892 Dinojo — MSM Djapanan — Bangsol Pohdjedjer Pandaan — '98 1899 Ngempit — '12

Kediri — KSM '97 — Goerah 1899 — '99 — Kawarsan 1898 — Konto — Poerwo-sari PsSM 1898 Winongan

1883 — KSM 1897 — Wates Djongkol — Kepoeng — 1878 — 1903 Singosari

1903 1879 — Blimbing 1901 Toempang

MALANG — MS

Toeloegagoeng — 1884 — Blitar — 1897 — Kepandjen — Boeloelawang '97 N MS 1898 1908 Toeren

Gondanglegi — 1899 Sedajoe Dampit

DvdS. 1-'19 Th.322

0 ———— 25
Km

Railways around Malang, 1931 (detail).

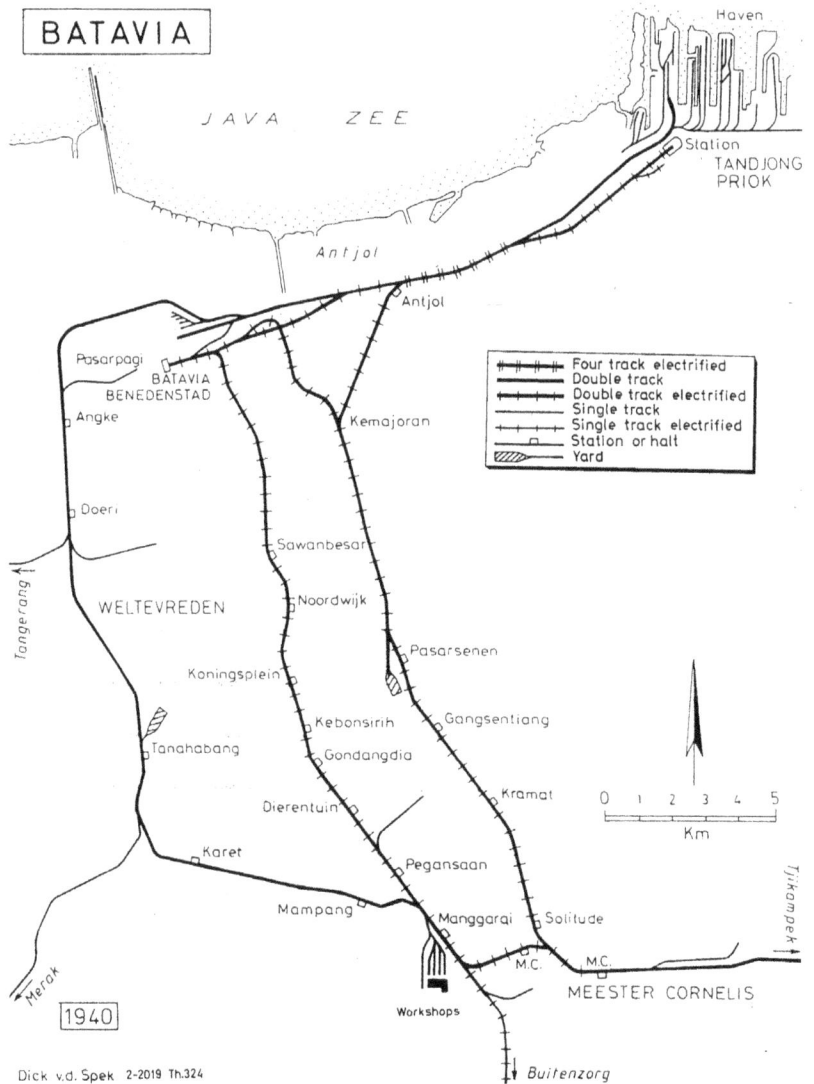

BATAVIA

JAVA ZEE

Haven

Station
TANDJONG
PRIOK

Antjol

Antjol

Pasarpagi
BATAVIA
BENEDENSTAD

Angke

Kemajoran

Four track electrified
Double track
Double track electrified
Single track
Single track electrified
Station or halt
Yard

Doeri

Sawanbesar

WELTEVREDEN

Noordwijk

Pasarsenen

Koningsplein

Tangerang

Gangsentiang

Kebonsirih

Gondangdia

Kramat

Tanahabang

Dierentuin

0 1 2 3 4 5

Km

Karet

Pegansaan

Mampang

Manggarai

Solitude

Tjikampek

Merak

M.C.

M.C.

1940

Workshops

MEESTER CORNELIS

Dick v.d. Spek 2-2019 Th.324

Buitenzorg

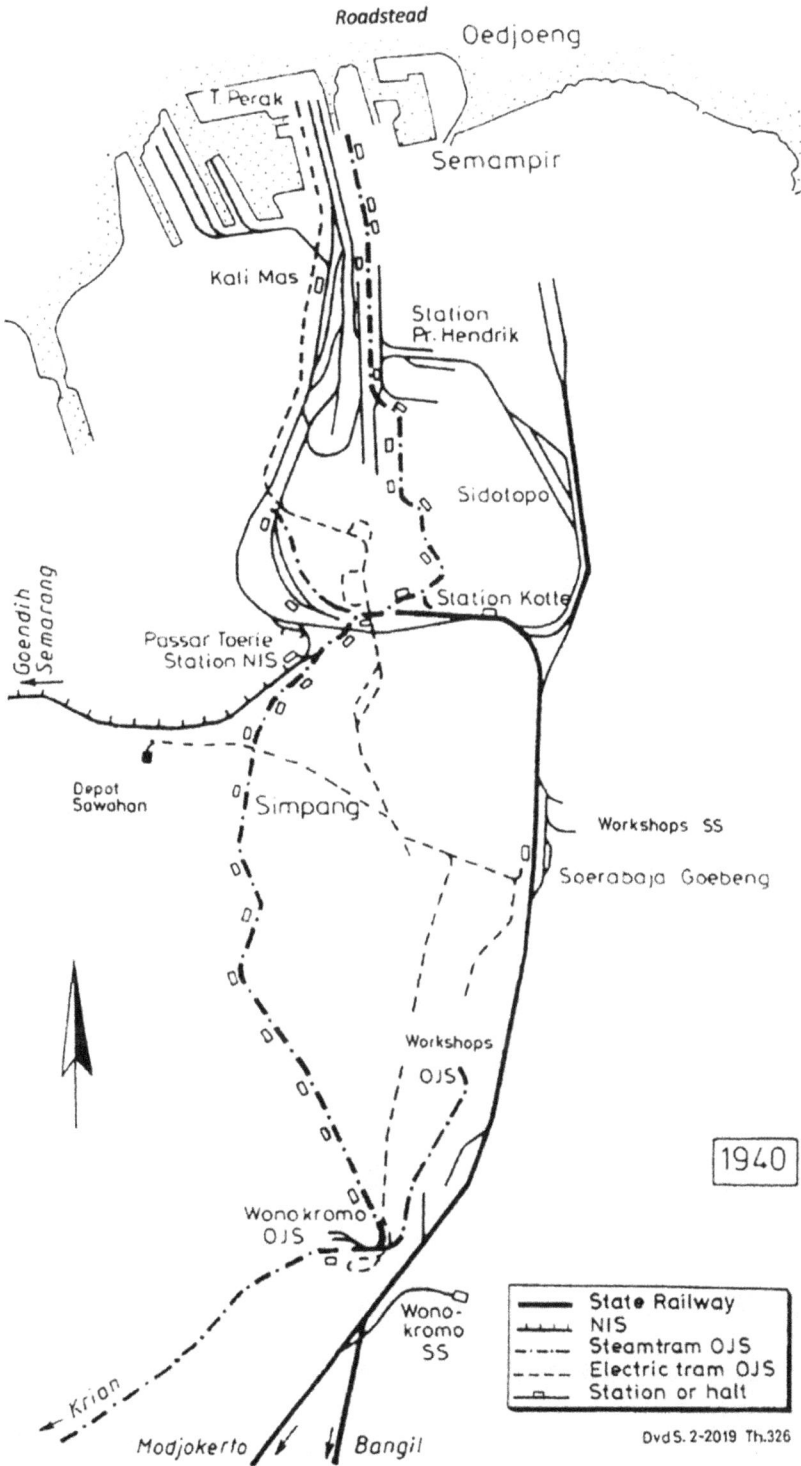

SOERABAJA

Roadstead
Oedjoeng

T. Perak

Semampir

Kali Mas

Station
Pr. Hendrik

Sidotopo

Station Kotte

Goendih
Semarang

Passar Toerie
Station NIS

Depot
Sawahan

Simpang

Workshops SS

Soerabaja Goebeng

Workshops
OJS

1940

Wonokromo
OJS

Wono-
kromo
SS

	State Railway
	NIS
	Steamtram OJS
	Electric tram OJS
	Station or halt

Krian

Modjokerto

Bangil

DvdS. 2-2019 Th.326

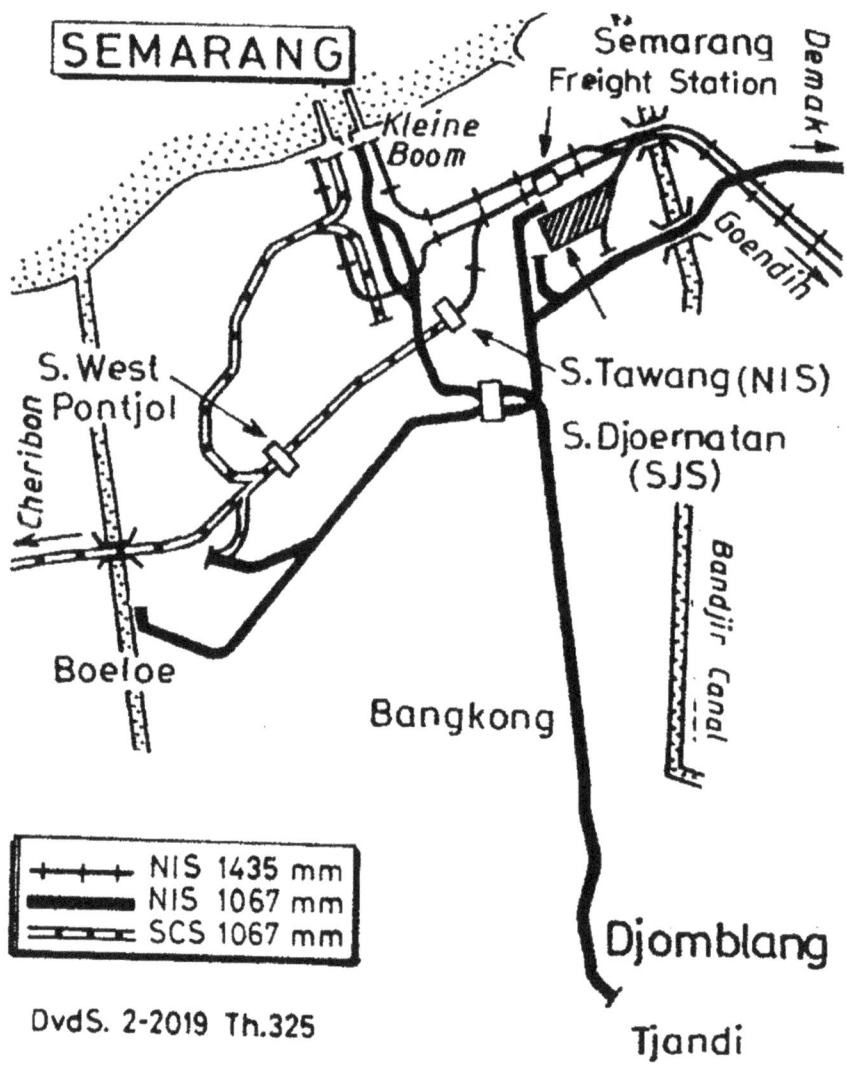

SEMARANG

Kleine Boom

Semarang Freight Station

Demak

Goendih

S. West Pontjol

Cheribon

S. Tawang (NIS)

S. Djoernatan (SJS)

Bandjir Canal

Boeloe

Bangkong

Djomblang

Tjandi

┼┼┼┼	NIS 1435 mm
▬▬▬	NIS 1067 mm
▤▤▤	SCS 1067 mm

DvdS. 2-2019 Th.325

TRAMLINES ON CELEBES

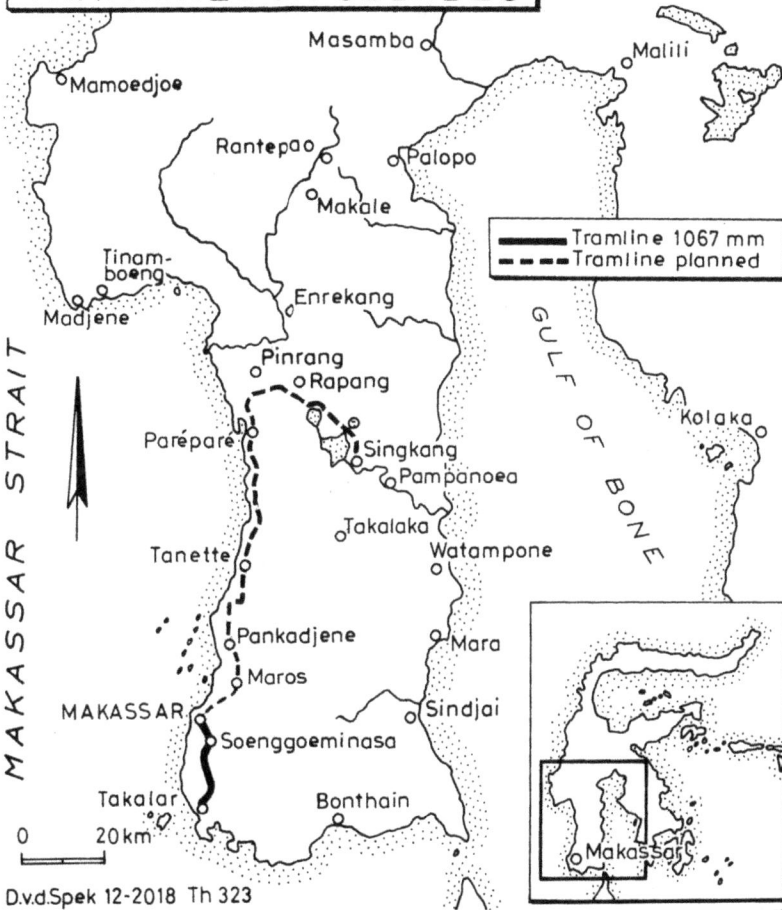

Masamba

Malili

Mamoedjoe

Rantepao

Palopo

Makale

Tramline 1067 mm
Tramline planned

Tinam-
boeng

Enrekang

Madjene

MAKASSAR STRAIT

Pinrang

Rapang

GULF OF BONE

Parépare

Singkang

Pampanoea

Kolaka

Takalaka

Tanette

Watampone

Pankadjene

Mara

Maros

MAKASSAR

Sindjai

Soenggoeminasa

Takalar

Bonthain

0   20km

Makassar

GAZETTEER

Geographical names used in the book and present-day names
(B) = Borneo, (C) = Celebes, (J) = Java, (M) = Madoera, (S) = Sumatra

Anei River (S)	Anai	Deli (S)	Deli
Anjer Kidoel (J)	Anyer Kidul	Deli Toewa (S)	Delitua
Atjeh (S)	Aceh	Djatibarang (J)	Jatibarang
		Djember (J)	Jember
Babat (J)	Babat	Djokja, *see* Jogjakarta	
Balapoelong (J)	Balapulung	Djombang (J)	Jombang
Bali (island)	Bali		
Balikpapan (B)	Balikpapan	Emmahaven (S)	Telukbayur
Banda Islands	Banda Besar		
Bandjar (J)	Banjar	Fort de Kock (S)	Bukittinggi
Bandjarnegara (J)	Banjarnegara		
Bandjermasin (B)	Bandjarmasin	Goendih (J)	Gundih
Bandoeng (J)	Bandung	Goentoer (mountain, J)	Guntur
Bangil (J)	Bangil	Grissee (J)	Gresik
Banjoewangi (J)	Banyuwangi		
Banka Island	Bangka	Idi (S)	Idi
Bantam (J)	Bantam	Indramajoe (J)	Indramayu
Batavia (J)	Jakarta		
Bekassi (J)	Bekasi	Joana (J)	Juana/Djoewana
Belawan (S)	Belawan	Jogjakarta (Djokja, J)	Yogyakarta
Bengkalan (M)	Bengkalan		
Besitang (S)	Besitang	Kalibodri (J)	Kalibodri
Billiton (island)	Belitung	Kalipoetjang (J)	Kalipujang
Bindjei (S)	Binjei	Kaliwoengoe (J)	Kaliwungu
Blang Mé (river, S)	Blangme	Kamal (M)	Kamal
Blitar (J)	Blitar	Kediri (J)	Kediri
Blora (J)	Blora	Kedoeng Djati (J)	Kedungjati
Boekit Asam (coal mines, S)	Bukit Asam	Kendal (J)	Kendal
Boenoet (S)	Bunut	Kertapati (S)	Kertapati
Borneo	Kalimantan	Kertosono (J)	Kertosono
Brossot (J)	Brosot	Kisaran (S)	Kisaran
Buitenzorg (J)	Bogor	Koeala Simpang (S)	Kualasimpang
		Ko(t)ta (Koeta) Radja (S)	Banda Aceh
Celebes	Sulawesi	Krawang (J)	Karawang
Cheribon (J)	Cirebon	Kroja (J)	Kroya

Laboean (J)	Labuhan	Prabamoelih (S)	Prabamulih
Lahat (S) Lahat		Preanger (highlands, J)	Priangan
Lampong District (S)	Lampong	Probolingo (J)	Probolinggo
Langkat (S)	Langkat	Proepoek (J)	Prupuk
Lawang (J)	Lawang		
Lho Seumawe (S)	Lhokseumawe	Rambipoedji (J)	Rambipuji
Loeboek Linggau (S)	Lubuklinggau	Rantau Padjang (B)	Rantaupajang
Losari (J)	Losari	Rantau Prapat (S)	Rantauprapat
		Rembang (J)	Rembang
Madioen (J)	Madiun		
Madjenang (J)	Madyenang	Samarang, Semarang (J)	Semarang
Madoera Island	Madura	Sasaksaat (J)	Sasaksaät
Magelang (J)	Magelang	Sawah Loento (S)	Sawahlunto
Makassar (C)	Makassar	Serajoe River (J)	Seraju
Manggarai (Batavia, J)	Manggarai	Setjang (J)	Secang
(Jakarta)		Seuleimom (S)	Seuleimeum
Maos (J)	Maos	Siak (S)	Siak
Maros (C)	Maros	Sidoardjo (J)	Sidoardjo
Medan (S)	Medan	Sigli (S)	Sigli
Meester Cornelis (Batavia, J)	Jatinegara	Si Maloer (island)	Simeuluë
(Jakarta)		Singaparna (J)	Singaparna
Meloewoeng (J)	Meluwung	Soekaboemi (J)	Sukabumi
Menado (C)	Manado	Soenda Strait	Selat Sunda
Mentawai Islands	Kepulauan Mentawai	Soerabaja (J)	Surabaya
Merak (J)	Merak	Soerakarta (Solo) (J)	Surakarta (Solo)
Merapi (volcano, J)	Merapi		
Modjokerto (J)	Mojokerto	Takalar (C)	Takalar
Moeara Enim (S)	Muaraenim	Tandjong Priok (J)	Tanjung Periak
Moendoe (J)	Mundu	Tanggoel (J)	Tanggul
Moluccas (islands)	Maluku	Tangoeng (J)	Tangung
		Tanjoeng Karang (S)	Tanjungkarang
New (Nieuw) Guinea (island)	Irian Jaya	Tasikmalaja (J)	Tasikmalaya
		Tebing Tinggi (S)	Tebingtinggi
Olehleh (S)	Ule Lhee	Tegal (J)	Tegal
Oosthaven (S), *see* Pandjang		Teloek Betong (S)	Telukbetung
		Teloek Niboeng (S)	Teluknibung
Padalarang (J)	Padalarang	Ternate Island	Ternate
Padang (S)	Padang	Timbang Langkat (S)	Timbanglangkat
Padang Pidji (S)	Padangtiji	Timor Island	Timor
Pajakombo (S)	Payukumbuh	Tjepoe (J)	Cepu
Pakan Baroe (S)	Pakanbaru	Tjiandjoer (J)	Ciandjur
Palembang (S)	Palembang	Tjibadak (J)	Cibadak
Pandjang (Oosthaven) (S)	Panjang	Tjibatoe (J)	Cibatu
Pangkalan Brandan (S)		Tjikampek (J)	Cikampek
Pangkalanbrandan		Tjilamaja (J)	Cilamaya
Pangkalan Soesoe (S)	Pangkalansusu	Tjilatjap (J)	Cilacap
Parakan (J)	Parakan	Tjitjalengka (J)	Cicalengka
Pasoeroean (J)	Pasuruan		
Poeger (J)	Puger	Weltevreden (Batavia, J)	Jakarta Gambir
Poerwodadi (J)	Purwodadi	Willem I (J)	Ambarawa
Poerwokerto (J)	Purwokerto	Wonosobo (J)	Wonosobo
Ponorogo (J)	Ponorogo		
Pontianak (C)	Pontianak		

ABBREVIATIONS
USED IN THIS BOOK

AC alternating current

AEG Allgemeine Elektrizitäts Gesellschaft, Berlin

ALCO American Locomotive Company, Schenectady, New York

ASS Atjeh Staats Spoorweg (Atjeh State Railway)

AT Atjeh Tram (Atjeh Tramway)

BB Binnenlands Bestuur (internal civil government)

BDSM Babat-Djombang Stoomtram-Mij. (Babat-Djombang Steamtram Cy.)

BOS Bataviasche Oosterspoorweg-Mij. (Batavia Eastern Railway Cy.)

BOW Burgerlijke Openbare Werken (public works dept.)

BP Beyer Peacock & Company, Manchester, England

BPM Bataafsche Petroleum Maatschappij, The Hague, Netherlands

BTM Bataviasche Tramweg Mij. (Batavia Tramway Cy.)

Cy. company

D&B Du Croo & Brauns, Locomotieffabriek, Weesp and Amsterdam, Netherlands

DC direct current

DSM Deli Spoorweg Mij. (Deli Railway Company)

GIP Great Indian Peninsula Railway

GM Gouvernements Marine (government navy)

GWR Great Western Railway, England

HVA Handels Vereeniging Amsterdam (Trading Cy. Amsterdam, Netherlands)

JSM Java Spoorweg-Mij. (Java Railway Cy.)

JSS Java Staats Spoorwegen (Java State Railways)

KITLV Koninklijk Instituut voor Taal-, Land- en Volkenkunde, Leiden

KNIL Koninklijk Nederlandsch-Indisch Leger (Royal Netherlands Indies Army)

KNILM Koninklijk Nederlandsch-Indische Luchtvaart Maatschappij (Royal Netherlands Indies Airline Company [Daughter of KLM Royal Dutch Airlines])

KPM Koninklijke Paketvaart Mij. (Royal Packet Navigation Company)

KSM Kediri Stoomtrammaatschappij (Kediri Steamtram Cy.)

MIJ   Maatschappij Company

MS   Malang
Stoomtrammaatschappij
(Malang Steamtram Cy.)

MSM   Modjokerto
Stoomtrammaatschappij
(Modjokerto Steamtram Cy.)

MT   Madoera Stoomtram Mij.
(Madoera Steamtram Cy.)

NHM   Nederlandse Handel
Maatschappij (Netherlands
Trading Cy., Amsterdam,
Netherlands)

NIH   Nederlandsch-Indische
Handelsbank (Netherlands
Indies Commercial Bank,
Amsterdam, Netherlands)

NIL   Nederlandsch Indisch Leger
(Netherlands Indies Army)

NIS   Nederlandsch-Indische
Spoorweg Mij. (Netherlands
Indies Railway Cy.)

NISM   Nederlandsch-Indische
Stoomvaart Mij. (Netherlands
Indies Steam Navigation Cy.)

NITM   Nederlandsch-Indische
Tramweg Maatschappij
(Netherlands Indies Tramway
Cy.)

NS   Nederlandse Spoorwegen
(Netherlands Railways)

NSM   Nederlands
Spoorwegmuseum, Utrecht

OJS   Oost-Java Stoomtram-Mij.
(East Java Steamtram Cy.)

O&K   Orenstein & Koppel, Berlin,
Germany

PbSM   Probolinggo Stoomtram-Mij.
(Probolingo Steamtram Cy.)

PsSM   Passoeroean Stoomtram-Mij.
(Passoeroean Steamtram Cy.)

SCS   Semarang-Cheribon
Stoomtram-Mij.
(Semarang-Cheribon
Steamtram Cy.)

SDS   Serajoedal Stoomtram-Mij.
(Serajoe Valley Steamtram
Cy.)

SJS   Samarang-Joana Stoomtram
Mij. (Samarang-Joana
Steamtram Cy.)

SLM   Schweizerische Lokomotiv
Fabrik, Winterthur,
Switzerland

SNR   Stichting NVBS
Railverzamelingen,
Amersfoort

SSS   Staats Spoorweg Sumatra
Westkust (State Railways
Sumatra West Coast)

VOC   Verenigde Oostindische
Compagnie (United East
India Company)

WW   World War (One and Two)

ZSS   Zuid Sumatra Staats
Spoorweg (South Sumatra
State Railway)

Note: The names of the several steam tram companies have been written as printed on their bonds and shares. The reader will note several versions of "stoomtram maatschappij," as one word or as two and hyphenated or not, but the spelling as given here is correct. Passoeroean with double *ss* is probably a mistake of the Dutch incorporators or the printers of the securities, as Pasoeroean was the established spelling of the town in colonial days.

SOURCES AND SUGGESTIONS FOR FURTHER READING

The vast archives of the Ministry of the Colonies are kept in the National Archives at The Hague. The archives of the Java State Railways are being preserved in Bandung, Java, out of my reach. Of the Zustertrammen, most archives are preserved in the National Archives in The Hague. The annual reports of the several railway companies have been consulted for figures and facts. The Railway Museum in Utrecht has a good collection of those for the researcher. Most of the available literature about the railways and tramways in the former Dutch East Indies is in Dutch, of course, and I have used everything accessible, most of it from my personal library. I understand that for English-speaking readers the Dutch titles below will have little value, but I wanted to show what I have used and where my information comes from. Fortunately, there are a number of books and articles in English available for those who want to know more about the railways of the former Dutch East Indies and the present Republic of Indonesia—more than I have been able to describe in brief in this single volume.

FURTHER READING

Abbott, Rowland A. S. *The Fairlie Locomotive*. Newton Abbot: David & Charles, 1970.

Amstel, Henry van. "Madoera Stoomtram Maatschappij." *Op de Rails* 85 (May 2017): 244–48.

Asselberghs, Henri. *Beijnes: Een Eeuw van Arbeid*. Haarlem, 1938.

Baas, P., and H. B. Roos. *Catalogue of Issued Stocks and Bonds of Railway Companies in [the] Netherlands Indies between 1863 and 1942*. Utrecht, 2017.

Baddeley, G. E. *The Continental Steam Tram*. London: Light Rail Transit Association, 1980.

Bakker, Michel. "Free Extending over the Bandjir: Building Bridges for Roads and Railways." In Ravesteijn and Kop, eds., *For Profit and Prosperity*, 137–92.

Ballegoijen de Jong, Michiel van. *Spoorwegstations op Java*. Amsterdam: Bataafsche Leeuw, 1993.

——. *Stations en Spoorbruggen op Sumatra 1876–1941*. Amsterdam: Bataafsche Leeuw, 2001.

Beaton, Kendall. *Enterprise in Oil: A History of Shell in the United States*. New York: Appleton-Century-Crofts, 1957.

Berckel, H. E. van. "De Zeehaven voor Batavia te Tandjong Priok." In *Gedenkboek KIVI*, 305–07.

Bergmann, Uwe. *Die Dampflokomotiven der indonesischen Werkbahnen*. Hamburg: Bahn Werk-Verlag Peter Lindemann, 2017.

Beyen, K. H. "De nieuwe Spoor-en Tram-
wetgeving voor Nederlandsch-Indië."
Spoor- en Tramwegen 1, no. 5 (1928):
127–29; no. 6, 162–64.

Boomgaard, Peter. "Het Javaanse boerenbedrijf, 1900–1940," *NEHA Jaarboek
voor economische, bedrijfs- en techniek-
geschiedenis*, 62 (Amsterdam: NEHA,
1999), 173–85.

Bordes, J. P. de. *De spoorweg
Samarang-Vorstenlanden*. 's Gravenhage: M. Nijhoff, 1870.

Bosma, Ulbe, and Kees Mandemakers.
"Indiëgangers: sociale herkomst
en migratiemotieven (1830–1950)."
*Bijdragen en Mededelingen betreffende
de Geschiedenis der Nederlanden / The
Low Countries Historical Review* 123-2
(2008): 162–84.

Boxer, C. R. *The Dutch Seaborne Empire,
1600–1800*. London: Hutchinson, 1965.

Boyd, J. I. C. *The Festiniog Railway*, 2 vols.
Lingfield: Oakwood, 1959.

Brink, E. A. B. J. ten, and C. W. L. Schell.
*Geschiedenis van de Rijkstelegraaf
1852–1952*. The Hague: PTT, 1954.

Brown, John K. *The Baldwin Locomotive
Works, 1831–1915*. Baltimore: Johns
Hopkins University Press, 1995.

Brownlee, W. Elliot. *Dynamics of Ascent:
A History of the American Economy*, 2nd
ed. Chicago: Dorsey, 1988.

Brugman, H. P. "Beveiliging van het
Treinverkeer op de Staatsspoorwegen
in Ned.-Indië." *Spoor- en Tramwegen* 1
(1928): 332–34.

Bruin, Jan de. *Du Croo & Brauns Locomotieven*. N.p.: Stichting Rail Publicaties,
1987. (Text in Dutch and English.)

——. *Het Indische spoor in oorlogstijd.
De spoor- en tramwegmaatschappijen
in Nederlands-Indië in de vuurlinie,
1873–1949*. N.p.: Uquilair, 2003.

Bude, Roland, Klaus Fricke, and Martin
Murray. *O&K Dampflokomotiven. Lief-
erverzeichnis 1892–1945*. Buschhoven:
Railroadiana Verlag, 1978.

Campo, M. à. *Koninklijke Paketvaart
Maatschappij: Stoomvaart en Staats-
vorming in de Indonesische Archipel
1888–1914*. Hilversum: Verloren, 1992.

Carey, Peter. *The Power of Prophecy: Prince
Dipanagara and the End of an Old Order
in Java*. Leiden: KITLV, 2013.

Chapelon, André. *La Locomotive à Vapeur*,
translated by George W. Carpenter.

Rode, near Bath: Camden Miniature
Steam Services, 2000.

Charité, J., ed. *Biografisch Woordenboek
van Nederland*, 6 vols. The Hague: M.
Nijhoff / Instituut voor Nederlandse
Geschiedenis, 1992–2008.

Clark, Christopher. *The Sleepwalkers:
How Europe Went to War in 1914*. London: Penguin Books, 2013.

Cluysenaer, J. L. *Het Hellend Vlak van
Agudio en de Stangenbanen*. The Hague:
Department of the Colonies, 1878.

Consten, Paul, *I. D. Fransen van de Putte
[1822–1902]: Het leven van een selfmade
politicus*. Nijmegen: Vantilt, s.a.

Dambly, Phil. *Vapeur en Belgique*, 2 vols.
Brussels: Blanchart, 1989–1994.

Davies, Harold. *North American Steam
Locomotive Builders and Their Insignia*.
N.p.: TLC, 2005.

Davies, W. J. K. *Light Railways, Their Rise
and Decline*. London: Ian Allan, 1964.

Derbyshire, Ian. "The Building of India's
Railways: The Application of Western
Technology in the Colonial Periphery."
In Ian J. Kerr, ed., *Railways in Modern
India*. Oxford: Oxford University
Press, 2001, 268–303.

Doorn, J. A. A. van. "De eerste spoorweg
op Java." In M. L. ten Horn-van Nispen,
H. W. Lintsen, and A. J. Veenendaal,
Jr., eds., *Nederlandse Ingenieurs en hun
Kunstwerken: Tweehonderd jaar civiele
techniek* (Delft: Stichting Historie der
Techniek / Zutphen: Walburg Pers,
1994).

——. *De laatste eeuw van Indië: Ontwikkeling en ondergang van een koloniaal
project*. Amsterdam: Bert Bakker, 1994.

Dröge, Philip. *Pelgrim: Leven en Reizen
van Christiaan Snouck Hurgronje*.
Houten-Antwerpen: Spectrum, 2017.

Duparc, H. J. A. *De Elektrische Stadstrams
op Java*. Rotterdam: Wyt, 1972.

Durrant, A. E. *The Mallet Locomotive*.
Newton Abbot: David & Charles, 1974.

——. *PNKA Power Parade: Indonesian
Steam Locomotives: Locomotives of the
Perusahaan Negara Kereta Api*. Kenton:
Continental Railway Circle, 1971.

Ellis, C. Hamilton. *British Railway History: An Outline from the Accession
of William IV to the Nationalisation
of Railways*, vol. 1. London: Allen &
Unwin, 1954.

Elsasser, Kilian T., ed. *Gnom: Niklaus Riggenbach - der Bergbahnpionier und seine Zahnrad-Dampflok "Gnom."* Zürich: AS Verlag, 2002.

Elson, R. E. *Village Java under the Cultivation System 1830–1870.* Sydney: Allen & Unwin, 1994.

Encyklopädie des gesamten Eisenbahnwesens, vol. 6. Wien: Carl Gerold, 1894.

Farwell, Byron. *Queen Victoria's Little Wars.* New York-London: Norton, 1972.

Fasseur, C. *Indischgasten.* Amsterdam: Bert Bakker, 1997.

Gaastra, F. S. *De geschiedenis van de VOC.* Haarlem: Fibula-Van Dishoeck, 1982; 2nd printing Zutphen: Walburg Pers, 1992.

Galloway, J. H. *The Sugar Cane Industry: An Historical Geography from Its Origins to 1914.* Cambridge-New York: Cambridge University Press, 1989.

Gedenkboek samengesteld ter gelegenheid van het vijf en twintig-jarig bestaan der Samarang-Joana Stoomtram-Maatschappij. 's Gravenhage: Couvée, 1907.

Gedenkboek uitgegeven ter gelegenheid van het vijftigjarig bestaan van het Koninklijk Instituut van Ingenieurs 1847–1897. 's Gravenhage, 1897.

Gerretson, F. C. *Geschiedenis der "Koninklijke,"* 4 vols. Haarlem: Bohn, 1932–1941.

Gladwin, David. *A History of the British Steam Tram,* vol. 1. Brora, Sutherland: Adam Gordon, 2004.

Gölsdorf, Karl. *Lokomotivbau in Alt-Österreich 1837–1918.* Wien: Slezak, 1978.

Gonggrijp, G. *Schets ener economische geschiedenis van Indonesië,* 4th ed. Haarlem: Erven F. Bohn, 1957.

Goor, J. van. *De Nederlandse Koloniën: Geschiedenis van de Nederlandse Expansie 1600–1975.* The Hague: SDU, 1994.

———. *Prelude to Colonialism: The Dutch in Asia.* Hilversum: Verloren, 1994.

Graaf, Ton de. *Voor Handel en Maatschappij: Geschiedenis van de Nederlandsche Handel-Maatschappij, 1824–1964.* Amsterdam: Boom, 2012.

Gratama, B. M. "De Nederlandsch-Indische Spoorwegmaatschappij, 1863–1896." In *Gedenkboek Koninklijk Instituut van Ingenieurs,* 287–91.

Guleij, Ron, and Gerrit Knaap, eds. *The Dutch East India Company Book.* Zwolle: W Books, 2017.

Helsdingen, W. H. van, ed. *Daar wèrd wat groots verricht: Nederlandsch-Indië in de XXste eeuw.* Amsterdam: Elsevier, 1941.

Hentschel, Volker. *Wirtschaftsgeschichte der Maschinenfabrik Esslingen AG 1846–1918.* Stuttgart: Klett, 1977.

Herder, Hans de. *Nederlandse industrielocomotieven: De normaalsporige stoomlocomotieven van de niet-openbare spoorwegen.* N.p.: Uquilair, 2007.

Herwerden, J. D. van. *Een spoorwegnet over Java.* 's Gravenhage: M. Nijhoff, 1872.

Hills, R. L. *Beyer Peacock Locomotive Order List.* London: British Overseas Railways Historical Trust, 1997.

Hilton, George W. *American Narrow Gauge Railroads.* Stanford, CA: Stanford University Press, 1990.

Hilton, George W., and John F. Due. *The Electric Interurban Railways in America.* Stanford, CA: Stanford University Press, 1960.

Holland's Colonial Call: Means of Transport in the Dutch East Indies / De Koloniale Roeping van Nederland: De Middelen van Verkeer in Nederlandsch-Indië. The Hague: Dutch-British Publishing Company, 1930.

Hoogstraten, Constance van, ed. *Gloria Mundi: Een wereldreis in 1913–1914.* Zutphen: Walburg Pers, 2011.

Horn-van Nispen, Marie-Louise ten. "The Road to a New Empire: Road Construction, Organisation and Techniques." In Ravesteijn and Kop, eds., *For Profit and Prosperity,* 69–89.

Hughes, Hugh. *Indian Locomotives: Part 1 – Broad gauge 1851–1940.* Harrow: Continental Railway Circle, 1990.

———. *Indian Locomotives: Part 2 – Metre gauge 1872–1940.* Harrow: Continental Railway Circle, 1992.

Hurd, John. "Railways." In Ian J. Kerr, ed., *Railways in Modern India* (Oxford: Oxford University Press, 2001), 147–72.

Ido, Victor. *Indië in de goede oude tijd.* 's Gravenhage: Van Hoeve, s.a.

Israel, Jonathan I. *Dutch Primacy in World Trade, 1585–1740.* Oxford: Oxford University Press, 1989.

Jacobs, Els M. *In Pursuit of Pepper and Tea: The Story of the Dutch East India*

Company. Amsterdam: Netherlands Maritime Museum / Zutphen: Walburg Pers, 1991.

Jong, H. de. *De Locomotieven van Werkspoor*. Alkmaar: De Alk, 1986.

Jong, J. J. P. de. *De Waaier van het Fortuin: Van handelscompagnie tot koloniaal imperium: De Nederlanders in Azië en de Indonesische Archipel 1595–1950*. 's Gravenhage: SDU, 1998.

Jonker, Joost. *Merchants, Bankers, Middlemen: The Amsterdam Money Market during the First Half of the 19th Century*. Amsterdam: NEHA, 1996.

Kerr, Ian J. *Building the Railways of the Raj, 1850–1900*. Delhi: Oxford University Press, 1995.

Kerr, Ian J., ed. *Railways in Modern India*. Oxford: Oxford University Press, 2001.

Knaap, G. J. "Transport 1819–1940." In P. Boomgaard, ed., *Changing Economy in Indonesia: A Selection of Statistical Source Materials from the Early Nineteenth Century*, vol. 9 (Amsterdam: Koninklijk Instituut voor de Tropen, 1940).

De Koloniale Roeping van Nederland / Holland's Colonial Call. The Hague: Nederlandsch-Engelsche Uitgevers, 1930.

Kommer, A. van. "De Deli-Maatschappij aan de Oostkust van Sumatra gedurende de jaren 1900–1940." In Clemens and Lindblad, eds., *Het Belang van de Buitengewesten 1870–1942*, 97–122.

Korthals Altes, W. L. *Tussen cultures en kredieten: Een institutionele geschiedenis van de Nederlandsch-Indische Handelsbank, 1863–1964*. Amsterdam: NIBESVV, 2004.

Kuipers, Marietje E. *In de Indische wateren: Anske Hielke Kuipers gezaghebber bij de Gouvernementsmarine 1833–1902*. Werken uitgegeven door de Linschoten-Vereeniging XCVIII. Zutphen: Walburg Pers, 1999.

Lenstra, R. "Jacob Theodoor Cremer, het Koloniaal Beheer en het Nederlands Belang in Atjeh." In *Economisch en Sociaal-Historisch Jaarboek* 49 (Amsterdam: NEHA, 1986), 165–216.

Leusink, Anne, and Wiebe Sybesma, eds., *Op Reis met Pen en Penseel: Frans en Jan Hendrik Lebret als toerist naar Java, 1863*. Zutphen: Walburg Pers, 2017.

Lindblad, J. Th. "Between Singapore and Batavia: The Outer Islands in the Southeast Asian Economy in the Nineteenth Century." In C. A. Davids, W. Fritschy, and L. A. van der Valk, eds., *Kapitaal, Ondernemerschap en Beleid: Studies over Economie en Politiek in Nederland, Europa en Azië van 1500 tot heden* (Amsterdam: NEHA, 1996), 529–48.

——. "De Handel tussen Nederland en Nederlands-Indië, 1874–1939." In *Economisch- en Sociaal-Historisch Jaarboek* 51 (Amsterdam: NEHA, 1988), 240–98.

——. "De Opkomst van de Buitengewesten." In Clemens and Lindblad, eds., *Het Belang van de Buitengewesten 1870–1942*, 1–34.

Lintsen, Harry. *Ingenieurs in Nederland in de Negentiende Eeuw: Een streven naar erkenning en macht*. 's Gravenhage: M. Nijhoff, 1980.

Lowe, James W. *British Steam Locomotive Builders*. Hinckley: TEE, 1975.

Mayer, Max. *Lokomotiven, Wagen und Bergbahnen: Geschichtliche Entwicklung der Maschinenfabrik Eßlingen seit dem Jahre 1846*. Berlin: VDI-Verlag, 1924.

Meijer, H. *De Deli Spoorweg Maatschappij: Driekwart Eeuw Koloniaal Spoor*. Zutphen: Walburg Pers, 1987.

Meilink-Roelofs, M. A. P. *Asian Trade and European Influence in the Indonesian Archipelago between 1500 and about 1630*. The Hague: M. Nijhoff, 1962.

Messerschmidt, Wolfgang. *Lokomotiven der Maschinenfabrik Esslingen 1841 bis 1966*. Moers: Steiger, 1984.

——. *Taschenbuch Deutsche Lokomotivfabriken*. Stuttgart: Francksche Verlagshandlung, 1977.

Middleton, William D. *The Time of the Trolley*. Milwaukee: Kalmbach, 1967.

Miller, John A. *Fares Please! A Popular History of Trolleys, Horse-cars, Street-cars, Buses, Elevateds, and Subways*. New York: Dover, 1960.

Molhuysen, P. C., and P. J. Blok, eds. *Nieuw Nederlandsch Biografisch Woordenboek*, 10 vols. Leiden: Sijthoff, 1911–1937.

Mollema, J. C. *De ontwikkeling van het eiland Billiton en van de Billiton-Maatschappij*. 's Gravenhage: M. Nijhoff, 1922.

Moser, Alfred. *Der Dampfbetrieb der Schweizerischen Eisenbahnen 1847–1966.* Basel: Birkhäuser, 1967.

Oegema, J. J. G. *De stoomtractie op Java en Sumatra.* Deventer-Antwerpen: Kluwer, 1982.

Overbosch, S. *De Stoomlocomotieven der Nederlandse Tramwegen.* Amsterdam-Dieren: De Bataafsche Leeuw, 1985.

Pater, A. D. de. *The Locomotives Built by "Machinefabriek 'Breda' voorheen Backer & Rueb."* Leiden: Brill, 1970.

Pierson, Kurt. *Borsig: Eine Nahme geht um die Welt.* Berlin: Rembrandt Verlag, 1973.

———. *Hohenzollern-Lokomotiven 1872–1929: Geschichte des Lokomotivbaues in Düsseldorf.* Moers: Steiger, 1984.

Pieterse, Evelien. *Sporen van Smaragd: Per trein door Nederlands-Indië.* Zwolle: W Books, 2017.

Potting, C. J. M. "De muntvoorziening in Nederlands-Indië, 1877–1913." In *Economisch- en Sociaal-Historisch Jaarboek,* 50. Amsterdam: NEHA, 1987, 111–45.

Puffert, Douglas J. *Tracks across Continents, Paths through History: The Economic Dynamics of Standardization in Railway Gauge.* Chicago-London: University of Chicago Press, 2009.

Ramaer, R. *The Locomotives of Thailand.* Malmö: Stenvalls, 1984.

Ransome Wallis, P. *On Railways at Home and Abroad.* London: Spring Books, 1951.

Ravesteijn, Wim. *De Zegenrijke Heeren der Wateren: Irrigatie en Staat op Java, 1832–1942.* Delft: Delft University Press, 1997.

Ravesteijn, Wim, and Jan Kop, eds. *For Profit and Prosperity: The Contribution Made by Dutch Engineers to Public Works in Indonesia 1800–2000.* Zaltbommel-Leiden: Aprilis-KITLV, 2008.

Reiche, Günther. *Richard Hartmann und seine Lokomotiven.* Berlin: Oberbaum, 1998.

Reid, A. J. S. *The Contest for North Sumatra: Aceh, the Netherlands and Britain, 1858–1898.* Kuala Lumpur: Oxford University Press, 1969.

Reitsma, S. A. *Gedenkboek der Staatsspoor- en Tramwegen in Nederlandsch-Indië, 1875–1925.* Weltevreden: Topografische Inrichting, 1925.

———. *Korte geschiedenis der Nederlandsch-Indische spoor- en tramwegen.* Weltevreden: Kolff & Co., 1928.

———. *De Staatsspoorweg ter Sumatra's Westkust (S.S.S.).* 's Gravenhage: Moorman's Periodieke Pers, 1943.

———. *Van Stockum's Travellers' Handbook.* The Hague: Van Stockum, 1930.

Ricklefs, M. C. *A History of Modern Indonesia since c. 1300.* Houndmills: Macmillan, 1993.

Ross, David. *The Highland Railway.* Stroud: Tempus, 2005.

Satow, Michael, and Ray Desmond. *Railways of the Raj.* London: Scholar, 1980.

Schippers, Hans. *Van Tusschenlieden tot Ingenieurs: De Geschiedenis van het Hoger Technisch Onderwijs in Nederland.* Hilversum: Verloren, 1989.

Schmeiser, Bernhard. *Krauss-Lokomotiven: Mit vollständigen Lieferlisten der Werke München (1876–1931) und Linz (1881–1930).* Wien: Slezak, 1977.

Sillem, Agnes. *De reis om de wereld van Ernst Sillem 1888–1890.* Amsterdam: Van Soeren & Co., 1897.

Simmons, Jack. *The Railway in England and Wales 1830–1914.* Leicester: Leicester University Press, 1978.

Small, C. S. *Far Wheels: A Railroad Safari.* London: Cleaver Hulme / New York: Simmonds Boardman, 1959.

Spielhoff, Lothar. *Hanomag Lokomotiven.* Brilon: Podszun, 2004.

Stapel, F. W. *Geschiedenis van Nederlandsch-Indië.* Amsterdam: Meulenhoff, 1930.

Statius Muller, R. C., and A. J. Veenendaal Jr. *De Nederlandse Stoomlocomotieven.* Alkmaar: De Alk, 2005.

Teitler, G. "The Dutch East Indies: An Outline of Its Military History." In *Revue Internationale d'Histoire Militaire* 58 (1984), 129–49.

Termorshuizen, Gerard, and Coen van 't Veer. *Een Groots en Meeslepend Leven: Dominique Berretty, Indisch Persmagnaat.* Zutphen: Walburg Pers, 2018.

Theroux, Paul. *Deep South: Four Seasons on Back Roads.* London: Hamish Hamilton, 2015.

Thorner, Daniel. "The Pattern of Railway Development in India." In Ian J. Kerr, ed., *Railways in Modern India,* 80–96.

Townsley, D. H. *The Hunslet Engine Works: Over a Century and a Half of Locomotive Building.* Norwich: Plateway, 1998.

Tramwegen, de, op Java: Gedenkboek samengesteld ter gelegenheid van het vijf- en twintig-jarig bestaan der Samarang-Joana Stoomtram-Maatschappij. 's Gravenhage: M. M. Couvée, 1907.

Veenendaal, Augustus J., Jr. "The Baltic States: Railways under Many Masters." In Ralf Roth and Henry Jacolin, eds., *Eastern European Railways in Transition: Nineteenth to Twenty-first Centuries.* Farnham: Ashgate, 2013.

——. "De kennisoverdracht op het gebied van de spoorwegtechniek in Nederland 1830–1870." In *Jaarboek voor de Geschiedenis van Bedrijf en Techniek* 7 (1990), 54–82.

——. "The Locomotive of Modernity: Building the Network of Railways and Tramlines." In Ravesteijn and Kop, eds., *For Profit and Prosperity*, 93–135.

——. *Railways in the Netherlands: A Brief History, 1834–1994.* Stanford, CA: Stanford University Press, 2001.

——. *Slow Train to Paradise: How Dutch Investment Helped Build American Railroads.* Stanford, CA: Stanford University Press, 1996.

——. *Spoorwegen in Nederland van 1834 tot nu,* 2nd ed. Amsterdam: Boom, 2008.

Veenendaal, Augustus J., and H. Roger Grant. *Rails to the Front: The Role of Railways in Wartime.* Rotterdam: Karwansaray, 2017.

Veer, Paul van 't. *De Atjeh-oorlog.* Amsterdam: Arbeiderspers, 1969.

Veering, Arjan. "Nodes in the Maritime Network: The Formation of the Port System." In Ravesteijn and Kop, eds., *For Profit and Prosperity*, 192–237.

Vilain, Lucien Maurice. *Les locomotives articulées du système Mallet dans le monde.* Paris: Éditions Vincent, Fréal et Cie., 1969.

Vogel, Kaspar. *Die Schweizerische Lokomotiv- und Maschinenfabrik 1871–1997.* Luzern: Minirex, 2003.

Vries, Jan de, and Ad van der Woude. *The First Modern Economy: Success, Failure, and Perseverance of the Dutch Economy, 1500–1815.* Cambridge: Cambridge University Press, 1997.

Wal, S. L. van der, ed. *Besturen Overzee: Herinneringen van oud-ambtenaren bij het binnenlands bestuur in Nederlandsch-Indië.* Franeker: Wever, 1977.

Walraven, Willem. *Een maand in het boevenpak.* 's Gravenhage: Thomas & Eras, 1978.

Webb, Brian. *The British Internal-Combustion Locomotive: 1894–1940.* Newton Abbot: David & Charles, 1973.

Weisfelt, J. *De Deli Spoorweg Maatschappij als factor in de economische ontwikkeling van de Oostkust van Sumatra.* Rotterdam: Bronder, 1972.

Wertheim, W. F. *Indonesian Society in Transition: A Study of Social Change,* 2nd ed. The Hague: W. van Hoeve, 1964.

Westwood, J. N. *A History of Russian Railways.* London: Allen & Unwin, 1964.

White, John H. *A Short History of American Locomotive Builders.* Washington, DC: Bass, 1982.

Whitehouse, P. B., and Peter Allen. *Round the World on the Narrow Gauge.* London: Ian Allan, 1966.

Wijn, J. J. A., ed. *Tot in de verste uithoeken: De cruciale rol van de Gouvernements Marine bij het vestigen van de Pax Neerlandica in de Indische Archipel 1815–1962.* Amsterdam: Bataafsche Leeuw, 1998.

Winchester, Simon. *Krakatoa: The Day the World Exploded.* London: Penguin Books, 2003.

Wintle, Michael. *An Economic and Social History of the Netherlands, 1800–1920: Demographic, Economic and Social Transition.* Cambridge: Cambridge University Press, 2000.

Winton, John. *The Little Wonder.* Portmadoc: Festiniog Railway / London: Michael Joseph Ltd, 1975.

Zanden, Jan Luiten van, and Arthur van Riel. *Nederland 1780–1914: Staat, Instituties en Economische Ontwikkeling.* Amsterdam: Balans, 2000.

Zwaag, Jaap van der. *Verloren tropische zaken: De opkomst en ondergang van de Nederlandse handel- en cultuurmaatschappijen in het voormalige Nederlands-Indië.* N.p.: Feniks Pers, 1991.

INDEX

NB—All persons mentioned in this index are Dutchmen unless otherwise noted. All place names in the East Indies have the island added on which they are situated. Index pages in italics indicate illustrations.

motorbus, competition with railways, 247, 254
Mount Washington rack railway, USA, 101

Nacht Express, JSS, 250
Nagasaki, Bay of, Japan, 9
Napoleon, French emperor, 7, 13
Natal, South Africa, 46, 48
Nederland, Maatschappij, shipping company, Amsterdam, 82, 114
Nederlandsche Handel-Maatschappij, Amsterdam, 13–14, 25, 88–89, 148
Nederlandsch-Indische Handelsbank, Amsterdam, 25, 28, 151
Nederlandsch-Indische Spoorweg-Maatschappij, The Hague (NIS), 27–41, 53, 55, 67–70, 83, 131, 171, 178, 195, 202, 204; Batavia-Buitenzorg problem, 39–42, 69, 178–180; financial performance, 53, 131–132, 171–172, 202, 258–259; indigenous personnel, 32–35
Nederlandsch-Indische Stoomvaart-Maatschappij, shipping company, 17, 84
Nederlandsche Industrie, Soerabaja, engineering works, 162
Neilson & Co., locomotive works, Glasgow, Scotland, 36
Netherlands, Kingdom of, passim; Parliament of, 8, 26, 28–29, 55–56, 58, 68–70, 88–89, 102; railways of, 26, 28–29, 64, 221, 249, 259
Netherlands Indies Army (NIL). See Dutch East Indies
Netherlands Indies Tramway Company (NITM), 129
New Guinea, island, 11
New South Wales, Australia, 47
New Zealand, 48
Nienhuys, J., tobacco planter, 111
North British Locomotive Company, Glasgow, 76
Norway, 41, 47, 50, 171

Oebroeg, Java, hydroelectric power station, 222
Oerlikon, electrotechnical works, Switzerland, 261
Ombilin coal mines, Sumatra, 61–63, 101–102, 186, 193
oil, petroleum, oil refineries, 112, 137–138
Olehleh, Atjeh, 92, 96–97
Oosthaven, Sumatra, 122, 124–125
Oost Java Steam Tram Cy. (OJS), 137, 141, 203, 256

Orenstein & Koppel, locomotive works, Berlin, Germany, 240–244
Ottoman Empire, Turkey, 194
Outer Possessions. See Dutch East Indies
Overend Gurney Bank, London, 269
Overland Mail, Alexandria-Suez, Egypt, 9

Padalarang, Java, 71, 148, 154, 191
Padang, Sumatra, 9, 16, 101–102, 105, 255
Padang Pidji, Sumatra, 97
Padri War, 101
Pahud, C. F., minister for the colonies and governor-general, 20–21
Pajakombo, Sumatra, 103
Pakanbaroe, Sumatra, 105
Palembang, Sumatra, 122–125, 237–238, 254
palm oil, cultivation of, 234–236
Palmer, William J., American railway promoter, 48
Pandjang, Sumatra, 122
Pangeran Ario Prabo Prang Wedana, aristocrat and sugar planter, Java, 234
Pangka, Java, 147
Pangkalan Brandan, Sumatra, 112
Pangkalan Soesoe, Sumatra, 95, 113
Parakan, Java, 172
Parapattan coal company, Borneo, 237
Paris–Orléans Railway, 253
Pasoeroean, Java, 69, 184
Passoeroean Steam Tram Company (PsSM), 143, 182
Pematang Siantar, Sumatra, 114, 118, 236
pepper, 125
Pereire, Brothers, French bankers, 28
Perry, Matthew C., American naval commander, 8
Peto, Sir Samuel Morton, English railway contractor, 270
Peru, 80
Pihl, C., Norwegian railway engineer, 43, 47–48, 133
Pincoffs, L., Rotterdam businessman, 56
Pletterij Enthoven, engineering works, The Hague/Delft, 212, 214, 219, 222
Poeger, Java, 181
Poeloe Weh, island, Sumatra, 105
Poerwakarta, Java, 148, 191, 252
Poerwodadie, Java, 135
Poerwokerto, Java, 138, 147
Poerwosari, Java, 174, 261
Ponogoro, Java, 180
Pontianak, Borneo, 125
Poolman, W., railway promoter, 25–26, 43n1
Port Said, Egypt, 9

DR. AUGUSTUS J. VEENENDAAL, JR., (1940) is a professional historian who worked for the Institute of Netherlands History of The Hague, Netherlands, where he edited the vast correspondence (1702–1720) of Anthonie Heinsius, Grand Pensionary of Holland. His other interest is the history of railroads worldwide. He published extensively in this field, in Dutch and in English, chiefly covering the railroads of his home country and those of the United States, including the financial involvement of Dutch investors in the building of railroads in the United States. Before his retirement in 2005, he served four years as historian of Netherlands Railways (NS) and wrote a comprehensive history of this company and its predecessors. He was also a visiting professor at several American universities, where he taught Dutch and American Economic History.